CUTS AND CRIMINALITY

Cuts and Criminality

Body Alteration in Legal Discourse

THEODORE BENNETT
University of Western Australia, Australia

Routledge
Taylor & Francis Group
LONDON AND NEW YORK

First published 2015 by Ashgate Publishing

2 Park Square, Milton Park, Abingdon, Oxfordshire OX14 4RN
52 Vanderbilt Avenue, New York, NY 10017

Routledge is an imprint of the Taylor & Francis Group, an informa business

First issued in paperback 2020

British Library Cataloguing in Publication Data
A catalogue record for this book is available from the British Library.

The Library of Congress has cataloged the printed edition as follows:
Bennett, Theodore Edward, author.
Cuts and criminality : body alteration in legal discourse / by Theodore Bennett.
pages cm
Includes bibliographical references and index.
ISBN 978-1-4724-4511-7 (hardback)
1. Human body – Law and legislation. 2. Human body – Law and legislation – Criminal provisions. I. Title.
K564.H8B46 2015
345'.025–dc23

2014045276

ISBN 978-1-4724-4511-7 (hbk)
ISBN 978-0-367-59925-6 (pbk)

Contents

Acknowledgements

My research into the material within this book began in 2008 and has developed in various stages over the course of the intervening years. Throughout this time I have benefited greatly from the assistance provided to me by a number of people and institutions, without whom this book would not have been possible.

I would like to acknowledge the financial assistance that my initial research received through the award of a Baillieu Research Scholarship, which enabled me to focus my efforts. I would like to thank the University of Western Australia Law School for the support that I received throughout this entire process. In particular, I thank Associate Professor Daniel Stepniak for his guidance and feedback on earlier versions of this work. I am also indebted to Winthrop Professor Mark Israel, Associate Professor Catherine Kelly, Winthrop Professor Holly Cullen and my colleagues in the Law and Society Research and Teaching Network for their advice.

I have benefited from the opportunity to present my thoughts on aspects of this research at the Somatechnics Research Centre Conference in 2009, and to present on some of my related research at the Australian Society of Legal Philosophy Pre-Conference Workshop in 2011 and at the Law, Literature and the Humanities Association of Australasia Conference in 2013. I thank my fellow attendees at these conferences for the helpful feedback that I received. I also thank Professor Carl Stychin and Associate Professor Nikki Sullivan for their feedback and encouragement on earlier versions of this work.

A number of other people have given me assistance at different points in time throughout the gestation of this book. I am grateful for the various contributions made by Dr Tracey Summerfield, Eddie Marcus, Cheyne Beetham and Xander Bennett, which ranged from academic inspiration to proofreading to thought-provoking philosophical debate. I especially thank my parents, Martin Bennett and Rebecca Bennett, for their love and support, and for instilling in me a passion for the law by making it a dinner-table topic throughout my life.

I would like to acknowledge that in the course of my general research on the body alterations considered in this book, I have explored a number of different lines of thought that fall outside the scope of the analysis that will be developed here. Some of these alternative ideas have been published as peer-reviewed journal articles and I have included their reference details in the bibliography (see: Bennett 2011; 2012a; 2012b; 2013; 2014). Whilst there is minimal overlap between these articles and this book, necessity requires that some of the same statutes and cases are referenced or explained because they are the key legal sources on these topics.

My gratitude and thanks to Ashgate Publishing, and in particular Alison Kirk, for being very efficient, professional and helpful throughout the publication and editing processes. I am also very appreciative of the time spent by the anonymous reviewer who provided me with useful and insightful comments on the manuscript for this book.

Finally, my utmost thanks go to my partner Lisel Avey for being a constant source of love and caring across the many years involved in developing this book. There is no one else in the world with whom I would rather have spent the time.

List of Abbreviations

AAP:	American Academy of Pediatrics
ACT:	Australian Capital Territory
BD:	Bondage and Domination
BDSM:	Bondage and Domination, Discipline and Submission, Sadism and Masochism
BIID:	Body Identity Integrity Disorder
Cth:	Commonwealth
D/s:	Discipline and Submission
DSD:	Disorder of Sex Development
FGCS:	Female Genital Cosmetic Surgery
FGM:	Female Genital Modification (in main text) or Female Genital Mutilation (in quotations from sources)
FTM:	Female to Male
GID:	Gender Identity Disorder
HIV:	Human Immunodeficiency Virus
MC:	Male Circumcision
NORM-UK:	National Organisation of Restoring Men – United Kingdom
NSW:	New South Wales
NT:	Northern Territory
Qld:	Queensland
SM:	Sadomasochism
S/M:	Sadomasochism
S&M:	Sadism and Masochism
Tas:	Tasmania
UNICEF:	United Nations Children's Fund
Vic:	Victoria
WHO:	World Health Organisation

Introduction

Overview

If you're reading this book, I can make a few assumptions about you with a high degree of certainty. I can assume that you're skimming these words and this page with your eyes and turning these pages with your hands. You're also breathing, swallowing, digesting, circulating blood and engaging in numerous other physiological processes at the same time. I can assume that you understand and internalise language as a system of describing and ordering concepts in your thinking and that you employ it on a day-to-day basis to communicate these thoughts with others who do the same thing. You're doing this right now as you read this sentence. I can also assume that you are located in a society governed by laws and regulations, and that you pattern your own behaviour and interactions with others around the restrictions and prohibitions found within these laws. For example, you probably did not steal this book. The reason that I can confidently make these assumptions is that they relate to conditions that apply to nearly all people. We are all necessarily embodied, and our bodies are the point at which we access and interact with our environment and with each other. We all draw on discourse as language to communicate and are all imbricated within discursive frameworks that structure our social realities. We are all subject to the various strictures of law and custom that not only deter and prohibit our individual actions but that also pattern our social structures and interactions.

This book is about each of these three topics: bodies, discourse and law. Taken individually, each of these topics plays an important part in the ways in which we conduct our lives and the ways in which society is organised. Indeed, they are all bound up in some way with what it means to be human at this particular point in time (leaving aside fantastical predictions of future possibilities about disembodied consciousness, and philosophical speculation about a hypothetical, lawless 'state of nature'). Taken together, the juncture between these topics – where they intersect and interact – is a theoretical area of prime concern. It is an area that we are all personally and necessarily invested in, for better or worse. It is in this critical juncture that this book is located.

The book focuses on one particular aspect of this juncture between bodies, discourse and law: the way in which discourse inflects and impacts on the criminal legal regulation of body alterations. In other words, it explores how language and conceptualisation structure the legality of the ways in which we literally shape our selves. Body alterations offer a key focus through which we can analyse the broader topics of bodies, discourse and the law, because whilst bodies will necessarily always be physical phenomena they are also never simply just physical phenomena. Whilst bodies 'have a material, substantial reality … the meanings of the body are facts of culture' and 'are provisional, multiple, ambiguous, shifting from context to context' (Sclater, 2002, p.6). Body alterations reflect and expose the cultural conditions that produce them because they are not exhausted by purely physical description and definition. The specific form, timing and extent of a body alteration constitutes a living testament to the cultural context in which it takes place. Cuts, scars and other kinds of marks can be understood as signs of past trauma and pain, markers of individuality and difference, reminders of grit and determination, or even locators of cultural belonging and identity. As their importance moves beyond their physicality, body alterations provide an analytical entry point for addressing various meanings about bodies and the processes of discourse that construct and maintain these meanings.

The physical cuts made during body alterations also provide an analytical entry point for addressing the operation of law. Some kinds of body alteration are lawful and other kinds of body alteration are criminal. However, the criminal law is not concerned simply with a physical account of cuts and incisions, instead legal sanctions are structured around and mobilised by various meanings about bodies that go beyond biological criteria. Why, as we shall see later in the book, do the cuts and bruises of the willing sadomasochistic participant attract criminal liability, whereas the cuts and bruises of the willing cosmetic surgery patient escape legal notice? Why, as we shall also see later in the book, do cuts and incisions into the genitalia of male and intersex infants escape legal notice, whereas cuts and incisions into the genitalia of female infants attract criminal liability? This book will attempt to unearth and reveal the conceptual understandings about bodies that underlie these divisions between lawful body alterations and criminal body alterations.

In these ways, body alterations provide literal and theoretical incisions which this book uses as analytical entry points in order to address discursive understandings about the body and the processes of law. If language and conceptualisation structure the legality of the ways in which we literally shape our selves, then conversely analysing the ways in which we literally shape our selves can provide us with a valuable way of approaching legality, language and conceptualisation.

Scope

Like most body alterations, the law is also something 'that *cuts*, that divides' (Derrida, 1992, p.24). This function is never clearer than it is in criminal law, where bright-line distinctions are drawn between criminal and lawful behaviour. Under the criminal law, this process of division becomes more than just a matter of legality and illegality. As connotations of morality, deviance and wrongdoing attach to this division it can be seen to cut and divide up social legitimacy as well. It is for this reason that this book focuses purely on criminal law. Rather than just providing a certain level of oversight on society, criminal law actively produces a particular type of society. By differentially legalising/legitimising some behaviours and criminalising/delegitimising others, the criminal law constructs a sociolegal reality wherein certain behaviours are performed more frequently than others and/or are performed only under specific conditions by specific people. Applying this understanding to the regulation of body alteration, the criminal law constructs a particular type of sociolegal reality that delimits the existence, frequency, location and production of certain types of bodies.

In a theoretical sense, there is an almost infinite variety of possible body alterations that any one person could undergo. These possibilities are extended every year by medical and scientific knowledge as well as by artistic and cultural innovations. In the same way that Botox injections and eyeball implants were literally unthinkable options for bodily configuration prior to the last few decades, we can only vaguely gesture towards the new and wondrous body alterations that may be developed and gain purchase in the somatic landscape of the future. But not all body alterations find fertile soil in which to flourish. The criminal law cuts and divides body alterations, authorising certain alterations as lawful and condemning other alterations as criminal. As a result, the criminal law also cuts and divides bodies, legitimising certain bodily configurations as socially appropriate and valued, and delegitimising and devaluing other configurations. In this way, the 'state's ability to legislate a person's relationship to their body can be seen as the ultimate expression of state authority' (Roberts, 2011, p.347), because by moulding the individual the law also moulds society. The criminal law not only restricts the capacity of individuals to control the changes they make to their own body, the criminal law also functions more broadly to foreclose the full range of human embodiment by preventing the actualisation of a wider variety of somatic possibilities within the community of bodies.

I have chosen to confine the analysis in this book to a specific range of body alterations. These body alterations will be closely addressed, explored and analysed as case studies, with a view to demonstrating different aspects of the operation of law and discourse within each study. Specifically, the body alterations considered here are sadomasochistic injuries, female genital modification, male circumcision, cosmetic surgery, body modification, genital normalisation surgery and sex reassignment surgery. These body alterations have been chosen for a number of reasons. Firstly, they all induce definitive and rapid shifts between bodily states, from the pre-altered to the post-altered state, and so they provide discrete corporeal material to work with and discrete analytical areas to work within. Secondly, they are all dealt with under a broadly similar criminal law framework. This allows less space to be spent setting out their legal status and more spent analysing the implications and underpinning conceptions of that status. Thirdly, as this book will argue as it progresses, the discursive framework in which these particular body alterations are enmeshed raises a variety of conceptualisations and understandings that are common to the whole range of body alterations, such as the predominant influence of medical discourse. Fourthly, despite these similarities these particular body alterations still raise a variety of different issues. For example, discussion of sadomasochistic injuries broadens the consideration of bodily alterations from 'permanent' and 'major' alterations to the body to also include more 'short-term' and 'minor' alterations. Finally, they provide a cross-section of body alterations that are accepted as lawful and condemned as criminal. This enables the analysis within the book to cover not only the discursive conditions that produce criminality but also those that produce lawfulness. As a general point, because this book considers a wide range of body alterations it is impossible for it to fully engage with every single aspect of each individual body alteration. There is sufficient analytical material for book-length engagement with each of these types of body alteration, and this obviously cannot all be entirely covered here. Instead, the book will focus on the aspects of each body alteration that are most pertinent to the analytical approach taken.

In engaging with the criminality and lawfulness of body alterations, this book will refer primarily to Australian law. This choice is a matter of practicality given that I live in Australia, and it is where I teach and conduct my research. However, the scope of the analysis moves far beyond Australia's borders. Discursive frameworks, legal principles and conceptual understandings about the body are not limited by traditional geo-political and jurisdictional boundaries. Instead, they span the globe. Legal and academic material from countries that share similar philosophical traditions and criminal law frameworks to Australia, such as the United Kingdom, New Zealand, Canada and the United States of America, will all be drawn upon and discussed as part of the book's broad analysis of the topic. These interrelations will become clear as the book moves through the various case studies. For example, common law principles from the United Kingdom around sadomasochism have been transplanted into Australian law, and medical models and arguments developed in the United States figure prominently in international discourse around male circumcision. Accordingly, the focus on Australian law here should not be understood as exclusionary but as exemplary. Whilst the lawfulness and criminality of the case studies considered in this book predominantly reflects the specific Australian criminal law position, the analysis of discourse that draws on and builds from this legal position reflects material of a more general international concern. This book reveals and analyses the ways in which legal processes, discursive frameworks and techniques of power function generally. These phenomena are not peculiar or unique to Australia but are key parts of sociolegal systems worldwide. Australian criminal law simply provides the specific example that illustrates a set of general interrelations between bodies, discourse and law.

Turning to the specifics of the Australian example, it is important to make clear at the outset that Australia does not have a unified national criminal legal system. Instead, the content of the criminal law varies from jurisdiction to jurisdiction. Broadly speaking, criminal law in Australia can be separated into two categories: the jurisdictions that follow a common law model (New South Wales, South Australia and Victoria), and the jurisdictions that have largely abandoned the common law by adopting a Criminal Code (the Australian Capital Territory, the Northern Territory, Queensland, Tasmania and Western Australia). This book will address the law in both the common law and Code law jurisdictions, but in order to avoid being drawn into the arcane idiosyncrasies of each different Code it will focus on Queensland and Western Australia as representative of the Code states more generally.

Key Questions

So far I have broadly addressed the general area in which this book is located and roughly foreshadowed the purpose it sets out to achieve. Here, I want to narrow down exactly what will be developed, argued and answered throughout the course of the book. It sets out to reveal and analyse the discursive processes through which some body alterations are discursively constructed as legitimate and are legally approved, whilst other body alterations are discursively constructed as illegitimate and are legally sanctioned. The focus of this book is on how discursive conditions produce the lawfulness and criminality of body alterations.

The criminal law does not construct its divisions between lawful and criminal body alterations in an arbitrary way. Rather the book argues that the timing, extent and consequences of these divisions are patterned around certain conceptualisations and understandings about the body and about society that find authoritative purchase within legal discourse. This book is 'not concerned with making truth-claims about particular modes and practices of embodiment' (Sullivan, 2009b, p.282), rather it is concerned with exploring, analysing and interrogating the content, positioning, construction and effect of such truth-claims as they circulate within and through legal discourse. Similarly, although the law will be shown to respond to the body alterations considered in this book in a variety of different ways, it is not concerned with proposing 'a scheme of law reform by which inconsistencies in the legal response to such practices can be ironed out or ameliorated' but is concerned primarily instead with the operation of the 'discourses surrounding them' (Kennedy, 2009, pp.211–212). The book reveals the techniques and processes of legal discourse that lead to the particular placement of divisions of legality/legitimacy and offers aetiological accounts explaining why legal cuts are made where they are. This book offers insight into specific instances of how, why and to what effect discourse moulds the sociolegal reality of embodiedness. It aims to 'unpack the unstated assumptions about the meanings (both natural and cultural) attributed to different forms of embodiment' (Karpin and Mykitiuk, 2011, p.118), through the specific lens of law's response to alterations of this embodiment. The underlying goal of this analysis is to lay bare the operational techniques of law and discourse and, in doing so, denaturalise the restrictions that law places on our relations to our bodies and open up room within legal discourse to allow for the possibility of a broader range of embodied expression.

In order to achieve these ends, a number of issues need to be addressed during the course of this book. I have framed these here as a series of key questions that will be answered as the book progresses across the various chapters:

- Under Australian criminal law, what is the current legal status of the body alterations that have been chosen as case studies?
- Through what discursive techniques and processes are those body alterations that are lawful divided from those that are criminal?
- How, and to what extent, does legal discourse draw on other discursive frameworks and conceptualisations – such as those existing around harm, medicine, sexuality and sex/gender – in order to construct and maintain these divisions?
- Do the legal divisions between different types of body alterations (re)produce a specific typology of bodies?
- Do the legal divisions between different types of body alterations marginalise certain kinds of discursive understandings about bodies?

The answers to these questions are complex and context-specific to the case studies addressed. As such, their answers are not easily translatable into a corresponding dot-point list, but are instead embedded within the course of the analysis as it progresses across the case studies.

Structure

The main content of this book is structured around an analysis of a series of case studies that address a variety of body alterations. Before this analysis can begin, however, it is important to first set out the key theories that inform this analysis and outline some of the major concepts that it draws on as it progresses. Moving forward from this theoretical and conceptual basis, each of the case studies will highlight the discursive processes that inflect and impact on the legal status of the body alterations that they consider.

Chapter 1 sets out the theoretical basis and key concepts that underpin the analytic approach taken during the course of the case studies in the book. In doing so it introduces core ideas from postmodernism, discourse theory and body theory, and links them to the overall book by explaining how they shape and inform the subsequent analysis. From postmodern theory, the book adopts a focus on subjectivity and pluralism in order to contest legal claims to a singular 'truth' and to justify the (re)presentation of a broader plurality of 'truths' about body alterations. From discourse theory, this book follows Foucauldian lines of thought around the permeable, contradictory and productive nature of discourse. In doing so it highlights the role of legal discourse in constructing and reifying, rather than simply representing or regulating, social phenomena. Different kinds of discourse analyses are distinguished and the analysis in the book is identified as a form of cultural discourse analysis. From body theory, this book outlines the inscriptive and performative models of reading bodies in order to open up body alterations to sociopolitical critique. It introduces and explains the key Foucauldian concept of disciplinary power that underlies the argument in the analysis that law and legal discourse around body alteration (re) produce 'docile' bodies and erase and marginalise 'unruly' bodies.

Chapter 2 opens with a brief description and explanation of sadomasochism, acknowledging but decoupling its pathologised roots in early sexological and psychological work. It proceeds to set out the criminal status of injurious sadomasochistic activities by reference to a number of key cases and statutes. The criminality of injurious sadomasochistic activities is then linked, through a close analysis of language, to the construction of sadomasochism within authoritative strands of legal discourse as non-consensual, violent and harmful. To contrast against this authoritative legal discursive construction of sadomasochism, alternative accounts of sadomasochism are offered that illuminate the meanings attached to sadomasochism outside legal discourse. These alternative accounts demonstrate how sadomasochism can be conceptualised in a multitude of different ways, including as being therapeutic, empowering, pleasurable, non-injurious, and an important part of personal and social identity. An explanation is offered as to why these alternative understandings of sadomasochism are marginalised within legal discourse;

sadomasochism generally challenges normative understandings about sexuality and bodies, and specifically challenges legal authority by appropriating the right to punish, highlighting connections between power and pleasure, and exposing the contingency of power. The criminalisation of sadomasochistic injuries is an attempt to defuse these challenges and recuperate the transgressive nature of sadomasochistic activities. The legal response to sadomasochism is thus argued to be the effect of law's disciplinary power exerted against the unruly bodies of sadomasochists.

Chapter 3 begins by offering an introduction to genital body alterations by explaining their various types, prevalence, geographical distribution, and the contexts in which they are typically performed. The book's focus on discourse necessitates delving into the academic debates about terminology that have characterised commentary around genital body alterations, in order to reveal the political stakes that have been attached to terms such as 'female genital mutilation' and 'male genital mutilation' and to show how language can be leveraged to position legal discourse in particular ways. Out of the troublesome terminological milieu, the terms 'female genital modification' ('FGM') and 'male circumcision' ('MC') are adopted in the book as the least-worst options. In keeping with international developments in other 'Western' liberal democracies, FGM is shown to have been explicitly criminalised under Australian criminal law, whereas MC is shown to be generally accepted as lawful even though it falls under a grey area of Australian criminal law. The rest of the chapter is devoted to demonstrating how discourse around FGM and MC separates and divides these body alterations to the extent that such a disparity in their legal treatment can develop. It reveals how this disparity is produced through the discursive deployment of medicalised understandings of 'harm' that erase sociocultural considerations, normative conceptions of sexuality and gender, and Othering models of culture that reify a reductive 'Western'/'African' divide. This discursive positioning is argued to marginalise alternative claims and understandings about the harms that can be caused by MC, and about the social and cultural benefits that can attach to FGM.

Chapter 4 focuses on how legal regulation is mobilised across the conceptual boundaries that are drawn within and between different body alterations in discourse. This chapter begins by offering brief definitions of what constitutes both cosmetic surgery and body modification and proceeds by charting their current legal status under Australian law, and in doing so discusses key precedents from the common law of England and Wales. Whilst cosmetic surgery is widely accepted as lawful, some body modifications are lawful, some hold a murky quasi-legality and others are criminal. The analysis then proceeds in three strands. Firstly, this legal differentiation frames the chapter's analysis of the internal discursive boundaries of both cosmetic surgery and body modification, an analysis that seeks to determine what constitutes 'acceptable' cosmetic surgery and body modification and explain why 'unacceptable' cosmetic surgery procedures remain lawful whilst 'unacceptable' body modifications face legal regulation. In doing so it delves into the sociocultural positions that each set of body alterations have historically occupied and explores how those positions have altered contemporaneously. Secondly, this chapter analyses the external discursive boundaries of cosmetic surgery and body modification, in order to determine the discursive forces that keep these categories conceptually separate from other body alterations, such as reconstructive surgery, FGM, exercise and dieting. The analysis here links back to legal regulation by demonstrating how the contours of the law are shaped to fit these discursive categorisations. Thirdly, this chapter explores the discursive boundary between cosmetic surgery and body modification by attempting to locate the practice of healthy limb amputation within these categories. Healthy limb amputation provides a problem case for the law because it simultaneously accords with and challenges the internal logics that typically dictate the categorisation of cosmetic surgery and body modification, and so it remains discursively unsettled. It is this liminality that enables the analysis of healthy limb amputation to reveal the discursive techniques that underpin both conceptual categorisations and the legal consequences at stake in this area. Ultimately, the chapter argues that the law demonstrates disciplinary power in its relative lack of regulation of cosmetic surgeries – discursively conceptualised as normative, high-status, socially valued body alterations performed under the venerable auspices of medicine – compared to body modifications – discursively conceptualised as non-normative, low status, socially oppositional alterations that demonstrate nonconforming individuality and/or subcultural affiliation.

Chapter 5 charts the discursive forces that have aligned to produce the lawfulness of genital normalisation surgeries performed on intersex people and sex reassignment surgeries performed on transsexual people, and interrogates the understandings about the body employed within legal discourse that serve to underpin the lack of criminal law regulation. In order to ground the analysis, the chapter begins by offering definitions of both genital normalisation surgery and sex reassignment surgery, and maps their current legal positions under Australian law. This chapter then denaturalises the lawfulness of these surgeries by comparing them to other body alterations already discussed in this book. Comparing these surgeries to FGM, cosmetic surgery and healthy limb amputation encourages reflexivity about why law treats the alterations to 'healthy' bodily tissue under the auspices of sex surgery differently from similar alterations that occur under these other discursive categorisations. To address this issue, this chapter then works through three of the dominant discursive frameworks that construct and position sex surgeries as lawful: medicine, sex/gender and notions of 'truth'. The conjunction of medical and legal discourse constructs intersex and transsexualism as medical 'conditions', which legitimates such surgeries as unproblematic medical 'treatment'. Normative notions of sex/gender fix a reductive focus on the creation of 'male' and 'female' bodies at the core of the legal response to potentially transgressive intersex and transsexual embodiment and identity. Such notions also motivate the legal search for a 'true' male or female sex/gender, the ideal of which is bolstered by the role of sex surgeries in crafting male and female physical attributes onto ambiguous bodies. Through this analysis, the chapter argues that legal discourse legitimises and (re)produces particular models of intersex and transsexual embodiment that accord with normative understandings about the body, whilst delegitimising alternative models of intersex and transsexual embodiment. Rather than encourage difference, this chapter argues that law uses such surgeries to erase potentially transgressive sex/gender identities, and that the lawfulness of sex surgeries relies upon legal discourse putting them to work in this disciplinary manner.

The Conclusion draws together the results of the analysis of the various case studies conducted throughout the book by engaging with three key common issues that cut across the material. Specifically, it considers the gaps in the legal coverage of these areas, the high level of medicolegal discursive collusion in this area, and the discursive marginalisation of alternative accounts of body alterations. Finally, it raises the possibility of utilising discourse analysis to reshape the processes of legal discourse around body alteration.

Chapter 1

Analytical Approach: Theoretical Basis and Key Concepts

Before beginning to engage in the proposed analysis of the case studies, it is necessary to first set out the theoretical understandings and key concepts that ground this book. If one of the outcomes I am seeking is to reveal and analyse the underpinning understandings about bodies that legal discourse employs and that law authorises, then it is important to lay out my own underpinning assumptions about discourse and the law with a high degree of transparency. The aim of this chapter is threefold. Firstly, I want to foreground the particular way in which the subsequent analysis will be conducted by providing a principled theoretical basis for its scope, content, method of approach and, ultimately, the types of conclusions that it reaches. This theoretical basis provides support and structure to the subsequent analysis but it is not the main feature of this book. The focus of the book is not directed specifically towards adding to, expounding upon, varying or critiquing the theory from which it draws: the focus is more on utilising such theory. Instead of being the object of analysis itself, this theoretical basis simply blends into and informs the shape of the case studies to come. Secondly, I want to introduce and explain a number of key concepts that this book will specifically draw on during the course of the subsequent analysis. Locating these concepts at the outset of the book allows the same concepts that arise within multiple case studies to be explained initially and in a central space, and it also assists the progress of the analysis within each chapter by obviating the need for lengthy segues into conceptual explanations that would distract from the case study at hand. Unlike the theoretical basis that blends into the analysis, these concepts will be explicitly addressed throughout the course of this book and their usage will be directly addressed in the Conclusion. Thirdly, certain theorists and thinkers have influenced this book and its approach towards the material. This chapter provides an opportunity to acknowledge the academic debts the book owes to these writers, as well as to locate it within the broader corpus of commentary in the area.

In working through the analytical approach taken in this book, the key areas of thought that need to be addressed are postmodernism, discourse theory and body theory. Brief explanations of these areas are offered, focusing on the relevant theories and concepts that underpin the analysis to come.

Postmodernism

The term 'postmodern' is notoriously difficult to define. The fact that it has been taken by some commentators to denote something as broad and as lofty as 'a range of cultural theories and practices which break with the unity and certainty of the Western intellectual tradition' (Shildrick 1997, p.5) indicates why its definitional borders lack clarity. This is further complicated by the different meanings postmodernism has within different academic contexts. Postmodernism has been employed differentially within areas as varied as art theory, critical literature studies, anthropology, sociology, science and philosophy. Any incoherence that may be seen to result from this is neatly defused by postmodernism's scepticism 'towards the separation and autonomy of … "spheres" of culture or separate "fields" of experts' (Turner, 1990, p.5). As Shildrick (1997, p.6) notes, part of postmodern theory is the assertion that the 'boundaries between hitherto discrete bodies of knowledge have blurred', allowing the exchange of theories and concepts across previously strictly demarcated lines. Any inconsistencies that arise between these various iterations of postmodernism do not threaten to destabilise or defocus it as a theory. Instead, they form an integral part of the theory. Coherence, truth and knowledge are considered to be fragmented. Objectivity and authenticity are portrayed within postmodern theory as mere claims made by a 'series of dispersed, competing and conflicting discourses' in an effort to claim authority (Shildrick, 1997, p.6). Instead, postmodernism recognises that 'different logics or paradigms, that is, different systems of discourse with their distinctive value axioms, can co-exist in the same social *space*' (Murphy 1994, p.4, emphasis in original). According to postmodern thinking, the idea that truth is a construction deflates appeals to higher-level, authenticating concepts, such as 'unified rationality or morality' (Shildrick, 1997, p.6). As a result, 'universal cultural meanings' are deprivileged by postmodernism and replaced with a 'recognition of local, particularised, and contradictory cultural configurations' (Stychin, 1995, p.23).

This postmodern focus on subjectivity is incorporated into the theoretical basis of this book. Instead of reading legal conclusions as objective pronouncements, or as based on basal and (purportedly) 'objective' principles such as justice, fairness or the *grundnorm*, focusing on subjectivity allows the law to be read as a system of internal truth-production. Considering law as self-authenticating and subjective opens it up to challenge. The 'truths' produced by legal systems of knowledge can be critically analysed and 'taken apart … so as to reveal that they are not universal truths but constructions' (Rahman and Jackson, 2010, p.126) Given that law holds no stronger claim to 'truth' than any other system of truth-production, its internal logic becomes susceptible to comparison to external logics and 'truths' with equally (in)valid claims to authenticity. As a result, this book is able to look beyond what would be considered 'traditional' legal texts in order to contest law and legal discourse. It employs this focus on subjectivity as a justification for drawing from other academic areas such as sociology, medicine, psychology, cultural studies and philosophy in order to contest legal claims to a singular 'truth' and to instead represent a broader plurality of meanings that cohere around body alterations.

Another key focus within postmodernism is pluralism. Societies organised on the basis of modernist principles operate through a system of homogeneity, taking 'the larger variety of human capacities or histories and transform[ing] them into a smaller number of possible outcomes or transform[ing] most of existing diversity into non-consequential variations' (Simon, 1996, p.12). In contrast, a postmodern society 'operate[s] in reverse, as identical points of origin give rise to many different outcomes and ... identical outcomes can be recognized as the product of a diversity of origins' (Simon, 1996, p.12). This is not only a principle of social organisation, it is also a key theoretical understanding. Postmodernism is deeply suspicious of unifying theories, grand narratives and the search for underlying 'hidden' truths and logics within and between topics. Such attempts are totalising as they construct, rather than recognise, similarities, and they elide, rather than dismantle, differences. In contrast, postmodernism is characterised by a 'desire to think in terms sensitive to difference', and to both recognise and legitimate diversity (Turner, 1990, p.5).

This postmodern focus on plurality has been incorporated into the theoretical basis of this book in two distinct ways. Firstly, it is incorporated in terms of content. The operation of criminal law tends towards singular, narrow constructions of people and events: lawful or criminal, guilty or not guilty, harmful or not harmful. Obviously, this can only be achieved at the expense of a much broader range of 'truths', stories and conceptions that circulate within law and discourse. This is a profoundly modernist characteristic of the legal system and this book shares Smart's (1989, p. 4) aim of exploring how and to what extent law 'resists and disqualifies alternative accounts of social reality', with a view to opening up space for the recognition of differences that are typically elided within legal discourse. In particular, the book is committed to recuperating alternative accounts about bodies. As it argues through the course of the various case studies, these accounts offer counter-discursive understandings that challenge the reductive monopolisation over meaning held by authoritative legal discourse and subvert the black-letter of the law. Secondly, it is incorporated in terms of form. The aim of this book is not to find, bring to light and reconcile 'hidden truths' about bodies that are submerged by the operations of law and discourse. The book does not work towards the modernist academic goal of guiding law closer to a more 'correct' understanding about bodies and body alteration, nor does it 'engage in the project of constructing a "grand theory"' (Beckmann 2009, p.6) that somehow draws together all the intersections between body alteration and law into a singular explanatory framework. Instead, like Beckmann (2009, p.6) I am 'committed to a critical exploration of significant concepts that serve as normativizing injunctions' within law and discourse. This book is about discovering, probing and dissecting multiple and competing understandings about bodies, how they are constructed and presented by various systems of discourse and how they are incorporated (or not incorporated) into criminal law. It does not make claims about which specific understanding about bodies that law and discourse should adopt and privilege, rather this book makes the pluralist claim that law and discourse should acknowledge a wider range of understandings about bodies.

It should be noted that the term '"postmodernism" is often used interchangeably with poststructuralism— and different writers will use either one of these terms to refer to the same body of theory' (Rahman and Jackson, 2010, p.125). Despite these terminological slippages within the broader commentary, this book refers to this body of theory as postmodernism. It should also be noted that postmodernism's body of theory stretches far beyond the focus on subjectivity and plurality that I have discussed here. A more thorough explanation of postmodernism would need to address the work of prominent theorists such as Baudrillard (1988a; 1988b; 1988c; 1988d), Derrida (1992), Foucault (1964; 1972; 1976; 1977; 1988a; 1988b; 1988c; 2003) and Lyotard (1984; 1988), as well as other key postmodern concepts such as deconstruction, simulacra and simulation, pastiche, irony and semiosis. To attempt a complete definition of postmodernism might even be a fool's errand. As Turner (1984, p.5) notes, given the very nature of postmodernism and its commitment to 'open textuality ... it is hardly possible to adopt a rigid or formal consensus about what [it] is'. Nevertheless, whilst this book deliberately adopts some core aspects of postmodernism it does not address other core aspects of postmodernism.

Narrowing down the broad range of postmodernism to what is relevant for the later analysis, one final part of the theoretical basis of the book must be touched upon: discourse. As Simon (1996, p.12) notes, if any one concept other than pluralism 'dominates discourse about postmodernism' it is the concept of '"discourse" itself'. Michel Foucault, who engaged with it at length in works such as *The Archaeology of Knowledge* (1972) and *Madness and Civilization* (1964), can be largely credited with developing and expanding the particular conceptions of discourse that this book draws on. Discourse is of such integral concern to the book that the next section of this chapter is devoted to an explanation of it. The purpose of mentioning discourse here is to locate this book's concern with discourse as a corollary to its adoption of other aspects of postmodernism.

Having explained the general influence of postmodernism on the book's analytical approach, it is still necessary to acknowledge and address the works that have informed the makeup of its theoretical basis. Whilst a number of texts provide valuable models of how to systematically incorporate elements of postmodernism into the discursive analysis of legal areas (such as Eisenstein, 1988; Smart, 1989), this book is indebted to two texts in particular: Carl Stychin's *Law's Desire: Sexuality and the Limits of Justice* (1995) and Alan Hyde's *Bodies of Law* (1997).

Stychin (1995) provides an illuminating example of how to embed postmodernism in his interrogation of the discursive construction of homosexuality within law and legal discourse. He closely reads and analyses homosexuality as a discursive category, revealing how homosexual identities are constructed and regulated within the law and demonstrating the ways in which such identities can be deconstructed and contested. He also offers an explicitly postmodern counter-point to the typical jurisprudential obsession with 'unearthing' and cultivating the internal logic of the legal system, stating that he cannot 'provide a singular "truth" in [his] examination' and must remain suspicious of claims to universal truth (Stychin 1995, p.1). The incorporation of postmodern thought in this book closely follows parts of Stychin's approach. Like Stychin (1995), the book treats elements of postmodern thought as a theoretical basis to achieve its analytical ends and will also highlight avenues for the contestation of authoritative legal discourse.

Hyde (1997) focuses on the use of language to reveal how law has developed a taxonomy of metaphor-centred, discursive conceptualisations of the body. For example, he identifies metaphors such as 'body-as-property' and 'body-as-machine' as being key concepts circulating within legal discourse. Tracing the development of these metaphors through time, Hyde (1997) elucidates the historical conditions for their existence and addresses the specific ways they inflect and function within legal reasoning. He rightly points out that these metaphor-constructions should be treated in a 'self-conscious' way, because they are neither 'natural' nor authentic, and that they should be regarded as 'strategic interventions' because they position and influence legal discourse in politically loaded ways (Hyde, 1997, p.235). Ultimately, Hyde (1997) argues towards what he names a postmodern state of 'body fantasia'. Within this state, the legal system would admit the artifice of these body metaphors, and begin using them reflexively as a means to move towards the 'larger goal of communication and understanding' the diversity of people (Hyde, 1997, p.263). Like Hyde (1997), this book argues that the conceptualisations of the body built up within legal discourse are thoroughly artificial as well as politically loaded. However, instead of arguing towards a state of 'body fantasia' where these conceptions of the body would still persist within the law (albeit in a more reflexive capacity), it works instead towards breaking down current restrictions on conceptions of the body by exposing them to alternative, counter-discursive accounts.

Hyde (1997, p.263) considers legal discourse to function in a reductive manner; he deplores the body metaphors used by law as 'the cumbersome euphemisms of people who cannot talk about the body, like sexless, joyless lawyers in their evasiveness'. The subtext here is that legal discourse is deficient in that it fails to capture some essential truth or authentic knowledge about the body. The problematic aspect of this subtext is that Hyde seems to slip from postmodern thought into a more modernist critique by figuring legal discourse as an inauthentic way of conceptualising the body. This necessarily implies objectivity, in that a conceptualisation of the body can only be inauthentic if there is an authentic conceptualisation of the body against which it can be measured and found wanting. Unfortunately, this modernist slippage seems crucial to the argument because it is necessary in order to justify his advocacy for the 'body fantasia' ideal: if current legal discourse isn't 'broken' in some way, then the 'solution' he offers would be superfluous. Unlike Hyde's (2007) approach, this book is more focused on the postmodern ideal of subjectivity and does not consider there to be an 'objective' truth about bodies that legal discourse should aim to approach or embody. Rather the book considers there to be a plurality of subjective truth-claims about bodies, and it reveals how legal discourse and law differentially authorise, marginalise and elide these accounts.

Discussing Discourse

Understanding the concept of discourse requires a shift away from seeing language 'simply as expressive, as transparent, as a vehicle for communication, as a form of representation', and towards seeing language as 'a system with its own rules and constraints, and with its own determining effect on the way that individuals think and express themselves' (Mills 1997, p.8). As such, the term 'discourse' has been used by commentators such as Foucault to 'more broadly… denote ways of thinking about and constructing knowledge of the world' (Rahman and Jackson, 2010, p.42). Language exists within different types of verbal and non-verbal texts and can be broken up into component parts, such as utterances, sentences and statements. Collections of component parts that have a discernible regularity in terms of their 'objects, types of statements, concepts, or thematic choices' (Foucault, 1972, p.38) are called discursive formations or discursive structures (Mills, 1997, p.17). Such collections are governed by their own idiosyncratic internal logics that regulate the form and content of their statements, as well as the requisite conditions under which such statements can operate and be communicated. Thus, attempting to determine whether a statement falls within the boundaries of a certain discursive framework requires comparing that statement to a collection of other statements generated within the discursive formation to determine if they result from a similar 'institutional pressure', if they have similar 'provenance or context' and if 'they act in a similar way' (Mills, 1997, p.62).

This book is concerned with discourse, and in particular with legal discourse. It is uncontentious to identify that the legal system produces an idiosyncratic discursive formation (Gibbons, 1994; Humphreys, 1995; Smart, 1992), and that this legal discourse, perhaps more so than other discourses, 'regulates the symbolic domain in order to maintain social order' (Gulerce, 2007, p.33). Legal discourse can be considered to be quite a 'fertile field' for discourse analysis both because it is highly verbal and because legal statements are carefully recorded and housed in the 'immense collections' of the law libraries, courts and internet databases (Shuy, 2003). The key agents who 'help to establish law as a discourse' include 'courts, judges, lawyers, and law professors' (Eisenstein, 1988, p.43) and the kinds of texts that make up legal discourse include statutes, cases, legal submissions, oral court records, transcripts, academic articles, academic books, and so on. This book focuses on written legal texts rather than on the various types of oral legal texts. This choice is simply one of convenience due to the easy availability of these written texts for research.

Exploring and analysing 'legal discourse' cannot be successfully carried out by adopting an approach that focuses purely on the 'law'. Legal discourse, like any discourse, is permeable because it intersects with other discursive formations. Isolating a particular discourse and determining what texts can be attributed to it is complicated by the fact that discursive formations do not function as discrete, self-contained wholes. They influence, and are influenced by, other discourses with which they share social space, and they are thus in a state of 'constant conflict … over questions of truth and authority' (Mills, 1997, p.19). As a result, the meanings and values assigned to the objects of discourse fluctuate with the varying authority held by certain discourses at certain times. Whilst legal discourse may be a relatively individuated formation, it is deeply interconnected with other discourses and institutions. Despite law's role as the sole 'institutionalised means of settling disputes and solving problems of social order' (Humphreys, 1985, p.250), legal discourse is only 'relatively autonomous' (Post, 1991, p.viii) as other discursive frameworks influence its operation. Concepts within political discourse, such as 'public order', influence the methods involved in policing and enforcement of laws at certain times and in certain spaces. Similarly, concepts within medical discourse, such as clinical definitions of 'insanity' and assessments of the level of physical injury, influence the extent of legal liability for actions. Legal discourse is thus sufficiently separate to be recognised as an individual discursive formation, but it is not separate enough to be free from the influence of other dominant discourses. Incorporating this understanding about the permeability of legal discourse into the theoretical basis of this book opens up the scope of the analysis. The analysis needs to be calibrated so as to encompass more than just legal discourse, and must also consider the range of other discursive frameworks that impact on legal discourse; law should not be 'seen unambiguously, in isolation, but in its relationship to [a] diverse range of social discourses' around the body (Sclater, 2002, p.1). Indeed, as Roberts (2011, p.351) recognises:

> To frame an issue within the context of legal discourse is not simply to resolve it or to make it solely a legal issue. Practices relating to the body cut across all the boundaries between social, political, legal, religious, medical, cultural and theoretical discourses exposing the ways in which each bleeds into the others and is in turn ruptured by the others.

Discourses are not only conflicted without, they are also conflicted within. Foucault (1972, p.155) warns us not to look for an 'ideal, continuous, smooth text' because discourses are characterised by dissension and contradiction. Discursive formations are malleable and responsive to internal and external pressures; their boundaries and logics are eternally changing and reshaping to accommodate shifts within other discourses and the wider culture. Discourse will necessarily never be free from competition for meaning. Whilst dominant and authoritative themes may strongly impact on the general flow of concepts within discursive frameworks, alternative conceptualisations are always simultaneously being pushed by counter-discursive currents.

Incorporating this understanding about the internal conflict within legal discourse into the theoretical basis of this book orients the scope of the analysis. The book cannot hope to analyse 'all' of legal discourse across time, but rather can only attempt to identify and engage with those key aspects of legal discourse that are identifiable by their relative authority, ubiquity and constancy within the contested discursive flux. Furthermore, the analysis must also account for the alternative counter-discursive currents that exist within legal discourse and that push back against the dominant authoritative discursive conceptions. Authoritative strands of legal discourse operate to 'disqualify other knowledges and experiences', determining who can speak and 'how they are allowed to speak', and who is 'silenced' (Smart, 1989, p11). This understanding is a key concept within the book. The tension and contradiction between dominant discursive conceptions and alternative discursive conceptions is an issue that will be revisited and directly addressed across multiple case studies within this book. It will be expounded upon at length in terms of how certain discursive conceptions construct and maintain their dominance, how and why other discursive conceptions are marginalised, and also in terms of identifying promising avenues for future potential change in discourse. These kinds of Foucauldian understandings about discourse can be and have been used in a variety of contexts, such as around sex/gender and sexuality, to demonstrate 'how identities are potentially multiple and unstable, but are disciplined into dominant versions' (Rahman and Jackson, 2010, p.43). Indeed, feminist legal writing has 'commonly rehearsed' and strongly established the proposition that law and legal discourse often 'fails to reflect women's lives and experiences' (Conaghan, 2013, p.47). However, this book moves beyond feminism's particular analytic focus on sex/gender and demonstrates how the lives and experiences of a variety of people are marginalised within legal discourse around body alteration.

The value of discourse theory comes in recognising that discursive formations are not merely representational, they are also productive; '[d]iscourses generate meaning rather than manifest pre-existing meaning' (Eisenstein, 1988, p.9). Discourse is inherently caught up in the '*social construction of reality*', where the 'texts we write and speak both shape and are shaped by [social and cultural] practices' (Paltridge, 2006, p.9, emphasis in original). Because it mediates an individual's apprehension of reality, the influence of discourse moves beyond framing texts to also constructing particular 'ways of thinking and behaving' (Mills, 1997, pp.17–18). Discourse is 'constraining, deviation-correcting, order-producing [and] disciplining' (Gulerce, 2007, p.32), because it limits and frames the minds and bodies of individuals in accordance with its content. Thus, when a discursive formation is organised around a single 'logic or a scientific, ideological, or any other belief' it reproduces thinking and behaving along that line (Gulerce, 2007, p.32). As such, discursive conceptualisations are an intrinsic part of our social reality. Things can be said to only exist contextually 'under the positive conditions of [the] complex group of relations' that make up the discourse around them (Foucault, 1972, p.45). But the discursive power to construct reality is also limited by this need for contextualisation.

Incorporating this understanding about the productive nature of discourse into the theoretical basis of this book requires the recognition that law does not passively represent or reproduce social phenomena when it puts them on trial. Instead, legal discourse actively constructs a particular model of reality. That is, the power of law is 'creative' and not just repressive (Smart, 1989, p.7). This enables comparisons to be drawn between various constructions of subjects under various discourses. In Chapter 2, for example, it allows for the identification of authoritative legal discourse as constructing a particular model of sadomasochism as harmful, non-consensual and violent, which is shown to compete with alternative discursive conceptualisations of sadomasochism as an enjoyable and meaningful pursuit. In turn, this enables analytical engagement with the processes and techniques of discourse that produce and position these competing conceptualisations.

So far, I have addressed what 'discourse' means and have offered some very specific examples of how it is incorporated into my analysis. It is also important to take a step backwards in order to address how discourse is used to structure the analytical approach in a very broad sense as well. The variety of ways in which academics have utilised discourse as an analytical tool has resulted in the phrase 'discourse analysis' becoming 'polysemie' (Scollon and Scollon

2003). Discourse analysis can generally mean either a close linguistic analysis of a specific text or collections of texts, or it can mean a broader, cultural analysis of the ways in which discourse operates within society. It seems like it should be easy to determine the particular type of analysis being conducted by the way in which the material is addressed in a work, but, as Mills (1997) recognises, many writers slip in and out of different types without explicitly stating they are doing so. Any compartmentalisation between linguistic and cultural analysis falls apart as even strict linguistic analyses still tend to situate themselves 'within a broader sociocultural or historical context', and cultural analyses still tend to 'ground themselves in the close analysis of concrete texts' (Scollon and Scollon, 2003). The analysis in this book is not a close analysis of the type favoured by academic linguists who identify as 'discourse analysts'. The analysis in the book is a cultural analysis of how discourse operates broadly in the context of law, but it does draw connections to the use of specific terms and phraseology. The analysis herein is sympathetic to the ideas evident in what discourse analysts term 'critical discourse analysis', which emphasises exploring the 'connections between the use of language and the social and political contexts in which it occurs' (Paltridge, 2006, p.179), with a view to the 'critique of dominant discourses and genres that effect inequalities, injustices and oppression in contemporary society' (Van Leeuwen, 2009, p.278). Primary issues of concern in critical discourse analysis include 'tracing underlying ideologies from the linguistic features', 'unpacking' meaning and inter-relations (Paltridge, 2006, p.179), and determining how the techniques of 'framing' (the presentation of content), such as 'foregrounding' (what content is emphasised) and 'backgrounding' (what content is deemphasised), are utilised (Paltridge, 2006, p.45).

As the analysis in this book progresses it alters scope between focusing on language use to a broader form of cultural discourse analysis. All chapters carry elements of both forms but Chapters 2 and 3 are more focused on the specific use of language than Chapters 4 and 5. This is partly a result of differences within the subject matter, but predominantly this shift is made in order to explore and reveal more about the various processes and techniques of law and discourse.

How to Read Bodies

As Turner (1984, p.1) notes, 'there is an obvious and prominent fact about human beings: they have bodies and they are bodies. More lucidly, human beings are embodied, just as they are enselved. Our everyday life is dominated by the details of our corporeal existence.' The relatively recent upsurge of academic interest in bodies within disciplines such as cultural studies, philosophy and anthropology possibly stems from the modern feminist movement's 'reprioritisation' of the female body as a site of political struggle (Lacey, 1998, p.114). Indeed, 'the body is a perennial in feminism' (Fox and Murphy 2013, p.250), with a large amount of feminist legal work having been built up around the construction and deployment of 'the body' and bodies within law and legal discourse (Braidotti, 2011; Bridgeman and Millns, 1995; Conaghan, 2013; Eisenstein, 1988; Fox and Murphy, 2013; Grbich, 1991; Lacey, 1998; Naffine and Owens, 1997; Smart, 1989; 1995). Whilst much early feminist legal work was concerned primarily with 'the female body', Fox and Murphy (2013, pp.252–253, emphasis in original) identify a 'turn towards *bodies* and, more recently, towards *embodiment*'. Work on the body now extends beyond the female body by touching on other analytic sites such as the disabled body (Campbell, 2001), the fat body (Murray, 2007), the homosexual body (Dalton, 2006), the male body (Thomson, 2008; 2011), reproductive and biotechnologies and 'variant corporeality' (Karpin and Mykitiuk 2011). Contemporary anthologies typically deal with a wide range of different body types and bodily issues (Bainham, et al., 2002; Cheah, et al., 1996; Hyde 1997).

Accompanying the diversity in the sites of body analysis is diversity in the ways in which bodies are analysed and read. Some theorists focus on the material body, dealing primarily with the 'physical aspects of experience', such as the 'corporeal body, the literal implementation of institutional control [and] the impact of the social environment' (Ussher, 1997, p.1). Other theorists focus on the body within discourse, dealing with issues such as body 'talk', 'visual representation', 'ideology, culture and power' (Ussher, 1997, p.1). The 'cultural turn' within critical scholarship over the last few decades has been identified as contributing to a general shift away from materialist engagement with the body and towards postmodern-inspired constructionist approaches that focus not 'on the body per se but on discourses *around* and *about* the body' (Conaghan, 2013, p.40, emphasis in original). Bottomley (2002, p.144) has argued that this focus on 'cultural representation' has been seen as a 'seemingly safer' way to analyse the body due to the 'fears of essentialism and determinism' that attach to engagement with the corporeality of the body, particularly feminist engagement with the 'female' body. However, the emergence of a 'New Materialism' in recent work has been taken to suggest a possible re-engagement with materiality and physicality within body work (Conaghan, 2013), and the 'resurgence of interest in how the body figures in theories and sexuality' has been read as 'challenging' the absence of the material body in postmodern and certain sociological writing (Rahman and Jackson, 2010, p.130).

Braidotti (2011, p.127) understands the body as 'neither a biological nor a sociological category, but rather as a point of overlap between the physical, the symbolic ... and the sociological', and these same vectors also overlap around body alterations. This book falls more strongly within the discursive, postmodern type of analysis popularised by the 'cultural turn', but because of this overlap it also engages at some points with the corporeality of bodies. In order to address both the discursive and physical elements of body alteration, the analysis within this book needs to be able to draw on a theoretical framework that assists in reading and understanding bodies. The particular understandings that are drawn on here conceptualise bodies as both inscriptive and active, and as being subject to disciplinary pressure.

As Grosz (1995, p.33, emphasis in original) argues, there has been a strong school of thought that conceives of bodies as being a '*hinge* or threshold' between a person's 'psychic or lived interiority' and the 'socio-political exteriority'. Accordingly, some cultural theorists have identified bodies as being 'inscriptive', meaning that bodies can be read and understood as 'surface[s] on which social law, morality, and values are inscribed' (Grosz, 1995, p.33). Under this model of bodies, culturally specific norms about bodily markings and adornment are materially (re)produced in the bodies of societal members and thus their bodies mark them as members of that culture. The inscriptive body is understood as a threshold between the self and culture, meaning that body markings and practices are 'emblems, heralds, badges, theatres, tableaux, of social laws and rights' (Grosz, 1994, p.118). There is a tendency to join this inscriptive model of the body with a form of interpretive body-reading. An individual's bodily signs and features are read as not only indicative of the social ordering that produces them, but also as indicative of the extent to which that individual has internalised the social order. Thus, non-normatively marked bodies tend to be read as indicating psychically non-normative individuals. Urla and Terry (1995, p.4) see this in the insistent idea that 'individuals who deviate from [social ideals] are morally and socially inferior, and that their social or moral disruptiveness is always somehow embodied'.

Whilst this inscriptive model conceptualises bodies as being representative of both social forces and psychic interiority, in doing so it relegates the body to the role of a 'passive medium' that is worked upon (Butler, 1990, p.129). This idea of the body as 'inert matter' is drawn from a particular, dated Cartesian paradigm (Butler, 1990, p.129). If the body is conceived merely as flesh that is inscribed and moulded from within by the self and from without by external social forces, then two undesirable presuppositions can be drawn out. Firstly, the inscriptive model seems to imply that there is a 'naturalistic' body that pre-dates and is covered over by inscription. This idea of an unchanging, 'natural' ideal body is a dominant bodily conception that has persisted throughout time and cuts across multiple discursive frameworks, figuring prominently in both legal and medical discourse. Butler (1990) has dismantled this conception of a pre-discursive body, arguing that physical features, like the genitalia, are always already coded and culturally positioned in certain ways, with the result that they cannot be separated from their representational effect. In relation to the distinction often drawn between sex and gender, Butler (1990, p.8, emphasis in original) even reverses normative cultural body logic by asking the question: '[t]o what extent does the body *come into being* in and through the mark(s) of gender?' On her account, 'bodies, as we understand them, come into being – materialize – through the reiteration of regulatory norms', they do not and cannot exist 'outside or prior to discourse' and are instead 'a discursive creation' (Conaghan, 2013, p.40). Secondly, the inscriptive model frames the body as a kind of canvas: something that is merely worked upon and presented to signify certain meanings. Butler (1990) argues that the body is not just a passive medium for inscription but rather actively takes up and performs body activities in order to position itself in culturally-meaningful ways within discursive frameworks of signification. The body does not just display the marks of its struggle with external social forces, rather the body is itself the site where cultural body knowledge is worked through, negotiated, (re)produced and/or challenged. Whilst this argument may have originally been made with specific regard to the performance of gender, it can be extended to cover other identity-formations constituted around, or signified by, particular body practices such as body alteration.

Incorporating these understandings of bodies as being both inscriptive and active into the theoretical basis of this book connects bodies to discourse. If bodies are 'sites of struggle and resistance' between personal and cultural forces (Grosz, 1995, p.36), then body alterations constitute important battlegrounds within this conflict. Body alterations have the potential to allow bodies to embody or transgress social norms and expectations, where such norms and expectations are the products of dominant forces within the discursive frameworks that enmesh the embodied subject. Body alterations that uphold normative models of embodiedness can thus be discursively read as being conservative because they both reflect, reify and reproduce dominant discursive understandings about bodies. Conversely, body alterations that challenge normative models of embodiedness can thus be discursively read as being transgressive because they both reflect, reify and produce alternative discursive understandings about bodies. Not only does this understanding connect bodies to discourse, it also provides a methodology for reading the political significance of body alterations. This methodology will be adopted throughout the case studies.

Foucault (2003, pp.240–242) identifies that 'State control of the biological' manifests in two related but distinct 'techniques of power that [are] essentially centered on the body'. Firstly, he argues that bodies are subject to 'disciplinary power' as they are 'controlled, identified and reproduced' by disciplinary mechanisms (Turner, 1984, p.34), which spatially distribute, organise, render visible and 'take control' of individual bodies (Foucault, 2003, p.242). Historically, such mechanisms operated overtly through relatively unsophisticated means such as violence and torture. Contemporaneously, however, these mechanisms are far more likely to operate in a manner that is 'calculated, organized, technically thought out', far more 'subtle' and yet still of the 'physical order' (Foucault, 1977, p.27). Such mechanisms may make use of the insistent repetition of spatiotemporal routines and movements, such as in the discipline of 'universities, secondary schools, barracks [and] workshops' (Foucault, 1976, p.140). Other mechanisms constitute and employ particular knowledges of the body that are 'not exactly the science of its functioning' (Foucault, 1977, p.27), such as medical discourse's tradition of pathologising bodies that take pleasure in non-normative sexual practices. These mechanisms of disciplinary power operate not only externally upon subjects but, insidiously, also operate internally within subjects. Once particular routines and knowledges about the body are internalised through repetition and pressure, individuals become self-disciplining. Secondly, he argues that bodies are also subject to 'bio-power', by which he meant the 'numerous and diverse techniques for achieving the subjugation of bodies and the control of populations' (Foucault, 1976, p.140). The difference between bio-power and disciplinary power is that bio-power is focused on the control of bodies at a far more generalised level than disciplinary power's focus on the individual: it is concerned not with 'man's body' but with the broader concept of 'man-as-species' (Foucault, 2003, p.242). It focuses on issues of 'birth, death, production, illness and so on', and seeks to measure and regulate 'processes such as the ratio of births to deaths, the rate of reproduction, the fertility of a population and so on' (Foucault, 2003, pp.242–243). Bio-power, then, 'deals with the population … as a political problem' that is also at the same time 'a biological problem' (Foucault, 2003, p.245).

Foucault acknowledges that his twin concepts of disciplinary power and bio-power are not mutually exclusive, but rather coexist and somewhat 'dovetail' because whilst they operate at different levels and on different scales and make use 'of very different instruments' (Foucault, 2003, p.243), they are both centred around techniques of control exerted over bodies. To the extent that these concepts can be disentangled this book is concerned primarily with disciplinary power, as the analytic focus of this work is on particular body alterations undergone by individual bodies rather than on population-level control mechanisms focused on humanity as a species. The concept of disciplinary power thus needs some further unpacking. Heyes (2007b, p.6) understands disciplinary power as 'a system of management in which all it touches participate; it operates on the population and on the body, fostering techniques of control, intervention, and regulation often presented as working to mutual benefit'. In doing so, disciplinary power 'functions to consolidate identities by managing the body's movements, its surface, and even our lived experience' (Heyes, 2007b, p.7). She explains further that '[d]isciplinary power is constitutive of the subject rather than external to it; it creates – rather than being imposed upon – types of individual' (Heyes, 2007b, p.6). It does not simply regulate individuals, it also 'makes individuals; it is the specific technique of power that regards individuals both as objects and as instruments of its exercise' (Duncan, 1995, p 328). Through disciplinary power the 'multiple resources and capacities of the body' are 'socialized into purposeful productivity' (Braidotti, 2011, p. 167) as the kind of individual that disciplinary power works towards making is one whose 'forces … have been rendered both useful and docile' (Foucault, 2003, p.249) A 'docile' body is a body that is thoroughly 'subjected and practised' (Foucault, 1977, p.138). Docile bodies have social utility, they are more economically productive because their labour power is more focused and they are less likely to be politically disobedient (Foucault, 1977 p.138). Disciplinary power thus prioritises the (re)production of normativised and conformist 'docile' bodies.

The concepts of disciplinary power and docile bodies are key ideas that are used in this book. Law is an exemplary disciplinary mechanism, functioning not only overtly, such as through the use of authorised police force and systems of incarceration, but also through more sophisticated mechanisms of internalisation and routine, such as the ways in which society is structured around legal restrictions and prohibitions. The idea of disciplinary power reveals that law does not just regulate bodies, it actively produces normativising knowledges about bodies and certain types of socially valuable bodies through the 'differential disciplining of differentially constructed bodies' (Duncan, 1995, p.345). Naffine (1997, p.84) recognises that 'law's approach is always, and inevitably, constitutive rather than simply reactive', and that it 'helps to constitute and organise our very sense of the nature and activities of the body. It shapes our understanding of the body, obliging us to think of bodies in certain ways, and not in others.' Thus we can understand law's relationship with the body as at once 'creative' and 'regulatory' (Cheah, Fraser and Grbich, 1996, p.xviii), in the same way as disciplinary power. A body that has been thoroughly subjected by law is a docile body. Indeed, the existence of the 'subjected body' can be considered to be a 'condition of possibility of the law' (Cheah, et al., 1996, p.xvii). If we accept that law embeds discursive understandings about bodies and society, then the body that is subjected by law is also subjected by dominant and authoritative aspects of the wider discursive framework. Revealing the discursive techniques and processes through which law produces docile bodies is an ongoing goal throughout the case studies. Correlatively, this book also charts the related issue of how law marginalises 'unruly' bodies, that is those bodies who contest their legal subjection and resist or challenge the disciplinary power of law.

Fully Equipped

Having extracted the relevant aspects of postmodernism, discourse theory and body theory, this book is now fully equipped to engage in its analysis of the body alteration case studies chosen for consideration. This chapter has set out the theoretical basis that provides support and structure to this analysis. This analysis adopts a postmodern focus on subjectivity and pluralism, reflects the permeable, externally conflicted and productive nature of legal discourse, and reads bodies and body alterations as both inscriptive and active. These theories and ideas will shape and influence the book as it progresses. This chapter has also introduced and explained the key concepts that will be explicitly drawn upon throughout the analysis. The internally conflicted nature of discourse is a key concept that highlights the discursive tensions within legal discourse, and this book will demonstrate how authoritative discursive conceptualisations construct and maintain their dominance despite facing constant pressure from alternative conceptualisations. The docile body is another key concept that connects bodies, discourse and law together as the form and effect of normative disciplinary pressure. This book will address how both docile and unruly bodies are constructed, de/valued and regulated by legal and discursive forces.

Chapter 2
Sadomasochistic Injuries: Harmful Crime or Harmless Pastime?

Sadomasochism is not merely a bodily activity, it is also a form of body alteration. Whilst sadomasochistic activities can be stopped or started at whim, they can also have ongoing physical effects. The cuts, bruises, burns, grazes, or any other injuries left after participation in sadomasochistic activities literally alter the masochist's body for the duration of their healing. Sadomasochistic activities cannot be understood in isolation from the injuries they can cause and such injuries cannot be understood in isolation from the sadomasochistic activities that cause them. Both are a function and effect of the other. Newmahr (2010, p.396) identifies sadomasochism as being 'a carnal experience. It is enacted, performed, processed, lived, and experienced on and through the body. Bodily manifestations and consequences of SM, such as bruises, scratches, and scars, are deeply entwined in ideologies of power.' But sadomasochistic activities and their effects are not only deeply imbricated at the physical and theoretical levels, they are also legally conjoined. As will be discussed below, the law only typically intervenes to regulate sadomasochistic activities where they result in bodily alteration of some kind: an alteration that legal discourse conceptualises as a form of harmful injury. Thus this book's focus on the body altering aspects of sadomasochism has particular resonance in relation to the law. This chapter will analyse 'sadomasochism' in the sense of a necessarily simultaneous analysis of both sadomasochistic activities and injuries, because sadomasochism is a type of bodily activity that is conceptually, literally and strongly legally interlinked with body alteration.

Sadomasochism has attracted a multitude of interpretations, being seen variously as criminal, pathological, pleasurable, painful, pro-feminist, anti-feminist, progressive, conservative, transgressive, *passé*, cathartic, sinful, spiritual, and so on (Califia, 1987; Freckelton, 1994; Hanna, 2001; Jeffreys 1993–1994; 1994; Stear, 2009). As a category, sadomasochism is marked by 'instability' (Khan, 2014, p.15): it defies easy characterisation and its evocative nature ensures both contestation around its meaning and a certain level of heatedness in this contestation. If we recognise sadomasochism as an unstable category then we should be wary of accounts of sadomasochism that fail to recognise this range of meaning, particularly those that disregard the meanings attached to sadomasochism by sadomasochists themselves. This charge can be levelled against the conceptualisation of sadomasochism within various discursive frameworks, from the psychological pathology model put forward by medical discourse (Freckelton, 1994), to the reified patriarchal power model put forward by radical feminist discourse (Linden, et al., 1982), to the disrupted development model put forward by psychoanalytic discourse (Hanly, 1995). The conceptualisation of sadomasochism embedded within authoritative legal discourse also exemplifies such a failure.

Legal discourse confines discussion of sadomasochism to preset modes of delivery, dealing only with certain issues and employing a terminology coloured by pejorative associations. Sadomasochism is conceptualised within legal discourse in terms that focus only on certain aspects of its practice, such as the physical acts involved and the physical consequences that result. As a result, authoritative legal discourse constructs sadomasochism as non-consensual, injurious, violent crime. Within legal discourse, masochists become pitiable victims who should be protected from their own desires, sadists become violent assaulters who hurt others and sadomasochistic injuries become bodily harms that always degrade and disable. Alternative, more positive, discursive understandings of sadomasochism are marginalised within legal discourse and erased from the operation of the law.

Clashes between discursive understandings are common and inevitable. As Mills (1997, p.19) notes, 'discourses do not exist in a vacuum but are in constant conflict with other discourses and other social practices which inform them over questions of truth and authority'. Indeed, discourses may be seen as being defined by their standpoint positions in relation to other discourses, and a discourse necessarily 'concerns itself with certain objects and puts forward certain concepts at the expense of others' (Macdonell, 1986, p.3). But there is no meaningful 'clash' of discourses here. Law's 'monologic formulatio[n] do[es] not leave space for other equally valid discourses' and instead becomes a 'too[l] of subjection' (Beckmann, 2009, p.39). Authoritative legal discourse holds a monopoly over legal meaning and legal power, so this 'clash' is more accurately understood as the subjugation and attempted recuperation of alterity. Ultimately, this exemplifies how law and legal discourse operate as a disciplinary power that constructs and (re)produces docile bodies and that sanctions unruly sadomasochistic bodies.

The legal focus of this chapter is on how sadomasochism is treated within criminal law as a violent offence, based on legal concepts of 'consensual assault' that Australia has inherited from and subsequently shared with the common law of England and Wales. The analytical focus of this chapter is on revealing the processes through which legal discourse constructs sadomasochism as criminal, and on demonstrating how authoritative legal discourse marginalises alternative discursive understandings about sadomasochism. This chapter begins by defining sadomasochism and identifying its legal status, and then moves to reveal the operation of legal discourse around key concepts such as consent, violence and harm. A critical counterpoint is then raised by detailing alternative discursive constructions of sadomasochism drawn from sadomasochists themselves and from non-legal academic studies of sadomasochistic subculture. The ultimate argument within this chapter is that the non-normative qualities of sadomasochism position it as a form of body alteration whose transgressive potential prompts the discursive erasure and legal recuperation of unruly sadomasochistic bodies in order to uphold dominant cultural norms surrounding concepts such as sex, violence and the body.

Sadomasochism

The term 'sadomasochism' combines two distinctly different, but conceptually related, words: 'sadism' and 'masochism'. Both words were coined by Richard von Krafft-Ebing and they gained widespread recognition after the dissemination of his book *Psychopathia Sexualis* in the late 1800s. He defined sadism as 'the experience of sexual pleasurable sensations (including orgasm) produced by acts of cruelty' (Krafft-Ebing, 1885, p.53) and the 'desire to cause pain and use force' (Krafft-Ebing, 1885, p.86). He named it after the Marquis de Sade, Donatien Alphonse François (1740–1814), who was a French nobleman and writer of fiction with sadistic elements, such as *The 120 Days of Sodom* and *Justine, or the Misfortunes of Virtue*. Krafft-Ebing (1885, p.86) defined masochism as 'the wish to suffer pain and be subjected to force', to be treated like a servant, 'humiliated and abused'. He named it after Leopold von Sacher-Masoch (1836–1895), who was an Austrian writer whose fictional works contained masochistic themes, such as *Venus in Furs*.

Originally, 'sadism' and 'masochism' were medical terms. Krafft-Ebing was an early psychiatrist and *Psychopathia Sexualis* comprised his attempt to identify and catalogue sexual disorders and deviations. Contemporaneously, these words have entered popular vogue and their current usage is looser and only contingently sexual. For example, Bibbings and Alldridge (1993, p.359) have identified that the word sadism is used in some American legal cases to mean merely 'gratuitously cruel', 'bullying' or non-sexual enjoyment from 'inflicting pain'. Chancer (1992) follows the Freudian psychoanalytic tradition by relabelling Krafft-Ebing's 'sadomasochism' as 'sexual sadomasochism', which she identifies as separate from the everyday 'sadomasochism' apparently found in many non-sexual relationships such as between friends and between employers and employees. A dynamic of relative power/powerlessness between two people seems sufficient for Chancer to use the term. However, sadomasochism has not wholly escaped its medicalised roots. 'Sexual Sadism Disorder' and 'Sexual

Masochism Disorder' remain diagnosable under the paraphilia section of the 5th edition of the *Diagnostic and Statistical Manual of Mental Disorders* (American Psychiatric Association, 2013).[1]

One further important connotation that has since been attached to sadomasochism is that of consensuality. For decades, the consensual nature of sadomasochistic activity has been a core feature of sociological and psychological studies within this area. Weinberg, Williams and Moser's (1984) widely cited operational definition of sadomasochism includes consensuality as a key component, and it has been noted that the mottoes adopted by the sadomasochistic subculture, such as 'Safe, Sane and Consensual' (SSC) and 'Risk Aware Consensual Kink' (RACK), clearly identify consent as integral to sadomasochists themselves (Downing, 2007). Indeed, a large proportion of academic writing on sadomasochism assumes consent as a given (Kleinplatz and Moser, 2006; Weinberg 1995). The primacy of consent within these discursive constructions of sadomasochism does not feature in all discourses around sadomasochism. Khan (2014, p.245) identifies that within both law and popular culture representations of sadomasochism, there is a 'conflation between sexual dominance in an s/m context, and sexual sadism in a non-consensual context'. Indeed, consent has proven to be a highly contested issue within legal discourse in this area. This legal contestation will be addressed at length below, but for the purposes of this chapter the discussion of sadomasochism will proceed on the basis of consent being freely given to sadomasochistic activities by all parties involved.

In contemporary usage, the word 'sadomasochism' can be located within the wider practice of BDSM, an acronym that stands for bondage and domination (BD), discipline and submission (D/s), and sadomasochism (SM).[2] BD entails physical restraint, bodily training and the imposition of physical force. D/s entails mental control, the use of verbal commands and the roleplaying of dominant/subservient archetypes. Within BDSM, sadomasochism specifically refers to the consensual infliction and receipt of pain. However, while there might be clear theoretical distinctions between these areas, in practice there is

---

1 However, in order to be diagnosed under these categories the individual's sadistic or masochistic 'sexual urges or fantasies [must] cause clinically significant distress or impairment in social, occupational, or other important areas of functioning' (American Psychiatric Association, 2013, pp.694–695). This requirement breaks with previous editions of the *DSM* by differentiating between sadistic/masochistic paraphilias (which do not automatically justify or require clinical intervention) and sadistic/masochistic paraphilic disorders (which do).

2 Legal and non-legal sources use a variety of abbreviations to refer to sadomasochism, including 'SM', 'S&M', 'S & M', 'sado-masochism' and 'sadism and masochism'. This book uses the word 'sadomasochism', but the original wording used in quotations from other sources has been preserved.

no bright dividing line and they frequently co-occur. Hence BDSM generally is brought before the courts when cases of sadomasochism are prosecuted, such as in *R v Brown* [1994] 1 AC 212 (hereafter '*R v Brown* [1994]') (p.236) where Lord Templeman deviated from his decision on the legal issues to conjecture that manacles were employed so 'that the sadist could enjoy the thrill of power and the victim could enjoy the thrill of helplessness'. The trappings of BDSM are also paraded before the court in sadomasochism cases even when not particularly legally relevant, to the effect that legal proceedings '[take] on the air of a carnival, with the prosecution exhibiting shackles, clamps and other equipment' (Ridinger, 2006, p.199). Because BDSM and sadomasochism are so closely interconnected, population participation figures are available only for BDSM. A study of sexually active Australian people aged 16–59 years indicated that approximately 1.8 per cent had participated in some form of BDSM in the past year (Richters, et al., 2008).[3] Despite this intertwining of sadomasochism and BDSM, the criminal law's concern with injuries that occur in the context of these practices ensures that legal attention is brought to bear predominantly on the sadomasochistic elements of BDSM.

So far only a broad description of what the term 'sadomasochism' covers has been offered without providing any details of what it entails in individual, physical specifics. This is because part of the contention in this chapter is that it is reductive to describe and understand sadomasochism as a mere taxonomy of physical acts. An observer's simple recitation of the visible bodily actions, reactions and injuries in a sadomasochistic encounter does not fully encapsulate what can be understood as a complex intersubjective event where the mental states of the participants and their contextualisation of the physical acts are also highly significant. However, with the proviso in place that this will be dealt with later in this chapter, some examples of physical specifics will be provided.

Sadomasochists employ a diverse variety of methods to cause pain, each resulting in different injury profiles – including no injury, superficial injury, temporary injury and (far less commonly) permanent injury. This chapter, and the law relating to 'consensual assault', is concerned primarily with injurious sadomasochistic activities. Spanking, whipping, beating, clamping, piercing, the pouring of hot wax, the use of fire/ice, slapping, pinching, the insertion of needles, cutting, the use of elastic bands, wrestling and cupping, are all techniques that can be utilised in a sadomasochistic encounter. Specialised equipment is readily commercially available for sadomasochists, including floggers, riding crops, low melting-point candles, Wartenberg pinwheels, violet wands, electrical

---

3 In contrast, American studies have indicated that as many as 5–10 per cent of Americans have experienced BDSM at some point in their lives (Apostolides, 1999, cited in Pa, 2001, p.59).

units and canes. Specific examples of sadomasochistic activities that have come before the courts include:

- cutting, slapping, punching, kicking, whipping, striking with a belt and the insertion of pins into the breasts and nipples (*R v Keeble* [2001] EWCA Crim 1764);
- caning of the legs and buttocks (*R v Donovan* [1934] 2 KB 498);
- branding of the genitals and thighs with heated wire, burning of the nipples with matches, insertion of pins into the buttocks, beating of the genitals with a ruler, flogging with stinging nettles, flogging with a cat o'nine tails, caning, biting and the application of hot wax to the genitals (*R v Brown* [1994]);
- whipping of the torso, back and buttocks (*People v Samuels* 250 Cal.App.2d 501 (1967);
- cutting of the breasts and back with a razor (*R v W* 2006 BCPC 300);
- beating of the back with a riding crop (*Commonwealth v Appleby* 380 Mass. 296 (1980)); and,
- burning of the breasts with lighter fluid and asphyxiation with a plastic bag (*R v Emmett* [1999] EWCA Crim 1710).

These specific legal cases should not be understood as being representative of sadomasochism more generally. The sadomasochistic activities that provide the factual matrices underlying these cases provide only a miniscule sampling from the potential thousands of sadomasochistic encounters that occur each year. Furthermore, because of the rarity of such sadomasochistic encounters being policed and/or prosecuted, these legal cases suffer from severe selection bias. Sadomasochism 'tends to come in front of the court when something goes wrong, when there is a complaint, or when it is attached to other stigmatized or unlawful behavior, such as prostitution, or other legal matters, such as child custody' (Khan, 2014, p.225), or where there is some atypical or uncommon feature of the sadomasochistic activities in question, such as the 'extreme' nature of the activities or the severity of the injuries caused.

The Legal Status of Sadomasochistic Injuries

As Ridinger (2006, p.197) points out with regard to the law in America, so too in Australia 'the codes and ordinances of … government at all levels lack clearly stated articles of law explicitly defining and prohibiting or limiting SM actions or practices'. There are no easily referrable statutory sections or legislative instruments that deal specifically with sadomasochistic activities or injuries. As a social phenomenon, sadomasochism intersects with a number of different areas of law (Bennett 2012a; Ridinger 2006; Weait 2007). However, when sadomasochistic activities have been brought before the legal system they have typically been treated as violent offences under the criminal law, because they involve physical touching and (sometimes) injury. In order to explain the legal status of sadomasochistic activities it is necessary to begin by broadly outlining the legal principles that underpin these violent offences, particularly those around assault law.

Technically, the word 'assault' has a different meaning under common law and Code law. Common law has historically differentiated between assault and battery, where 'a battery involves an unlawful and unwanted contact with the body of another, while an assault involves causing another to apprehend the possibility of imminent unlawful contact' (Herring, 2012, p.326). By contrast, Code law has conflated actual touching and the threat of touching under its definition of 'assault':

> A person who strikes, touches, or moves, or otherwise applies force of any kind to the person of another, either directly or indirectly, without the other person's consent, or with the other person's consent if the consent is obtained by fraud, or who by any bodily act or gesture attempts or threatens to apply force of any kind to the person of another without the other person's consent, under such circumstances that the person making the attempt or threat has actually or apparently a present ability to effect his purpose, is said to assault that other person, and the act is called an *assault*. (*Criminal Code Act 1899* (Qld) schedule 1, s245, emphasis in original)[4]

Baker (2012, p. 237) has identified that the distinction between assault and battery under common law makes it 'awkward' to write and talk about the law in this area, and this effect would be even more pronounced if I were to attempt to use the word 'assault' to refer to two different things in relation to common law and Code law. As such, the term 'assault' will be used in this book in 'the wide sense', (Baker, 2012, p. 237) as covering both actual physical contact and the threat of physical contact.

Another problem with the definition of assault arises because of the Code law's explicit inclusion of a lack of consent as an element of the definition of 'assault'. Given that some contemporary discourses partly define sadomasochism by its consensuality, the use of this area of law to regulate sadomasochistic activities therefore seems odd. As the Queensland Supreme Court stated in *Schloss v Maguire* (1897) 8 QLJ 21 (p.22), the notion of consensual assault is somewhat oxymoronic as 'the term assault of itself involves the notion of

4 The definition contained in *Criminal Code Act Compilation Act 1913* (WA) schedule, s222 is identical except that it refers to a male person, rather than being neutrally worded.

want of consent … assault with consent is not an assault at all'. However, even though the recipient of an assault may subjectively consent to that assault, it does not necessarily follow that this will protect the assaulter from prosecution. Under common law principles stretching back hundreds of years, this subjective consent is only legally effective to prevent criminal liability if the assault takes place within certain circumstances. To clarify the discussion of these issues, this chapter will adopt the terminology used by Egan (2007, p.1619) who draws a useful distinction between 'factual consent', a term that denotes the presence of subjective consent, and 'legal consent', a term that denotes the legal recognition of consent as a complete or partial shield to criminal liability.

It is clear that sadomasochistic activities fulfil the legal requirements to constitute an assault, especially given that this chapter is concerned with sadomasochistic injuries which can only possibly be caused if physical contact is somehow involved. Accordingly, sadomasochistic activities could give rise to criminal liability for the offence of 'simple assault', or if they cause a certain level of physical injury they could give rise to criminal liability for other offences such as 'assault occasioning bodily harm', 'wounding', or 'grievous bodily harm'. Whether or not these additional offences are relevant depends on the level of physical injury caused by the sadomasochistic activities. At common law, bodily harm has its 'ordinary meaning' and includes 'any hurt or injury calculated to interfere with the health or comfort of the [recipient]' that is 'more than merely transient and trifling' (*R v Donovan* [1934] 2 KB 498, at p.509).[5] In Code States, bodily harm means 'any bodily injury which interferes with health or comfort' (*Criminal Code* (Qld) s1; *Criminal Code* (WA) s1(1)) Examples of bodily harm include 'a fractured bone, a broken nose, severe bruising or burning, a deep cut or cuts, or multiple minor injuries' (Syrota, 1996, p.172), and the standard is not met by mere pain alone (*Scatchard v The Queen* (1987) 27 A Crim R 136). The legal requirement for wounding is that both layers of the skin (the dermis and the epidermis) are broken, leading to free bleeding (*R v Devine* (1982) 8 A Crim R 45; *Vallance v R* (1961) 108 CLR 56). The definition of grievous bodily harm under common law is 'really serious bodily harm' (*DPP v Smith* [1961] AC 290), whilst under Code law it means 'any bodily injury of such a nature as to endanger, or be likely to endanger life, or to cause, or be likely to cause, permanent injury to health' (*Criminal Code* (WA) s1), and also includes 'the loss of a distinct part or an organ of the body' and 'serious disfigurement' (*Criminal Code* (Qld) s1).

It would be very rare for sadomasochistic injuries to reach the legal threshold for grievous bodily harm, but it is not unlikely that certain sadomasochistic

5 However, there is some suggestion that the 'transient *and* trifling' element of this test has since been broadened to cover 'transient *or* trifling' injuries (*R v Morris (Clarence Barrington)* [1998] Cr App 386).

activities would result in injuries that met the legal definitions of bodily harm or wounding. The question that must be answered is whether sadists can successfully protect themselves from criminal liability in some way, and the key issue is whether or not the masochist's consent provides them with a legal shield. In cases where the sadomasochistic activities fail to cause injury, or cause only superficial injury insufficient to reach the legal threshold for bodily harm, wounding or grievous bodily harm, the masochist's consent will protect the sadist from criminal liability (*Mosley v News Group Newspapers Limited* [2008] EWHC 1777 (QB), paragraph 115). Where sadomasochistic activities cause injury, the legal effect of the masochist's consent is less clear-cut.

Before seeking to determine the legal effect of consent to an injurious assault, it is important to flag three issues that prevent the criminal law in this area from being clear. Firstly, the broad framework of the criminal law differs substantially across the different Australian jurisdictions. As mentioned in the Introduction, the Australian Capital Territory (*Criminal Code 2002* (ACT)), the Northern Territory (*Criminal Code Act* (NT) schedule 1 (hereafter '*Criminal Code* (NT)')), Tasmania (*Criminal Code Act 1924* (Tas) schedule 1 (hereafter '*Criminal Code* (Tas)')), Queensland (*Criminal Code Act 1899* (Qld) schedule 1 (hereafter '*Criminal Code* (Qld)')), and Western Australia (*Criminal Code Act Compilation Act 1913* (WA) schedule (hereafter '*Criminal Code* (WA)')), have all codified their criminal laws, whilst the remaining jurisdictions have retained common law offences and definitions. Accordingly, the application of authorities from common law jurisdictions to Code jurisdictions is suspect, and *vice versa*. Thus, the laws relating to assault potentially differ across jurisdictions, and precedent might not provide a levelling effect. Secondly, there is a 'dearth of Australian case authority … on this aspect of the law' (Anon., *Editorial: Consensual Harm*, 2005, p.197). The result of this lack of local legal consideration of sadomasochism and consent to assaults is that courts and academics have looked predominantly to English case law for guidance, reflecting the 'widely-held assumption that the English common law position on consent applies equally in Australian common law jurisdictions' (Anon., *Editorial: Consensual Harm*, 2005, p.197). Even for Code jurisdictions, it has been said that English common law still provides 'a formidable and highly persuasive line of authority' (*R v Holmes* (1993) 2 Tas R 232, p.236 per Wright J). The result is that it is unclear whether to apply Australian or English authorities in particular cases, and what relative weight to give to cases from each jurisdiction. Thirdly, the law around consensual assaults has itself been described as 'uncompromising' (Kell, 1993, p.199), 'unclear' (Syrota, 1996, p.169), and 'unprincipled and incoherent' (Nash, 1996, p.382). It has developed on 'an ad hoc and often unconceptual basis' (Freckelton, 1994, p.59), perhaps because consensual assault has been treated by the courts through a 'case by case' approach 'rather than upon general propositions' (Nash, 1996, p.382). The legal treatment of consensual sadomasochism as a violent offence transposes the general lack of clarity that permeates the whole area of consensual assault law onto the specific legal status of sadomasochistic activities.

Leaving these problems to one side, the legal status of consensual assaults relies heavily upon a handful of oft-cited twentieth-century English common law authorities. Lord Hewart CJ, Swift and Du Parcq JJ in *R v Donovan* [1934] 2 KB 498 (p.507) decided that a criminal act 'cannot be rendered lawful because the person to whose detriment it is done consents to it. No person can license another to commit a crime.' Somewhat circularly, the Court exempted 'harmless and lawful' acts which only become unlawful when 'consent is absent' (*R v Donovan* [1934] 2 KB 498, p.507). However, the Court did offer the general rule, subject to some unspecified but 'well established' exceptions, that 'it is an unlawful act to beat another person with such a degree of violence that the infliction of bodily harm is a probable consequence, and when such an act is proved, consent is immaterial' (*R v Donovan* [1934] 2 KB 498, p.507). This legal line drawn at bodily harm was reinforced in *Attorney-General's Reference (No 6 of 1980)* [1981] 1 QB 715 in a judgment by Lane CJ, Phillips and Drake JJ. They concluded that 'it is not in the public interest that people should try to cause, or should cause, each other actual bodily harm for no good reason … it is an assault if actual bodily harm is intended and/or caused' (*Attorney-General's Reference (No 6 of 1980)* [1981] 1 QB 715, p.719). They also expanded on the unspecified exceptions mentioned in *R v Donovan* [1934] 2 KB 498, noting that their formulation of the law was not 'intended to cast doubt upon the accepted legality of properly conducted games and sports, lawful chastisement or correction, reasonable, surgical interference, dangerous exhibitions, etc' (*Attorney-General's Reference (No 6 of 1980)* [1981] 1 QB 715, p.719).

The common law, however, treats sadomasochism differently from these other contexts. In the case of *R v Brown* [1994], a 3 to 2 majority of the House of Lords held that the consent of the masochist did not negate the criminal liability of the sadist for assaults occasioning bodily harm that occur in a sadomasochistic context. Lord Templeman, for the majority, stated that consent provided a full defence to simple assault, but consensual assaults that inflict 'actual bodily harm, wounding or serious bodily harm' could only be lawful if inflicted in the course of certain activities such as surgery, '[r]itual circumcision, tattooing, ear-piercing and violent sports including boxing' (*R v Brown* [1994], p.231). He considered that 'policy and public interest' issues prevented him from treating sadomasochism in a similar way (*R v Brown* [1994], p.234). Similarly, Lord Jauncey of Tullichettle noted a number of 'well known exceptions' in which factual consent constituted legal consent, such as 'organised sporting contests and games, parental chastisement or reasonable surgery', but did not treat sadomasochism as such an exception (*R v Brown* [1994], p.245). Lord Lowry, the final member of the majority, considered 'whether there is any good reason to add sado-masochistic acts to the list of exceptions contemplated in *Attorney-General's Reference*' and answered simply 'No' (*R v Brown* [1994], p.255). Whilst a predominant focus of the majority judgments within *R v Brown* [1994] was the defendants' homosexuality and the group nature of their sadomasochistic activity, the same legal result was reached in *R v Emmett* [1999] EWCA Crim 1710 which was a case involving sadomasochistic activities engaged in by a heterosexual couple (Herring, 2012, p.375).

These United Kingdom authorities on consensual assault have been incorporated into Australian common law. In *R v McIntosh* [1999] VSC 358 (p.3), Vincent J adopted *R v Brown* [1994] and summarised what he saw to be the current state of the common law in Australia regarding sadomasochism:

> First, it is not, of itself, and I repeat that expression, of itself, in the case of consenting adult persons, contrary to the law of this jurisdiction to engage in activities that could be described as bondage or sexual sadomasochism.
>
> Second, the possibility that an activity involves the application of physical force to another and is accompanied by a real risk of even quite serious injury does not, of itself, render that activity unlawful. If that were the case many sporting contests would become unlawful.
>
> Third, apart from some special circumstances which the law has guarded carefully, and which are not present here, no recognition will be accorded to the consent of an individual to the infliction of significant physical injury upon himself or herself.
>
> In my opinion, if the sadomasochistic activity or bondage activity to which a victim consents involves the infliction of any such injury or the reckless acceptance of the risk that it will occur, then the consent of the victim will not be recognized.

In Kellam J's judgment in *R v Stein* (2007) 18 VR 376 (p.381), Vincent and Neave JJ agreeing, this passage was extracted in full and described as 'an accurate statement of the current law as it applies in Australia, the United Kingdom and Canada'. Kellam J also favourably cited both *R v Brown* [1994] and *R v Emmett* [1999] EWCA Crim 1710 in his judgment. However, the recent case of *Neal v R* (2011) 32 VR 454 does somewhat question the authority of *R v Brown* [1994] in Australia. In *obiter dicta* the Court critiqued the reasoning of the majority judges in *R v Brown* [1994] and commented positively on Lord Slynn's dissenting judgment in that case, which advocated the recognition of consent as a defence to all bodily harm occurring in private, stating that logically it 'is to be preferred' (*Neal v R* (2011) 32 VR 454, pp.469–472). Importantly, however, the Court did not press this as an issue and decided the case before them on alternative grounds. In contrast to *Neal v R* (2011) 32 VR 454, the authoritative position of the traditional common law approach was upheld in *Davis v Chief of Army* (2011) 205 A Crim R 521 (p.530), as the Tribunal in the case decided that the

ACT Criminal Code had preserved the common law formulation of assault and interpreted this common law position in a manner 'consistent with the majority opinion in *R v Brown*'.

Despite the suggestion in *Neal v R* (2011) 32 VR 454 that Australian common law could break with the common law in England and Wales,[6] the weight of authority strongly indicates that the legal status of sadomasochistic activities is the same under both systems. As such, in Australian common law jurisdictions if injuries amounting to at least bodily harm are inflicted in the course of consensual sadomasochistic activities, then the sadist can be held criminally liable.

The legal status of sadomasochism in Australian Code law jurisdictions is more difficult to determine. By the very fact that they are Code law jurisdictions they are no longer bound by the decisions or principles that have historically influenced the development of the common law. This does not automatically mean, however, that the law in Code jurisdiction will necessarily differ from that in common law jurisdictions. Although Code law judges are not legally required to follow common law lines of authority and reasoning, they may do so anyway or otherwise reach similar legal conclusions on the basis of the wording of the relevant Code. There is certainly the possibility that Code law could mirror the common law around consensual assault, given that the Codes explicitly state that the 'application of force by one person to the person of another may be unlawful, although it is done with the consent of that other person' (*Criminal Code* (Qld) s246; *Criminal Code* (WA) s223). Indeed, when deciding on consensual assault matters, some judges in Code jurisdictions have referenced and drawn on the common law to bolster their conclusions. For example, Connolly J in *R v Raabe* [1985] 1 Qd R 115 (p. 199) adopted a construction of the Code law that 'would bring the law into line with the current law of England. It is the preferable view from a social point of view, as discouraging violence.'[7] Similarly, Wright J in *R v Holmes* (1993) 2 Tas R 232 (p. 236) stated that he was 'compelled to the conclusion that the law of Tasmania as expressed in the *Code* … coincides with the principle established by the English and Canadian decisions'.

Nevertheless, in the course of applying the specific wording of the Codes, and in the absence of the restrictive effect of common law precedent, case authority has developed that holds that factual consent will provide a defence for all Code offences of which assault is an element. This position is supported

6 As New Zealand did in *R v Lee* [2006] 3 NZLR 42.

7 Connolly J may have been part of the 2:1 majority, but Thomas J, the other member of the majority, declined to comment on whether consent could be used to defend a charge of assault occasioning bodily harm. However, as Devereaux (1987, p.159) recognises, it is worrying that the summary of the reasoning contained in the case's headnote seems to reflect the views of only one out of the three judges.

by two Queensland authorities: *Lergesner v Carroll* [1991] 1 Qd R 206 and Derrington J's judgment in *R v Raabe* [1985] 1 Qd R 115. Both cases support the general proposition that because the absence of consent is explicitly articulated as an element of the Code definition of assault, the prosecution is required to 'negative consent beyond reasonable doubt' in order to make out an assault-based offence such as simple assault or assault occasioning bodily harm (*Lergesner v Carroll* [1991], p.212 per Sheperdson J). This legal position stands in contrast to the common law, in which the 'absence of consent is not an element of the offence', and these Queensland decisions 'depend upon' the particular formulation of the relevant 'statutory provisions' of Code law (*Davis v Chief of Army* (2011) 205 A Crim R 521, p.530). Similarly to the Queensland authorities, a trend has been identified in the Northern Territory towards interpreting consent as an element of the offence and which accordingly must be disproved by the prosecution (*R v Minor* (1992) 2 NTLR 183; *Police (NT) v Segeyara* [2008] NTMC 19).

One implication of this line of authority in Queensland and the Northern Territory is that the factual consent of the recipient of the assault would defend any charge of simple assault or assault occasioning bodily harm levelled against the assaulter. As a result, it has been argued that in Code law jurisdictions the common law approach to consensual assault, which only recognises factual consent as constituting legal consent in certain circumstances, 'is not available' (Devereux and Blake, 2013, p.280). The other implication of this line of reasoning is that consent is an irrelevant consideration for Code offences of which assault is not an element, such as wounding and grievous bodily harm. If we transpose these general principles about the operation of Code law to the specific case of sadomasochistic activities, this suggests that in Code law jurisdictions the sadist can be held criminally liable if injuries amounting to at least wounding are inflicted in the course of consensual sadomasochistic activities.

Sadomasochism as Harmful Crime

Under Australian law, then, sadists are indefensibly criminally liable for sadomasochistic injuries that either cause at least bodily harm (in common law jurisdictions) or cause at least wounding (in Code law jurisdictions) (Bennett, 2012a, p.205). This criminality is a product of the ways in which sadomasochism is discursively constructed and positioned within legal discourse. This section will focus on three key conceptions within legal discourse around sadomasochism that work simultaneously to construct and position it as criminal: (non) consensuality, violence and harm. The goal here is to examine how legal discourse constructs a particular model of sadomasochism and to reveal the discursive techniques employed in embedding this model within the law. Whilst this section will at times digress to consider how authoritative legal discursive conceptualisation of sadomasochism conflict with alternative accounts, this issue will be the primary focus of the next section.

Conceptions of (Non)Consensuality

The factual consent of sadomasochists to participation in sadomasochistic activities has not only been classified as legally ineffective by the criminal law, it has also been challenged within legal discourse. Even in cases where the presence of factual consent is definitively disposed of by the operation of law or the evidence of witnesses it is continually raised as an issue that requires comment and consideration. Lord Templeman, for example, summarised *R v Donovan* [1934] as being a case where the 'appellant in private beat a girl of 17 for purposes of sexual gratification, *it was said* with her consent' (*R v Brown* [1994], p.233, emphasis added). Similarly, whilst commenting on *R v Brown* [1994], where the presence of factual consent was not in issue, Hanna (2001, p.265) opines that 'the extent to which the "victims" willingly submitted to the encounters remained unclear'. Whilst discussing *R v Emmett* [1999] EWCA Crim 1710, Hanna (2001) raises further concerns about both battered wives syndrome and domestic violence. She argues that we 'have no way of knowing if the victim, like many abused women, was afraid to testify' in this case (Hanna, 2001, p.274). The underlying issue for Hanna (2001) is that false claims of consensual sadomasochism may be cynically used to mask instances of non-consensual violence. Whilst this fear may be justified as a possibility in certain individual cases, Hanna (2001) uses it as a generalisable basis for legally treating all claims of consent to sadomasochistic activities with intense suspicion. She argues that this fear justifies law's current failure to recognise the factual consent of the masochist as legal consent, because this approach 'facilitates' the 'important policy goa[l]' of 'protect[ing] the victim if she did not consent' (Hanna, 2001, p.274). In this way, all instances of sadomasochism are tainted by fear of non-consensuality: every masochist should be treated as being a 'victim', even (or perhaps especially) when they say they are not.

Not only is the factual consent of sadomasochists directly challenged, it is also more subtly undermined through the imputation that masochists are psychologically deficient and incapable of giving consent in any event. Freckelton (1994, p.73), commenting generally on self-mutilation but here comparing it to sadomasochism, even argues that it 'must be conceded that there is a danger that consent, if provided, may not be entirely voluntary and informed, even if given by adults who are not intoxicated, not intellectually disabled and not diagnosably mentally ill'. He supports this statement by making the claim, without citing any empirical evidence, that 'those who fulfil the masochistic side of the compact are likely to be psychologically vulnerable individuals' (Freckelton, 1994, p.73).

Similar imputations have also come from the bench, with Shoemaker J in *People v Samuels* 250 Cal.App.2d 501 (1967) (pp.513–514) writing that: '[i]t is a matter of common knowledge that a normal person in full possession of his mental faculties does not freely consent to the use, upon himself, of force likely to produce great bodily injury'. In addition to this general lack of 'mental faculties' to provide factual consent to sadomasochistic activities, imputations of short-term mental impairments that would vitiate consent have also been made through judicial references to the use of alcohol and drugs by sadomasochists (*R v Brown* [1994], p.236 per Lord Templeman), thereby also stigmatising sadomasochism by associating it with 'substance abuse' (Khan, 2014, p.230). Indeed, sadomasochism is conceptualised within legal discourse as something that is itself 'addictive' (Stychin, 1995, pp.127–132), which suggests that any choice to participate in sadomasochistic activities is not made entirely freely but is instead the result of an uncontrollable compulsion.

The autonomous rational actor that sits at the heart of legal thought in contract, medicine and other areas of law, is replaced in legal discourse around sadomasochism by the notion of the feeble-minded, irrational or otherwise impaired sadomasochist. Factual consent is discursively constructed as necessarily absent due to the mental 'incapacities' built into this conception of the 'sadomasochist'. The boundary between factual consent and legal consent is strategically blurred here by legal discourse's refusal to accept the willingness of sadomasochists to participate in sadomasochistic activities. Indeed, the law's refusal to recognise the legal effectiveness of the factual consent of the masochist is reified into the absence of such consent through this discursive process.

Complementing this construction of sadomasochism as mental infirmity is the medicalised positioning of sadomasochism as sickness through the use of conceptual linkages with illness and contagion (Stychin, 1995, pp.134–138). 'Discursively, blood flowed from the bodies in *Brown*' carrying with it the 'presence of moral and health dangers' (Houlihan, 2011, p.55). Although there was no evidence of any link to the offences alleged, or even to sadomasochism generally, the majority in *R v Brown* [1994] expressed concern about the threat of the spread of HIV and other blood-borne illnesses between sadomasochists. Other concerns mentioned included the risks of septicaemia, infection and urinary tract infections allegedly posed by certain sadomasochistic activities. Compounding this discursive association between sadomasochism and sickness is the construction of sadomasochism as contagious. Semi-public displays of sadomasochism were conceptualised as presenting a public threat through the danger of 'corruption of young men' (*R v Brown* [1994], p.246 per Lord Jauncey of Tullichettle). Lord Lane CJ, who heard *R v Brown* [1994] at the Court of Appeal level, recounted the story of the 'corruption of a youth K' by the sadomasochistic group on trial, noting that it 'is some comfort at least to be told, as we were, that K. has now it seems settled into a normal heterosexual relationship' (referred to in *R v Brown* [1994], p.235 per Lord Templeman). Khan (2014, p.230) identifies the focus on the 'youth' of K and other young participants within this case as being an attempt to 'cast doubt' on the consent given, through the 'insinuat[ion] that since some were corrupted as adolescents, their current decisions cannot hold legitimacy'. The use of the language of 'corruption', and its contrast towards the implicitly 'healthy' normality, can also be read as presenting sadomasochism as a kind of contagious illness that can be passed to others through exposure and proximity. Raising medical issues such as illness and contagion within the context of a discussion of sadomasochism implicitly evokes its historical (and, to a lesser extent, contemporary) characterisation as a mental disorder. But the legal discourse here goes further by explicitly linking sadomasochism with physical ailments as well, constructing sadomasochism as a holistic sickness of both the mind and the body. It legally flows from this construction of sadomasochism as sickness that the consent of sadomasochists, when constructed as being necessarily given under the influence of such an affliction, would be worthless. The factual consent of masochistic participants is discursively constructed as the consent of the ill, that is, not 'real' or valid consent at all.

Interestingly, although sadomasochism is constructed as being a disabling sickness, legal discourse only conceptualises masochists as needing protection from this illness. The various legal discursive assaults on consensuality are centred around the 'consent' of the masochist, and work selectively to ensure that 'the pleasure and agency of the submissive is disavowed' (Khan, 2014, pp.229–230). The sickness and irrationality conceptualisations of sadomasochism are not deployed to mitigate the liability of the sadist; there is no corresponding discursive construction of a sick, irrational sadist who should not be legally held accountable for their actions due to their 'affliction'. The medicalisation of legal discourse around sadomasochism works against the conceptualisation of sadomasochistic activities as the free and consensual exchange of pain and pleasure, and instead conceptualises sadomasochism as the physical domination of the mentally and physically vulnerable. Masochists 'suffer … from these desires' (*Leitner v State* 631 So.2d 273 (Ala.Cr.App. 1993), p.279 per Taylor J), as one would suffer from any other 'illness'. This selective conceptualisation of sadomasochism as a masochistic illness smoothes over the anomaly of the masochist's factual consent not translating to legal consent by the discursive rewriting of the masochist as being incapable of giving factual consent at all. Shortcircuiting the possible characterisation of law as intrusively over-reaching into the autonomous choices of rational actors, law alternatively presents itself 'as the defender of this weak and easily corrupted bunch' (Khan, 2014, p.231), at least as far as masochists are concerned.

There is, however, another strand of legal discourse that deals with consent and sadomasochism. In reaction to the obvious paternalism inherent in the current legal approach, liberal theory has been used to argue that the consent of the masochist should carry weight and provide a defence to assault (Allen, 1994; Athanassoulis, 2002; Green, 2001; Sullivan, 2009). These types of arguments typically draw on John Stuart Mills' harm principle, that is that the state is only justified in limiting the freedom of individuals to the extent of preventing actions that harm others. They argue that because sadomasochism is consensual sadomasochistic activities do not meaningfully harm the masochist, and therefore, regardless of whether one thinks that sadomasochism is grotesque or immoral, it should be lawful. This account of sadomasochism carries strong discursive associations with contemporary human rights theory, particularly issues such as privacy and freedom of sexuality, but despite being invoked as early as 50 years ago (Williams,1962) it has had little to no impact on the status of the law. As such, it has been relegated to a position as a counter-discourse pushing back against the authoritative legal account of sadomasochism.

Conceptions of Violence

Whether or not sadomasochistic activities should be conceptualised as a form of violence has been a highly contested topic within the legal discourse around sadomasochism. Some key legal texts conceptualise sadomasochism as a form of violence. Lord Templeman in *R v Brown* [1994] (p.236) provides an archetypal example, noting that: 'there is a difference between violence which is incidental and violence which is inflicted for the indulgence of cruelty. The violence of sado-masochistic encounters involves the indulgence of cruelty by sadists and the degradation of victims.' This construction of sadomasochism as violence has been oft-repeated (Anon., *Assault and Battery*, 1968, p.1340; Chandra-Shekeran, 1997, p.588; Hanna, 2001; R v *Dica* [2004] EWCA Crim 1103, at p.1269 per Judge LJ; *R v Donovan* (1934), p.507 per Swift J). Other legal texts, usually academic commentary, conceptualise sadomasochism as a form of sex, a point often made to directly resist sadomasochism's construction as violence. For example, Wadham (1996, p.1812) argues alternatively that '[s]ado-masochism is a form of mutual sexual expression, not a type of violence'. Lord Mustill even opened his dissenting judgment in *R v Brown* [1994] (p.257) with a declaration that whilst the majority treated it as a case about violence 'it should be a case about the criminal law of private sexual relations, if about anything at all'. This construction of sadomasochism as sex has also been oft-repeated (Bronitt, 1995, p.67; Egan, 2007, p.1642; Kell, 1993, p.199). Other legal texts adopt approaches with finer distinctions, conceptualising sadomasochism as being either a form of sex with violent aspects, or a form of violence with sexual aspects (Bibbings and Alldridge, 1993, p.360; Bradwell, 1996, p.1682; Freckelton, 1994, p.51; Pa, 2001, p.71). Markwick (2002, p.162), as an example, argues that 'it is difficult to believe that … sado-masochism is not concerned with both sex and violence'. Why is this particular issue within the discursive conceptualisation of sadomasochism so important? What turns on it?

It would be naïve to describe these terminological divergences as nothing more than a situation where the 'same activity can … be described in a number of ways' (Bix, 1993, p.542). The very fact that this discursive contestation exists constitutes tacit acknowledgement of the contingent nature of sadomasochism's criminality, that sadomasochism's legal status relies on constructing it in a particular, partisan manner. Indeed, a number of commentators have argued that if sadomasochistic activities were conceptualised as sex, then sadomasochists would be charged with sex offences rather than violent offences and factual consent to sex offences typically functions as a legally effective defence to liability (Cowan, 2012; Murphy, 2011; Pa, 2001). At a discursive level, the conceptualisation of sadomasochism as sex or violence also shapes the kinds of discursive frameworks brought to bear on sadomasochism. This framing is strategically valuable as it supplements and authenticates particular legal positions. This is evidenced by the link between those who construct sadomasochism as a form of violence generally supporting stricter legal limits to consensual assault, and those who construct sadomasochism as a form of sex generally arguing that law has 'no business' interfering with such private activities (Cowan, 2011, p.73). If sadomasochism is constructed as violence, then it becomes loaded with culturally specific negative connotations such as pain, non-consensuality, harm and victimhood. If sadomasochism is constructed as sex, then it becomes loaded with positive connotations such as pleasure, consensuality, expression and mutuality (Law Commission, 1995, p.144, submission by Professor D. Feldman).

Much ink has been spilled contesting whether sadomasochism should be conceptualised as violence or sex. Whilst this contestation continues between commentators, the construction of sadomasochism as a form of violence currently dominates legal discourse and inflects the criminality of sadomasochistic acts. My concern in this section is to unpack some of the discursive processes used to construct this conceptualisation within legal discourse. If we explore the rhetorical techniques underpinning this conceptualisation of sadomasochism-as-violence we can identify a number of conceptual linkages that have been successfully leveraged to solidify this position within legal discourse. In particular, I want to focus on the imputation that sadomasochism is atavistic, that is, it is symptomatic of the 're-emergence of primitive tendencies in otherwise civilised people' (Ridinger, 2006, p.191).

Like other 'perversions' sadomasochism is 'figured as a regression backward in time to the "prehistory" of racial "degeneration" … the degeneration of the race writ as an individual pathology of the soul' (McClintock, 1993, p.90). This discursive imputation is employed directly, through the use of words with associations to primitivism to describe sadomasochism and the legalisation of sadomasochism. For example, 'barbarity' and 'cult' (*R v Brown* [1994], p.235 per Lord Templeman), 'brutalize' (Hanna, 2001, p.289), 'regressive' (*R v Jobidon* [1991] 2 SCR 714, p.763 per Gonthier J) and '*natural* human aggression' (Hanna, 2001, p.256, emphasis added). This imputation is also constructed indirectly, through contrasts made between sadomasochism and words with associations of advancement and sophistication. This is evident in the statements that '[c]ruelty is uncivilised' (*R v Brown* [1994], p.237 per Lord Templeman), 'it is idle for the appellants to claim that they are educated exponents of "civilised cruelty"' (*R v Brown* [1994], p.255 per Lord Lowry), '[e]rasing longstanding limits on consent to assault would … retard the advance of civilized norms of conduct' (*R v Jobidon* [1991] 2 SCR 714, p.763 per Gonthier J), and '[t]o suggest that anyone should have the right to … escape culpability under a theory of sexual consent violates our deepest notions of freedom, human rights, and *civility*' (Hanna, 2001, p.289, emphasis added).

Through these linguistic processes, sadomasochism is discursively constructed 'as a macabre, barbaric pseudo-religion, antithetical to the implied values of civilization' (White, 2006, p.173). This atavistic imputation represents sadomasochists as savage degenerates, who take perverse pleasure in 'serious physical injuries [being] inflicted in the course of a sexual frenzy' (Syrota, 1996, p.189). Sadists become uncivilised, cruel barbarians who are ruled by their baser instincts and bodily processes. Thus, they are easily 'carried away by sexual excitement or by drink or drugs' and the only thing saving the masochist from serious injury is 'good luck rather than good judgment' (*R v Brown* [1994], p.246 per Lord Jauncey of Tullichettle). Masochists, by contrast, are constructed as weak-willed beings, who give in to their bodily desires for strong sensations and who have apparently given up their higher intellectual functions because they are oblivious to the clear danger that sadists pose to them.

The authoritative legal discursive conceptualisation of sadomasochism as violent and as uncivilised is antithetical to alternative constructions of sadomasochism put forward by sadomasochistic participants and non-legal academics who have studied sadomasochism. There is 'ubiquitous evidence' that sadomasochism is a 'complex and multifaceted [ritual] of staging sexuality' (Attias, 1995). This construction of sadomasochism is primarily based on the acknowledgement that it is heavily invested in the manipulation of symbolism and the utilisation of the weight of meaning and cultural associations behind particular objects and practices. For this reason, it has been identified as an activity that is monopolised by 'well-developed civilizations' (Gebhard, 1976, p.166). Furthermore, even within these well-developed civilisations, studies have shown that sadomasochism is most commonly practiced amongst the more highly educated and highly paid members of the citizenry (Moser and Levitt, 1995; Yost, 2007). However, this alternative construction of sadomasochism as post-literate and highly developed is marginalised within legal discourse, which instead privileges a particular understanding of sadomasochism that doesn't place any importance on its depth of (inter)subjective meaning. The legal discursive conceptualisation of sadomasochism as 'uncivilised' here 'effectively dismisses the … experiences and the understandings of consensual "SM" practitioners' that give 'a different impression of their interactions' (Beckmann, 2009, p.154). In doing so, the discursive linking of sadomasochism with savagery and excess authenticates the legal conceptualisation of sadomasochism as violence. Indeed, if the discursive framework within which sadomasochism was embedded instead carried these alternative links to refinement and civility, it would be much more difficult for such a construction to take hold.

Conceptions of Harm

Some physical injury to sadomasochists is an almost inevitable result of general sadomasochistic activities. Whilst some forms of 'light' sadomasochism may entail only very superficial physical marks, other forms of sadomasochism will result in bruises, lacerations, cuts, piercings, cane marks and other injuries that reach the legal definition of 'bodily harm' or 'wounding'. Sadomasochistic activities and sadomasochistic injuries become inextricably legally intertwined at this point, as the criminal law regulates sadomasochism where it becomes a form of body alteration. This is why comments such as Weait's (2007, p.64) that 'S/M is not a crime … there is no "law against" being a sadist or a masochist', and Vincent J's that it is not 'contrary to the law of this jurisdiction to engage in activities that could be described as bondage or sexual sadomasochism' (*R v McIntosh* [1999] VSC 358, p.3), are misguided. Sadomasochism cannot be divorced from its practice: it is not merely an internal psychological predilection or an ontological status, rather it is an active inter-personal and intersubjective process. One cannot 'be' a sadomasochist without 'doing' sadomasochism, and 'doing' some forms of sadomasochism is clearly criminal where such sadomasochistic activities alter the body.

Matching the legal preoccupation with sadomasochism when it becomes a form of body alteration, some texts attempt to create distinctions between 'authentic' sadomasochism, which is conceived of as non-injurious, and 'inauthentic' sadomasochism, which is injurious. The latter is characterised as being a '[p]erversion … of S/M, or not by the book S/M' (Hanna, 2001, p.286), and its illegality is purportedly justified because it is constructed as outside '"normal" sadomasochism' (Sullivan, 2009, p.226). Instead of placing sadomasochism-involving-injury within the same discursive category as sadomasochism-not-involving-injury, the division created by the legal line drawn at bodily harm is reified and the 'separateness' of these two practices is invoked, in a display of circularity, to justify the original legal division. Claims that there exists an 'authentic' or 'normal' model of sadomasochism are clearly suspect, especially given the wide variety of sadomasochistic practices and the broad range of meanings that sadomasochists attach to them (as discussed below), and it is not clear in any case why causing physical injury would preclude something from being 'authentic'/'normal' sadomasochism. What this attempt at discursive boundary-drawing reveals, however, is the central importance of concepts of harm to discursive accounts of sadomasochism, particularly within legal discourse.

Injuries inflicted in the course of sadomasochistic encounters are conceptualised as harms. In order to ground this conceptualisation sadomasochistic activities are decontextualised, stripped of the subjective and intersubjective meanings they hold for sadomasochistic participants and represented purely by physical taxonomies of bodily actions and reactions. For example, Edwards (1993, p.406) describes the facts of *R v Brown* [1994] simply as a case involving:

> [W]hipping, genital torture, the insertion of fish hooks through the penis, the cutting of the penis with a knife, branding a man with initials using wire heated by a blow lamp, taping matches to the victims' nipples, clamping and pinning the scrotum to a board, nailing the foreskin to a board *ad nauseum ad infinitum*.'

This is not a holistic description of the sadomasochistic activities that took place between the sadists and the masochists in *R v Brown* [1994], rather it is simply a laundry list of some of the physical activities that occurred. Lord Jauncey of Tullichettle's description of the activities within *R v Brown* [1994] (p.246) is even more pared back as he reduces the legal question simply to deciding whether or not:

> [S]uch activities as the nailing by A of B's foreskin or scrotum to a board or the insertion of hot wax into C's urethra followed by the burning of his penis with a candle or the incising of D's scrotum with a scalpel to the effusion of blood are injurious neither to B, C and D nor to the public interest.

The underpinning logic here is that the meaning of sadomasochistic activities is exhausted by the sheer physicality of the cut of the scalpel and the drip of the wax. The answer to the question posed by Lord Jauncey of Tullichettle is already contained in the way it is formulated; if one describes the sadomasochistic activities that A, B, C and D participated in in terms that construct them merely as physically harmful acts, then by necessity they must be injurious to B, C and D. Importantly, the entire subjective content of the sadomasochistic activities has been evacuated, including 'the negotiations involved in enacting the scene, the consent and enthusiasm of the hypothetical persons of A, B, C, and D, and the pleasures they extract from the activity' (Khan, 2014, p.236). Indeed, the sadomasochists themselves are so legally irrelevant that they have been anonymised, reduced from human beings in the full richness of their subjecthood to mere letters used as placeholders. An equivalent description of boxing, for example, would be a fight between two people who attempt to inflict as much blunt force trauma to the torsos and heads of their opponents as possible or to land a punch to their opponent's head causing internal injury to the brain sufficient to incapacitate them (*R v Brown* [1994], p.265 per Lord Mustill). This description of boxing seems alien and inappropriate because it conflicts with widely-known discursive constructions of boxing that include associations with strategy, technique, skill, fairness, consensuality and celebrity. The reductive nature of legal descriptions of sadomasochistic activities is less readily accessible because of the lack of mainstream awareness of sadomasochism, as well as the naturalisation of these kinds of descriptions within legal discourse. The gap in meaning created by the reductive nature of legal descriptions of sadomasochism is instead filled by the discursive association of sadomasochistic injuries with mutilation and limitless violence.

The conceptual linkage made between sadomasochism and mutilation within legal discourse is clearly evident in Freckelton's (1994) article, tellingly entitled 'Masochism, Self-mutilation and the Limits of Consent'. Other consensual assault circumstances that involve actual or potential injury to the body, such as sport and surgery, are not coloured by the same pejorative association. The professional athlete, for example, who spends hours in the gym every day hurting their body and who suffers injuries every season, ranging from the minor (such as bruises or sprains) to the severe (such as torn ligaments or broken bones), is free to engage in their own 'self-mutilation' without being subjected to the sanction of the criminal law or the moralising diatribes of commentators. These kinds of inconsistencies within legal discourse are highlighted by contrasting the cases of *R v Brown* [1994] and *R v Wilson* [1997] QB 47. In both cases, the branding of a person by a heated wire provided the basis of at least one of the alleged offences. However, despite these identical physical facts, the legal results differed with regards to these particular offences. Consent was held to provide a defence to the branding in *R v Wilson* [1997] QB 47 (p.50) because it occurred in a desexualised, heterosexual, married, monogamous context, so the branding was interpreted to be merely the 'acquisition of a desirable piece of personal adornment'. Consent could not provide a defence in *R v Brown* [1994] because the branding was explicitly sexualised, and it occurred in a non-monogamous, group and homosexual context. The same physical acts and consequences can be described alternatively as desirable or mutilatory, but this latter construction is reserved for sadomasochism. Again, in *R v Emmett* [1999] EWCA Crim 1710, the court evidenced a concern about the mutilatory aspect of sadomasochism by noting that it was pleased that the burn injury received by the masochist had healed over without scarring. There is something about sadomasochism as a form of body alteration that makes it particularly troubling for the law. Sadomasochistic injuries are not constructed within legal discourse as necessary by-products of the practice (as they are for sport), nor as desirable adornments (as they are for some forms of body modification: see Chapter 4), nor even as marks of achievement to be worn with pride, but rather as disabling harms that mar and degrade the masochist.

The spectre of uncontrolled, 'limitless violence' haunts legal discourse around sadomasochistic injury (White, 2006, p.176), as '[a]ll bodies are vulnerable within the narrative of s/m crime' (Houlihan, 2011, p.59). Careful legal control of specific sadomasochistic acts is portrayed as necessary to protect society from a general 'cult of violence' (*R v Brown* [1994], p.237 per Lord Templeman). Legalisation of sadomasochism, and the correlative unleashing of this 'cult', is constructed as threatening not only the masochistic participants themselves but also 'youths and nonconsenters' (Anon., *Assault and Battery*, 1968, p.1340). Sadomasochism is constructed as posing the threat of uncontrolled violence that could spill out from sadomasochistic participants and harm the rest of society. Bradwell (1996, pp.1682–1683) envisions a literal orgy of violence if consent were recognised as a defence to assault occasioning bodily harm, arguing that this would apparently give men *carte blanche* to begin (or expand) the widespread sexual abuse of women, sadistically abuse underage female prostitutes, and bash homosexuals, and would even encourage teachers to get sexual satisfaction from a return to corporal punishment in schools. The law is constructed as evolving to 'control … male violence' and this is argued to be, 'overall, a good thing' (Hanna, 2001, p.254). The physical injuries of the masochist are constructed as synechdochic; they come to represent the threat of harm not just to the masochist but also the threat of widespread, limitless harm to all of society. The operation of legal discourse around sadomasochism here is similar to legal discourse around female genital modification which, as will be addressed in Chapter 3, is also conceptualised as embodying a threat of harm to the entire body politic.

Sadomasochistic injuries are discursively constructed as representing the limitless danger that sadists pose to masochists. Whilst no direct link is made between sadists and murderers within academic or legal argument, there is strong recurring oblique implication that the two are somehow connected. Freckelton (1994, pp.57–58) puts them on the same continuum of behaviour, which stretches from sadists who are 'comparatively harmless' to 'those finally who impose their fantasies on others without any semblance of consent from their victims'. Hanna (2001, pp.262–263) slots two pages of discussion about the infamous serial killer Jeffrey Dahmer into her article on sadomasochism for no readily apparent reason. Hanna (2001, p.259) also takes pains to note that in *People v Samuels* 250 Cal.App.2d 501 (1967):

> [I]t is troubling to know that the 'victim' was not identified. There was no way to know if [the sadomasochistic activity] was consensual … [W]ithout any witnesses there was no way to prove that the acts were consensual. Even assuming that the [sadist] was truthful in his statements that the injuries were staged, it should indeed give us pause for concern as to what actually happened to the 'victim'.

This last sentence is particularly ironic given that the law, as we have seen, has very little regard for masochists. It doesn't really matter what 'actually happened' to the masochist: their consent, their pleasure from the sadomasochistic encounter, and the meanings they attribute to both sadomasochism and their injuries, are all marginalised within legal discourse. Instead, within legal discourse sadomasochistic activities are 'overdetermined as intrinsically harmful practices' and 'the mental state of the participants, i.e., whether the actors themselves feel harmed, is irrelevant' (Khan, 2014, p.186).

Sadomasochistic activities are constructed within legal discourse as a form of violence which is an 'addiction' and which 'escalates' (Stychin, 1995, p.129), with the 'brutal and inevitable' consequence that it will end in death (Stychin, 1995, p.138). Sadomasochistic injuries are read as degrading harms because they break the easy functioning of the body's physiological processes, regardless of how they are perceived by the masochists themselves (Weait, 2007, p.67). The infliction of sadomasochistic injuries on others is conceptualised as antithetical to the social order and harmful both to the masochist and to the broader society. Harm to a body that constitutes part of the body politic becomes harm to the body politic. The sadist is constructed as having some darker, deeper agenda involving the degradation and/or destruction of the masochist and, by discursive extension, society.

Alternative Accounts of Sadomasochism

The previous section of this chapter dealt primarily with 'how' authoritative strands of legal discourse construct the meanings attached to sadomasochism within the law and the particular discursive processes and devices used to establish this model of sadomasochism as authoritative and legitimate. This section will expand on this analysis by exploring exactly 'what' is being marginalised by the authoritative legal discursive account and 'why' these alternative accounts are excluded.

To deal with the issue of 'what' has been excluded by the operation of legal discourse, a descriptive account is provided of other competing discursive understandings of sadomasochism that have historically been marginalised within law. Not all discursive understandings of sadomasochism compete with the legal construction outlined above, indeed Khan's (2014) recent monograph comprehensively details the extensive overlap between conceptions about sadomasochism that circulate within and through medical discourse, certain feminist discourses, popular culture and legal discourse. The account in this chapter is drawn alternatively from understandings about sadomasochism within work generated by the writings of sadomasochists themselves and from the writings of non-legal scholars who have studied the sadomasochistic subculture.

Whilst these alternative understandings are not typically present within law itself they do appear in broader legal discourse, such as within legal academic commentary. The response from commentators who have recognised that the meanings attached to sadomasochism by sadomasochists have been marginalised within law has typically come in the form of a call for law to treat sadomasochism as a form of 'sex' rather than as a form of violence (Athanassoulis, 2002; Bamforth, 1994; Cowan, 2011; Egan, 2007). It has been argued that this conceptual shift reflects how sadomasochists understand their own activities and, as mentioned above, it has been suggested that this shift would loosen legal restrictions on sadomasochism by allowing law to recognise the consensual, pleasurable and erotic nature of sadomasochistic activities (Egan, 2007). I have not adopted this kind of approach here. I agree with Khan's (2014, p.277) assertion that in the context of the current legal 'master narrative' of violence, the 'legal recognition of s/m as a sexuality does complicate the jurisprudence and may create unwitting discursive space for s/m practitioners to assert their own truth-claims about their desires'. However, replacing the law's current totalising construction of sadomasochism as violent crime with another equally totalising construction of sadomasochism as sexual variation (or allowing the two to sit uneasily side-by-side), simply replicates the same conceptual problem that I consider to be plaguing the surrounding legal discourse. Sadomasochism holds multiple conflicting and individual meanings to different sadomasochists, and it is this broader range of 'subjugated knowledges' (Beckmann, 2009) – importantly plural rather than singular or dual – that should be recognised.

Giving content and expression to alternative constructions of sadomasochism, by reproducing them here in this book, denaturalises authoritative legal discourse's conceptualisation of sadomasochism and aids in the process of loosening its hold over the legal meaning of sadomasochism. I refer somewhat flippantly to these alternative accounts in the section and chapter headings as conceptualising sadomasochism as a 'harmless pastime', but I will also explore how sadomasochism can become a serious and meaningful aspect of sadomasochists' lives and identities. To further unpack this issue, I will also offer an aetiological account explaining 'why' law and authoritative legal discourse conceptualises and constructs sadomasochism in the way in which it does. This account will be grounded in an analysis of the broader cultural positioning around sadomasochism. Ultimately, this chapter argues that whilst sadomasochism's cultural positioning as a non-normative bodily alteration attracts the attention of disciplinary institutions generally, the unruly sadomasochistic body also offers specific, idiosyncratic challenges to the authority and power of law. Law and authoritative legal discourse respond by silencing these challenges through marginalisation and erasure to defuse the threat of sadomasochism and recuperate unruly sadomasochistic bodies.

Competing Constructions

Houlihan (2011, p.38) identifies that the narrow account of sadomasochism that is embedded within the law functions to obscure the 'heterogeneous and complex' nature of sadomasochism. Sadomasochism is not a single, monolithic practice with minor variations to encompass the tastes of different practitioners. Rather, sadomasochism is comprised of a 'cluster of circulating genres, some of which are distinct, some of which overlap' (McClintock, 1993, p.98). Correlatively, there 'is not simply one SM community but multiple communities with contrasting and contested versions of SM identities' (Langdridge, 2006, p.383). The legal discursive construction of sadomasochism, then, is simply one possibility amongst a multitude of conceptualisations about what sadomasochism can mean, and sadomasochism holds a range of different meanings to different sadomasochistic individuals and communities.

What sadomasochism means to sadomasochists

Even a cursory glance over the literature on sadomasochism reveals that, in the words of one sadomasochistic respondent to the Law Commission (1995, p.140), sadomasochism can 'mean a lot of things. It can be light hearted but exhilarating fun between two people who barely know each other. But it can be far more than that.' For some people, sadomasochism is merely about game-playing and fun. Foucault (1988c, p.299) wrote of sadomasochism as resembling a game of 'chess', which the sadist played by 'respond[ing] to the needs and trials of his victim', and that the masochist played by standing up to 'the challenge thrown at him'. Other people treat sadomasochism as a pastime or hobby. Williams (2009, p.209) regards sadomasochism as being comprehensible as 'serious leisure', with participants spending hours 'planning events, making "toys" and equipment, learning, and practicing various activities'. This light-hearted, almost frivolous, conceptualisation of sadomasochism as a game or a hobby contrasts sharply with the *gravitas* with which it is approached at law.

For other people, however, sadomasochism does hold significantly more importance. It has been used as a form of quasi-medical psychotherapy. Barker, Gupta and Iantaffi (2007, p.197) recognise the recent emergence of multiple 'healing narratives', where BDSM is constructed as providing a 'safe space to explore issues that might traditionally have been brought to contexts such as counselling and psychotherapy'. This point is echoed by professional dominatrixes in the interviews conducted by Lindemann (2013). Easton (2007, p.228), a licensed therapist and sex educator who works with abuse survivors, even advocates the use of 'S/M roles and stimulation to travel to the roots of our emotional realities and the core of our sense of identity'. Whether sadomasochism is an appropriate medium for working through psychological issues is not the issue here, my point is simply to contrast legal discourse's conceptualisation of sadomasochism as a form of 'harm' towards the mentally 'ill' with alternative accounts of sadomasochism as a form of mental health treatment. Indeed, this latter conceptualisation has seen widespread cultural recognition in the Golden Globe nominated film *Secretary* (2002) (Barker, Gupta and Iantaffi 2007). These alternative accounts of '"SM" as an experience of healing, clearly contradict not only scientific stereotypes of "Sadomasochism" but further challenge the courts' conventional understanding of consensual "SM" that appears to associate it ... intimately with the production of "harm"' (Beckmann, 2009, p.94). Sadomasochism has also been used as a source of spirituality, with sadomasochistic activities being regarded by some as quasi-religious experiences. For Vesta (2004), female domination of male masochists can replicate a form of Goddess worship, whilst for Norman (2004, p.279) the use of 'ritual, rites of passage, initiatory practices' and 'ordeals' are common to both sadomasochism and shamanic training.

One dominant thread throughout alternative accounts of sadomasochism relates to desire and eroticism. To eroticise sadomasochistic activities, sadomasochists must have access to the polymorphous perversity required to 'break open, shatter, stretch, expand, seduce, coerce, force – if necessary – one's *own* ability to imagine alternatives to the rigid, limited, and impoverished sites of desire' (Hart, 1998, pp.67–68, emphasis in original). Sadomasochism can be about expanding the limits of the erotic, sexualising the non-sexual and taking pleasure where it is not normatively found. It can offer participants a 'different kind of erotic narrative, one whose organization is aleatory and paratactic rather than direct and hypotactic, preferring fore-pleasures to end-pleasures, and browsing to discharge' (Silverman, 1992, p.186). Whilst sadomasochism 'is not – at least not simply – about sex' for every sadomasochist (Newmahr, 2011, p.68), it does hold a strong sexual meaning for some.

What is revealed by these alternative accounts is that there is no set importance or meaning given to sadomasochism by its practitioners, instead there is a multitude of varying and competing meanings and sadomasochism's importance to each practitioner depends upon the specific meanings they adopt and employ. In contrast to legal discourse's conceptualisation of sadomasochism as violent and degrading, sadomasochism may be accompanied by strong, positive emotional connections forged between the participants. Indeed, preliminary research data have indicated that engaging in sadomasochistic activities increases feelings of relationship closeness (Sagarin, 2009).

Sadomasochism and identity

Within the range of meanings attached to sadomasochism, identity is a dominant theme in alternative discourses. Newmahr (2011), in a four-year ethnographic study of the organised sadomasochistic subculture (known as the 'scene'), identifies sadomasochists as frequently being social outsiders with long-held feelings of difference and alienation. A participant's entry and acceptance into the scene, when placed 'against [this] backdrop of marginality … creates and constitutes feelings of intimacy' (Newmahr, 2008, p.634). Sadomasochism can thus be used as a way to adopt and create a social identity that affords participants social access and connections. This construction of sadomasochistic social identity is readily apparent in texts dealing with the homosexual 'leather' subculture of 1950s–1970s in New York, Chicago and San Francisco wherein themes of family and brotherhood consistently recur (Mains, 2002).

In addition to social identity, sadomasochism can also influence and constitute private identity. Baumeister (1998, p.36) argues that the appeal of masochism lies in its ability to provide a 'powerful method of removing high-level, abstract self-awareness'. By refocusing the masochist on themselves in a 'physical, low-level immediate manner', sadomasochistic activities free them to 'create a new, fantasized identity that is fundamentally different from the self that is escaped' (Baumeister, 1998, p.36). Sadomasochism can be seen as providing cathartic relief from the stresses and anxieties of everyday identity and allowing participants to create short-term, pleasurable identities to adopt and discard. But sadomasochism can also contribute to participants' long-term private identities. The mind and the body, constructed as disconnected by dominant Western culture, are re-connected by sadomasochism. By playing with physical and mental perceptions and experiences, sadomasochism joins 'people and their stories to their bodies' (Williams, 2009, p.209). Through sadomasochism the body is no longer an object to be internally disciplined, an obstacle to overcome or a medium through which to interact with the world, but rather it becomes a reintegrated part of the self. Unlike legal discourse, sadomasochism is conceptualised here as enhancing and enabling, rather than maiming or destroying, the masochist.

Sadomasochism and pain

The meanings attached to pain and injury in sadomasochism can also differ from those in legal discourse. Whereas in law the 'paradigm case of injury sustained by stabbing, shooting, punching and kicking [is] during aggressive and unwanted confrontation', in sadomasochism the parties' 'inter-subjective understanding of what those consequences and effects may mean *for them*' is different (Weait, 2007, p.67, emphasis in original). Sadomasochism is not about the taking of pleasure in activities traditionally considered painful. By this I mean that the concept of sadomasochism is not exhausted by the mere phenomenological substitution of the *qualia* of pleasure for the *qualia* of pain. Rather, sadomasochism is concerned with framing and contextualising pain in a way that strips it of the negative Western dominant cultural associations with fear and suffering, and recasts it to have positive associations with sexual pleasure or achievement. As Gebhard (1976, p.163) notes, apparently counter-intuitively, 'pain *per se* is not attractive to the masochist, and generally not to the sadist', unless it is properly contextualised. Hence, a masochist who stubs their toe, or who trips and falls whilst running for a bus, is no more likely to enjoy their experience than a non-masochist, because the pain incurred here is outside the transformative sadomasochistic setting.

Within the sadomasochistic setting, pain and injury in sadomasochism can take on 'multiple complex meanings … A cut not only produces pain but also offers a sense of release, an exchange of power, a feeling of trust, loss of selfhood and so on: the possibilities are almost limitless' (Langridge, 2007, p.90). Undergoing intense pain may be characterised as indicative of strength of will or of eagerness to please the sadist, and the infliction of bruises or cuts might serve as reminders of dominance or as badges of a masochist's pride in their achievement. Some masochists may take pleasure in the pain itself, some may suffer pain as a mark of submission, some may endure it as an unfortunate by-product (Newmahr, 2011, pp.134–142), and some may use it as a method to achieve 'sub-space' (a pleasurable state of mind speculated to be the result of a rush of endorphins released by the body during physical stress) (Mains, 2002). In sadomasochism, pain is still felt and injury is still suffered, but they are not tinged by the traditional cultural associations of negativity, hostility and harm. Instead, they can be reframed to have positive associations.

Accounting for Legal Discourse's Construction of Sadomasochism

The authoritative legal conceptualisation of sadomasochism, then, is markedly different from alternative conceptualisations of sadomasochism drawn from sadomasochists and other discourses. Sadists and masochists are alternatively constructed as equal and free partners who engage in sadomasochistic practices for a multitude of possible reasons, including sexual pleasure, identity-formation, psychic enjoyment, therapeutic healing and emotional connection. Injuries and pain are not automatically considered to be disabling and contemptuous, but can rather be enabling and enhancing. But 'criminalisation in this area' has occurred 'without proper regard to … the range of complex socio-sexual practices that are labelled as SM, and the meaning of such practices to participants' (Cowan, 2011, p.61). Hoople (1996, p.186) persuasively argues that 'SM practitioners were never really represented in *R v Brown*', and that the model of sadomasochism that emerges from the law is deliberately and almost wholly divorced from the accounts of sadomasochists themselves. These alternative accounts of sadomasochism are 'subjugated knowledges' because they lack the recognition, acceptance and authority of other accounts generated by discourses such as law and medicine (Beckmann, 2009).

These alternative discursive understandings are incommensurable with authoritative legal discourse; the idiom of sadomasochism offered by these alternative accounts runs counter to the idiom of sadomasochism that dominates authoritative legal discourse and that informs the black-letter of the law. Claims that masochists are freely consenting and experience pleasure from their participation in sadomasochistic activities are not legible under the law. Instead, the factual consent of the masochist is substituted for legal non-consent and the injuries that they endure are conceived of as nothing other than harmful and degrading. An important question remains to be answered: if sadomasochism has been constructed in such positive ways within these alternative accounts, why has it been conceptualised so negatively within authoritative legal discourse?

Sadomasochism as transgression

The transgressive qualities of sadomasochistic activities are downplayed by some commentators who believe that sadomasochism has been incorporated into the dominant culture. Hanna (2001, pp.243–244) argues that 'S/M is so trendy it is almost *passé*', citing examples of it within popular culture such as the prevalence of people wearing black leather, articles about it appearing in magazines, the popularity of Anne Rice's novels, personal ads in newspapers, sadomasochistic books being stocked in chain book stores, sadomasochistic equipment being available in sex stores and the ease of attending sadomasochistic conferences or joining sadomasochistic organisations. Sadomasochistic imagery is indeed commonplace in 'movies, television, music videos, and magazine advertisements' (Donnelly and Fraser, 1998, p.392), and BDSM fetish fabrics (such as leather, latex and rubber) and styles (such as corsets, collars and high heeled shoes) have also either experienced a resurgence of popularity or otherwise become contemporary staples of the fashion industry (Steele, 1996).

Beckmann (2009, p.2) rightly identifies that 'elements of "SM" and of fetish culture have become part of capitalist consumerism and thus of mainstream society'. But whilst it may be true that representations of sadomasochism have 'saturated popular culture', not all of these representations are favourable and they are generally intended to titillate rather than promote acceptance of alternative sexualities (Weiss, 2006, p.104). Pa (2001, p.55) argues that these cultural images are usually 'hackneyed', and that 'cultural curiosity with S/M stems' from 'a desire to ogle what is perceived as aberrant sexual conduct'. Even if one understands such pop culture representations as positive endorsements, the normalisation of a limited selection of some sadomasochistic practices as socially 'acceptable' implicitly reinforces the position of the remaining sadomasochistic practices as socially 'unacceptable' (Barker, Gupta and Iantaffi, 2007, p.198). 'Kinky sex' in the sense of some occasional light-hearted fun with handcuffs, a blindfold or a soft whip, may have indeed been normalised and commercialised in some (or some parts of) Western societies (Beckmann, 2001). However, there is markedly less cultural acceptance of sadomasochistic-identified individuals and those who practice sadomasochism in more 'extreme' forms. A 2008 survey by the National Coalition for Sexual Freedom (an American-based organisation which supports alternative sexualities) found that 22.2 per cent of respondents had suffered some kind of violence or harassment because of their sadomasochistic practices (Wright, 2008, p.14). That Madonna's *Sex* book sold well and *Secretary* recouped more than its budget is no indication that sadomasochism is socially accepted or mainstream. It merely means that some consumer objects or advertisements with sadomasochistic themes are commercially viable in an easily titillated but perennially jaded marketplace. Egan's (2007, p.1638) observation that despite 'the public fascination with the trappings of the SM lifestyle, many people react with disgust to the actual practice of SM', seems wholly accurate.

This section does not contend that all sadomasochists are sex radicals, anarchists or otherwise politically extreme. Though this may be the case for some, it is undoubtedly not the case for all. Whilst transgression 'has long been recognised as an important part of the appeal of SM, for some at least ... this is not all there is to SM and indeed may not be terribly relevant to some practitioners' (Langdridge, 2006, p.383). This section does contend, however, that sadomasochistic activities themselves are transgressive regardless of the political motivations of the participants behind them. Transgression here does not require an element of intention, it is merely a product of function. Sadomasochism can be considered transgressive in a number of ways.

Firstly, sadomasochism is transgressive because it challenges both the normative construction of sexuality and the normative boundaries of sexualisation. Those sadomasochists who attach sexual meanings to their sadomasochistic activities make no pretence about eschewing the 'naturalistic' model of sex as a utilitarian method of production and are instead concerned with indulgence in pleasure rather than the efficient production of new citizens. Indeed, if the non-sadomasochistic pursuit of sexual pleasure can be seen as the extravagant squandering of 'physical resources on non-productive activity', then it 'is arguable that sadomasochistic sex', which can be very time-consuming, utilises costly specialised equipment and generally injures and tires the body, 'takes this to its logical extreme' (Weait, 1996, p.169). The sheer excessive and inefficient nature of sadomasochistic sex crosses the normative boundaries of sexuality to open up new space for sexual freedom and expression. Furthermore, sadomasochism also extends the traditional concept of sexuality beyond a mere focus on genitalia and opens it up to the use of objects, the use of the brain and, indeed, the 'use of every part of the body as a sexual instrument' (Foucault, 1988c, p.299). It utilises pain and the trappings of power, normally conceived of as antithetical to the pleasure and freedom of sex, and eroticises them. The transgressive threat of sadomasochistic bodies to the dominant culture is the possibility they raise that any item or scenario, regardless of the negativity built into its cultural associations, can be transformed into sex. This revelation calls into question the socially constructed nature of normative sexuality and the disciplinary institutions that produce and replicate it, as well as freeing sexuality from its status as 'subservient to the requirements of the state' (Taylor, 1997, p.119). The sadomasochist's rejection of the 'mainstream, heteronormative, and strictly boundaried model of sexual citizenship' is thus 'dissenting and confrontational' (Cowan, 2011, p.76). Whilst sadomasochism can hold a range of non-sexual meanings for sadomasochists, where sadomasochism does become intertwined with sexuality it constitutes a challenge to normative models of desire and eroticism. This transgressive character of sadomasochism-as-sex partly accounts for the 'marked differences in the crimino-legal treatment of sadomasochism (s/m) from that of other sexualities, especially the heteronormative and procreative' (Houlihan, 2011, p.32).

Secondly, sadomasochism is transgressive because it reverses typical body-logics and challenges normative understandings about embodiedness. As Chan (2006, p.195) recognises, '[p]ain and pleasure do not co-exist in the mindset of a normal citizen'. The adoption of medical technological advances has transformed the Western world into an 'anaesthetic society ... [where f]ew of us could contemplate our teeth being drilled without injections, or an operation without gas' (Weait, 1996, p.171). As has been discussed, the experience of pain is an integral part of sadomasochistic activities and does not involve the substitution of pain for pleasure but rather involves the re-characterisation of pain as desirable and enjoyable. Sadomasochistic activities break the cultural nexus between pain and undesirability, and radically devalue the nexus between pleasure and desirability. Pain is no longer 'viewed as intrinsically evil' (Mains, 2002, p.69), but can be recast in any light the participants want. As such, the sadomasochist who 'actually appreciates or enjoys pain ... seems both illogical and deeply disturbing' to society (Beckmann, 2009, p.54). The negative dominant cultural associations between injury and harm are also broken, as injuries can be recast as marks of pride or achievement. The threat of sadomasochism is that it offers different understandings of embodiedness to those widely accepted within dominant culture, and that these understandings free the body from social convention and allow it to attach whatever associations it chooses to particular sensations and bodily states. In particular, the Western cultural conceptualisation about the body typically idealise smooth functioning, unbroken and unmarked skin and continuous, uninterrupted bodily processes.[8] By seeking out brokenness, visible marking and discontinuity in bodily processes, sadomasochists invert this key, normative bodily value-system. Beckmann (2009, pp.164–165) identifies sadomasochism as requiring 'open bodies' – both physically open in terms of cuts and open orifices, and also subjectively open in terms of interpersonal connection – the existence of which 'disrupts the notion of a "closed", self-possessed and therefore "safe" body'. It is this body altering aspect of sadomasochism that is so incomprehensible and problematic for the law, which treats sadomasochism's opening up of the body as a form of violent rending rather than as a form of pleasurable and consensual sharing.

Thirdly, sadomasochism is transgressive because it reveals the socially constructed and contingent nature of power. Sadomasochism can be read as a microcosmic theatrical simulation of macrocosmic social power. As Hopkins (1994, p.123) argues:

> SM participants do not rape, they do rape scenes. SMists do not enslave, they do slave scenes. SMists do not kidnap, they do capture and bondage scenes … SM is constructed as a performance, as a staging, a production, a simulation in which participants are writers, producers, directors, actors, and audience.

This simulation has been characterised as highly theatrical, because the power of the sadist comes from the adoption and acceptance of an openly artificial imbalance of power created by the participants working together to construct their fantasy. This sadomasochistic power does not follow dominant cultural conceptions about the proper exercise of such power. For example, sex/gender is not determinative of who holds the 'power' within sadomasochism, as a number of studies demonstrate that male masochists are approximately as common as male sadists (Moser and Levitt, 1995; Yost, 2007). Accordingly, Hoople (1994, pp.209–210) describes sadomasochistic power as being 'structural and not essential', by which he means that 'the attributes accorded to each role are structurally imposed rather than essential characteristics of the persons who occupy these roles at any given point in time'. As such, this power is not necessarily attached, nor integral, to the participant who initially plays the role

8 This conception coheres in the common assumption of the 'natural, properly healthy body as [being] pristine or unmodified' (Pitts-Taylor, 2007, p.21). This conception also explains why, for example, cosmetic surgery (as discussed in Chapter 4) has historically strived towards the 'natural look' and has hidden its own traces (Fraser, 2003, pp.70–71). The scar tissue from such surgeries must be concealed or managed so that the 'operated body' can appear to be 'natural, that is to say, woundless' (Kinunnen, 2008, p.35), because this is a more culturally valuable bodily state to be in or to be perceived to be in.

of the sadist. A number of sadomasochists freely swap between participating as a sadist and as a masochist (they are known as 'switches'). The flexibility of power is also evident in the ability of sadomasochists to drop in and out of their sadomasochistic roles at different times. As McClintock (1993, p.87) notes: '[t]he economy of S/M is the economy of conversion: slave to master, adult to baby, pain to pleasure, man to woman, and back again'.

Power, then, is constructed within sadomasochism as contingent, reversible and flexible. But the scandal of sadomasochism is that its commentary on power does not end at the bedroom/dungeon door. In order to construct its fantastical imbalance of power, 'S/M borrows its decor, props, and costumery (bonds, chains, ropes, blindfolds) and its scenes (bedrooms, kitchens, dungeons, convents, prisons, empires) from the everyday cultures of power' (McClintock, 1993, p.89). The threat of sadomasochism is that it challenges social authority by revealing that all power is the specific result of particular patterns of social positioning. Sadomasochism thus refuses everyday power's 'legitimacy as nature' (McClintock, 1993, p.91), undermining its authority by demonstrating that it too is a theatrical performance (albeit more widespread) without an authentic or ontological basis.

Because of sadomasochism's transgressive nature, it has attracted the attention of disciplinary institutions that label and deal with it as an example of 'deviance'. Sadomasochism's history of pathologisation within the medical sphere and its criminalisation by the law are both examples of this. Claims that sadomasochism is *passé*, or otherwise socially accepted, are sharply undercut by the mobilisation of these social institutions to prevent and condemn its practice. Sadomasochistic activities, characterised by excess, inefficiency and social/sexual non-normativity, create unruly bodies. The cuts, bruises, welts and burns on the bodies of sadomasochists are somatic markers of transgression. The legal regulation of sadomasochism flows from a clear disciplinary concern about the 'threat of sadomasochism' (Beckmann, 2009, p.182), and is 'dependent upon the degree to which the behaviours are politically dissident and undermining of hegemonic notions of "normal sex"' (Taylor, 1997, p.108). The criminalisation of sadomasochistic injuries is an attempt to normalise unruly sadomasochistic bodies by rehabilitating them into docile bodies.

Sadomasochism's Specific Challenge to Law

In addition to exposing everyday institutional power as inauthentic and contingent, sadomasochism also specifically undermines the exercise of judicial power. While we can identify judicial power as shifting from a punitive to a disciplinary model (Foucault, 1977), the authoritative right to punish the transgressions of citizens and the accoutrement of such punishment are still specific to the judiciary. They function both as methods of social control and as authorising links to the judiciary's history of social control. The threat of sadomasochism to the legal system is that it 'borrows directly from the juridical model, while radically disarranging the right-to-punish' (McClintock, 1993, p.107). The accoutrement of judicial punishment is adopted by sadomasochists in order to enhance their activities, with common items including handcuffs, chains, cages, canes and stocks. As Weait (1996, p.167) notes with regard to the activities in *R v Brown* [1994]:

> What is immediately striking about the injuries which these men inflicted on each other is their similarity with the forms of corporal punishment which the criminal courts used to sanction. The men were tied down, they were beaten, they were clamped to wood and they were branded. What they did was organised, planned and executed.

By simulating judicial authority in this way, Weait (2007, p.74) sees sadomasochism as infringing on the authority of law because:

> Not only do [sadists] place themselves in the position of the law (by inflicting the pain and/or injury that will satisfy their desire) but [masochists] ridicule the power of law by actively enjoining the [sadist] to engage in the discipline and ritual humiliation upon which the law depends for its authority.

Indeed, what possible weight can the 'punitive symbolism of the criminal law' carry when it becomes 'a celebration of sadomasochistic desire'? (Houlihan, 2011, p.47).

Whilst the physical enactment of punishments within sadomasochistic and legal activities may be similar, sadomasochism constructs a markedly different aetiological model of punishment. The trial is constructed within the law as a truth-finding exercise, and where the truth that is found conflicts with legal standards then punishment is used to repair the damaged social fabric, rehabilitate the offender and deter future offences. Punishment within the legal system is deliberate and purposive, an impersonal and almost automatic mechanism that is used for calibrating behaviour. In contrast, punishment within sadomasochism has no purpose other than to fulfil the subjective desire for punishment by the participants themselves. It is deeply personal, sometimes sexualised and nearly always divorced from all but the flimsiest conception of wrong-doing. Sadomasochism's revelation that punishment is not necessarily the by-product of wrong-doing, and that punishment is something that can be desired and enjoyed, threatens a juridical order based on the use and threat of negative punishment to control wrong-doing. Indeed, McClintock (1993, p.107) argues that 'it is as subversive of the modern penal economy to enjoy a punishment without having first committed a crime, as it is to commit an unpunished crime'. Legal discourse's negative construction of sadomasochism is symptomatic of the 'jealous wrath of the penal bureaucracy challenged in its punitive monopoly' (McClintock, 1993, p.108), and the debasing treatment of sadomasochists by legal officers and processes in some cases demonstrates a similar 'jealous need to establish the justice system's monopoly on meting out humiliation' (Khan, 2014, p.271). Underpinning this legal jealousy is an anxiety around keeping punishment/humiliation discursively constructed as negative phenomena within dominant culture, lest law lose the value and efficacy of its techniques of social control. Law desperately tries to foreclose the question raised by sadomasochism that 'if it is possible to derive pleasure from pain, which the law has assumed people wish at all costs to avoid, what is left for law to use?' (Weait, 1996, p.170).

Sadomasochism also threatens to expose the connection of the exercise of power to the experience of pleasure. Connections between sexual pleasure and power are made explicit within some sadomasochistic activities, and in doing so this highlights the same connections within the exercise of judicial power. There is undoubtedly a certain scopophilic enjoyment in forcing an alleged offender to reveal the secrets of their actions and life, a forced confessional pleasure that derives from 'exercising a power that questions, monitors, watches, spies, searches out, palpates, brings to light' (Foucault, 1976, p.45, as noted in Bibbings and Alldridge, 1993, p.359). This is generally hidden quite deeply beneath the legal façade of objectivity and propriety, but some cracks in this façade do exist. As Bibbings and Alldridge (1993, p.359) identify, when *R v Brown* [1994] was still before the Court of Appeal, Lord Lane CJ lamented that it was 'unhappily, necessary to go into a little detail about the activities which resulted in the various counts being laid against these men', before delivering a legally unnecessary but 'detailed and salacious account of the counts on the indictment, which spread over nearly two whole pages'. Similarly, in *R v Robinson* (2001), 53 O.R. (3d) 448 (Ont. C.A.) (paragraphs 35 and 38) Rosenberg JA noted that counsel for the Crown 'repeatedly made use of … evidence' about the alleged offender's sex life being 'out of the ordinary [and including] bondage, three-way sex, anal sex, mutual urination, and use of various sexual aids' to make him seem like 'a demented sexual pervert'. Through the almost 'obsessive' collection and presentation of details about the non-normative sex lives of alleged sadomasochistic offenders, 'the sex trial reveals itself as deployed about the archival exhibition of the fetish. Under his purple robes, the judge has an erection' (McClintock 1993, p.103). Khan (2014, p.25) has built on these kinds of earlier observations by engaging in far more extensive detail with what she regards as the 'vicarious kinks' that 'are produced when s/m is rendered an object of knowledge'. She argues that the various discourses – medical, feminist, pop cultural, legal – that engage with sadomasochism 'reap epistemic enjoyment in discerning, delineating, and determining the truth of s/m' (Khan,

2014, p.305). In particular relation to law, she contends that '[w]hile often being repressive and punitive, socio-legal discourses on s/m effectively proliferate pleasure as they traffic in the excitement and the incitement of new knowledges of sex' (Khan, 2014, p.305).

It seems that 'the only legitimate dominant/submissive relationship is that which exists between the law and the legal subject' (Weait, 1996, p.170), and in particular the sadomasochistic subject, who can be alternatively exposed, defined, known, controlled and punished at law's pleasure. But these kinds of legal pleasures are pleasures that the law desperately does not want to be questioned, monitored, searched out or brought to light, because it would undermine the justice system's carefully cultivated air of detached and neutral analysis. The explicit connection between power and pleasure for some sadomasochists threatens law because it hints at law's own implicit, and hidden, connection between the two. As a result, sadomasochists are regulated and their activities and pleasures are criminalised/delegitimised so that that law's own guilty pleasures can stay safely in the proverbial closet.

Sadomasochism's status as theatrical simulation also provides a challenge to the authoritative basis of the law. Sadomasochistic activities can be argued to not be replicating violent acts but merely simulating them (Hopkins, 1994, p.123) in a particular self-conscious, parodic way (Pa, 2001, p.78). To argue that the 'slave' in a BDSM fantasy roleplay is actually enslaved in any meaningful way, or that the sadist actually has any meaningful power whilst the masochist does not, would be to 'read theatre for reality … to play the world forward' (McClintock, 1993, p.87). Legal discourse reads sadomasochism's simulation of violence as real violence because it questions, like Plant (2007, p.549, emphasis in original), whether 'there is *some* distinction between simulation and reality; between what one *is* and what one is capable (and/or willing) of *doing* or *pretending to be*'.

Hopkins (1994) identifies a passage from Baudrillard as being relevant to helping us understand why law cannot recognise a differentiation between simulation and reality in sadomasochism. In this passage Baudrillard (1988c, p.178) asks the reader to:

> Go and organize a fake hold up. Be sure to check that your weapons are harmless, and take the most trustworthy hostage, so that no life is in danger … Demand ransom, and arrange it so that the operation creates the greatest commotion possible. In brief, stay close to the 'truth', so as to test the reaction of the apparatus to a perfect simulation. But you won't succeed: the web of artificial signs will be inextricably mixed up with real elements (a police officer will really shoot on sight; a bank customer will faint and die of a heart attack; they will really turn the phoney ransom over to you). In brief, you will unwittingly find yourself immediately in the real, one of whose functions is precisely to devour every attempt at simulation, to reduce everything to some reality: that's exactly

> how the established order is, well before institutions and justice come into play. In this impossibility of isolating the process of simulation must be seen the whole thrust of an order that can only see and understand in terms of some reality, because it can function nowhere else … The challenge of simulation is irreceivable by power.

'Real' (non-simulated) crimes are less serious than simulated crimes because they operate within the conceptual framework of, and thus implicitly affirm, the criminal justice system. However, simulated crimes are 'infinitely more dangerous' because they always suggest that '*law and order themselves might really be nothing more than a simulation*' (Baudrillard, 1988c, p.177, emphasis in original). If the entire purpose of criminal law is to draw a distinction between transgression and obedience, but no distinction can be drawn between simulated transgression and simulated obedience, because they are both merely simulations, then this '*cancels out the difference upon which the law is based*' (Baudrillard, 1988c, p.178, emphasis in original).

Hopkins (1994, pp.137–138) relegates his discussion of this passage to an endnote, and in doing so I think he overlooks its importance to the legal regulation of sadomasochism. If sadomasochism simulates violence for its own ends, then the 'threat' of sadomasochism goes to the very heart of the law because it challenges the basis of legal authority by undermining the fundamental distinction between transgression and obedience on which law operates. Law's only defence to the challenge of sadomasochism's theatricality is to 'reinject realness and referentiality everywhere' (Baudrillard, 1988c, p.179). Sadomasochism cannot be constructed as simulation within legal discourse, it is imperative that legal discourse constructs sadomasochism's parodic simulation of violence as real (non-simulated) violence in order to protect the authority of law even though such a position strongly contradicts the discursive understandings of sadomasochist participants. Ironically, the 'reality' of sadomasochism for sadomasochistic participants is lost within the law when legal discourse reads sadomasochism's simulation of violence as 'real' violence.

Conclusion

Inflicting injury in the course of consensual sadomasochistic activities is a criminal offence and this legal position is underpinned by a conceptualisation of sadomasochism within legal discourse that is both reductive and profoundly negative. Masochists are conceptualised as mentally and morally ill, unable to give consent and helpless without the intervention of the law to protect themselves from being harmed. Sadists are conceptualised as uncivilised, exploitative degenerates who pose an unlimited threat of violence to both the masochist and society. As a result, the body alterations caused by sadomasochistic activities are conceptualised as non-consensual, violent and harmful injuries. This conceptualisation inflects the treatment of sadomasochism by the law. The discursive conceptualisation of sadomasochism as non-consensual and not consensual, violence and not sex or something else, and harmful and not beneficial, all feed into and inform the broader legal division of sadomasochistic activities as criminal and not lawful.

But authoritative legal discourse can only construct and maintain this particular conceptualisation of sadomasochism by marginalising and eliding alternative accounts of sadomasochism that conceptualise it in markedly different ways. There is a disjunction between 'how SM practitioners "see" and represent themselves and their practice … [and] how others "see" them, and thus there is a struggle over how to represent SM, a struggle with potentially dire consequences for practitioners' in legal terms (Hoople, 1996, p.190). The elision of the subjectivity of the masochist within the black-letter of the law reflects the broader elision of alternative accounts of sadomasochism that contest the narrow, pejorative model constructed within legal discourse. These alternative accounts undermine the legal conceptualisation of sadomasochism as non-consensual, harmful and violent at least partly through their sheer variety and multitude. Contrasting models of sadomasochism are many and varied, with the body alterations caused by sadomasochistic injury being alternatively conceptualised as a form of cathartic therapy, as markers of identity, as by-products of pleasure and desire, as consensual, as a form of play or leisure, and as marks of pride and achievement. The failure of the law to more fully incorporate these alternative, positive accounts into the legal discourse around sadomasochism constitutes a wilful blindness to viable sources of meaning that could be drawn on to generate a more holistic construction of sadomasochism.

This blindness can be explained by taking into account the normative functions of the law and the symbolic threat of sadomasochism. The discursive marginalisation of these alternative accounts is necessitated by law's need to regulate sadomasochistic activities. This need arises because of the structural role of law in society and the transgressive nature of sadomasochism. Sadomasochism is 'in a very real sense against the law', because it parodies legal power and authority and challenges the 'logic upon which law depends' (Weait, 2007, p.78). The criminalisation of injurious sadomasochistic activities and the negative conceptualisation of sadomasochism within legal discourse are both directed towards defusing and rehabilitating the general transgressive nature of sadomasochism, the unruly bodies of sadomasochists and the specific challenges that sadomasochism poses to legal authority. Law and discourse in this area work strategically to bolster law's disciplinary function; *R v Brown* [1994] and the common law tradition should be understood as 'the selective regulation of "unruly bodies"' (Beckmann, 2009, p.77).

Regardless of whatever strategic value discourse may have to the law, authoritative legal discourse's monopolisation over the conceptualisation of sadomasochism within law marginalises the accounts of sadomasochists themselves. Sadomasochists' own understandings of sadomasochism are incommensurable with these authoritative understandings, and as a result they are not only relegated to the status of alternative counter-discursive accounts but the insights they offer also fail to be reflected in the black-letter operation of the law. *R v Brown* [1994] stands as explicit precedent for the evacuation of the (inter)subjective content of sadomasochistic activities from legal consideration. Specific evidence about the factual consent of the masochist to injurious sadomasochistic activities is overridden by the declaration of consensual assault law that this does not constitute legal consent. Given the exclusionary and reductive nature of the law's treatment of sadomasochism, commentators have identified that the legal construction of sadomasochism as violent crime works to obscure the violent operation of law itself here (Khan, 2014, p.305; Moran, 1995). From a discursive standpoint, of all the activities considered within this chapter this legal 'violence' may be the most harmful.

Chapter 3

Genital Cutting: The Disparity Between Female Genital Modification and Male Circumcision

For thousands of years humanity has performed various body alterations on the genitalia. Male circumcision 'is or has been ritualistically practiced by a wide variety of primitive as well as advanced peoples throughout the history of the world', including the ancient Egyptians, Aztecs, Indigenous Australians and American Indians (Lightfoot-Klein, 1989, p.184). There is even some suggestion that it dates back to the Stone Age (Miller, 2002, p.512). Whilst the origins of the different forms of female genital modification are 'not known' (Queensland Law Reform Commission, 1994, p.15), they are 'generally accepted as having pre-dated Islam, Christianity and other major religions' (Family Law Council, 1994, p.9). These genital-based body alterations also continue to be carried out today. They are not antiquated relics, which appear only in museums or in accounts from history books, they exist in the living bodies of millions of people. The World Health Organisation (2007, p.1) ('WHO') estimates that approximately 30 per cent of all males have been circumcised, and the United Nations Children's Fund (2013) ('UNICEF') estimates that approximately 125 million females have undergone some form of 'traditional' female genital modification.

Despite their extensive lineage, these genital body alterations received little Western academic attention, outside anthropological and medical studies, until relatively recently. This tardiness has been more than made up for in the sheer volume and vehemence of material that has since been produced, particularly in relation to work on female genital modification within certain strands of feminist thought after its 'rediscovery by the West' in the 1970s (Boddy, 2007, p.52).[1] Much of this material is tinged with a sense of immediacy: describing the

1 Obviously, the notion of 'the West' is a reductive and Othering conceptualisation that is inherently problematic. It does, however, have particularly strong discursive resonance around the issue of female genital body alterations. As such, whilst notions

debate around such issues as 'urgent' (Silverman, 2004, p.419), seeking to evoke a widespread 'cry for urgent change' (Gruenbaum, 2001, p.1), or comprising a *Call for Global Action* (Toubia, 1993). The contemporaneity of this urgency suggests that the cultural and theoretical prerequisites for conceptualising these body alterations as harms have only recently been met by Western writers. That is, the conceptual framework through which the genitally-altered body is constructed has somehow shifted. This chapter analyses the discursive formations that have built up around the genital modifications since this surge of academic interest.

The aim of this chapter is to reveal and interrogate the ways in which male circumcision and female genital modifications are discursively conceptualised and legally treated as entirely different, even oppositional, practices. These body alterations hold radically differing legal positions: female genital modification is criminal whereas male circumcision is lawful. However, this chapter considers them together. Rather than handling them as separate topics, it interweaves discussion of their history, practice and the discourses that enmesh them. Such a coupling is contentious. Whilst numerous commentators consider male circumcision to be incomparable to the various female genital modifications, other commentators argue that they are almost identical. This debate structures this chapter, channelling its analysis into an engagement with the discursive techniques that are employed to construct and maintain the dissimilarities between the two. Unpacking the discursive forces behind the legal disparity between female genital modification and male circumcision segues what could devolve into a mere summary of the 'histories and geographies' of genital body alterations into an interrogation of the '[W]estern assumptions and traditions' that produce the differing legal status of these body alterations at this specific point in time (Green and Lim, 1998, p.382).

This chapter begins by setting out a brief definition of female genital modification and male circumcision, and proceeds by engaging with the discursive stakes involved in the terminological debate around how these body alterations should be named. This chapter then charts the legal status of both alterations under Australian law, contrasting the blanket criminality of female genital modification to the widely accepted lawfulness of male circumcision. Ultimately, this chapter demonstrates how particular conceptualisations about the body, sex/gender and culture, are all deployed in order to effect the discursive and legal separation of female genital modification from male circumcision.

---

of 'the West' will be employed in this chapter, this will be done reflexively and critically, and with the intention merely to reflect the discourse rather than to make truth-claims about fundamental divides in systems of knowledge or the sociocultural state of the world.

Genital Cutting

Whilst genital modifications are body alterations, their significance does not stop at the skin. They are culturally and socially meaningful, with strong connections to religion, sex/gender, and society. By offering physical information about how these alterations change the body and empirical information about where and how often such practices are carried out, this section does not seek to exhaustively define these body alterations. Rather, it merely presents one aspect of these alterations. The definitions offered here should be read in conjunction with the additional sociocultural material presented in the course of the analysis throughout the rest of this chapter.

Female Genital Modifications

The female genitals can be, and have been, modified in numerous ways. Some of these methods go beyond the scope of this chapter, such as genital piercing and genital cosmetic surgery (see Chapter 4), genital normalisation surgery and sex reassignment surgery (see Chapter 5). This chapter deals with one particular set of modifications that has drawn sufficient attention in recent years to generate the 'discursive construct' most commonly known as 'Female Genital Mutilation' or 'FGM' (Sullivan, 2007, p.400). WHO (2008a, p.4) has categorised these particular female genital body alterations into a widely cited schema:

> Type I: Partial or total removal of the clitoris and/or prepuce (clitoridectomy).
> Type II: Partial or total removal of the clitoris and the labia minora, with or without excision of the labia majora (excision).[2]
> Type III: Narrowing of the vaginal orifice with creation of a covering seal by cutting and appositioning the labia minora and/or labia majora, with or without excision of the clitoris (infibulation [or Pharaonic circumcision]).
> Type IV: All other harmful procedures to the female genital for non-medical purposes, for example: pricking, piercing, incising, scraping and cauterisation.

Historically, these body alterations have been carried out predominantly within African countries, and that is where the majority of such alterations are performed today. However, their estimated prevalence differs drastically across the different African countries. For example, it is estimated that the prevalence is 98 per cent in Somalia, 96 per cent in Guinea, and 91 per cent in Egypt, whereas it is estimated that the prevalence is 44 per cent in Chad, 27 per cent in Nigeria and just 4 per cent in Ghana (UNICEF, 2013, p.27). Different types

2 Interestingly, the reference to labia majora under the Type 2 heading was not part of earlier WHO classificatory schemas (WHO, 1998).

of female genital body alterations are practised in these different locations, for example infibulation is generally practised only in 'Djibouti, Egypt (Nubians), Ethiopia, Mali (among a few ethnic groups), Somalia and Sudan' (Ras-Work, 1997, p.143). Similarly, not all the types occur with equal frequency. Type III infibulation accounts for only 10 to 15 per cent of all of these female genital alterations, whereas Types I and II are performed far more frequently (Boddy, 2007, p.48; The Public Policy Advisory Group on Female Genital Surgeries in Africa 2012, p.22). The age at which females undergo this body alteration varies 'from region to region, from community to community' (Ras-Work, 1997, p.140), but typically ranges 'from infancy to late adolescence' (The Public Policy Advisory Group on Female Genital Surgeries in Africa 2012, p.21). Slack (1988, pp.442–443) notes that in 'Mauritania, Nigeria and Ethiopia, the operation is performed on newborns, or within the first few weeks following birth', whereas in 'Kenya and Tanzania, young women are excised on their wedding night' and in 'Mali, the operation may be performed on married women after they have had their first child'.

These body alterations are also practised in some Asian countries, such as India, Indonesia and Malaysia (Patrick, 2001, p.17). Furthermore, there are reported cases in Western countries including Australia, Canada, Denmark, France, Italy, Netherlands, the United Kingdom, the United States, Sweden and Spain (Coello, 1999, p.218). This has been attributed to the 'immigration and settlement of practicing communities' in the West (Khalafzai, 2008a, p.3). In Australia, the introduction of female genital modification has been blamed primarily on immigration from 'Horn of Africa countries, such as Eritrea, Somalia, Ethiopia and Sudan' (Queensland Law Reform Commission, 1994, p.11). The 'extent to which any form of female genital mutilation is practised in Australia, if at all, is not known' (Queensland Law Reform Commission, 1994, p.17). However, Dr Ted Weaver from the Royal Australian and New Zealand College of Obstetricians and Gynaecologists ('RANZCOG') has been quoted as saying that:

> It's hard to gauge the actual numbers because it's prohibited by legislation and it's something that is performed in an underground way ... [But t]here is some evidence to suggest that it does happen in certain parts of Australia ... [and] certainly there have been reports of children being taken to hospital after having the procedure done with complications from that procedure. (Bourke, 2010)

The quality of the instruments, the hygiene of the conditions and the use of anaesthesia varies across locations: unsterilised 'kitchen knives', 'broken glass' or 'sharp stones' may be used in rural African villages, whereas sterilised scalpels may be used in 'local health clinics' (Slack, 1988, p.442). The person who carries out the modification may be a doctor, a nurse or a lay person. In most African countries it is typically carried out by 'traditional practitioners', but in some countries, such as Egypt, it is more common for it to be carried out by health personnel such as a doctor (UNICEF, 2013, pp.44–45). There is some evidence that in Western countries, like Italy, some doctors may clandestinely carry out these body alterations in a clinical medical setting (Gallo, et al., 1999).

Male Genital Modifications

As with female genital modification, there are a number of traditional body alterations that continue to be practised today on the male genitalia, including subincision, penile cutting, skin flaying, epispasm, infibulation, urethral routing and cauterisation, duct resection and castration (Miller, 2002, pp.510–511). Particular practices are specific to certain geographies and ethnic groupings, for example, Povenmire (1998–1999, p.116, footnotes omitted) lists the Hottentot tribe of Africa as practising partial castration by removing one testicle, the Ysidi tribe in Yemen as practising skin flaying from the navel to the anus, and the Massai and Kikiuyu of Africa as practising a form of circumcision that keeps the 'lower part of the flesh of the foreskin to remain attached in a "bib" of atrophied flesh'. Wallerstein (1980, p.7) notes that skin flaying is also practised by 'some Bedouin Arabs', who call it *salkh* or *selkh*, and for them it 'consists of flaying the skin from below the navel to the upper thigh'. In Australia, there is a history of subincision amongst the Aboriginal people and this continues to be practised in certain areas (Williams, 1997, p.189). Subincision involves the lengthwise slitting of the penis through to the urethra, a wound that is then 'not permitted to close so that the urethra remains exposed' (Wallerstein, 1980, p.7).

Despite this variety, the literature around male genital body alteration focuses overwhelmingly on circumcision, a practice involving the removal of the foreskin. This will be the focus of this chapter's analysis as well. Not all male circumcisions are the same. Darby and Svoboda (2007) have developed a five-point scale to measure the amount of tissue removed during a circumcision. This scale ranges from Type 1 circumcision – 'excision of the part of the foreskin which extends beyond the glans' – to Type 5 circumcision – 'excision of the foreskin at the point where the foreskin joins the main penis shaft, removing the frenulum and frenular nerves' (Darby and Svoboda, 2007, p.308). Circumcision is commonly practised in a diverse range of places including Israel, Canada, New Zealand, 'much of the Middle East', Central Asia and West Africa, but is uncommon in East and Southern Africa (WHO, 2007, p.1). Take up rates are especially high in the United States, where they were around 90 per cent in the 1980s (Brigman, 1984–1985), but have since dropped to around 60 per cent (Royal Australian College of Physicians, 2004b), and in South Korea, where they are around 90 per cent (Waldeck, 2003–2004, p.457). The circumcision rate in Australia peaked at 40 per cent in the 1970s before dropping to around

10 per cent in the 1990s (Darby, 2001). It is now estimated at being around 12 per cent (Australian Federation of AIDS Organisations, 2009, p.3). The results of a survey of Australian males found that 58.7 per cent were circumcised, but that this dropped to 31.6 per cent for males between the ages of 16 and 19 (Richters, 2006a). Like subincision, circumcision is also a traditional and ongoing part of Australian Aboriginal culture in some areas (Queensland Law Reform Commission, 1993, p.8).

The age at which males undergo this body alteration varies. Circumcisions in Western countries are typically performed as a neonatal procedure at a doctors' surgery or a hospital within a few months of a boy being born. In Australia, the vast majority of circumcisions take place on newborns (Queensland Law Reform Commission, 1993, p.13; Tasmania Law Reform Institute, 2012, p.1). However, circumcision can also be used to treat adult males for medical conditions such as phimosis and balanitis xerotica obliterans. Outside this medical context, the age of circumcision can vary, with the Waibiri people of Central Australia carrying out these body alterations on boys aged between 11 and 13 years old (Queensland Law Reform Commission, 1993, p.9), and Philippinos performing it on boys aged 10 to 14 years (WHO, 2007, p.5). The conditions under which it is performed also vary. If carried out within a medical setting in the West, the circumcision is usually performed by a doctor, the boy may be anesthetised and sterilised equipment such as scalpels, clamps and bandages are used. If carried out in a non-medical setting – as is typical in Pakistan where circumcisions are generally performed by non-medically trained people – this body alteration may take place without stitches or sterilised instruments, and alternatives to bandages, such as ashes, may be used to stop bleeding (Rizvi, et al., 1999, p.14).

Male circumcision is also closely tied to the religious practices of both Islam (Rizvi, et al., 1999), and Judaism (Glass, 1999). Indeed, in Judaism it is considered to be 'a parent's duty [to] have [their] child circumcised ... on the eighth day after birth' (Bridge, 2002, p.280). Whilst the Muslim community typically have circumcisions performed by health care practitioners in hospital, the Jewish community are not reliant 'on the state health system for the circumcisions of body as the Jewish community includes *mohelim*, men who are specially trained to perform circumcisions' (Khalafzai, 2008, p.8). Jewish ritual circumcision performed in synagogues or private homes provides an alternative, non-medical context in which male circumcision takes place in Australia. However, given that only 0.5 per cent of Australians identified Judaism as their religious affiliation in the 2011 Australian Census (Australian Bureau of Statistics, 2012), it is apparent that ritual circumcision accounts for only a very small proportion of the circumcisions that are carried out in Australia. Indeed, in Tasmania 'less than one circumcision a year is performed on average ... by a traditional Jewish circumciser' (Tasmania Law Reform Institute, 2012, p.8).

It is clear that '[m]ost circumcisions performed in Australia are performed in hospitals' or otherwise 'by medical professionals in day surgeries and in general practice offices' (Tasmania Law Reform Institute, 2012, p.6). As such, the more common medical rather than ritual circumcisions will be the main focus of this chapter.

Troublesome Terminology

The casual reader thumbing their way through a handful of papers on female genital modification could be forgiven for thinking that each writer had their own idiosyncratic terminology for the same set of body alterations they all discuss. The kinds of body alterations covered by WHO's four-part schema outlined above have been variously referred to as:

- female circumcision (Sussman, 1998);
- female genital mutilation (Khalafzai, 2008a);
- female genital surgery (Mason, 2001);
- traditional female genital surgeries (Lane and Rubinstein, 1997);
- female genital alteration (Darby and Svoboda, 2007);
- female genital operations (noted in Gruenbaum, 2001);
- female genital modification (Oboler, 2001);
- female genital ritual (Nnamuchi, 2012);
- female genital cutting (Wade, 2009); and,
- clitoridectomy (Bowra, 1994).

Sorting through this tangle of wording and settling on what to use is neither an idle nor an unimportant task. Terminology works to inflect the broader discourse by determining the terms of the debate, the types of arguments and the information that can be brought forward and given validity within the discursive framework. For example, arguments based on the liberal notions of freedom and agency seem not only inappropriate but almost inconceivable when the choice is phrased as a decision to 'mutilate' or 'not mutilate' a child's genitals. Similarly, arguments about the cultural importance of such body alterations are incompatible with considering them as a form of 'surgery', a classification typically turning on questions of medical necessity. As terminology can constitute, rather than just communicate, the debate, this choice is important and should be fully considered as an essential component of how the discourse in the area functions.

The same point can be made regarding male circumcision. Although the literature on male genital body alteration overwhelmingly employs 'circumcision' to describe the practice, and 'uncircumcised' to describe a male who has not undergone it, there have been some calls to adopt different terminology (Darby and Svoboda, 2007). For this chapter, presenting my working through of the terminological options to arrive at a choice is valuable in the context of the larger work as it demonstrates what factors are taken into account by commentators, the connections this choice has with their arguments, and how their arguments frame the wider discourse. Discourse is inextricably linked to language, and this book cannot analyse the former without close scrutiny of the latter.

Working Through the Options

The 'most well-known and commonly used term' to describe these female genital body alterations is female genital mutilation (Skaine, 2005, p.2). It is argued that the word mutilation 'adequately describes the practice' (Hughes, 1996–1996, p.321), because it recognises it as 'intrinsically an infringement on the physical and psychosexual integrity of women and girls and as a form of violence against them' (Patrick, 2001, p.16), and because it refers specifically to the fact that 'most variants of the practices entail damage to or removal of healthy tissues or organs' (Gruenbaum, 2001, p.3). This term has been widely adopted by writers within certain strands of feminist thought, as well as a number of important international organisations such as the WHO, the United Nations and various United Nations sub-bodies.

Despite its widespread usage, 'female genital mutilation' is a problematic terminological option. Although the term mutilation is 'technically accurate' – though perhaps only if used to describe *some* of the practices (Nnamuchi, 2012, p.91) – and does not carry pejorative associations in a strict dictionary-definition sense, 'for most people, [it] implies intentional harm and is tantamount to an accusation of evil intent' (Gruenbaum, 2001, p.3). In contrast, within those communities where female genital modification is practised it is usually something that is 'done out of love and caring' (Queensland Law Reform Commission, 1994, p.58), something that is done *for* the female rather than *to* the female. As such, the use of the term can deeply offend particular communities, not least of all the women who have undergone the body alteration and who may not consider themselves 'mutilated' (Gruenbaum, 2001, p.4).

Irrespective of the concern that it may alienate some women who have undergone FGM, many anti-FGM writers see strategic value in propagating this term. If these body alterations are constructed as 'female genital mutilation', then those opposing their continuation can easily claim the moral high ground. Arguments that cultural reasons, such as tradition or religion, might justify this body alteration ring hollow when faced with the rejoinder that what they propose is a form of disfiguring violence (Wellerstein, 1999–2000, p.101). As Green and Lim (1998, p.369) note, referring to it as female genital mutilation loads the debate because 'no one would choose to be … mutilated'. Although this term is commonly used, it will not be adopted in this chapter for two reasons. Firstly, because it is such a 'strongly value-laden term' (Patrick, 2001, p.16), adoption of it is tantamount to complicity with a particular aspect of the discourse around FGM. The term itself 'begins with the presumption of an antipathy toward the practices, and … resists dialogue' (Rogers, 2013, p.71), thus it would not be conducive to the kind of analysis that this book is engaged in. Secondly, it is reductive. The term 'female genital mutilation' disregards the different meanings, contexts and types of female genital modifications and instead 'forges a single decontextualized fact' out of them, that it imbues with one particular significance (Boddy, 1998, p.80). It levels out the differing severity across the numerous types of procedures, so that ritual nicking or scraping (Type IV) becomes the discursive equivalent of infibulation (Type III). Such an approach is disingenuous, as it not only fails to account for such difference but actively works to put it under erasure. Those writers who shorten female genital mutilation to 'the more clinical-sounding FGM' (Gruenbaum, 2001, p.4), perhaps in an attempt to make the term less evocative and denigrating, fail to overcome this additional problem.

The terms 'female genital operations' and 'female genital surgeries' can be criticised for lending 'an air of legitimacy or medical necessity to the practice[s] which cannot be supported' (Hughes, 1995–1996, p.321), and for evoking certain inaccurate notions about the conditions under which these body alterations are performed. However, in response to a similar criticism of their choice of wording in an earlier article, Lane and Rubinstein (1997, p.5) argue that the 'gloss of the term surgery to mean a valued, aseptic, therapeutically necessary treatment, carried out by an authorized practitioner … is embedded in a particular cultural tradition' and is a Western biomedical understanding of the term. They go on to note that 'traditional female genital surgeries are carried out by a culturally authorized practitioner and are meant to improve – not hurt – the life chances of the girls involved', so they qualify as a form of 'surgery' within a non-Western biomedical understanding of the term (Lane and Rubinstein, 1997, p.5). Whether or not this is true, if a Western audience is anticipated to make up a portion of an author's readership it seems imprudent to adopt terminology that carries such a risk of misinterpretation. Accordingly, whilst these terms 'can be used in some contexts' (Gruenbaum, 2001, p.4), they will not be used in this chapter.

The use of the term 'female circumcision' to describe these body alterations has proved highly contentious. There is a general trend of those who support the cessation of female genital modification dissociating the two, arguing that male circumcision is incomparable for various reasons (Dixon, 1996; Khalafzai, 2008a; Toubia, 1993; Trueblood, 1999–2000; Wood, 2001). Conversely, those who advocate fostering a deeper tolerance towards female genital modification, and those who support the cessation of male circumcision, generally tend to construct the two as comparable (Boyle, 2000; Chessler, 1997; Svoboda, Van Howe and Dwyer, 2000). Given that the bulk of the analysis later in this chapter is devoted to exploring how these dis/similarities between the two are constructed through discursive representation, it is not necessary to go into detail here. Briefly, however, such arguments include statements that the term circumcision is inappropriate because it makes female genital modifications seem 'nonmutilating' (Chessler, 1997, p.558), when they are claimed to be 'far more invasive, and without any medical benefit' (Khalafzai, 2008a, p.1), and because they involve 'cutting [that] is much more severe and extensive, often impairing a woman's sexual and reproductive functions' (Trueblood, 1999–2000, p.441). Others argue that the term circumcision is appropriate because both types of body alteration involve the cutting and disfiguring of the genitals (Richards, 1996, p.372), it is the term 'usually preferred by women in the communities that engage in this practice' so its use is 'culturally sensitive' (Sussman, 1998, p.197), it is the term actually used by 'members of cultures who practice the procedure' (Skaine, 2005, p.2), and because they both cause similar harms to the person undergoing them (Svoboda, 1999).

The discursive importance of this comparison depends upon the context in which it is employed. If it is employed by a Western anti-female genital modification writer who argues that these body alterations are dissimilar, the effect is to render female genital modifications less acceptable. By directing their Western audience away from the comparison to male circumcision, the possible transference of positive cultural sentiment from male circumcision – which is legal, commonly practised and widely accepted in the West – to female circumcision is foreclosed. The aim appears to be to prevent those 'who support male circumcision … [from] rethink[ing] their opposition to female genital mutilation' (Miller, 2002, p.503). Similarly, any cognitive dissonance that may be experienced as a result of condemning one set of body alterations and embracing the other may be defused. Alternatively, if this comparison is employed by an anti-male circumcision writer who argues that these body alterations are similar, the effect is to render male genital modification less acceptable. Tapping into the associations built up around female genital modifications in popular Western discourse – like mutilation, human rights violation, and unjustifiable violence, all backed by the condemnation of international bodies – elevates the importance of male circumcision and helps construct it discursively as a wrong. Seeking only to comment upon and analyse this comparison, rather than take sides in this ongoing debate, this chapter will not use the term 'female circumcision'.

Not only has the term 'female circumcision' been criticised when used to describe female genital body alterations, so too has the term 'male circumcision' been criticised when used to describe body alterations that remove the foreskin of the penis from the male. Goldman (1997, p.51) notes that 'circumcision' is a 'symbol' or 'euphemism' for the body alteration that lessens its 'emotional impact' and accordingly functions strategically to position parents as more likely to accept it being carried out on their son. Rogers (2013, p.78) incisively recognises that 'the practices of circumcision on men are not referred to as 'male genital circumcision', which both obscures the corporeal nature of the practice and disjoints the practice from cultural associations about the genitalia. Instead, it has been argued that a more accurate term than 'circumcision', one which more fully conveys the physical significance of this body alteration, would be 'mutilation'. Because it necessarily entails 'the removal of a conspicuous part of the body', 'inflicts an irreparable injury and alters the appearance of the penis', calling it mutilation is 'clinically accurate and objective' (Denniston, Hodges and Milos, 1999, pp.vi–vii). Whilst, technically, 'the word "mutilation" as defined in its ordinary sense, as well as by medical dictionaries, is wholly apt to describe the result of this procedure' (Price, 1996), similar issues regarding the negative connotations of violence and disfigurement that pertain to the female genital modification naming debate apply here also. The term 'male genital mutilation' has strategic value for advocates of the cessation of male circumcision, and similar counter-arguments to the ones discussed above also apply. For example, circumcision is rarely, if ever, done with malice, and circumcised men may not identify themselves or want others to identify them as 'mutilated'. Goldman (1997, p.52) offers a less pejorative term when he writes that 'circumcision is foreskin amputation', though he also seems to dismiss this term because amputations generally only occur 'if there is an incurable localized condition present that may threaten the rest of the body or result in a serious irreparable injury' if the amputation is not carried out (see, however, the discussion of healthy limb amputation in Chapter 4). Accordingly, neither of these other terms are appropriate for this chapter.

The Choice of Terms

So, what terms will be adopted here? Throughout the rest of this book I will use 'female genital modification' (hereafter 'FGM') and 'male circumcision' (hereafter 'MC'). For ease of expression I have chosen the singular rather than the plural forms of both of these terms, but I still want to highlight the wide variety of physical practices, physical effects and cultural understandings that these terms incorporate, and so I flag this as an issue here. The use of 'modification' is an effort to adopt more neutral, non-evocative, and non-partisan language to describe an already heated debate. Adopting the identical acronym to female genital mutilation, that is 'FGM', carries the benefits of name-recognition as well as evoking the discursive dominance of the conceptualisation of FGM as being 'mutilatory'. By using 'MC' instead of the full words 'male circumcision', I am seeking to open up some critical distance in order to promote reflexivity about the culturally embedded nature of circumcision's general acceptance in the West. I readily admit that my choice of terminology may be an imperfect solution to the terminological problems in this discursive area. However, given that no terminological choice will ever carry a 'neutral' loading of meaning and that adding to the already bloated terminological array is not a viable option, the terminology I have adopted here is the least problematic of all possible choices. Although these specific terms will be used in this chapter, the terminology used in quotations from other authors will not be changed. As previously discussed, one's choice of terminology reflects not only the message of one's work but also the wider discursive framework, and thus in order to properly analyse the discourse it is necessary to preserve the specific use of terminology in an effort to capture how it may function strategically in its context.

The only remaining terminological question to resolve is how to refer to those males and females whose genitals have not been altered by FGM or MC: should they be described as 'intact', 'uncut', 'uncircumcised', 'unmutilated', and so on? 'Intact' is an inappropriate reference term because it denies the range of other body alterations that can affect the genitalia, such as genital piercing and cosmetic surgery (see Chapter 4), sex reassignment surgery and genital normalisation surgery (see Chapter 5). Furthermore, it seems to implicitly invoke a problematic conceptualisation of the body as natural, separated from culture and 'whole' in its 'naturalness'. The terms 'uncut', 'uncircumcised' and 'unmutilated' can also be rejected for the reason that they situate the cut, circumcised and mutilated bodies, respectively, as the default bodily state. This sets these bodies up as 'the norm, the standard', from which to measure (Goldman, 1997, p.51), which correlatively legitimises the production of these bodies by naturalising them within the discourse. Instead, this chapter will refer to such people as non-Circumcised, for the males, and as non-Modified, for the females. The aim of retaining the upper-case letters is to make it clear that it merely denotes that this particular sub-set of genital body alterations have not been carried out (regardless of whether other genital body alterations have), to draw attention to the social meanings of these alterations and to indicate not only the physical but also the discursive changes wrought on the body by FGM and MC. By reinserting awareness of the discursive character of the body, my hope is that no form of bodily state is seen as 'default' but rather as merely one possibility within a plurality.

The Legal Status of Genital Cutting

Whilst whether or not FGM and MC should be conceptualised as comparable body alterations remains a discursively contested issue, their legal positions are definitively settled. Legally, they have been adjudged to be dissimilar; FGM is criminal whereas MC is lawful.

The Legal Status of FGM

FGM has been explicitly criminalised in most Western countries over the last few decades. For example, it became an offence in the United Kingdom in 1985 with the passage of the *Prohibition of Female Circumcision Act 1985* (which has since been replaced by the *Female Genital Mutilation Act 2003*), a federal offence in the United States in 1996, and an offence in New Zealand in 1996 through the amendment of the *Crimes Act 1961*. Despite these new laws, the number of prosecutions for FGM is extremely low. In the United States, from 1996 to 2004 there were only two prosecutions (Mendelsohn, 2004, p.1011). In the United Kingdom, there had only been one arrest and two instances of doctors losing their medical licence for agreeing to perform FGM by 2010 (Boyle and Corl, 2010, p.200). Further, in the initial 12 years after FGM's criminalisation in the United Kingdom, no prosecutions were brought despite evidence of its continuing practice (Skaine, 2005, p.66).

In Australia, '[d]ebates around female circumcision ... were not present in Australian legal discourse until the 1990s', when media reporting on FGM picked up and subsequently spurred the various levels of government to respond (Rogers, 2007, p.138). Specific statutory sections now exist in every State and Territory prohibiting FGM. Arguably, these reforms were unnecessary, as 'the weight of legal opinion' suggests that FGM was already criminal on the basis of pre-existing assault law (Ierodiaconou, 1995–1996, p.565). The Queensland Law Reform Commission (1994, pp.30–35), tasked with investigating the appropriate legal response to FGM, noted that even without specific legislation FGM would likely constitute unlawful wounding or grievous bodily harm, and that it was doubtful that the medical benefit defence would apply to it.

Whilst the various Australian statute sections are worded slightly differently they each have the same legal effect: the blanket criminalisation of FGM. Regardless of the consent of the female on whom it is performed, carrying out 'female genital mutilation' is a criminal offence in all State and Territory jurisdictions (*Crimes Act 1900* (ACT) ss74(1)–(2); *Crimes Act 1900* (NSW) ss45(1) and 45(5); *Criminal Code* (Tas) ss178A(1)–(2); *Criminal Code* (NT) ss186B(1) and 186D; *Criminal Code* (Qld) ss323A(1)–(2); *Criminal Law Consolidation Act 1935* (SA) ss33A(1)–(2); *Crimes Act 1958* (Vic) ss32(1) and 34; *Criminal Code* (WA) ss306(2)–(3)). Similarly, it is an offence in every State and Territory jurisdiction to remove a person from that jurisdiction in order for them to undergo 'female genital mutilation' somewhere else (*Crimes Act 1958* (Vic) s33): in some jurisdictions this only applies if that person is a child (*Crimes Act 1900* (ACT) s75; *Criminal Code* (NT) s186C; *Criminal Code* (Qld) s323B; *Criminal Law Consolidation Act 1935* (SA) s33B; *Criminal Code* (Tas) s178B; *Criminal Code* (WA) s306(3)), whilst in other jurisdictions this applies if that person is ordinarily a resident of that jurisdiction regardless of their age

(*Crimes Act 1900* (NSW) s45(2); *Criminal Code* (NT) s186B(2)). In the Australian Capital Territory, New South Wales and Tasmania 'female genital mutilation' is statutorily defined as including the excision, infibulation or mutilation of any part of the labia majora, labia minora or clitoris (*Crimes Act 1900* (ACT) s73; *Crimes Act 1900* (NSW) s45(1)(a); *Criminal Code* (Tas) s1), and in the remaining jurisdictions this definition is extended to also include any procedure to narrow or close the vaginal opening (*Criminal Code* (NT) s186A(3); *Criminal Code* (Qld) s323A(3); *Criminal Law Consolidation Act 1935* (SA) s33; *Crimes Act 1958* (Vic) s15; *Criminal Code* (WA) s306). These various legal definitions clearly cover FGM Types I, II and III from the WHO classificatory schema. There are a number of limited exceptions to the criminalisation of FGM, including surgical operations performed for therapeutic reasons by recognised medical practitioners and sex reassignment surgeries (discussed in Chapter 5) (*Crimes Act 1900* (ACT) ss75(1)–(3); *Crimes Act 1900* (NSW) ss45(3)–(4); *Criminal Code* (NT) ss186B(3)–(4); *Criminal Code* (Qld) s323A(3); *Criminal Law Consolidation Act 1935* (SA) ss33(1)–(2); *Criminal Code* (Tas) ss178C(1)–(2); *Crimes Act 1958* (Vic) ss34A(1)–(2); *Criminal Code* (WA) ss306(1)(d)–(e)).[3] In Victoria, an additional exception exists where only the clitoral hood of a consenting adult woman has been removed (*Crimes Act 1958* (Vic) ss3 and 32(2)). Despite the criminalisation of FGM Australia-wide, these laws have historically had merely a symbolic effect as 'very few, if any, female genital mutilation offences have been successfully prosecuted in Australian courts' (Attorney-General's Department, 2013, p.4).

Arguably, FGM also constitutes a violation of numerous international treaties and covenants, most of which Australia is a party to, such as the *Universal Declaration of Human Rights* (1948), the *Convention on the Elimination of All Forms of Discrimination Against Women* (1979), and the *Declaration on Violence Against Women* (1993) (Mason, 2001, p.62). Indeed, the United Nations General Assembly (2012) recently passed a resolution calling on countries to eliminate FGM on the basis of health and human rights concerns. The issue of FGM under international law and human rights law has been well-canvassed by other commentators (Sussman, 1998; Swensen, 1995; Trueblood, 1999–2000; Wellerstein, 1999–2000; WHO, 2008a), and as it is outside the scope of this book's focus on criminal law it will not be further addressed. There has been some suggestion that the wide scope of anti-FGM provisions in Australian law may criminalise other forms of body alterations that affect the female genitalia, such as female genital cosmetic surgery and female genital piercing, and these issues will be addressed in Chapter 4.

3 In all jurisdictions, the 'therapeutic reasons' exception explicitly excludes 'cultural reasons' from being regarded as being 'therapeutic'.

The Legal Status of MC

MC holds an unsettled position under Australian law. The Tasmania Law Reform Institute (2012, p.15) recently reported that '[t]here has never been significant legal action relating to, or legislative regulation of, male circumcision anywhere in Australia. There is no governing Circumcision Act. There has never been a circumcision test case. Uncertainties abound in the application of the general law to circumcision.' However, the lawfulness of MC is typically not questioned within the Australian legal system. Given the current circumcision rate of around 12 per cent (Australian Federation of AIDS Organisations, 2009, p.3), thousands of these body alterations are performed every year and there have been no criminal convictions of doctors for non-negligently performing MC with the consent of the patient or their parents. This generally assumed lawfulness of MC is well entrenched. For example, when South Australia amended the *Criminal Law Consolidation Act 1935* in 2005 they inserted a list of examples of situations when one can lawfully consent to assault. The revised s22(3)1 now reads: 'A person may … consent to harm that has a religious purpose (e.g. male circumcision but not female genital mutilation).' In other words, the lawfulness of MC is so strongly assumed that it is used to literally exemplify a lawful action in a statute. This trend carries through into case law, with Nicholson CJ in *Re Jane* (1988) 85 ALR 409 (p.40, emphasis added) noting with regards to surgical intervention that 'some non-therapeutic procedures are *generally accepted* and are performed as a matter of routine for religious or social purposes. In this category would fall male circumcision (although arguably, it may also have a therapeutic purpose).' The Law Commission (1995, p.119) has bluntly stated that '[m]ale circumcision is lawful under English common law', which, as we saw in Chapter 2, has close links to Australian law.

Whilst these sources try to foreclose any questioning of the legality of MC, other commentators argue that MC's legal position is actually more complex (Boyle, 2000; Gilbert, 2007; Price, 1996). Although circumcision is widely practised and has a generally assumed lawfulness, there is room for this to be challenged. Technically, because MC necessarily entails the cutting and removing of part of the body, it *prima facie* fulfils the legal requirements for charges of assault, wounding, grievous bodily harm and even child abuse (Tasmania Law Reform Institute, 2009). In order for the person performing MC to avoid criminal liability, they must show that either their conduct falls under an exception, such as that for medical procedures, or that the patient consented to MC and that their consent is legally effective to excuse liability. These legal tactics to absolve the person who performs MC from liability can be resisted at three levels.

Firstly, it can be argued that the medical procedure exception does not apply to MC in Code jurisdictions. In both Queensland and Western Australia a person is not criminally responsible for administering surgical or medical treatment, in good faith and with reasonable care and skill, to another person for that person's benefit (*Criminal Code* (Qld) s282(1)(a); *Criminal Code* (WA) s259(1)(a)). MC, performed routinely as a neonatal medical procedure, is a form of surgical treatment and is undoubtedly carried out in good faith and with reasonable care and skill in the majority of cases. Thus, whether or not MC falls under this exception depends primarily on whether or not MC can be considered as being for the male's benefit. The medical literature on benefits has seen heated debate (Morris, et al., 2006; Royal Australian College of Physicians, 2006; Royal Australian College of Physicians, 2010; Van Howe, 1999b). Arguably, however, since the Royal Australian College of Physicians' (2010, p.5) official position is that 'the frequency of diseases modifiable by circumcision, the level of protection offered by circumcision and the complication rates of circumcision do not warrant routine infant circumcision', this type of MC may not be considered as being for the male's medical benefit. Whether or not the purported cultural benefits of MC, such as access to one's 'cultural heritage and identity' for children of Jews and Muslims (Freeman 1999, p.74), can make up for this deficit is undecided at law. O'Regan (1990, pp.75–76) contends that it is 'doubtful whether the word "benefit" in this context would be given any wider meaning than "therapeutic" benefit', and concludes that MC 'seems to be outside the protection' of this defence. The Tasmanian Law Reform Institute (2009, p.27) reaches much the same conclusion, noting that the medical treatment defence might not apply to MC cases as it is questionable whether MC actually benefits the male.

Secondly, it can be argued that the consent provided in the typical Australian case of MC is invalid. If MC is performed against the male's wishes or without their consent, in other than an emergency medical situation, those performing the operation will clearly be criminally liable (Queensland Law Reform Commission, 1993, p.13). However, the legal position becomes more complicated where the male is incapable of giving consent to MC and instead their parents/guardians purport to give consent. This is typical in Australia, as MC is predominantly performed as a routine neonatal procedure and infants are incapable of giving legally valid consent. It can be argued that this parental consent is legally invalid on the basis of certain legal restrictions found in *Secretary, Department of Health and Community Services v JWB and SMB (Marion's Case)* (1992) 175 CLR 218 (hereafter '*Marion's Case* (1992)'). When considering the rights of parents to consent to medical procedures for their children in *Marion's Case* (1992) (p.240), the majority judgment of Mason CJ, Dawson, Toohey and Gaudron JJ found that 'the overriding criterion of the child's best interests is itself a limit on parental power'. They distinguished between therapeutic surgery, which was clearly in the child's best interests and to which parents could validly consent for their children, and non-therapeutic surgery, the benefit of which was more difficult to determine and to which parental consent was not automatically legally valid (*Marion's Case* (1992), p.250). They held that non-therapeutic surgeries that were 'invasive, irreversible, and major', such as sterilisation, require court authorisation where there is a significant risk of making the 'wrong decision' about the best interests of the child and where 'the consequences of [such] a wrong decision are particularly grave' (*Marion's Case* (1992), p.250).

MC could be legally considered to be non-therapeutic. MC provides no clear health benefits that are undisputed in the medical literature and Boyle (2000) argues that where such benefits are equivocal it should be considered to be non-beneficial. Whatever benefits are argued to exist will typically only have effect 'many years in the future', which is difficult to weigh against the 'immediate "best interests" of the child' (Fox and Thomson, 2012, p.275). Indeed, the Queensland Law Reform Commission (1993, p.39) argued that where there is no 'immediate health benefits to a particular child from circumcision, it is unlikely that the procedure itself could be considered as therapeutic'. Even if benefits are found to accrue in a particular case, a blanket presumption that benefit therefore accrues in all cases should not be made. As the Tasmanian Commissioner for Children Paul Mason (2009b, p.3) points out: '[w]hether or not non-therapeutic male circumcision was "for the benefit of the child" and was reasonable in all the circumstances would need to be assessed on a case-by-case basis in relation to the presenting medical needs of the patient'.

MC can also be considered medically invasive as it necessarily involves the cutting of skin, and as major because it is usually performed with local or general anaesthesia (Royal Australian College of Physicians, 2006, p.25), and typically involves the removal of 30–50 per cent of the total penile skin (Kim and Pang, 2006, p.619), which is approximately 15 square inches of area in the adult penis (Price 1996). Despite the fact that there are various foreskin restoration techniques available, I disagree with Freeman's (1996, p.75) assertion that MC 'may not be irreversible'. Surgical restoration techniques typically involve skin grafting from the scrotal area and carry with them a number of problems: they are very expensive and often fail (Griffiths, 1999, p.301), they are subject to various surgical complications, they necessarily cause further scarring of the penis (Warren, 1999, p.305), and the grafted skin is 'likely to be insensitive, thicker than normal penile skin, hairy, and immobile' (Warren, 1999, p.305). The dominant non-surgical technique involves repeated stretching of the remaining penile skin, either manually or with an elastic or weighted device, until it covers the glans of the penis (a technique dating back to ancient Greco-Roman times) (Schultheiss, 1999). This is a very slow process the success of which is dependent on the amount of foreskin removed from the penis and the male's commitment to the stretching. The National Organisation of Restoring Men – United Kingdom (NORM-UK), an 'uncircumcision' charity organisation, notes that 'a few men will achieve reasonable results in one to two years, but most will take longer' (Warren, 1999, p.309). At a practical level, then, MC should be considered an irreversible procedure.

Arguably there is significant risk that a parent will make a wrong decision about the best interests of the child if they give consent for MC to be performed. Given the marked lack of consensus with the medical literature about whether MC provides any appreciable medical benefit to a male at any point throughout their life, it is likely that MC is not in their best interests because it exposes them to the possible risks of the procedure and guarantees them the loss of their bodily tissue without necessarily providing anything in return. It is more difficult to determine the question of whether the consequences of a wrong decision are particularly grave for MC. In *Marion's Case* (1992, p.250), the question of gravity was determined with reference to 'the fact of being acted upon contrary to one's wishes or best interests', and included an assessment of the impact of the 'social and psychological implications' of such a 'violation' as well as the 'far-reaching consequences of a general rule of law allowing [such consent] to all kinds of medical treatment'. The general legal rule that would be set by allowing parental consent to MC is not one that should be widely promoted: cultural or religious standards or a belief in an ambiguous benefit should not be the basis for an incompetent person's bodily tissue to be surgically excised, regardless of whether this comprises part of their genitalia or any other part of their body. However, given that MC is undertaken on an area of the body that is typically culturally encoded as very personal, the 'violation' involved in MC should also be considered to be greater than if it took place on any other part of their body. Gauging the social and psychological implications of such a 'violation' would be very difficult to do in an abstract, generalised way, but the mere existence of un-circumcision groups such as NORM-UK demonstrates that MC can have negative implications for at least some people.

Because MC arguably fails to fulfil the criteria set out in *Marion's Case* (1992), parental consent to MC for their male children could possibly be legally invalid. If parents cannot validly give legal consent to MC they should make an application to the Family Court for court-ordered approval that it be carried out (Queensland Law Reform Commission, 1993, p.38). It is possible that MC carried out without this approval is legally non-consensual, and thus it 'cannot be said with certainty whether a parent's consent for the performance of a non-therapeutic circumcision on their child will relieve a circumciser of criminal liability' (Tasmania Law Reform Institute, 2009, p.25). As such, 'those who perform, assist in or instigate a circumcision do so without knowing the extent to which they are protected from criminal liability' (Tasmania Law Reform Institute, 2012, p.18).

Thirdly, MC may be unlawful because it can be argued that even if the person himself does give consent to MC this factual consent is legally ineffective. Normally, if a person is an adult then they are capable of giving valid consent to a medical procedure. Furthermore, even if they are a minor they can still be capable of giving valid consent to a medical procedure if they fulfil the competency requirements set out in *Gillick v West Norfolk and Wisbech AHA* [1986] AC 112 (which was subsequently adopted into Australian law in *Marion's Case* (1992)). In order to fulfil these requirements, a minor must show that they are 'capable of understanding what is proposed, and of expressing [their] own wishes' (*Gillick v West Norfolk and Wisbech AHA* [1986] AC 112, p.169 per Lord Fraser of Tullybelton). However, even if an adult male or legally competent minor purports to give consent to MC, this consent might not be legally effective to protect the person who performs MC from criminal liability.

As discussed in Chapter 2, under the common law the factual consent of the recipient of an injurious assault is not recognised as legal consent unless it occurs within certain specific contexts. Thus, as we saw, a sadist can still be held criminally liable for sadomasochistic injuries inflicted on a consenting masochist. MC falls within this same general set of legal rules and accordingly many of the same legal issues regarding sadomasochism in Chapter 2 are imported here. Thus, consent to MC may be irrelevant in Code jurisdictions in relation to criminal charges that lack an assault element, such as wounding or grievous bodily harm. For common law jurisdictions, and for criminal charges with an assault element in Code jurisdictions, situating MC within the long line of 'consensual assault' cases within English law becomes important. Lord Templeman specifically lists '[r]itual circumcision' in *R v Brown* [1994] (p.231) as one of a number of body practices he identifies as 'lawful activities'. This alone has been enough for some commentators to consider that consent to MC provides a 'good defence to a criminal prosecution' (Haberfeld, 1997b, pp.104–105), but Price (1996) rightly points out that this is simply the viewpoint of one majority judge and that MC went unmentioned by the rest of the majority. Situating MC within the legal logic employed by consensual assault cases requires looking at the public interest in MC, its medical and cultural benefits and whether it should be considered as a form of 'violence'. As MC has not been judicially considered in this way under Australian law, its legal position remains unsettled. As such, it is unclear if factual consent to MC by an adult or a legally competent minor is legally effective.

Ultimately, the current legal status of MC under Australian criminal law is problematic. This stems from the fact that 'there has been no reasoned decision in the English-derived common law about the validity of parental consent to medically unnecessary circumcision' (Mason, 2009b, p.3). Under Code law provisions and general common law legal principles, it is *prima facie* an offence to carry out MC and non-specious legal arguments can be raised against the validity of either the medical treatment defence or consent being used to deflect criminal liability. However, the multitude of MC procedures being carried out every day are not prosecuted because medical interventions 'are not regarded in practice as *prima facie* illegal' (Somerville, 1980–1981, p.96). To those who advocate against it, this lapse in strictly enforcing the law results from a cultural failure to acknowledge MC as a form of abuse (Brigman, 1984–1985). Goldman (1997, p.169) describes this lapse in controversial terms: 'the public defines fondling a child's genitals as child sexual abuse yet cutting off a piece of the penis is not'. Other commentators have described the widespread acceptance of MC as an 'artefact of … cultural tolerance' (Van Howe, 1999a, p.69) and as the result of 'an untutored perception of the reality of the harm caused' (Price, 1996). Comparing this tolerance of MC to the widespread Western condemnation of FGM has led some legal commentators to argue that legislation outlawing FGM but failing to prevent MC is sexually discriminatory, because it fails to offer equal protection to males and females (Baer, 1997; Boyle, 2000; Macdonald, 2004, p.253; Povenmire, 1999; Price, 1996). Ultimately, despite the legal arguments that can be raised regarding the potential criminality of MC, it retains its generally accepted legality in everyday life. Although it is not available in Australian public hospitals as an elective procedure (except in Queensland) (Cooper, Wodak and Morris, 2010, p.318), the federal government offers a Medicare rebate of around $70 for MC (Australian Federation of AIDS Organisations, 2009, p.3).

Constructing and Maintaining the Disparity

There is a clear disparity between the legal status of FGM and the legal status of MC. FGM is thoroughly and comprehensively criminalised by statutory sections that specifically target it, whereas MC may possibly be criminal under the general application of nonspecific legal principles but is instead widely treated and regarded as lawful. This section reveals and critically analyses how this legal disparity is constructed and maintained by the discursive conceptualisation of FGM and MC as markedly different types of body alteration.

Thomson (2008, p.20) identifies that 'contemporary legal responses to the issue of male circumcision … construc[t] a simplified oppositional relationship between male and female circumcision whereby male circumcision is self-evidently different from the practice of female circumcision'. However, as Kennedy (2009, p.211) incisively recognises, the naturalisation of the varying ways in which law responds to body alteration practices can mask the underlying operation of 'disciplinary practices that imprint and inscribe the body, and, in so doing, reproduce themselves'. If we unpack the discursive processes and techniques that underpin the 'self-evident' 'differences' between FGM and MC, we can begin to appreciate the complex webs of signification and understanding that are involved in constructing, maintaining and naturalising this oppositional relationship. The discursive dis/similarity of FGM and MC relies heavily on a number of key 'differences' that have been disputed in recent years: differences in physical effect, differences in sexual effect, and differences in cultural location. This section takes each of these 'differences' individually, sets out the discursive contestation around it, and analyses this contestation with a view to exposing how particular understandings and concepts about the body are deployed/employed and to what effect. The aim here is to explore to what extent, and in what ways, this discursive framing informs the legal response to these body alterations. This chapter argues that the current authoritative legal discursive understanding of the dissimilarity of FGM and MC is underpinned by normative conceptualisations about harm, sexuality and culture. However, this chapter also notes the growing strategic viability of counter-discursive accounts that seek to construct FGM and MC as being comparable.

Conceptions of Harm

There is a marked discursive tendency to background and deemphasise the harm caused by MC and to foreground and emphasise the harm caused by FGM (Fox and Thomson, 2005, p.163l; Thomson, 2008, p.20). FGM is recognised as causing harm 'of a very serious kind', whereas whilst MC might have 'some medical risk involved ... some prophylactic benefits of the removal of the foreskin are evident' (Haberfeld, 1997b, p.104). Discourse here constructs conceptual dissimilarities between FGM and MC by establishing a hierarchy of harm with FGM located far above MC. This discursive process is informed by a reductive over-reliance on medical discourse as providing a totalising account of both FGM and MC.

Differences in physical effects

FGM is discursively conceptualised as being different from MC because it is 'far more invasive, and without any medical benefit albeit with numerous and frequent complications' (Khalafzai, 2008a, p.1), due to the 'much more severe and extensive' cutting involved (Trueblood, 1999–2000, p.441). Lists of the negative, medical side-effects of FGM are commonplace, and such complications are often extensively reproduced to the point of fixation. Swensen (1995, pp.28–29) lists damage to and bleeding from adjacent organs, haemorrhage, shock, infection, pain, death, increased susceptibility to HIV and AIDS, neuromas, vulvar abcesses, cysts, urinary tract infections, urine retention, menstrual difficulties, obstetric difficulties, psychological trauma, and scarring, to which can be added pain during sexual intercourse and sexual dysfunction (Mendelsohn, 2004, pp.1013–1014), tetanus, sepsis, open sores, bladder infections, infertility and the need for later surgeries to increase the vaginal opening (WHO, 2008). Hicks (1993, p.11, emphasis added) finishes up her addition to this compiling tendency with septic anemia, 'keloid and fistula formation, *etc*'.

This final point on the list betrays the strategic value of the obsessive listing of FGM's 'dizzying range of potential health impacts' (Kennedy, 2009, p.218): it constructs FGM as a source of limitless harm. The pain and suffering of women who have undergone FGM knows no boundaries as its harm does not end with the healing of the wounds but rather stretches through time to make them suffer a 'life of pains and illnesses' (Coello, 1999, p.225). It is a 'kind of torture that remains with a mutilated woman' (Wellerstein, 1999–2000, p.128). '[T]he scar of FGM is not transient' but is 'life-long' (Nnamuchi, 2012, p.101); discursively, it is a cut that never stops harming. This construction of FGM is totalising as it presents the pain and suffering caused by FGM as the only relevant factors to account for when determining whether FGM should be legal, inducing closure on alternative issues such as culture and religion.

The literature on MC diverges in its construction of the physical effects. Those who advocate the continuation of MC background the harm, whilst those who advocate its cessation seem, at times, to attempt to match the severity of the constructions of harm associated with FGM. The former approach argues that MC only 'causes discomfort (and this fleeting) rather than pain' (Freeman, 1999, p.75), and has historically been quite widespread within the medical profession (Van Howe, 1999a). As a result, anaesthesia was not traditionally used in neonatal circumcision procedures (although this has undergone recent change) (Miller, 2002). The long-term negative complications of MC are backgrounded in favour of foregrounding the various, potential medical benefits it purportedly brings to the circumcised male. Indeed, Fox and Thomson (2012, p.267) argue that the risk of complications has tended to 'be erased or downplayed when infant circumcision is discussed in the West'. In contrast, the purported benefits are writ large. MC has been argued, over the last 150 years, to cure and prevent epilepsy, cure and prevent the spread of sexually transmitted diseases, cure and prevent cancer of all sorts (including cancer of the penis, tongue, prostate, and of the female cervix), prevent HIV infection (Hodges 1997, p.36), and prevent Urinary Tract Infections in infants (Morris 2006). More recent developments in discourse emphasise the purported benefits of MC in potentially inhibiting the spread of HIV/AIDS in areas where it is a public health pandemic, such as sub-Saharan Africa (Fox and Thomson, 2012). However, the latter approach, that MC is painful and harmful, is gaining traction. More current research identifies that infants do feel significant pain from MC, and that anaesthesia should be used (Van Howe, 1999a). Over the years, the purported medical benefits of MC have been vigorously questioned, and more attention has been paid to the attendant risk of negative side-effects, which include *inter alia* pain, bleeding, haematoma, swelling, infection, anaesthesia-related events, delayed healing, excessive removal of skin, insufficient removal of skin, problems with urination, problems with appearance, erectile dysfunction, injury to glans (WHO, 2007, p.18), haemorrhage, meatal stenosis, gangrene (Rizvi, et al., 1999, p.15), buried penis, partial or complete penile amputation, urethral fistula, phimosis, and even death (Svoboda, Van Howe and Dwyer, 2000, pp.103–109). This medicalised recounting clearly replicates the anti-FGM discursive strategy of seeking to over-determine MC as a form of harmful violence to the body, and by utilising a similar method of discursive conceptualisation it seeks to draw FGM and MC together and render them comparable.

A number of other discursive strategies are employed that construct FGM and MC as different on the basis of the level of harm they cause their subject. WHO's four-point typology of FGM demonstrates a broad range of physical cutting and manipulation of the body, and hence in the severity of the injury they can cause, but FGM writing is commonly marked with discursive slippages between the different types in order to maximise rhetorical effect. Thus, Toubia (1999, p.4) recognises that '[m]any falsely hold up infibulation (the most extreme form, which constitutes only 15 per cent of the total) as representing all female circumcision'. Mackay (1983, p.717, emphasis added) is not only complicit in this strategic elision, but goes further by stating that the 'term circumcision is not restricted to clitoridectomy … but also includes the much *more common* "Pharaonic" circumcision'. When infibulation is utilised to 'stand for female genital cutting, *tout court*' (Boddy, 2007, p.48), it weights the construction of FGM as overly harmful and invasive. Thus when Bashir (1995–1996, p.442) sympathetically argues that FGM should be considered a threat to life or freedom in asylum cases, she cites statistics estimating that 15–30 per cent of all girls and women die from bleeding or infection: statistics drawn from a study that is tellingly entitled *Pharaonic Circumcision of Females in Sudan*

Another discursive strategy that foregrounds the harm of FGM whilst backgrounding the harm in MC, involves conflating the risks of FGM with the risks of the way FGM is performed within rural settings in African countries. Clearly, the risk of serious complications is greatly increased when FGM is 'undertaken in unhygienic conditions, by inexperienced providers with inadequate instruments' (Toubia, 1999, p.21). Whilst the harms caused by the 'non-hygienic conditions of performance' may provide a 'case for regulation of the conditions under which the operation is performed' (Obiora, 1996–1997a, p.369), it has been argued that they do not provide a valid comparator to the risks of MC when practised 'in sterile [Western] hospitals by trained medical practitioners' (Svoboda, 1999, p.456). For example, data from Pakistan, an area in which '90–95% of circumcisions are performed by traditional circumcisers, village barbers, paramedical theatre staff and technicians', may prove more appropriately matched (Rizvi, et al., 1999, p.14). In the study of 330 MC procedures in Pakistan, 52 per cent of boys suffered haemorrhage, 8.2 per cent infection, 7.2 per cent meatal stenosis, and 0.6 per cent gangrene

(Rizvi, et al., 1999, p.15), figures which show the harm of MC as being far more comparable to that typically claimed of FGM. As another example, data from South Africa indicates that there 'were more than 100 deaths and 200 penis amputations between 2001 and 2006' in the Eastern Cape area (Peltzer, 2008, cited in Tasmania Law Reform Institute, 2012, p.24). Toubia (1999, p.5) supposes that if an 'appropriate comparison' based on evidence collected from procedures 'performed under similar conditions' were carried out, that the 'range of clinical complications (such as bleeding and infection) will not differ dramatically between male and female circumcision except in the case of infibulation'. Further, whilst discussion of the harms caused by FGM in rural, non-Western settings may be appropriate for work that deals with those areas, it is frequently transplanted into discussions of whether FGM should be legal in Western countries. Thus, we find detailed references to traditionally-performed unhygienic FGM and the African rural 'village environment' in the Family Law Council's (1994, pp.7–9) report into the adequacy of Australian laws regarding FGM. This rhetorical technique functions to construct FGM as a body alteration whose harms are universal and exist regardless of context.

The reductive deployment of medical discourse

FGM is discursively conceptualised as an alteration *qua* harm, whose risks are so great they transcend both place and conditions to inevitably cause pain and suffering for the entirety of a female's life. The discursive conceptualisation of MC is fragmented: one strand of discourse argues that it does not cause harm and that its inherent injuries are minor and outweighed by prophylactic benefits, whilst the other strand of discourse argues in parallel to FGM discourse by attempting to over-determine MC as always and only harmful. The feature that unifies all strands of discourse in this area is the heavy reliance on medical considerations, which conceptualise these body alterations as either harmful or beneficial in purely physical terms. The underlying, medicalised assumption implicit in this discussion is that the validity of both FGM and MC can be determined by subjecting them to a physical cost-benefit analysis (Fox and Thomson, 2009, p.195), where if the physical benefits outweigh the physical harms then the body alteration is justified. The current legal status of these body alterations reflects this discursive construction. Indeed, Bridge (2002, p.284) proposes that if a 'risk/benefit analysis were undertaken it would totally support the current prohibitive legislation'. Trueblood (1999–2000, p.452) non-reflexively sums up this situation in a quote from one Dr Trudy Smith of South Africa that 'male circumcision makes physiological sense, but FGM makes no sense whatsoever'. However, the only possible sense that FGM or MC could make within this medicalised discursive framework is physiological sense.

Where medical discourse interweaves with the discourse around FGM and MC it totalises the methods of presentation and truth-values within the debate.

Arguments around these body alterations demonstrate a tendency to descend into mere litanies of the complication rates and possible side-effects, rather than being open-ended discussions that touch on additional issues such as religion, culture and personal choice. It seems simply that the 'excision of healthy flesh from a healthy child is acceptable if scientific studies say it is so' (Dritsas, 2001, p.308). This point has marked similarities with the rationale behind the genital normalisation surgeries carried out on intersex infants, as discussed in Chapter 5. Moral and philosophical answers are disregarded in preference to those that are 'purely scientific' (Toubia, 1999, p.3), because only those types of answers can be reconciled with the discursive framework put in place to conceptualise these body alterations. For example, Nnamuchi (2012, p.98) is convinced that if 'FGM defenders' 'educate themselves', 'think seriously' and 'critically', and 'honestly and carefully evaluate' the practice, then they will see that the mental and physical harm caused by FGM makes it 'indefensible on that ground alone'. But surely if one were to think seriously, critically, honestly and carefully about FGM, one needs to move beyond a close focus on medicalised models of harm and move towards a broader analysis of other factors? Sole recourse to medical discourse is reductive, as it prevents other considerations from being weighed or valued, but it is also powerful, as it channels the authority of medicine as a dominant cultural institution that imports its own epistemological framework and truth-making. Underlying medical discourse is a set of particular understandings about the body that are (re)produced within FGM and MC discourse, and to which this chapter will now turn.

Those writers who construct FGM and MC as harmful frequently make reference to the non-Modified and non-Circumcised body as the idyllic bodily state. Arguments that these body alterations need to be stopped in order to preserve the 'physical integrity' (Gilbert 2007, p.288), 'bodily integrity' (Povenmire, 1998–1999, p.113; Toubia, 1999, p.2), 'somatic integrity' (Silverman, 2004, p.420), or 'genital integrity' of the child (Boyle, 2000, p.304) implicitly affirm the idea of the 'whole body' as the ideal bodily form. These are simply fancier ways of phrasing what others call 'natural, intact, the ways males are born' (Goldman, 1997, p.52), the 'natural features' (Slack, 1988, p.466), and the 'natural state' (Lane and Rubinstein, 1996, p.35). As mentioned in Chapter 2, the whole, enclosed body is paradigmatic within the Western conception of the body, and takes on particular importance within medical discourse. In the same way that sadomasochism's opening up of the body is conceptualised within law as a kind of rending violence that marks the body as incomplete, so too the cuts and incisions of FGM are automatically equated to harmful injuries to the body. The body alteration involved in FGM is conceptualised as harmful because it doesn't meet the narrow confines of justification set out under medical discourse and mars the body's 'natural' state. In contrast, the body alteration involved in MC is seen as justified because it provides prophylactic benefits against diseases that place the body in an 'unnatural' state, like HIV/AIDS. Some commentators disagree with this conceptualisation of MC, like Chessler (1997, p.565) who argues that '[t]he penis, like a woman's genitalia, is formed at birth without the need for alteration or "improvement"'. These are typically anti-MC proponents, who use 'naturalness' strategically, like anti-FGM writers, to position MC as a harm (Miller, 2002).

The 'natural' body in the West, then, is the female body that has not undergone FGM, whereas male bodies may still be considered 'natural' even if they have undergone MC. The 'natural' body becomes the 'normal' body under this paradigm. Povenmire (1998–1999, p.93) tellingly collapses the two when he states that it is 'possible that the next generation will accept the natural, whole penis, as normal', indicating how the naturalisation of MC has led to the Circumcised penis being regarded as the default, 'normal' state. Representing the body in terms such as 'natural' is problematic because it reifies the conception of an abstract, idyllic, untouched body. This construct is contradicted by the theoretical understanding of the active and productive body, which both continually constitutes and is constituted by culture. Instead of seeing the body as a medium upon which negotiations between cultural influences and personal choices are played out, the Western medical ideal of the body replicated here is inert, static and vulnerable, such that any unjustified interference to it can only ever cause harm. This operates within FGM and MC discourse to 'close down any discussion of [these] body practices' (Green and Lim, 1998, p.368).

The effect of this conceptualisation on the law is the reading of harm onto the body of the female who has undergone FGM, regardless of whether she considers herself to be harmed, let alone 'mutilated', simply because her body has been altered by FGM and is thus marked as 'unnatural' or 'abnormal'. This is reflected in the law by the blanket criminalisation of FGM within Australia, where its practice constitutes an offence with or without the consent of the female and regardless of whether any negative or unwanted side-effects are caused. The allegation that for some women FGM is 'endowed with psychological benefits' and that it can even be an event 'that young girls look forward to in excited, and even in some cases pleasurable, anticipation' (Slack, 1988, pp.449–450), cannot possibly have any legal relevance even if it were to provide an accurate description of a case before the court. In this way, 'the speech of the mutilated woman is foreclosed upon when she says she is not mutilated' (Rogers, 2013, p.152). Legally, this discursive construct also works to erase any harm from the body of the male who undergoes MC. Regardless of whether or not he consider himself to have been harmed or mutilated by it, MC is not treated as a criminal offence. Even if it causes severe harm to the male it may, at most, give rise to a civil suit, but only if performed negligently and not simply because it was performed. This is because MC 'enters the male child into a pact with western biomedicine that renders the circumcised subject a "healthy subject'" (Rogers, 2013, p.58), regardless of the actual health of the subject. A male who has been non-negligently circumcised and who suffers, as some men do, from ongoing 'low self-esteem' and 'shame' because he feels he has been mutilated can find no recourse at law for the harm he subjectively has suffered (Warren, 1999, p.304). Claims that MC is physically injurious and constitutes harm to a male, and claims that whilst FGM may be physically injurious it might not constitute harm to a female, are incommensurable with authoritative legal discourse. They are incapable of being voiced within a legal system that fails to recognise the terms of reference through which they are made. The idiom that the law adopts is one that only recognises FGM as an irredeemable harm and MC 'as a standard and benign medical practice' (Thomson, 2008, p.18).

Another effect of the impact of medical discourse within this area has been the increasingly medicalised scrutiny of the comparison between FGM and MC. Resolving the comparison has descended, for some commentators, into purely physical minutiae. Thus, the equivalent of removing the tip of the clitoris has been said to be removal of the glans of the penis (Asefa, 1998, p.92; Hosken, 1993, p.46), the equivalent of clitoridectomy has been said to be amputation of all or part of the penis (Asefa, 1998, p.92; Bashir, 1995–1996, p.420; Hosken, 1993, p.46; Toubia, 1993, p.9), and the equivalent of infibulation has been said to be removal of all the penis, its roots of soft tissue and part of the scrotal skin (Asefa, 1998, p.92; Toubia, 1993, p.9). In contrast, the Family Law Council's (1994, p.19) report noted that clitoridectomy had no male equivalent because the penis, unlike the clitoris, has both sexual and reproductive functions. Hosken's (1993, p.47) bizarre contribution to this issue was that fertility was 'not impaired' by the 'excision of the penis' because conception could take place through 'artificial insemination, which can be accomplished with simple tools, for instance, a spoon'. This quote exemplifies the reductive physical fixation of medical discourse that pares back the terms of the debate. Arguments about the 'embryonic development' of genitalia (Hosken, 1993, p.46), and whether different parts of the genitalia are functionally or anatomically analogous (Darby and Svoboda, 2007, pp.309–310), fail to recognise that the body alterations could be regarded as being physically similar (not identical) and as both having negative side-effects (that can be serious or minor), and that their similarity or difference might be better or further evaluated by reference to factors beyond simple biology. The cultural reasons behind these body alterations and the meanings Modified genitals carry within various societies may reflect similarities that would otherwise be elided if one were to only conduct a physiological comparison of FGM and MC. Comparing the two sets of body alterations through a strict medical paradigm not only works to disclaim the similarities between the two, it is also a method of preventing other sources of meaning from being adequately presented. Medical discourse functions as a totalising idiom that precludes further investigation into possibly fruitful avenues of debate and discussion around cultural and social meaning, a feature of medical discourse's intersections with legal discourse that also strongly reoccurs in debates around genital normalisation surgery and sex reassignment surgery (as discussed in Chapter 5).

The authorising power of medical discourse in the debate around FGM has the possibility, however, to work against the criminalisation of FGM. In order to control and minimise the physical risks and harms associated with FGM, it may seem like the 'lesser of the two evils' would be to allow FGM to take place 'in a controlled hospital environment, under sterile conditions with anaesthesia' (Khalafzai, 2008a, p.2). The lure of the 'medicalization of FGM' has been resisted, however, on the basis that 'acquiescence to FGM in any form is unacceptable' (Khalafzai, 2008a, p.2; Hosken, 1993), and is underpinned by anxiety that any such medicalisation may become a 'further factor potentially contributing to the perpetuation of the practises' (Royal Australian College of Obstetricians and Gynaecologists, 1997, p.15). There is a discursive dynamic at work in the outright refusal of many anti-FGM commentators to countenance this possibility that became very visible amidst the uproar caused by a recent announcement by the American Academy of Pediatrics ('AAP'). In 2010, the AAP Committee of Bioethics released an amended policy statement on the 'ritual genital cutting of female minors'. In the statement, they acknowledged that '[m]ost forms of FGC are decidedly harmful' and suggested that, in order to prevent greater harm and to 'build trust between hospitals and immigrant communities', it might be 'more effective' for paediatricians to offer a 'possible compromise' rather than simply refusing to perform any form of FGM outright (AAP, 2010a, p.1092). This proposed 'compromise', which was similar to the so-called 'Seattle compromise' that was debated in the 1990s, would be to offer a 'ritual nick': a form of 'pricking or incising [of] the clitoral skin' so as to 'satisfy cultural requirements' but not to cause any physical harm (AAP, 2010a, p.1092). This policy statement generated significant backlash, including an international joint statement from WHO, UNICEF, the United Nations Population Fund ('UNFPA') and the United Nations Development Fund for Women ('UNIFEM') which aimed to 'strongly encourage AAP to revise its policy statement' (WHO, 2010). In the international joint statement it was argued that:

> By suggesting that a 'nick' could be performed by medical personnel, the AAP statement opens a loophole that partially legitimizes the practice of FGM and creates an opening for more invasive procedures. Allowing such a cut with a doctor's assistance may make parents think it is acceptable or medically beneficial. It may also serve to institutionalize the procedure as medical personnel often hold power, authority and respect in society and lead health care providers to develop a professional and financial interest in upholding the practice. (WHO, 2010)

In response to the public pressure, the AAP quickly put out a subsequent policy statement reaffirming 'its strong opposition to female genital cutting (FGC)' and explicitly dealing with the controversy by stating that the 'AAP does not endorse the practice of offering a "clitoral nick". This minimal pinprick is forbidden under federal law and the AAP does not recommend it to its members' (AAP, 2010b, p.191).

Rogers (2013, p.35) identifies a 'strange seeming hypocrisy' in the negative response from 'anti-fgm advocates' to proposals that call for a ritual nick instead of a more severe form of FGM, because such advocates 'are so concerned with impairment and injury, but completely unassuaged by a lack of both' (Rogers, 2013, p.35). She explains this response as being the result of the symbolic overinvestment of FGM with a conception of harm that moves beyond the physical: 'the injury imagined by the anti-fgm advocate is not to the skin, it is to the subject *as subject*' (Rogers, 2013, p.35, emphasis in original). If all forms of FGM are 'symbolic of total castration', then FGM of any kind is conceptualised as being harmful 'irrespective of quantity of flesh' (Rogers, 2013, p.35). This is one of the important discursive dynamics at play here, but the arguments made in the international joint statement reveal another discursive dynamic as also underpinning the negative response to the AAP's compromise. The 'ritual nick' proposed by the AAP is based around a harm-minimisation strategy that functions in purely physical terms around minimising the extent of body altering cuts made to female bodies. In contrast, the international response to the AAP's compromise works at a discursive level as it is concerned with the role that medical authority plays in determining and guiding the sociolegal il/legitimacy of FGM. The AAP's compromise posed more than just a perceived threat to female bodies or female subjects, it posed an actual threat to the well-entrenched conceptualisation of FGM as always and necessarily a harmful injury: a conceptualisation that was constructed and is maintained by medical discourse's influence on the overlapping sociolegal discourses around FGM. If medical practice were to fracture around FGM, authorising some forms of FGM but not others, the focused power of medical discourse's totalising construction of FGM as always and necessarily harmful would be diffused. The quick international response to shut down this alternative possible conceptualisation of some forms of FGM as non-harmful (or less harmful) demonstrates the strategic importance to anti-FGM efforts of both medical discourse itself and the circulation of certain kinds of constructions of FGM within medical discourse.

Fox and Thomson (2012) have charted recent movement within the discourse around MC that raises a related issue. They identify a new discursive trend within certain areas of political, medical and legal commentary to frame widespread MC initiatives as a viable 'public health response' in the ongoing efforts to curb the pandemic of HIV/AIDS in 'sub-Saharan Africa' (Fox and

Thomson, 2012, p.257). They argue that this trend towards conceptualising MC within a 'broader public health context' could move discussions about MC beyond the restrictive boundaries of 'traditional medical law discourses' that typically have constructed it as a private, familial medical decision (Fox and Thomson, 2012, p.269). Instead, this public health context could make visible 'the multiple interests at stake' and actors at play in the performance of MC, including 'NGOs, private philanthropic organisations, procircumcision activists and national governments' (Fox and Thomson, 2012, pp.256–257). They argue that MC should be situated within this public health discourse in a particular way: it should be grounded in a broader 'social justice paradigm' that will make 'visible the political, social and cultural dimensions of debates around male circumcision', and this will 'open … up space to address issues of social disadvantage and vulnerability' (Fox and Thomson, 2012, p.269).

The AAP's 'compromise' was a discursive gesture that contained the potential for recalibrating how FGM was conceptualised within medical discourse, and this 'public health' trend contains the same kind of possibility for MC. Whilst the AAP's 'compromise' failed to alter the discursive terrain and its potential was quickly defused, whether or not the 'public health' trend can alter orthodox medical discursive constructions of MC remains to be seen. Even if the 'public health' trend does gain traction, it may not have the broadening effect on discourse around MC that Fox and Thomson (2012) argue for. Instead, it may simply re-entrench the current, narrow medical models of MC. Fox and Thomson (2012, p.259) themselves identify that the 'public health' trend around MC has resulted in a 'discernible "blowback" effect' in the West, with various Western medical bodies considering whether to use 'African trials showing that the procedure may reduce the risk of HIV infection for adult men' as simply a newer, stronger basis for 'recommending the routine circumcision of infant boys in the USA'. This 'public health' issue could thus be merely the latest shift in the ever 'fluctuating biomedical opinion on male circumcision which has suggested that the practice is *for or against* "medical necessity" at different times and with different opinions' (Rogers, 2013, p.58). However, even if the 'public health' trend does move discourse around MC away from 'private health' associations, the common underlying denominator remains the conceptualisation of MC as an issue of 'health' and medicine. In both the AAP's 'compromise' and the 'public health' trend, the possibilities for discursive change around FGM and MC remain bounded by the inescapable centrality of medical discourse.

Conceptions of Sexuality

Authoritative legal discourse conceptualises FGM as inherently damaging to female sexuality and MC as being neutral, or even beneficial, to male sexuality. This conceptualisation elides alternative accounts about the possible enhancement of culturally specific models of female sexuality through FGM as well as alternative accounts about the harmful effects of MC on the sexuality of some males.

Differences in sexual effects

Because FGM involves the cutting and removal of part of the female genitalia, it is conceptualised as making it 'physically impossible for an operated woman to be sexually stimulated by intercourse or respond to touch in the genital area' (Hosken, 1993, p.46). When the clitoris is removed, 'no orgasm can be achieved' (Dixon, 1996, p.280). As the flesh of the clitoris and/or labia is cut away, FGM is conceptualised as 'attenuating women's sexual desire' (Trueblood, 1999–2000, p.449), and 'depriving them of their freedom to have a healthy sex life' (Coello, 1999, p.225). This effect has been characterised by some as purposeful and deliberate, leading anti-FGM writers within certain strands of feminist thought to condemn it as a patriarchal tool for the broad control of female sexuality (Asefa, 1998; Bashir, 1995–1996; Hosken, 1993; McBride, 2001; Toubia, 1993). In contrast, as the Law Commission (1995, p.119) opines, it 'is generally accepted that the removal of the foreskin of the penis has little, if any, effect on a man's ability to enjoy sexual intercourse'. The foreskin is presented as 'merely a protective part of the male sexual apparatus', which can be likened to an eyelid (Toubia, 1999, p.4). Even where some reduction in penile sexual tactility is conceded (as the inevitable result of the removal of part of the penis) this is reconceptualised as sexually beneficial rather than sexually harmful because loss of sensation may potentially increase 'ejaculatory latency time', allowing the male to 'last longer' during sex (Morris, 2006, p.19).

The arguments contesting this discursive positioning work to bridge the gap between the sexual effects of FGM and MC by undermining the construction of all forms of FGM as always (and always severely) harmful to female sexuality and by articulating the possible negative effects MC can have on male sexuality. There is empirical evidence that women who have undergone FGM do suffer sexual effects but are still capable of experiencing sexual pleasure, including orgasm. Rosenberg's (2009, p.5) pilot study of 260 sexually active women, half of which had undergone some form of FGM, found that there were no differences in terms of their libido or pain indexes, but that 'women with genital cutting had lower scores on indexes for arousal, lubrication, orgasm and satisfaction'. Similarly, a recent meta-analysis of studies in this area found evidence to substantiate 'the proposition that a woman whose genital tissues have been partly removed is more likely to experience increased pain and reduction in sexual satisfaction and desire' (Berg and Denison, 2012, p.41). Nevertheless, it is still clear that 'a high percentage of women who have had [FGM] have rich sexual lives, including desire, arousal, orgasm, and satisfaction', regardless of whatever type of FGM they have undergone (The Public Policy Advisory

Group on Female Genital Surgeries in Africa, 2012, p.22). Lightfoot-Klein (1989, p.80, emphasis in original) reports in her study of infibulated Sudanese women that approximately 90 per cent 'claimed to regularly achieve *or had at some times in their lives* achieved orgasm', even though infibulation is typically conceptualised as the most physically invasive and harmful type of FGM. First-hand accounts from women who have undergone FGM also contradict the construction of FGM as destroying all sexual pleasure. Suaad, an infibulated Sudanese woman, states that:

> [M]y infibulation did not eliminate my desire to have sex ... As a grandmother now ... I have sex five times a week. It is very enjoyable and I know too about orgasm, *tharwa*. I have *tharwa jinsia*, that indescribable sense of pleasure that gives one the feeling of touching the sky. It makes one shiver. (Abusharaf, 2001, cited in Sullivan, 2007, p.405)

Clearly, then, blanket statements about the 'devastating negative effects of FGC on ... sexuality' should be viewed critically (Dopico, 2007, p.246). Indeed, the removal of the clitoral hood (prepuce), which would be classified as Type 1 FGM on WHO's four-part schema, has been constructed alternatively as being sexually 'beneficial' (Nnamuchi, 2012, p.94) and is even sometimes performed in the US in order to treat women who suffer from anorgasmia, the failure to attain orgasm (Obiora, 1996–1997a, pp.298–299).

Some commentators have made claims that the foreskin plays a 'useful if not important role in coitus' and gives the un-Circumcised male greater sexual pleasure and sensation (Wallerstein, 1980, p.53). MC necessarily involves the 'loss of nerve endings' from the penis (Kim and Pang, 2006, p.619). Indeed, it has been recognised that 'the densest concentration of blood vessels and nerves is found in the foreskin itself, whereas the glans is relatively insensitive and equipped mainly to detect discomfort and pain' (Darby and Svoboda, 2007, p.309). Additionally, the foreskin is said to stimulate the penis of the un-Circumcised male via a gliding action (wherein the foreskin slides up and down over the glans) during intercourse and masturbation, which the circumcised male cannot experience because of his deficit of skin (Warren, 1999, p.304). Medical studies have demonstrated that circumcision decreases a male's masturbatory pleasure and sexual enjoyment whilst increasing masturbatory difficulty (Kim and Pang, 2006), and that a circumcised male's female sexual partners are less likely to have a vaginal orgasm, less likely to have multiple orgasms and are more likely to report vaginal discomfort either often or occasionally (O'Hara and O'Hara, 1999, p.80). The disparate discursive construction of FGM as always sexually harmful and MC as always sexually neutral or beneficial, is problematised by these kinds of alternative conceptualisations.

The conflation of sexuality and genitalia

Underpinning the arguments about the effects of FGM and MC on sexuality are a number of Western cultural assumptions about the body that work to position the discourse in particular ways. One of the most prominent is the conflation of sexuality and genitalia. The analysis of the impact of FGM and MC on sexuality over-invests genitalia by conceptualising them as exhaustively defining what 'sexuality' is. Thus, when FGM is seen as removing much of the external female genitalia so too is it seen as removing the 'sexual identity of women' (Wood, 2001, p.371). On this account, one's sexual identity is reducible to one's genitalia. A female who has undergone FGM is incapable of being 'sexual' in a normative sense because she cannot provide physiological evidence that she possesses the sexual biology that is marked by dominant Western culture as inherent to 'sexuality'. Alternative models of sexuality that employ methods of sexual behaviour that may bypass the genitalia altogether (like some forms of sadomasochism, as discussed in Chapter 2) or that eroticise other areas of the body, are erased from the debate. Other erogenous zones on the body include the lips, anus, ears, neck, nipples and thighs, all of which can be 'sexually sensitive' depending on the individual (Gruenbaum, 2001, p.150). The presence or absence of the foreskin or clitoris may have no bearing on the type or quality of sensation felt in these other areas.

Furthermore, the reduction of sexuality to merely an embodied experience, one mediated by nerve endings and the rushing of blood, denies the connections between sex and the mind. The role of desire, fantasy and mental context in one's sexual life is clearly important, but this is elided within a discursive construction that reduces sex simply to a form of mechanical interaction reliant on friction between biologically 'intact' genitalia. Pleasure and desire can be understood as 'culturally if not individually specific' and 'contingent on location, environment, relationship, performance of one's partner and the quirks of fantasy' (Rogers, 2013, p.29). Indeed, what one might find pleasurable might vary over time, with other important factors associated with orgasm and sexual satisfaction including 'relationship variables, individual dimensions, and general ecological factors' (Dopico, 2007, p.246). These understandings are not captured by a close fixation on physiological genital 'wholeness' as the basis for sexuality.

The idyllic notion of the whole, natural, intact body clearly impacts this aspect of the debate, but more connections can be drawn. The discursive framework of the debate here has links to disciplinary power. The castigation of FGM can be read as the production and preservation of a normative form of genital sexuality that eliminates pleasurable excess in favour of a docile, slavish conformity to a more restrictive sexual model. Sexuality is tightly regulated, relegated to particular bodily apparatuses and strictly cordoned off from other areas. When these apparatuses are seen to be 'damaged' the discursively impelled response is to consider sexuality as also having been 'damaged'. The law mirrors this by protecting female genitalia from any 'damaging' bodily interference in order to preserve 'normal sexual function' (WHO, 1998, p.3). The more laconic traditional approach to MC that reads it as non-harmful has preserved the lawfulness of MC so far, but the recent alternative construction of MC as sexually harmful has been coupled with legal calls for its criminalisation.

Complementing the construction of sexuality as solely genital-oriented within FGM and MC discourse is the correlative construction of the genitals as solely sex-oriented. The social value given to sexual pleasure is culturally contingent and discourse in this area typically reflects the Western allocation of high social value to genital sensation, almost to the exclusion of recognising the genitalia as having any other kind of possible function. 'Damaging' the capacity for sexual response by modifying the genitals is presented as an unalloyed wrong and normative genital-based sexual pleasure is constructed as a good-in-itself that needs no social justification. This Western position is represented as universalisable, an acultural truth that ontologically just is. However, Rogers (2013, p.20) reminds us that '[b]odies are not transparent pages upon which universally meaningful social markings are inscribed … The particular body being marked will … adopt a specific position within the society where the markings have cultural significance. Placed in another culture those markings take on another significance.' Dominant Western understandings about the significance of genitals and genital alterations can be challenged by alternative non-Western discursive conceptualisations about genitalia.

Within many African communities where FGM and MC are traditionally practised, and within the African diaspora in Western countries, genitalia can take on a range of meanings and are usually closely associated with gender and fertility (Atoki, 1995, pp.230–232). Modifications to the genitalia, on these accounts, are about more than just sex. Admittedly, Boddy (1998, p.93) is correct when she notes that 'the reasons for performing circumcision are legion; they vary by society and are usually complex'. My point, however, is not that all non-Western groups believe the same things about FGM and MC but rather that a range of different cultural/bodily associations attach to these issues. Within Western society gender identity is generally regarded as congruently following biological sex (though this issue is problematic: see Chapter 5) and thus a body's 'natural' male sexual organs signify its male sex/gender. In some African communities, however, one only becomes gendered by bodily alterations such as FGM and MC.

One traditional belief, stemming from the 'bisexuality of the gods', is that 'males and females have both masculine and feminine souls that are represented in their sexual characteristics' (Slack, 1988, p.447). The foreskin is seen as the feminine part of the male and the clitoris as the masculine part of the female, and these parts need to be removed before one can take their place as an adult of a particular gender (Slack, 1988, p.447). FGM and MC in these communities can be seen as body-technologies employed in order to negotiate and construct gender out of biology (Boddy, 2007; Hosken, 1993).[4] In this way they are similar to other body-technologies – such as breast implants, genital normalisation and sex reassignment surgery (discussed in Chapters 4 and 5) – that physically (re)inscribe culturally-specific conceptualisations of appropriate sex/gender through normativising alterations to biological features. Understood in this way, rather than being damaging to sexuality, the body alterations involved in FGM and MC may be beneficial because they function as culturally desirable sexual features or even prerequisites for sexual behaviour. As Atoki (1995, p.230) identifies, in some cultures FGM is performed to ready the body for sex, not to deny the body sexual sensation. The effects of FGM might be damaging on the basis of judgement from a Western construction of sexuality, but this construction is not universal. The Modified genitals here break the nexus between genitalia and sex by also playing a role as social signifiers that can indicate sex/gender, status and desirability within a community.

Other social constructions of the meaning of genitalia downplay their role in producing sexual pleasure, and instead value them for their capacity for reproduction. FGM is conceptualised within some cultures as something that increases fertility (Oboler, 2001, pp.313–314), an issue which in some African contexts is more closely linked to sexuality than orgasm is (Atoki, 1995, p.231). A Western focus on the 'need to derive pleasure from sexual intercourse' is a secondary consideration in many FGM-practising cultures where reproduction 'is the primary purpose' (Atoki, 1995, p.231). Embedding the Western dominant cultural model of sexuality into the discursive framework, and presenting it as the universal, neutral standpoint from which to analyse FGM and MC, fails to account for alternative models of sexuality. Claims that FGM and MC enhance sexuality by readying the body for sex or by conforming to a model that sees fertility-as-sex are marginalised within legal discourse. FGM is a criminal wrong regardless of any claim that the female's 'sexuality' has not actually been harmed. Any such claim is rendered legally irrelevant by the legislative framework which encapsulates FGM. Whilst MC may be lawful, it does not go unregulated because

---

4 A similar point has been made by Richters (2006a, p.251) about MC in a Western context, that is that it makes the penis 'more unambiguously phallic' and that it:

> [R]emoves the foreskin and its awkward ambiguity, its feminine capacity to function as a receptive space (for objects such as the partner's tongue) and as a receiver of sensory stimulation ... It could also be argued that the circumcised penis resembles an erect penis even when flaccid, as the difference between a circumcised and an uncircumcised penis is less apparent when they are erect and the foreskin is retracted behind the coronal sulcus. This effect too makes the circumcised penis more 'phallic', more symbolically expressive of its purpose.

of respect for alternative models of sexuality but rather because MC is not currently seen as sexually harmful under the Western dominant cultural model.

Sex/gender and victimhood

Unpacking the differential recognition of both the physical/sexual harms of FGM and MC requires closer attention to Western concepts of sex/gender and how they relate to the body. The Western cultural tradition of viewing women as helpless victims, requiring intervention from a stronger third party in order to be saved, partly explains the 'hypersensitivity' to FGM as a violation of female human rights, 'at the expense of male human rights' (Chessler, 1997, p.557). The discursive construction of women who undergo FGM is that they are 'unenlightened', 'passive' and 'in need of rescue' (Sullivan, 2007, p.407). This is typified in narrative 'accounts' of the carrying out of FGM that recur throughout anti-FGM writing (Hughes, 1995–1996; Wellerstein, 1999–2000; Wood, 2001), where the subject is invariably portrayed as a helpless girl-child, even though FGM is also performed on teenagers and sometimes adult women. Certain kinds of images or narratives of FGM circulate within and gain traction in the Western imaginary and strongly inform how FGM is debated and responded to (Rogers, 2013). In particular, the idea of the helpless female 'child' plays a central and important role within the discourse around FGM (Green and Lim, 1998, pp.376–378), and the specific ideation of 'a child is being mutilated' simultaneously underpins urgent 'calls for law to intervene' and causes '[o]pportunites for consultation or conversation' around FGM to 'disappear' (Rogers, 2013, p.45). The female body that is threatened with FGM within discourse is conceptualised as vulnerable, helpless and 'girlish', and thus the potential harms suffered by this body are readily converted into discursive facts.

Another reason why FGM is so readily conceptualised as harm is that the non-Modified female body is constructed as empowered and as embodying agency. Since the 1970s the clitoris, for some Western feminists at least, has become 'a metaphor for women's power and self-determination' (Lane, 1996, p.35). It is still glorified today, constructed as central to concepts of female sexuality and freedom (Gruenbaum, 2001; Sullivan, 2007). Removal of the clitoris is tantamount to removal of selfhood; it becomes the 'quintessential loss' as the clitoris is heavily invested with ideas of desire, subjectivity, agency and autonomy (Rogers, 2013, p.27). FGM in these symbolic terms is not only seen as violating the individual female's human rights, but as also violating 'the dignity and worth of every woman, indeed every human being' (Hosken, 1993, p.6). These kinds of sex/gender-specific bodily associations function to foreground harms and negative effects to the female body by making them easy to identify and easy to condemn, especially when they are seen as directed towards the female genitalia.

Conversely, the pain and negative effects suffered by male bodies are obscured by Western bodily associations. As Zoske (1998) discusses, an inherent part of masculinity within Western culture is the long-standing set of cultural tropes that present men as bulletproof heroes, able to easily shrug off pain and hardship. The male body has not traditionally been constructed as helpless, nor as a victim, instead it has been conceived of as 'bounded (or impermeable) and invulnerable, with the female body constructed in opposition to this' (Thomson, 2011, p.144). This disparate discursive construction makes the recognition of any physical or sexual harm to the male body more difficult than to the female body. Masculinity in the West is partly defined by the ability to withstand 'physical pain or psychological distress' (Waldeck, 2003–2004, p.494), a construction which downplays the potential harms of MC as just one more thing that a male should 'take like a man'. This is especially so regarding the male genitalia, which, within contemporary culture, is usually 'objectified, viewed as a joke or a weapon, and often reduced to being either a giver or receiver of pain' (Zoske, 1999, pp.280–281).

Drawing on this cultural background, discourse's traditional lack of recognition for the negative sexual effects of MC is clearly explicable. The differential between the easy recognition of the harms caused by FGM to female sexuality and the difficulty of recognising the harms caused by MC to male sexuality can be attributed to Western associations with the sexed/gendered body. The female body is discursively constructed as easily harmed and victimised, whereas the bulletproof male body is constructed as both impervious to such harm and incapable of being a 'victim'. Fox and Thomson (2005, pp.175–176) identify this discursive construction as carrying on into legal work, suggesting that 'within law the role of abuse victim is feminised … produc[ing] a greater acknowledgement of harms perpetrated against girls'. In the context of FGM and MC, the cultural loading of male and female bodies with these kinds of understandings means that it is 'more difficult to uncover harms to boys – a contention which seems to be borne out by the tendency of Anglo-American commentators to minimise the harms inflicted on boys by circumcision with a concomitant propensity to exacerbate the risks occasioned by less invasive forms of female circumcision' (Thomson, 2008, pp.35–36). The disparity in the legal position of FGM and MC reflects this discursive disparity in sex/gender victimhood; the criminalisation of FGM and the lawful status of MC replicates and reifies 'discourses that constitute women and girls as victims and men and boys as … heroes' (Roberts, 2011, p.353).

The sex/gender conceptual disparity which underlies the disparity in the legal treatment of FGM and MC also played itself out publicly in the aftermath of the AAP's 'compromise' (as discussed above). In the wake of the release of AAP's policy statement, in May 2010 RANZCOG announced that they were going to discuss the proposal at one of their upcoming meetings (Murphy and Sikora,

2010). This announcement was quickly followed by public condemnations of FGM, such as by the then Sex Discrimination Commissioner for the Australian Human Rights Commission Elizabeth Broderick, who described FGM as 'violence against women', as well as former Commissioner Pru Goward, who described it as 'a form of child abuse' (Tatnell, 2010). Notably missing from the response to this announcement was any substantive engagement with the idea that the superficial cut that would take place in the course of the proposed 'ritual nick' would be far less physically invasive than that involved in MC. Indeed, part of the reasoning behind the AAP's original proposal that a 'ritual nick' of the female genitalia be possibly allowed was their contention that '[s]ome forms of FGC are less extensive than the newborn male circumcision commonly performed in the West' (AAP, 2010a, p.1089). RANZCOG did not adopt the AAP's 'compromise'.

Conceptions of Culture

Whilst addressing the physical/sexual effects of FGM and MC, this chapter has also indirectly touched on some of the cultural understandings about these body alterations, the social significance they hold and the reasons that they are carried out. In this section, these issues will be addressed more directly by critically exploring how FGM and MC are discursively constructed as originating from opposed cultural locations.

Othering and Westernisation

Numerous academic commentators have identified that discourse tends to locate FGM outside Western culture, constructing it as an alien practice of the African Other. Oppositions are set up between Africa and the West, playing the former off as the dangerous and barbaric home of FGM and the latter as enlightened in its refusal to follow this harmful practice (Silverman, 2004; Wade, 2009). This discursive positioning draws on Western cultural myths about Africa that stem from colonial-era times (Green and Lim, 1998), such as that of Africa as being 'the dark continent, heart of darkness, literally and figuratively' (Fraser, 1994, p.149).

In practical terms, this conceptualisation plays itself out as an 'anti-immigrant and refugee sentiment' that tends to coalesce around FGM debates within Western countries, where the African diaspora is condemned as the 'deviant Other' (Buhagiar, 1997, p.184). The totalising, monolithic construction of FGM that collapses the numerous differences of meaning and practice is complemented here by the monolithic construction of Africa and African woman, presenting them as all the same. Ieradioconou (1995–1996, p.584, footnote omitted) identifies this in news footage that broadcast on the Australian Broadcasting Corporation (ABC) television channel showing 'Eritrean women talking about female genital mutilation whilst [playing] a "file tape" of Somalis undergoing female genital mutilation.' Some academic commentators non-reflexively employ this model of FGM as culturally Other, comparing it to other archetypal non-Western practices like Chinese foot binding (Khalafzai, 2008a, p.4), Indian *sati* (widow-burning) (Queensland Law Reform Commission, 1994, p.56), and utilising it as an example of when one could employ a 'cultural defence' to criminal prosecution in the same article as discussions of Japanese parent-child suicide, Chinese honour killing, and Hmong marriage-by-capture (Mendelsohn, 2004). FGM, then, is discursively constructed as non-Western. Indeed because it is so alien and Other it is constructed as almost anti-Western.

In contrast, MC has typically been conceptualised as a 'normal' Western cultural practice (though Fox and Thomson's (2012) recognition of the new 'public health' trend generated by discussions of MC in Africa may indicate a discursive shift in this regard). Absences or gaps in discourse are as meaningful as the presence of texts, and the absence of much considered academic evaluation of MC within Western legal discourse demonstrates its widespread acceptance. Commentators have wondered at the 'very limited body of case law' (Fox and Thomson, 2008, p.283), the 'surprising paucity of thoughtful analysis' (Price, 1996), and the general lack of legal work on MC (Haberfield, 1997, p.93; Tasmania Law Reform Institute, 2009, pp.5–6). This, however, is easily explicable: because it is so common and because it is so widely accepted, 'the fact that men are circumcised scarcely merits comment' (Gruenbaum, 2001, p.15). Much the same standpoint underlies the disparity between MC's technical criminality and the failure to enforce it. Because MC has a generally accepted legality, it effectively becomes 'legal' as instances of MC are not prosecuted. In the US, MC takes on even more cultural importance as it is constructed as quintessentially American. This importance is reflected in such claims as '[i]t's the All-American way to be circumcised, to be a regular guy' (Price, 1999, p.430). This importance is self-perpetuating, as Wallerstein (1980, p.2) determines that the fact that 'everybody does it' is one of the major social reasons for its continued practice. In this way, MC becomes more than just a practice carried out in the West, and instead becomes a 'Western practice'. It is something that has been discursively linked to particular countries, especially America and, historically, Australia. The result is that, in the West, FGM is conceptualised as something that 'they do' whilst MC has historically been uncritically conceptualised as something that 'we do'.

The purported discursive division between the cultural location of FGM as non-Western and MC as Western is easily problematised. There is a cultural history of FGM within Western countries, including the United Kingdom, Australia and the United States of America. From the mid-1800s, clitoridectomies were carried out by medical practitioners on females for various reasons (Barker-Benfield, 1975), including being used to treat masturbation, lesbianism and hysteria (Lightfoot-Klein, 1989, pp.179–181).[5] This continued to as late as the 1950s (Obiora, 1996–1997a, p.298), with a certain Dr Rathman from California publishing pieces up until 1959 that advocated for 'wide-scale female circumcision' (Hodges, 1997, p.29). Whilst some commentators identify this cultural link, many others tend to gloss over it or downplay it. For example, Mason (2001, p.67) dismisses this Western form of FGM as being only 'very minor, because it was never routine and uniform', whilst Koso-Thomas (1987, p.15, emphasis added) notes that it 'involved *only* clitoridectomy'. Morgan (1997, pp.93 and 105) more blatantly describes FGM as a 'nonexistent issue for Western medicine' until immigration brought it to American shores, mentioning its Western history only in passing 12 pages later. However, the discursive ramifications of this connection are clear; the construction of FGM as African and Other relies on placing the West's own cultural history under erasure, a telling denial of fact strategically employed to preserve the channelling of xenophobia into anti-FGM sentiment. Recognition that 'African women were reported to undergo clitoridectomy for reasons similar to those for which doctors recommended it in Europe and the United States' (Boddy, 1998, p.91), undermines the construction of the West's 'enlightened' rejection of this 'barbaric' practice. This reveals that whilst FGM may be something 'they do', it is also something 'we have done' and for similar reasons.

Similarly, MC cannot be culturally located simply as a Western practice. 'In almost all societies where there are customary female genital surgeries, there are also customary male genital surgeries' (The Public Policy Advisory Group on Female Genital Surgeries in Africa, 2012, p.23), with the effect that African societies that perform FGM almost invariably also perform MC or some kind of equivalent (Boddy, 2007, p.60).[6] Many of those cultures and communities that are discursively presented as alien and Other when discussing FGM also carry out the exact same male genital body alteration that is discursively presented as Western and as a quintessential part of American identity. Some two-thirds of all Circumcised males over 15 years are Muslim, living mainly in Asia, the Middle East and Africa (WHO, 2007, p.7).

5 Testing for the 'disease of desire' required clitoridectomists to induce orgasm by 'manipulating [the] clitoris and breasts' of their patients (Barker-Benfield, 1975, p.295). This concept is disturbing not only because of the overtones of sexual exploitation but also because of the pathologisation of what is generally seen as a 'natural' physiological reaction.

6 Although the reverse is not true; whilst 'almost all group that circumcise females also circumcise males', it is only the case that many 'groups that circumcise males also circumcise females' (Wallerstein, 1980, p.53).

Body politics

The construction of disparities between the reasons why 'non-Western' FGM and 'Western' MC are performed helps maintain this culturally-oppositional conceptualisation. The reasons for FGM are discursively presented as primitive superstitions, ridiculous or blatantly false, and completely inadequate as justifications. For example, the typical non-Western claim that FGM increases the beauty of the female genitalia (Royal Australian College of Obstetricians and Gynaecologists, 1997, p.16), by making it 'flat and smooth', and free from 'unsightly … [f]leshy encumbrances' (Atoki, 1995, p.228), is treated with scorn. Toubia (1993, p.15) describes genitals that have undergone FGM as bearing 'more resemblance to cured hide than to human tissue' because of the 'tough scar tissue', whilst Koso-Thomas (1987, p.10) characterises infibulated genitals as bearing 'ugly' scars and having a 'horrifying appearance'. The aesthetic claim has itself even been dismissed as a 'myth' in the Family Law Council's report to the Attorney-General (1994, p.10).

This aesthetic claim is not a 'myth', it is a culturally-located statement about culturally-specific standards of beauty. This claim can only be dismissed as a 'myth' if one loses sight of the fact that 'the West *has* and *is* a culture' itself (Kennedy, 2009, p.219, emphasis in original), and that Western standards of beauty are also cultural standards of beauty. The totalisation of discourse by Western standards allows FGM to be portrayed as barbaric and primitive, whilst masking the culturally-specific nature of the standards of beauty that underpin body alterations within Western culture (on this issue, see the discussion of cosmetic surgery in Chapter 4, particularly in relation to beauty standards for women). Through the processes of cultural Othering that operate within the discourse here, the practice of FGM, 'once constructed as mutilation, is always already a very different practice from western practices – even if the practices involve cosmetic or biomedical cutting' (Rogers, 2013, p.92). However, some of those Western women who were clitoridectomised by their doctors in the late 1800s and early 1900s 'considered their scars "as pretty as the dimple in the cheek of sweet sixteen"' (Barker-Benfield, 1975, p.295). This 'myth' has in the past held the status of a cultural 'truth' for these Western women. The Western cosmetic claim that MC makes the penis 'look better' (Wallerstein, 1980, p.2), could also be dismissed as a myth, with the Circumcised penis described as ugly and scarred. However, the Circumcised aesthetic is naturalised within Western popular discourse, such as in the *Sex and The City* episode 'Old Dog, New Tricks' (1999) where the character Charlotte characterises the non-Circumcised penis as looking like a Shar-pei.

Moving beyond aesthetics, we can also look towards the motivations behind FGM and MC as a point of similarity. Whilst we should remember that the 'meanings and motives associated with the practice [of FGM] vary … and are not necessarily shared by every ethnic group' (The Public Policy Advisory

Group on Female Genital Surgeries in Africa, 2012, p.21), Lightfoot-Klein's (1997) illuminating comparative analysis of African FGM and American MC found that they typically 'occur for the same reasons'. Lightfoot-Klein (1997, pp.132–134) notes similarities in attitudes about the two sets of body alterations regarding:

- claims that they beautify the genitalia;
- medical indications for their performance;
- claims that they help maintain hygiene;
- claims that they prevent future problems;
- claims that they improve sex;
- claims that they should be universalised (performed on everyone); and,
- denial of their long-term harms.

FGM and MC are not geographically separable into body alterations that occur in the West and in the non-West. Neither are they separable on the basis of the reasons for which they are carried out. The discursive construction of FGM as non-Western and MC as Western is reducible to an issue of simple 'cultural, religious and racial' boundary-drawing on seemingly arbitrary grounds (Denniston, Hodges and Milos, 1999, p.vii).

Despite the challenges that can be levelled against the disparate cultural location of FGM and MC within discourse, the discursive authority of the culturally-oppositional account still holds sway. Thus, FGM remains predominantly figured within discourse as creating unruly bodies. The Modified woman is an alien somatic type that enters into the West and insinuates itself, unseen and unmonitored, into the Western body typology. Because the scars of FGM are hidden under clothing, the problem itself becomes invisible, but this makes it only more dangerous as the rate at which it is spreading cannot be monitored. It is portrayed as a significant problem, as although 'no statistical studies reveal the prevalence of FGM in the United States' we can somehow still be sure that it is a 'common occurrence among immigrant communities' (Hughes, 1995–1996, pp.323–324 and 333–334).

The Modified female body is discursively constructed as a form of foreign somatic sickness that threatens to infect the Western 'body politic' (Fraser, 1994, p.150). Lane and Rubinstein (1996, p.38) disapprove of the use of the word 'eradication' by anti-FGM advocates to call for the cessation of FGM, arguing that it is 'public health language ... most often associated with germ theory and worldwide campaigns against infectious diseases like smallpox, malaria, and polio'. However, it is a term that has seen ubiquitous use (Bashir, 1995–1996; Funder, 1993; Gunning, 1991–1992; Hosken, 1993; Hughes, 1995–1996; Morgan, 1997). The implicit threat in this sickness metaphor is that the unruly, Modified female body will infect the enlightened West with barbarism and violence. As we saw in Chapter 2, discursive associations of atavism and contagion are also used in a similar way within legal discourse to condemn sadomasochistic bodies as dangerous and worthy of criminalisation. The difference with regard to FGM is that the Modified female body is discursively constructed as an external, rather than internal, threat. The West is figured as under attack by the 'increasing number of immigrants' who are bringing their 'primitive and even horrifying procedures' into the West, which must respond by 'grab[bing] hold of its fears and fac[ing] this issue head on' (Morgan, 1997, p.111). In contrast, the MC body is constructed within this discourse as docile. It is a 'natural' body type that functions as the norm or a neutral variation from the norm in Western countries. The body of the Circumcised male is read as local, unproblematic and as posing no threat to Western culture or cultural identity. Recognised as a familiar choice within normative body typologies, MC is uncontroversial and requires no further justification.

Connecting this discursive conceptualisation of FGM and MC to their disparate legal positions appears simple. Their legality seems to merely depend on whether they are discursively positioned as 'acceptable or 'unacceptable' in accordance with 'dominant societal conception[s]' (Mason, 2001, p.66). Given the negative conceptualisation of FGM as dangerous and Other, and the positive conceptualisation of MC as neutral or normative, the explicit criminality of FGM and the accepted lawfulness of MC merely reflect the discursive consensus. It might be a trite conclusion, but it seems inescapable that the legal system here has simply codified and enshrined the 'oppositional images' of FGM as Other and MC as Western (Gunning, 1994–1995, p.47). The 'threat' posed by the unruly Modified female body is constructed as a society-wide threat, an attack from the Other against the West as a whole. As such, an institution-level, organised response is of the same scale as the perceived threat and adequately protects the body politic from the unruly body. In contrast, the docile MC body poses no threat to either the social order or normative values and is correspondingly ignored at the institutional level. It is simply deemed to be lawful but is left with the ever-present shadow of the potential for the legal machinery to be turned against it if the counter-discourse that conceptualises it as a harm were to gain more traction.

Conclusion

The legal disparity between explicitly criminalised FGM and tacitly lawful MC is informed by the oppositional positioning of these body alterations within the broader discursive framework. This positioning is premised upon the strategic deployment of particular discursive conceptualisations about the body and society that work to separate and keep FGM and MC separated around issues such as harm, sexuality and culture. FGM is discursively constructed as a monolithic, singular harm to all women that destroys female sexuality and that originates from an Other/African cultural location. In contrast, MC is discursively constructed as a neutral or beneficial procedure that does not harm men either physically or sexually, and that originates from a Self/Western cultural location.

A number of commentators are invested in maintaining this current authoritative discursive account for advocacy purposes. The negative discursive conceptualisation of FGM is necessary to support calls for the continued criminalisation and future, potential 'eradication' of FGM. Relaxation of the strict discursive boundaries constructed between FGM and MC is seen as worrisome because it might draw attention to points of similarity between these body alterations, potentially causing pro-MC sentiment to erode anti-FGM sentiment. By foregrounding the physical and sexual harms of FGM and backgrounding the similar potential harms of MC, and by drawing sharp cultural distinctions between 'what they do' and 'what we do', the legal distinctions between these alterations are also naturalised and justified through discourse. Ironically, the failure to recognise that MC can also be conceived of as harmful may be damaging efforts to prevent the practice of FGM in non-Western countries. Zwang (1997, p.75) argues that to many Africans this double-standard is 'incomprehensible', as it 'seems inconsistent to them to be obliged to leave girls in their native state, while still being permitted to "correct" boys'. Thus the strategic value of maintaining the discursive dissociation of MC from FGM can be called into question.

A counter-discursive current continues to push back against the legal disparity between, and discursive separation of, FGM and MC. Variously seeking to tap into pro-MC sentiment to bolster support for partial deregulation of FGM or tap into anti-FGM sentiment to bolster support for the criminalisation of MC, other commentators draw points of comparison between these body alterations in order to construct them as being similar. By highlighting the desirable and beneficial nature of FGM for some specific women, by foregrounding the potential physical and sexual harms of MC, and by drawing attention to the reductive and artificial nature of the Othering that occurs in cultural boundary-drawing, the discursive barriers set up between FGM and MC can be challenged.

Nevertheless, the authoritative discursive account of the dissimilarity of FGM and MC informs the legal status of these body alterations. The current law disregards alternative accounts of FGM as not always harmful, or as a harm that may be seen as justifiable for aesthetic or fertility reasons. Legal discourse here colludes with medical discourse in framing FGM as harmful by placing weight on a reductive, purely physical-based view that accounts for complications and side-effects but ignores the social meanings attached to it by the relevant women themselves. The evidence from some specific women about their benefit, or lack of harm, from FGM is irrelevant to a legal regime that criminalises all forms of FGM even when it is performed consensually on adult women. As Rogers (2009, p.187) notes, Modified women cannot speak to the law but are necessarily merely 'in receipt of law's message' because of the 'impossibility of [their] speech acts … being recognised in legal discourse'. Authoritative discursive conceptualisations construct FGM as necessarily always a legal harm. Conversely, the law disregards the lived experiences of those males who consider themselves to have been harmed by MC. Their scarring, loss of sensation and pain may be subjectively experienced as harmful but this does not constitute a legal harm unless some additional factor is present, such as negligence in the performance of the surgery. If one's embodied experience of FGM or MC does not match the law's accounts of these body alterations, then no legal recourse is available. The benefits that FGM may bring to some and the harms that MC may bring to others are incomprehensible under the idiom of law that recognises FGM as always harmful and that always dismisses claims about the harmfulness of MC.

This striking contrast in the legal response to two sets of body alteration that share so many points of similarity is the result of their disparate relative positioning within the discursive framework. Despite the counter-discursive trends within this area of discourse, the disparate legal positions of both body alterations remain well-entrenched in Australian law. A recent Commonwealth Government review into Australia's legal response to FGM recommended an increase in the penalties for FGM offences in some jurisdictions, a broader scope of liability for these offences and stricter enforcement, with the purpose of more strongly dissuading and penalising this 'abhorrent practice' (Attorney-General's Department, 2013). These recommendations appear to have been taken up in NSW, with the passage of the *Crimes Amendment (Female Genital Mutilation) Act 2014* (NSW) through both Houses of Parliament in mid-2014. The Act, amongst other things, triples the maximum penalty (from 7 years to 21 years) for performing FGM under s45 of the *Crimes Act 1900* (NSW). In contrast, the recommendations made in a recent report by the Tasmanian Law Reform Institute into non-therapeutic circumcision demonstrate the traction gained by counter-discourses pushing back against authoritative legal constructions of MC. In the report, the Institute recommended the enactment of a new criminal offence in Tasmania to prohibit the non-therapeutic circumcision of a minor who is incapable of providing legal consent on their own behalf (Tasmania Law Reform Institute, 2012). However, the Institute also recommended that any such offence be made subject to substantial exceptions in order to 'accommodate established religious and ethnic circumcising traditions in Tasmania' (Tasmania Law Reform Institute, 2012, p.71). Although this recommendation has not yet been made into law (and may never be), that fact that such a recommendation has been made indicates the strength of the counter-discursive current pushing back against the discursive construction of MC as wholly neutral or beneficial, and thus as incomparable with FGM on this basis.

Chapter 4
Aesthetic Alterations: What Healthy Limb Amputation Can Tell Us About Cosmetic Surgery and Body Modification

The previous two chapters focused on body alterations that are either relatively rare or are declining in popularity in Australia: sadomasochistic injuries result from a niche, subcultural practice, even before FGM was explicitly criminalised it would probably only ever have been performed on a small number of females within certain communities, and the rate of neonatal routine MC has declined precipitously in the past few decades. The focus of this chapter, however, is on two sets of body alterations practised with increasing frequency since the 1970s. Cosmetic surgery's 'ever-increasing popularity' (Bridy, 2004, p.151) has led to a 'burgeoning' Australian cosmetic surgery industry (Cornwall, 2000, p.87). Although exact figures are not available, this industry is generally accepted to have doubled in size between 1994 and 1999 (Cosmetic Surgery Inquiry Committee, 1999, p.v). Similarly, the set of body alterations commonly termed 'body modification' is 'gaining in popularity' (Egan, 2007, p.1627), with a veritable 'explosion' in the take-up rate of tattooing and body piercing (Select Committee on the Tattooing and Body Piercing Industries, 2005, p.8).

The increase in the cultural visibility of cosmetic surgery and body modification has correlatively increased academic interest and output around these issues, and this has primed this area for discursive analysis. I am interested in these body alterations not simply because they are currently popular, but because their broadening exposure has recently cued the intrusion of societal mechanisms such as mass-market commercialisation, media exposure and legal regulation. The rise of these body alterations has been interpreted by some academic commentators as indicating a cultural shift towards conceiving of the body in different terms, such as being a vehicle for self-expression (Hewitt, 1997, p.1; Rosenblatt, 1997, p.317), or as being inherently malleable rather than having a fixed form (Bridy, 2004, p.151; Pitts-Taylor, 2009, p.126). However, Australian law has scrambled to reassert its authority over the boundaries of the body, such as through the introduction of legislation to prohibit these bodily alterations from being performed on children (*Children and Young Persons (Care and Protection) Amendment (Body Piercing and Tattooing) Act 2008* (NSW) and the *Health Legislation (Restriction on Use of Cosmetic Surgery for Children and Another Measure) Amendment Act 2008* (Qld)). As such, the legal status of cosmetic surgery and body modification, and the discourses that conceptualise and position them, are key sites for analysing contemporary social anxieties and understandings about body alteration as well as the encapsulation by the law of new types of bodies and the practices that produce them. In addition to their simultaneous rise in popularity and cultural visibility, cosmetic surgery and body modification also share an underlying aetiology: both sets of body alterations are concerned with predominantly aesthetic, rather than functional, changes to the body. They also invoke a common discursive framework of issues, such as those around bodily appearance and sex/gender, that makes them suitable to be analysed together.

The analytical focus adopted in this chapter takes a step back from the close discursive analysis in Chapters 2 and 3, which examined the specific linguistic and rhetorical techniques that structured legal discourse in those areas, and places more emphasis on the broader discursive formations that position cosmetic surgery and body modification within culture and society. This shift is partly attributable to the pre-existence of other secondary material that already engages in close discursive analysis of these body alterations, such as the extensive review of cosmetic surgery discourse in women's magazines, medicine, feminist writing and the law in Fraser's (2003a) book *Cosmetic Surgery, Gender and Culture*. This shift is also partly attributable to the nature of the subject matter itself. Cosmetic surgery is so deeply imbricated with 'tremendously complex and significant social trends concerning the body, gender, psyche, medical practice and ethics' (Heyes and Jones, 2009, p.2) that to approach it with a narrow analytical focus would risk failing to engage with the social meanings that make this body alteration politically significant. This kind of criticism has previously been levelled against other postmodern-inspired engagements with cosmetic surgery (Bordo, 1993). A similar issue can be raised in relation to body modification, which is arguably just as closely enmeshed with conceptions of sex/gender (Atkinson, 2002), psyche (Sullivan, 2001), and the body (Grosz, 1995). Whilst reference will still be made to some aspects of close discursive analytical work, shifting the focus towards the broader operation of discourse allows this chapter to compensate for the intertextuality of the material, more fully account for the cultural terrain and expand the scope of this book to demonstrate the broader ways in which discourse intersects with law.

The aim of this chapter is to critically explore the discursive boundaries that operate around cosmetic surgery and body modification, with a view to revealing how law is mobilised across these boundaries. This chapter begins by offering brief definitions of what constitutes both cosmetic surgery and body modification, and proceeds by charting their current legal status. Whilst all cosmetic surgery procedures are widely accepted as lawful, some body modifications are lawful, some hold a murky quasi-legality and others are criminal. This legal differentiation frames the subsequent analysis of the *internal discursive boundaries* of both cosmetic surgery and body modification, an analysis that seeks to determine what constitutes 'acceptable' cosmetic surgery and body modification and explain why 'unacceptable' cosmetic surgery remains lawful whereas 'unacceptable' body modification faces legal regulation. This chapter then analyses the *external discursive boundaries* of cosmetic surgery and body modification, in order to determine the discursive forces that keep these categories conceptually and legally separate from other body alterations such as reconstructive surgery, FGM, dieting and exercise. Finally, this chapter explores the *discursive boundary between cosmetic surgery and body modification* by attempting to locate healthy limb amputation within either of these categories. Healthy limb amputation provides a problem case for the law because it simultaneously accords with and challenges the internal logics that typically dictate assignation into the conceptual categories of 'cosmetic surgery' or 'body modification'. This liminality enables the analysis of healthy limb amputation to reveal the discursive techniques that underpin both conceptual categorisation and the legal consequences at stake in this area.

Aesthetic Alterations

Cosmetic Surgery

The terminological framework that surrounds the set of body alterations collectively known as 'cosmetic surgery' is complex and politically loaded. Plastic surgery (which takes its name from the Greek word *plastikos*, meaning to shape or mould: Haiken, 2000, p.82) is surgery undertaken for the purpose of altering the appearance of the patient. Another, less-common phrase used to refer to plastic surgery is 'aesthetic surgery' (Jones, 2008b, p.3), an epithet that highlights the discursive connection between appearance and beauty that dominates this area. Cosmetic surgery is typically described as one of two sub-fields within the broader medical practice of plastic surgery. The other sub-field of plastic surgery is known as reconstructive surgery, and it is in contrast to reconstructive surgery that cosmetic surgery is typically defined.

Under an orthodox account, reconstructive surgery is defined as work that seeks to 'repair catastrophic, congenital, or cancer-damage deformities' and is seen as restorative of a somehow damaged appearance, whereas cosmetic surgery is defined as 'entirely elective' work that is seen purely as enhancement of appearance (Balsamo, 1996, p.58). Cosmetic surgery is typically understood as simply being the 'aesthetic improvement of otherwise healthy bodies' (Davis,

1995, p.16), and is considered to be elective, in contrast to reconstructive surgery (Jones, 2008b, p.3), because it 'is initiated by the consumer rather than resulting from medical need' (Cornwall, 2000, p.88). Given that 'the content of medical diagnoses is shaped by social, economic, and political factors' (Irvine, 1995, p.314), the divide between reconstructive and cosmetic surgery is blurry and has invited criticism and challenge (Naugler, 2009). For the sake of clarity, this debate will not be engaged with now, but it will be returned to below in the analysis of the external conceptual boundaries of cosmetic surgery. Until then, highlighting these problems here should serve to prevent the distinction between reconstructive and cosmetic surgery from being naturalised within this chapter. The imprecise term 'appearance medicine' is also sometimes used to refer to both cosmetic surgery and some other 'treatments' that Scott (2009, pp.625–626) categorises as 'more akin to beauty therapy', such as dermabrasion, chemical peels and laser light skin treatments. However, these other 'treatments' have been defined elsewhere as 'cosmetic surgery' (Queensland Health Department, 2007, p.1), so the terms have also been used interchangeably. This chapter will proceed on the basis that these 'less invasive procedures' are 'distinct from cosmetic surgery' (Karpin, 2009, p.80) and will not focus on them.

Historically, plastic surgery has been performed since approximately 1000 BC, where the use of nose amputation as a form of punishment in India gave rise to a demand for nose reconstructions (Davis, 1995, p.14). Nose reconstructions were also performed in Europe in the sixteenth century after the outbreak of syphilis (Gilman, 1999), as were operations to repair facial scars resulting from duelling (Haiken, 2000, p.82). It was not, however, until the discovery of both effective anaesthetic and antisepsis in the 1800s that plastic surgery became more practically feasible (Gilman, 1999). Cosmetic surgery was performed in America in the 1920s and 1930s (Haiken, 1997), and Fraser (2003a, p.16) notes that it is possible Australian medical practitioners also performed 'cosmetic procedures such as nose jobs and facelifts during the early 1900s'. But the fate of cosmetic surgery in this time period was linked to that of plastic surgery in general, and that particular field of medicine only began to be more widely practised from the 1950s onwards. The rise of modern plastic surgery has been attributed to World War I, where the type of fighting engaged in – which involved trench warfare, the use of helmets and shrapnel weapons – resulted in large numbers of troops sustaining, but surviving, injuries to the face and neck (Haiken, 1997). New reconstructive techniques were developed in Europe in an effort to treat these soldiers, and the practice of reconstructive surgery was adopted by more surgeons. Similar development of these techniques continued through World War II, and a number of newly-skilled American and Australian surgeons took what they had learnt back to their home countries after the end of the war (Fraser, 2003a, p.15). Shortly thereafter, in 1955 plastic surgery was made a separate group within the Australasian College of Surgeons, and in 1956 the Society of Plastic Surgeons held their first meeting in Melbourne (Fraser, 2003a, p.16). With the rise of plastic surgery providing a skilled base of surgeons, as well as breaking down the stigma of vanity and frivolity previously attached to appearance-based medicine (Haiken, 1997), cosmetic surgery flourished. By 1999, in Australia alone there were some 350 doctors performing approximately 50,000 cosmetic surgical procedures per year, as well as 150 doctors and 50 nurses performing approximately 200,000 cosmetic medical procedures per year (Cosmetic Surgery Inquiry Committee, 1999, p.v).

The types of doctors performing cosmetic surgery today include not just plastic surgeons, but also cosmetic surgeons, cosmetic physicians, general practitioners, dermatologists, ophthalmologists, and otolaryngologists, who have been variously trained, accredited and represented by over ten specialist colleges and professional associations (Cosmetic Surgery Inquiry Committee, 1999, p.v). Data on the exact number of cosmetic surgeries, and the number of procedures by type, are unavailable in Australia, but the American Society of Plastic Surgeons (2009) found that in 2008 in the US alone 12.1 million cosmetic procedures were performed, of which 1.7 million were surgical, and that over $1 billion was spent on breast augmentations. From its position of relative obscurity a century ago, cosmetic surgery has grown to a multibillion dollar industry today.

A bewildering array of body alterations fall under the auspices of cosmetic surgery, including *inter alia*:

- cheek implants;
- chin augmentation (menoplasty);
- ear pinback (otoplasty);
- eyelid tightening (blepharoplasty);
- face-lift (rhytidectomy);
- hair transplantation;
- nose job (rhinoplasty);
- breast augmentation;
- breast reduction (mammoplasty);
- breast tightening (mastopexy);
- buttock-lift and thigh-lift;
- liposuction and lipectomy;
- male breast reduction;
- penile enlargement and implants; and,
- tummy tuck (abdominoplasty) (Gilman, 1999, pp.6–7).

These various body alterations are not performed with equal frequency. In the US in 2008 the five most popular surgical cosmetic procedures were breast augmentation (307,000 procedures), nose reshaping (279,000 procedures), liposuction (245,000 procedures), eyelid surgery (221,000 procedures), and tummy tuck (122,000 procedures) (American Society of Plastic Surgeons, 2009).

Body Modification

The beautification of the body has been practised by humans for thousands of years, 'most likely, since humans became human' (DeMello, 2007, p.xvii). DeMello (2007) draws a distinction between two types of beautifying practices, separating out body adornment from body modification. Body adornment refers to the physical enhancement of the body that is by definition and intention temporary, including 'styling and decorating the hair, painting and embellishing the fingernails, wearing makeup, painting the body, wearing jewellery, and the use of clothing' (DeMello, 2007, p.xvii). Body modification refers to alterations to the structures of the body that are 'typically permanent (but can also be temporary) made through the use of processes including surgery, tattooing, piercing, scarification, branding, genital mutilation, and implantation' (DeMello, 2007, p.xvii).

This distinction provides a good starting point, but it must be further refined. A literal understanding of the term 'body modification' would draw it so widely as to encompass all interactions that modify the structure of the body in some way. If we were to follow this reasoning then it could even be said that '[t]echnically, cosmetic surgery is a form of non-therapeutic body modification' (Bogdanoski, 2009, p.508). Indeed, Karpin (2008) refers to cosmetic surgery as 'cosmetic body modification'. This book will follow the trend set by some commentators and those who identify as 'body modifiers', such as Modern Primitives (Vale and Juno, 1989), by using the term 'body modification' to refer only to a certain category of body alterations that has been constructed, delimited, and positioned in particular ways within discourse. Fixing the limits of the definition of 'body modification' is both problematic and politically loaded, as it relies on dominant cultural conceptions about what constitutes appropriate and socially valued types of body alteration. These definitional problems will not be engaged with now, but will be returned to below in the analysis of the external conceptual boundaries of body modification. Whilst the exact limits of the definition of body modification may be contested, certain forms of body alteration are widely recognised as belonging to this category and these will be addressed here.

The general minimum set of body alterations included in the category of 'body modification' are 'piercings, brandings, scarification, splitting, and tattooing' (Egan, 2007, p.1615).[1] Each modification entails a different type, and process, of body alteration:

1 Other body alterations that might be considered part of the 'body modification' category include transdermal and subdermal implants – the difference being in the

- Piercing refers to the process whereby a needle, either guided by hand or by a piercing-gun, is passed into the skin and then out again in a different area to create a 'tunnel' in the flesh into which a piece of jewellery (commonly stainless steel) is inserted. The wound heals around the jewellery causing the 'tunnel' to line with scar tissue and eventually become semi-permanent, although the removal of the jewellery may cause it to close up over time. Many parts of the body can be pierced including the ear cartilage, the nose, the lips, the eyebrows, the neck, the nipples, the navel and the genitals.
- Branding refers to the process whereby a pattern is marked onto the skin through the medium of a heat burn, inflicted by 'a white hot steel "strike" or a medical cauteriser' (Law Commission, 1995, p.123), or a cold burn, inflicted by a liquid nitrogen-chilled metal 'strike'. As the burns heal they are covered over with scabs and scar tissue that cause the pattern to stand out.
- Scarification refers to the process of cutting a pattern into the skin with a sharp object, such as a medical scalpel, to cause the formation of scar tissue in the shape of the pattern (Law Commission, 1995, p.123). The cuts are 'usually approximately a quarter of an inch deep' (Uden, 2001, p.10). To cause sufficient scar tissue formation, the cutting process may be repeated numerous times, or the healing process may be interfered with by the removal of any scabs that form.
- Splitting refers to a process of bodily bifurcation performed by cutting a protruding area of tissue and separating it into two sections, but leaving both sections attached to the rest of the body. The cut where the sections were split then heals, leaving the two parts separated. This can take place on body parts such as the tongue, creating a literal forked tongue, or the penis.
- Tattooing refers to the process of depositing ink or ash beneath the uppermost layers of skin by way of the repeated insertion of a sharp object, whose end is dipped in the ink/ash, into the flesh. This sharp object may be inserted manually or, more commonly, through the use of a motorised tattooing 'gun'. Tattooing is an ancient form of body alteration, with archaeological evidence indicating it was probably practised during the Stone Age (Sanders, 2008, p.9).

former the implant is wholly under the skin, and in the latter it is only partially under the skin (DeMello, 2007, pp.155–156) – and the relatively newly developed process for the implantation of jewellery into the mucous membrane of the eye (Armstrong, 2005, p.42).

Similarly to cosmetic surgery, these body modifications are not performed with the same frequency. Certain types of piercing and tattooing are far more prevalent than other body modifications. Historically, piercing of the ear lobes, especially on women, has been popular in Western culture. An Australian study found that nearly 1 in 3 of the population aged 14 years and over had had their ears pierced at one point in their lives (Makkai and McAllister, 2001, p.69). However, the same study showed that only 6.7 per cent of people reported undergoing 'body piercing', defined as piercing not located on the ears, at some point in their lives (Makkai and McAllister, 2001, p.69). Furthermore, while approximately 1 in 10 Australian people have had a tattoo at some point in their lives (Makkai and McAllister, 2001, p.69), undoubtedly the number of arm or back tattoos far outweighs the number of facial or genital tattoos. As a general rule, body piercing, multiple piercings, scarification, branding and extensive tattooing, all body modifications popularly perceived as 'extreme', 'remain a good deal less widespread' (Benson, 2000, p.242).

Body modifications have been, and continue to be, performed in both DIY and professional contexts. For example, the modern practice of body piercing has historical roots in the sadomasochistic and punk subcultural communities, where sadists would pierce masochists in order to indicate ownership or as part of sadomasochistic activities (Rosenblatt, 1997, pp.310–311). Whilst body modifiers have long-existed, the recent explosion of mainstream popularity has resulted in the development of a fully-fledged industry to service the needs of those desiring such modifications (Jeffreys, 2000, p.409). Body modifications are now performed by 'tattooists, piercing specialists' and 'body modification artists' (Karpin, 2008, p.82), their services are readily available (for a fee) and they can be easily found in most cities.

The Legal Status of Aesthetic Alterations

The Legal Status of Cosmetic Surgery

Cosmetic surgery is a well-worked area within civil law, particularly in relation to the tort of negligence. The typical case scenario involves a cosmetic patient, who has undergone cosmetic surgery and who is unhappy with the result, suing their medical health practitioner for either negligently carrying out the procedure or negligently failing to warn them of a risk of the procedure that then materialised, for example *Dunning v Scheibner* (Unreported, NSW/SC, No 13776 of 1988, 15 February 1994). It is pertinent that whilst cosmetic surgery is a medical area that generates an inordinately high number of these kinds of civil legal claims (Fogg 2005), like the Law Commission (1995, p.110) before me, I 'have been unable to identify any [criminal] case in which the lawfulness of cosmetic surgery carried out by consent has been called into question'. Similarly, whilst there is a wide collection of legal commentary on the civil aspects of cosmetic surgery, engagement with its position under criminal law is scarce to non-existent, as it 'is rare for the criminal law to be invoked to resolve a medical treatment case' (Karpin, 2008, p.83). Despite the assertion that 'the only possible medical result of cosmetic surgery is harm' (Mantese, et al., 2006), it appears that this truism is only partially translatable into legal terms. Thus, whilst the law recognises that cosmetic surgery can physically harm the patient, where the patient consents to the procedure the intelligibility of this harm is limited to civil law. Turning now to the legal status of cosmetic surgery under criminal law, this legal positioning can be unpacked further.

Cosmetic surgery can involve body alterations such as the cutting of skin, the remoulding and reshaping of cartilage, the breaking of bones, the removal of tissue and the forcing of implants into cavities surgically created within the body. The damage done to the body of the patient undergoing cosmetic surgery varies from procedure to procedure, but healing and recovery time can be lengthy. For example, it is recommended that patients take two weeks off work to rest and abstain from physical exercise for six weeks after receiving a breast lift (Department of Health, 2006, p.38), and the final results from a nose job can take up to 12 months to become apparent because it can take that long to fully heal and resettle (Department of Health, 2006, p.96). Absent any legal excuse or justification, such interference with the body would normally be sufficient to constitute an offence of assault occasioning bodily harm, wounding or grievous bodily harm. However, the legal status of cosmetic surgery is complicated by the fact that these procedures are performed exclusively by health care practitioners, which allows the practitioner to use the medical or surgical treatment defence, and that it is usually consented to by the patient. Clearly, these factors raise very similar legal issues to those considered in relation to MC in Chapter 3, and thus I import into this chapter the general legal framework of cases and statute sections considered there (with the omission of the issue of parental consent which is atypical of cosmetic surgery). Whilst the legal framework may be broadly the same, the application of the law to cosmetic surgery differs from MC in two ways.

Firstly, regarding the medical treatment defence, whilst cosmetic surgery is self-evidently a form of surgical treatment and will usually be carried out in good faith and with reasonable care and skill, it is even more difficult than with MC to determine whether cosmetic surgery could be said to be done for the patient's benefit. Unlike MC, there are no claimed physical benefits (prophylactic or immediate) to the patient from the performance of cosmetic surgery. Conversely, there are well-established potential risks to the patient's health that can arise as complications of cosmetic surgery, for example whenever the skin is cut scarring and hypertrophic scarring can occur, implants can become encapsulated in scar tissue and/or leak, breast reductions can lead to nipple or fat necrosis, some forms of liposuction were linked to numerous deaths in the United States of America during the 1990s, and the use of anaesthetic in cosmetic surgery procedures can cause paralysis or death (Hodgkinson, 1999, pp.6–8). 'Since cosmetic surgery cannot be said to directly improve physical health' advocates of cosmetic surgery tout certain non-physical benefits to the procedures (Heyes, 2009, p.76). Such benefits are typically described as either aesthetic, in that they make the body of the patient more 'beautiful' and thus more socially/sexually valuable, or as psychological, in that they make the patient more confident and/or happy with their appearance. It is questionable whether or not these claimed benefits would be legally recognised as constituting a benefit for the purpose of the medical treatment defence (just like the claimed 'social benefits' of MC in Chapter 3). In cases where cosmetic surgery is used as a means of treating mental disorders such as Body Dysmorphia (Kennedy, 2009, p.214), there is a strong argument that any resulting psychological benefits should be recognised as therapeutic (Karpin, 2008, p.81). However, this is not a scenario that is reflective of the vast majority of cosmetic surgeries. Despite these claimed benefits, Elliott (2009, p.180) still struggles to find any 'therapeutic benefit in much cosmetic surgery'. Even if we do not dismiss these expanded conceptions of benefit as being 'nebulous' (Kennedy, 2009, p.214), Bogdanoski (2009, p.505) is of the opinion that 'the risks and side-effects associated with operating on a person where not otherwise medically indicated may not outweigh the benefits gained from an improved aesthetic outcome'. If non-medical benefits are legally recognisable and do outweigh the risks and side-effects of cosmetic surgery, then health care practitioners may be able to use the reasonable surgical treatment defence. If not, this defence would be inapplicable and in Code jurisdictions, given that consent is not an element of provisions without an assault element (as detailed in Chapter 2), cosmetic surgery that causes wounding or grievous bodily harm is arguably criminal.

Secondly, like MC, cosmetic surgery is not readily identifiable as falling under common law's list of categories in which the consent of the 'victim' absolves the assaulter of criminal liability. Turning back to the seminal consensual assault case of *R v Brown* [1994], although three of the five Law Lords explicitly considered surgery to be an example of a consensual assault context that was lawful, their conclusions differed. Lord Templeman opines that surgery is simply a 'lawful activity', despite involving intentional violence and sometimes serious bodily harm (*R v Brown* [1994], p.231). Lord Mustill similarly states that the consent of the patient or the presence of a medical emergency are important points in deciding that surgeons who carry out 'proper medical treatment … incur no liability' (*R v Brown* [1994], p.266). Lord Jauncey of Tulichettle describes 'reasonable surgery' as a 'well known exception' to the rule that assaults that occasion bodily harm cannot be legally consented to (*R v Brown* [1994], pp.244–245), but elsewhere gives the same endorsement to what he terms 'necessary surgery' (*R v Brown* [1994], p.242). The common law position is thus left muddled. Cosmetic surgery appears to be lawful under Lord Templeman's approach because it is a form of 'surgery'. It could be argued to fall under Lord Mustill's exception for 'proper medical treatment', however, whilst it is carried out predominantly by trained health care practitioners in hospitals and doctors' surgeries, and is therefore 'medical' in nature, it is difficult to identify what, exactly, cosmetic surgery is 'treating'. It is doubtful whether it would be considered 'necessary surgery' under Lord Jauncey of Tulichettle's formulation as there is no medical indication for elective cosmetic surgery. Similarly, it is doubtful whether it would be considered 'reasonable surgery' because the medical risks and non-physical benefits that attach to cosmetic surgery will always, necessarily, outweigh the (non-existent) physical benefits.

Other commentators have looked beyond the specific common law categories and have argued that cosmetic surgery fulfils the general test of public interest/good set out in *R v Brown* [1994]. Baker (2008, pp.36–38) argues that cosmetic surgery should be lawful on this basis because it is not intended to cause harm but rather to bring about long-term benefit, and that cosmetic surgery is usually a one-time thing unlike the sadomasochist who must repeat the harm constantly to gain a repeat of the benefit. Kennedy (2009, pp.213–214) alternatively contends that the claim of psychological benefit, when coupled with liberal rhetoric about autonomy, is sufficient to demonstrate the public benefit of cosmetic surgery. These arguments are speculative at best, so it remains unsettled at common law as to whether the patient's consent to cosmetic surgery is legally effective.

On the basis of the legal framework imported from the previous chapter, and the additional comments made here, it seems that cosmetic surgery might technically constitute a criminal offence in both Code and common law jurisdictions even when performed with the patient's consent. Clearly, this lack of legal clarity is not reflected in how cosmetic surgery is actually practised within Australia, with tens of thousands of procedures being carried out every year by hundreds of doctors. Like MC, cosmetic surgery has a generally accepted legality. As a broad principle, the 'de facto legality of cosmetic procedures is so firmly entrenched that it is almost inconceivable that any challenge on the basis of unnecessary treatment could be mounted or sustained' (Kennedy, 2012, p.353). But whilst the cosmetic surgery industry may lack criminal law oversight, it is still heavily regulated. Kennedy (2009, p.213) identifies that 'the practice of medicine, including cosmetic surgery, is subject to myriad legal and regulatory regimes directed at various aspects of the profession'. In addition to the general statutes and regulations that govern the practice of medicine and surgical procedures, professional accreditation boards (such as the Australian Medical Association), internal hospital/surgery review procedures and medical codes of ethics structure and limit the performance of cosmetic surgery (Karpin, 2008, pp.86–87). As such, the cosmetic surgery industry is primarily self-regulating (Bogdanoski, 2009, p.504). The law is content to regulate cosmetic surgeries through limited civil law means, but, despite technical arguments that such procedures constitute assault offences, it is loath to regulate it through the criminal law.

The rapid expansion of cosmetic surgery to include new types of patients and new types of body alterations has caused some shifts within this legal position. It is no longer the case that there are no 'legislative limits on parental capacity to consent to ordinary cosmetic procedures undertaken by a medical practitioner' on a child (Karpin, 2008, p.90). Responding to concerns that minors were increasingly being subjected to cosmetic surgery, the Queensland Parliament passed the *Health Legislation (Restriction on Use of Cosmetic Surgery for Children and Another Measure) Amendment Act 2008 (Qld)*. This act amended the *Public Health Act 2005* (Qld) and, under s213B, has made it an offence to perform a 'cosmetic procedure' on a child unless the person performing the procedure believes on reasonable grounds that the procedure is in the best interests of the child, having regard to the child's views, the child's parent's views, the physical and mental health of the child and the timing of the procedure. The term 'cosmetic procedure' is defined broadly to cover most typical cosmetic surgery procedures (*Public Health Act 2005* (Qld), s213A), with some omissions such as otoplasty and gastric banding (Cockburn, 2008). Whether or not this statute marks a change in the hands-off criminal law approach to cosmetic surgery is unclear, and depends on whether other Australian jurisdictions follow suit. At the very least it constitutes a partial reassertion of legal authority in this area.

The Legal Status of Body Modification

Even as certain types of body modifications have roots reaching back into ancient history, so do the regulations that govern them. Moses supposedly forbade the cutting of the flesh or printing of any marks on the body in the Bible (*Leviticus* 19:28), and tattooing has historically been banned by ancient Roman and Japanese Emperors (Armstrong, 2005, p.39), as well as the Catholic Church (Falk, 1995, p.100). Whilst there may not be any explicit ban on tattooing in contemporary Australia, what we can glean from this area of law – an area that has been described as 'uncertain' and lacking in cohesion and comprehensiveness (Select Committee on the Tattooing and Body Piercing Industries, 2005, Appendix 8) – is that performing certain other body modifications constitutes a criminal act.

Because body modifications break the skin and cause damage to the body they 'may constitute, prima facie, criminal assault by the artist' (Karpin, 2008, p.83), leading to a number of possible offences including assault occasioning bodily harm, wounding, and even grievous bodily harm. The specific charge they may attract depends on the type of body modification. A simple ear piercing might constitute assault occasioning bodily harm or wounding, whilst scarification or a tongue piercing may arguably be 'serious enough to constitute grievous bodily harm' (Watkins, 1998, p.373). The only available defence to criminal charges stemming from a body modification is that the consent of the recipient absolves the performer of the modification of criminal liability. Conversely, where a body modification is performed without consent it will clearly be a criminal offence.

As in the case of sadomasochism, whether consent can shield a body modifier from criminal liability in Code jurisdictions is questionable as a matter of law, and I import the discussion of this issue from Chapter 2 here. Consent in Code jurisdictions would arguably be irrelevant to charges of wounding (which would encompass basically all body modifications) and grievous bodily harm, and may also be irrelevant to a charge of assault occasioning bodily harm. Whether or not the recipient's consent to body modification is legally effective at common law is an issue that has received very little coverage in both case law and legal commentary. 'The courts in Australia have not yet been asked to rule on the commercial activities of tattooing and piercing' (Karpin, 2008, p.84, footnote omitted) let alone other body modifications such as scarification or branding. There are, however, a few sources to which we can turn. *R v Brown* [1994] once again provides a good starting point. In setting out the contexts in which factual consent is legally effective, both Lord Templeman and Lord Slynn of Hadley specifically listed tattooing and ear-piercing (*R v Brown* [1994] pp.231 and 277). Although this is simply the *obiter dicta* of a minority of the bench, it seems to have been accepted as an accurate statement of the common law (Select Committee on the Tattooing and Body Piercing Industries, 2005, Appendix 8).

Along with *R v Brown* [1994], three further cases help delimit the legal status of body modification under the common law. Firstly, in *R v Oversby* (Unreported, UK Central Criminal Court, Rant J, December 1990), a prominent body piercer and tattooist was charged with numerous counts of causing bodily harm for piercing his clients at his London clinic (Pitts 2003, p.95). The presiding judge, Rant J, held that whilst body piercing for cosmetic and decorative purposes was lawful and could be consented to, body piercing for the purpose of sexual gratification could not be the subject of legally effective consent (Dawkins, 1997, p.156). The piercer subsequently pleaded guilty to piercing his lover's penis and received a fifteen month suspended sentence (Bibbings and Alldridge, 1993, p.361). Given the dubious legal authority of an unreported, single judge case, it would be unwise to make sweeping conclusions about the effect of *R v Oversby* (Unreported, UK Central Criminal Court, Rant J, December 1990) on the law. Dawkins (1997, p.156) goes too far in claiming that as a result 'it is quite unobjectionable at English law to pierce any part of the body, whether above or below the neck, for decorative or cosmetic purposes'. The more cautious approach would be to recognise that body piercings that are sufficiently similar to the ear-piercing exception in *R v Brown* [1994], a far more authoritative decision, should be considered lawful (Watkins, 1998, p.384).

Secondly, in *R v Wilson* [1997] QB 47 (a case also considered in Chapter 2) a wife's consent to being heat-branded on the buttocks by her husband was held to be legally effective as it was for the purpose of decoration. This case adds branding to the lawful categories of tattooing and piercing. However, the underlying legal issue in this case seems to be the cordoning off of 'decorative' body modifications from 'sadomasochistic' body modifications. This case suggests that the purpose for which a body modification is undertaken has a significant impact on its legality; if done for decorative reasons then consent is legally effective, but if done for sadomasochistic pleasure then consent is legally ineffective as the body modification strays into the discursive framework surrounding sadomasochistic injury. In the earlier case of *R v Oversby* (Unreported, UK Central Criminal Court, Rant J, December 1990), Bibbings and Alldridge (1993, p.362, emphasis in original) identified a similar dynamic in play, in relation to which they claimed that '*eroticism makes a difference*' in the legal response to body alteration. However, it is doubtful that this sexual/non-sexual binary at play here is workable as a legal limit. Uden (2001, pp.30–31) tries to argue for the dissimilarity of sadomasochism and body modification by claiming that the injuries inflicted in body modification are merely 'incidental', that pain is minimised, and that the level of bodily interference is strictly worked out between the two parties prior to the procedure. However, she is eventually forced to admit that a 'sexual element is present within the context of body alterations, as some alterations are performed with the intention of improving sexual sensitivity or gratification' (Uden, 2001, p.31). Freckelton (1994, p.51) goes even further, opining that 'in psychoanalytic terms, self-injurious behaviour', here including body modifications like piercing, 'is invariably sexual in nature although not always in its direct expression'. Thus, whilst we can identify a legal focus on identifying the purpose behind body modifications, it seems doubtful that this is of much use.[2]

Thirdly, in *R v Adesanya* (Unreported, UK Central Criminal Court, King-Hamilton J, 16 July 1974) scarification was considered by the London Central Criminal Court when a 32-year-old woman was charged with assault occasioning bodily harm. The presiding judge, King-Hamilton J, ruled that scarification

2 Indeed, supposedly 'sadomasochistic' undertones can be easily located in many body alterations. Some commentators have identified what they see as an erotic element in cosmetic surgery, where the (almost invariably) male surgeon operates on the (statistically overwhelmingly) female patient, literally penetrating her body with medical instruments (Braun, 2009, p.176).

should be distinguished from the 'accepted practices of ear-piercing and ritual circumcision' on the basis of the possibility it held for serious injury, and was thus criminal (Law Commission, 1995, p.124). The applicability of this authority today is dubious because it has been overtaken by *R v Brown* [1994], which has since become the leading authority in consensual assault law, and because of additional legal considerations raised by the factual matrix that complicated the court's consideration of the legality of scarification. The scarification that was judicially considered in this case was performed by a mother on the cheeks of her two underage children in accordance with traditional Nigerian custom (*The Times*, 16 July 1974, p.3), raising a host of additional legal issues such as the ability of minors to give consent and the accommodation of 'foreign' customs within English law (Poulter, 1975). Given these complications, this case at best provides the mere persuasive suggestion that scarification will not be a body modification that can be legally consented to. Accordingly, the Law Commission (1995, p.119) has placed scarification into a 'grey area' of indeterminable legal status.[3]

Whilst these cases may help delimit the legal status of some types of body modifications, other modifications, such as tongue-splitting, have not been specifically addressed by the law. In determining whether consent to these body alterations is legally effective, Watkins (1998) offers a guide drawn from the factors considered in *R v Brown* [1994]. She notes that body modifications that are similar in nature and 'widespread social acceptance' to the category of tattooing and body piercing would be lawful, whereas body modifications that are dissimilar would likely be criminal (Watkins, 1998, p.384). Under this test, body piercing would be categorised as lawful as it is similar to ear-piercing, but

---

3 Whilst the New Zealand common law relating to consensual assault broke with the English and Australian tradition in *R v Lee* [2006] 3 NZLR 42 and thus has limited relevance, scarification was addressed in *R v Barker* [2009] NZCA 186. In *R v Barker* [2010] 1 NZLR 235 (p.249) Glazebrook J reflected that:

> It cannot be open to this Court to introduce into our law a general prohibition against scarification and its related activities of piercing, branding and tattooing. The Crown does not suggest that we should. Scarification can serve a variety of functions in different cultures. For instance, in some cultures, it may be used as a rite of passage in adolescence or to mark particular emotional states. It can have deep spiritual significance. Scarification may also operate as an 'identifier' in some instances. Many young people today adopt facial or body ornamentation, sometimes associated with scarring. The short point for present purposes is that in many societies, practices associated with, or similar to, scarification are an exercise of personal or tribal autonomy and have social utility.

splitting, implants, scarification, and other modifications seen as more 'extreme', would be unlawful because they are dissimilar.

Similarly to recent cosmetic surgery legislation, statute law has also been enacted to restrict the practice of body modifications on minors, though the level of restriction varies from jurisdiction to jurisdiction in a haphazard way. For example, whilst it is a statutory offence to tattoo a minor, even with their consent, in Queensland (*Summary Offences Act 2005* (Qld) s19(1)), Victoria (*Summary Offences Act 1966* (Vic) s42(1)), Tasmania (*Police Offences Act 1935* (Tas) s35A(3)), and South Australia (*Summary Offences Act 1953* (SA) s21C(1)), tattooing can lawfully be performed on a minor as long as parental consent is obtained in Western Australia (*Children and Community Services Act 2004* (WA) s103), New South Wales (*Children and Young Persons (Care and Protection) Act 1998* (NSW) s230(2)), and the Australian Capital Territory (*Children and Young People Act 2008* (ACT) s87(1)). Body piercing of a minor cannot lawfully be performed except with the consent of a parent in New South Wales (*Children and Young Persons (Care and Protection) Act 1998* (NSW) s230A(4)), Victoria (*Summary Offences Act 1966* (Vic) s44A(2)), and Western Australia (*Children and Community Services Act 2004* (WA) s104A(4)). It is an offence regardless of consent to pierce the intimate areas of a minor, understood as the genitalia and nipples in New South Wales and Queensland (*Children and Young Persons (Care and Protection) Act 1998* (NSW) s230A(2); *Summary Offences Act 2005* (Qld) s18(1)), as well as the perineum in Victoria and Western Australia (*Summary Offences Act 1966* (Vic) s44(2); *Children and Community Services Act 2004* (WA) s104A(2)), and also the uvula in South Australia (*Summary Offences Act 1953* (SA) ss21A and 21C(2)) and Tasmania (*Police Offences Act 1935* (Tas) ss35A(1) and 35A(4)(a)).[4]

Very little statutory regard has been paid to other types of body modification, an issue brought to the forefront in 2008 when the NSW Parliament enacted new laws to close what was seen as a 'loophole' in the legislation that prohibited the tattooing of minors but seemed to allow their scarification, beading and branding (Australian Associated Press 2008). Arguably, however, these processes were already illegal under the coupling of existing assault laws and the common law relating to consensual assault. As a result of this legislation, it is an offence in NSW to make any permanent mark on the skin of a minor, including scarification, beading and branding, without first obtaining parental consent (*Children and Young Persons (Care and Protection) Act 1998* (NSW) ss230(1)-(2)). In other jurisdictions, branding a minor is an offence unless parental consent is obtained in Western Australia (*Children and Community Services Act 2004* (WA) s103), and performing beading, branding, scarification or tongue splitting on a minor is an offence regardless of consent in Victoria (*Summary Offences Act 1966*

4 In layman's terms, the 'uvula' is the dangly piece of bodily tissue at the back of your throat.

(Vic) ss42(1) and 42(1AA)). In South Australia and Tasmania it is unlawful to perform a 'body modification procedure' on a minor or an intoxicated person, where 'body modification procedure' is statutorily defined to cover branding, subdermal implantation, earlobe stretching, tongue splitting, scarification and any other procedure prescribed in the relevant regulations (*Summary Offences Act* 1953 (SA) ss21A, 21B(1) and s21C(1); *Police Offences Act 1935* (Tas) ss35A(1) and 35A(3)). Whilst this legislative muddle cannot be taken as demonstrating a co-ordinated legal response to the recent rise in popularity of body modifications across the various Australian jurisdictions, it does demonstrate a general tendency to use the criminal law to regulate body modification.

Like cosmetic surgery, body modifications are also subject to a system of civil regulation (see Karpin, 2008, pp.85–87). This includes safety-based statutes and guidelines that govern the hygiene and general conditions of establishments for which the ordinary course of business involves the penetration of the skin (and hence carry the risk of spreading blood-borne pathogens). The exact content of these regulations differs from jurisdiction to jurisdiction. In Western Australia, for example, the *Health (Skin Penetration Procedure) Regulations* 1998 (adopted under the *Health Act 1911* (WA), ss344A(2) and 344A(3)) make it a statutory offence for a body modification artist to fail to comply with the *Skin Penetration Code of Practice*, which puts in place detailed requirements about *inter alia* the sterilisation of instruments, the level of lighting, the handling of tattoo ink, and the material composition of body piercing jewellery. Unlike cosmetic surgery, however, the civil law forms only part of the framework of legal regulation around body modification.

The Internal Discursive Boundaries

This section charts and accounts for the internal discursive boundaries that are constructed within the categories of cosmetic surgery and body modification. Specifically, the focus is on the discursive distinctions that separate out 'acceptable' or 'appropriate' forms of these body alterations from 'unacceptable' or 'inappropriate' forms. This section demonstrates that the conceptualisations about the body that underlie these discursive boundaries are informed by normative standards of bodily appearance and devalue alternative models of embodiment. These discursive boundaries mobilise the criminal law in specific ways so that the law prohibits breaches of normative appearance standards when achieved through body modification but not through cosmetic surgery. Unpacking and explicating the distinctions made between 'the legal, the questionable, and the illegal' here (Bibbings and Alldridge, 1993, p.356), reveals how the disparate legal statuses of cosmetic surgery and body modification are inflected by the broader system of social signification.

Cosmetic Surgery 'Successes' and 'Failures'

Given the strong discursive connections between cosmetic surgery and celebrity (Haiken, 1997; Pitts-Taylor, 2007), it is little wonder that the media is especially active in constructing and policing the internal conceptual boundaries of cosmetic surgery. With the rise of academic interest and coverage of cosmetic surgery, it would be trite to revisit such a well-worked area in any detail. Nevertheless, it should be noted that a lucrative section of the media industry has developed around identifying whether celebrities have undergone cosmetic surgery and publicly excoriating those results that do not meet the standard of 'acceptable' cosmetic surgery. These media attacks against celebrity targets – common targets have historically included Michael Jackson, Jocelyn Wildenstein, and Pamela Anderson – serve to reinforce a more general discursive understanding that constructs the internal conceptual boundaries of cosmetic surgery by negotiating the definition of what constitutes a cosmetic surgery 'failure' or 'disaster'. From the media attack pattern, we can discern that a successful, acceptable cosmetic surgery is that which is age-appropriate, correctly presents sex/gender (usually female/femininity), and embraces a normative aesthetic (Jones, 2008b, p.115). Conversely, a cosmetic surgery procedure that departs from any one or more of these criteria is capable of literally turning the patient into a 'monstrosity', one who becomes 'repulsed' and 'detestable' (Jones, 2008b, p.115). Jocelyn Wildenstein is typically used as an example of this. She has had multiple facelifts, facial collagen injections and eye surgery apparently in order to look more like a cat, and has been lambasted as one of cosmetic surgeries' 'junkies and fools' (Pitts-Taylor, 2009, p.124).

The distinction between successful/acceptable cosmetic surgery and unsuccessful/unacceptable cosmetic surgery seems to turn on two key factors: 'naturalness' and normalisation. Cosmetic surgery 'tries to hide its traces' (Strauss, 1989, p.158), and for a result to be 'natural' it should ideally be almost undetectable that a patient underwent surgery at all. Scar tissue growth should be minimal and confined to areas usually hidden from view (the hairline, under clothing, and so on), implants should be scaled proportionately to the patient's body size, and other possible tell-tale signs should be avoided, for example, facelifts should not be too tight lest they leave the patient with 'a "zombie" look … devoid of expression' (Gimlin, 2002, p.77). For a cosmetic surgery procedure to be normalised, it should accord with contemporary attitudes about what constitutes a socially valued, or at least accepted, body. For example, because of the Western sex/gender coding of breast size, breast augmentation is positioned as an inappropriate procedure for a male to undergo, whereas conversely, breast reduction surgery is positioned as appropriate if a male does develop breast tissue. There is little distinction between 'naturalness' and normalisation, as the 'natural-look' is normalised within Western society (Fraser, 2003a, p.71).[5]

Acceptable, successful cosmetic surgery is a body alteration that normalises appearance (Bordo, 1993, pp.25–26), enabling bodies that were previously marked as non-normative or aberrant to 'pass' as normative, or shifting already normative bodies into more socially valued categories (Gilman, 1999). For the breasted man, the un-breasted woman, the large-nosed, and the small-chinned, acceptable cosmetic surgery takes the alternatively-embodied and shapes them so that their flesh more closely resembles the standard or the ideal, and not a negative deviation. Conversely, unacceptable cosmetic surgery creates such deviations by shaping patients into alternative embodiment forms such as the gargantuan-breasted female, the zombie-faced, the heavily-scarred, and the octogenarian without wrinkles. Thus, the internal boundaries within cosmetic surgery are dependent upon normalised concepts of bodily appearance; acceptable, successful procedures are conceptualised as those that shift the patient's body closer towards the normative ideal, whilst unacceptable, unsuccessful procedures are conceptualised as those that shift the patient's body further away.

Mainstream and Non-Mainstream Body Modification

The internal boundary-drawing within body modification is based less on the results of the modification and more on the type of modification. A distinction typically drawn by commentators identifies two categories of body modification: 'mainstream' body modification and 'non-mainstream' body modification. Uden (2001) and Watkins (1998) both support this classificatory schema, locating ear-piercing and tattooing as falling within mainstream body modification, and all other forms of body modification as falling within non-mainstream body modification. Uden (2001, pp.6–8) justifies this distinction on the basis that the growing acceptance of tattooing and ear-piercing has made them socially 'legitimate form[s] of altering one's appearance'. Bibbings (1996, pp.180–181) supports the distinction between mainstream and non-mainstream body modifications on the basis of social acceptance, but appears to be somewhat reluctant to allocate tattooing and body piercing to the mainstream category because at the time of writing they had only recently gained more widespread popularity.

5 Heyes & Jones (2009, p.6) have observed that, recently, some young people are deliberately undergoing cosmetic surgery procedures in order to achieve physical results that clearly appear to be medically manufactured, that is 'fake' or 'unnatural', as a form of conspicuous consumption and status-seeking. Whether this trend will gain traction remains to be seen.

The accuracy of a conceptual division based on these notions of general acceptance and social legitimacy is questionable due to the lack of any clear supporting empirical evidence. Although certain types of body modifications such as ear piercings have undoubtedly achieved 'social acceptance', it is unlikely that other types of body modification, such as extensive facial or genital piercing, have achieved much (if any) social acceptance in Western society. The value of this boundary comes not in its practical use in strictly categorising different types of body modifications, but more in its signification that some body modifications are discursively constructed as socially unacceptable whilst others have come to fall within a range of 'tolerable deviance' from the norm (Atkinson, 2003). Whilst visible body modifications have historically been conceptualised within modern Western society as 'signs of deviance, marginality and perversion' (Strauss 1989, p.158), such stigma is increasingly detached from less 'extreme' forms of tattooing and piercing. This has occurred to such an extent that, as Fenske (2007, p.1) points out, '[e]ven Barbie has had a tattoo'.[6]

When a body modifier alters their body via tattooing or piercing, they are no longer automatically read as positioning themselves as a cultural 'outsider' or social 'deviant', but rather as enacting a form of appearance that might deviate from the norm but is not constructed with the same transgressive edge that it has held previously. Whatever the shift in cultural attitudes around tattooing and piercing, the social stigma remains linked to other types of body modifications, so that 'scarifications and brandings can [still] create horror and revulsion' (Pitts, 2003, p.34). Thus, tattooing and piercing create bodies that fall within a tolerable deviation of the norm, but other body modifications create bodies that are transgressively non-normative. Branded, scarred and implanted bodies are still conceptualised as transgressive forms of embodiment that differ from and challenge the standard. The nomenclature that labels this boundary-drawing within body modification is therefore apt. 'Non-mainstream' body modifications are socially unacceptable because they depart from and challenge normative standards of bodily appearance, whereas 'mainstream' body modifications are socially acceptable because they fall within a tolerable deviation of these standards.

This internal boundary-drawing within the conceptualisation of body modification matches the regulatory boundary-drawing of the criminal law. 'Mainstream' body modifications, such as tattooing and most types of piercing, maintain a generally accepted lawful status, whereas 'non-mainstream' body modifications, such as branding and scarification, are more likely to hold a quasi-legal or criminal status. The criminal law reinforces normative standards

6 However, the very fact that Barbie having a tattoo is noticeable and judged worthy of comment demonstrates that the non-tattooed body remains strongly embedded as the naturalised ideal.

of appearance by differentially regulating those body modifications that transgress these standards. However, it does not operate in the same way with regard to cosmetic surgery. Those cosmetic surgery 'failures' that lead to normative appearance-trangressing results retain the same lawful status as 'successful' cosmetic surgery. As Bogdanoski (2009, p.507) notes: 'there is no law that seeks to prevent people from having further cosmetic surgeries, even after such surgery has altered their bodies and faces beyond what is socially and culturally desirable'. If the internal discursive boundaries that separate out 'successful'/'mainstream' forms of cosmetic surgery and body modification from 'failure'/'nonmainstream' forms can be seen to be informed by a common reliance on normative standards of appearance, their differential criminal regulation is a notable disparity.

The Differential Legal Regulation of Cosmetic Surgery 'Failures' and Non-Mainstream Body Modification

Karpin (2008) has argued strongly that the twin conceptions of naturalness and normalisation are key legitimising aspects of the discourse that attach to cosmetic surgery but that do not attach to body modifications, and that this conceptual disparity explains the legal non-regulation of cosmetic surgery compared to the legal regulation of body modification. On her account of body altering practices, '[b]ecoming "normal" is valorized and encouraged' by a lack of regulation and the law is only 'motivated to act ... where non-normative body modification practices are involved' (Karpin, 2008, p.92). However, if the criminal law is mobilised by discursive divisions drawn from normative standards of bodily appearance, then why are all cosmetic surgery procedures, including those 'failures' that produce non-normative appearances, lawful? Why, as Bogdanoski (2009, pp.509–510) recognises, when 'cosmetic surgery itself can be transgressively used to go beyond socio-culturally accepted norms', is it legally the case that 'people are still free to have as much or little of it as they like'? Whilst Karpin (2008) is undoubtedly correct to point to naturalness and normalisation as important discursive factors at work in this area, more remains to be unpacked. Here I more fully account for and explain this discrepancy by reference to the cultural location of cosmetic surgery and body modification within the broader discursive framework. In particular, focus will be placed on two additional factors: the social positioning throughout time of cosmetic surgery and body modification as cultural phenomena, and the extent to which these body alterations are complicit with other key discursive frameworks such as those around sex/gender.

Social il/legitimacy

The historical development of cosmetic surgery under the aegis of medicine, and medicine's discursive connections to science, truth and health, informs its valued sociolegal position today. Conversely, the historical connection between body modification and crime, deviance, subculture and the lower class, informs its devalued sociolegal position today. This section will not provide an exhaustive historical account of these body alterations within Western society, but will simply offer links to the historical development of their social status in order to explicate their current discursive positioning and legal status.

The historical development of cosmetic surgery into a multibillion dollar industry has been briefly mentioned in the section above and this material will not be repeated here. It should be added to the previous overview that cosmetic surgery has not always enjoyed the widespread social acceptance it seems to have garnered during the 1990s and 2000s. Historically, cosmetic surgeons have had to fight 'long and hard to shed the pejorative label of "beauty doctor"' and the connotation that cosmetic surgery wasn't really medicine but just a form of indulgence' (Haiken, 2000, p.88). Previously, it was seen as 'the domain of the sleazy, the suspicious, the secretly deviant or the pathologically narcissistic' (Morgan, 2002, p.346), with patients going to lengths to hide their cosmetically altered status lest they be viewed as overly vain or frivolous. This opprobrium is still somewhat evident today in the denial by celebrities of self-evident cosmetic surgery results, and the push to pathologise body image concerns under diagnoses such as Body Dysmorphic Disorder (Cornwall, 2000). However, the single most important legitimating factor that has remained constant throughout cosmetic surgery's historical development is its discursive location within medicine.

Cosmetic surgery procedures are unlike other medical procedures because, by definition, they have no physical therapeutic value. Historically, cosmetic surgery has been justified on the basis that it does provide some kind of health benefit to the patient in the form of improved mental health (Pitts-Taylor, 2007, p.115), such as through increased confidence and freedom from anxiety about appearance, but it remains a medical area that contradictorily specialises in surgeries that are medically unwarranted. The uniqueness of the cosmetic surgery industry within the field of medicine is also demonstrated by its relatively excessive commercialisation. Cosmetic surgery 'is the one area of medicine that makes widespread use of the term *client* rather than *patient*' (Gilman, 1999, p.5, emphasis in original), reflecting its status as almost a 'wholly separate market' from traditional medicine (Mantese, et al., 2006, p.27). Cosmetic surgeons play a role more akin to a 'service provider' than a health care practitioner (Heyes and Jones, 2009, p.6), with 'clients' seeking cosmetic surgery on an 'on demand' basis for treatment of an often self-diagnosed issue (Bogdanoski, 2009, p.509). The rightness or wrongness of classifying cosmetic surgery as a type of medicine aside, this classification has significant ramifications for the ways in which cosmetic surgery is discursively positioned.

Cosmetic surgery's status as a form of medicine gives it a cultural legitimacy that body modification lacks. Built into the discursive construction of medicine within Western culture are strong, positive associations with concepts such as science, truth, healing and non-maleficence. The medical industry is a self-authenticating and self-authorising network that bases its claim to objectivity on internal systems of training, licensing, reporting and research. The enmeshment of cosmetic surgery within medical discourse imports the *gravitas* of the entire medical system into every cosmetic surgery procedure, providing it with social and discursive legitimacy. This grants the cosmetic surgeon a certain high level of status, as the patient who submits themselves for surgery is actually submitting to 'someone whose authority derives from the state – someone who represents modernity, technology, and the achievements of the West' (Rosenblatt, 1997, p.321). The cosmetic surgeon breaks social taboos by inducing pain, handling the bodies of others, and working with blood and bodily fluids, but is 'insulated from the stigma of unclean work by a medical degree' (Sanders, 2008, p.92). Not only is the surgeon protected from social stigma, their location within 'medicine' also seems to function as a legal shield that protects them, unlike the body modification artist, from criminal prosecution (Bibbings and Alldridge, 1993, p.361). Ironically, the level of bodily damage the surgeon inflicts on the patient in procedures like a breast augmentation 'would be considered savage if … carried out at a body modification convention' (Jeffreys, 2005a, p.49), because 'the alterations undertaken are of a far more invasive nature than "non-mainstream" body modifications' (Watkins, 1998, p.380).

The historical development of cosmetic surgery as a form of medicine plays a significant role in how it is regulated by the criminal law today. The high social value assigned to medicine, and the high social status assigned to medical personnel, inflects how cosmetic surgery is dealt with by dominant social institutions. It is especially telling that the criminal law legalises cosmetic surgery procedures to the extent that 'they are performed by a qualified medical practitioner' (Bibbings, 1996, pp.184–185), but such legal protection is not extended to unqualified lay people even if performing identical surgical procedures. Legal discourse seems to respect medicine's system of internal regulation, and demonstrates this by failing to implement a system of criminal regulation governing the practice of cosmetic surgery.

The way in which the law here colludes with medicine by failing to regulate cosmetic surgery demonstrates the discursive effect of medicalisation that underpinned the anxiety about the AAP's 'compromise' discussed in Chapter 3. The anti-FGM backlash against the suggestion that doctors perform a 'ritual nick' was a manifestation of the concern that if any form of FGM becomes medicalised then this would provide an impregnable discursive defence, bolstered by medicine's social authority, to any subsequent challenge. As with FGM, some feminist commentators have identified cosmetic surgery as being a form of physical violence against women and have argued against it on this basis. However, cosmetic surgery's lawful legal status has proven immune to this line of critique. This immunity is at least partly attributable to the innoculatory effect of cosmetic surgery being socially authorised in the West because it falls within the aegis of medicine.

Conversely, the historical development of body modification as a marginal cultural practice discursively interlinked with conceptions of criminality and deviance predicates its current social illegitimacy and illegality. There is little value in canvassing the ancient roots of body modification here, but even within the last few hundred years body modification has been used as a form of punitive measure, with convicted criminals being branded or tattooed with letters or symbols that (typically) indicated the nature of their crime (Caplan, 2000). This practice, coupled with the voluntary adoption of these stigmatising marks by criminal subcultures themselves, such as the Yakuza in Japan and Russian gang members, can perhaps be partly identified as causative of the modern discursive connection between body modification and criminality. Early criminologists read the presence of tattoos as an indicator that the bearer was criminally-inclined. Lombroso saw tattoos as a literal mark of the criminal's atavistic nature, arguing that the presence of a tattoo 'often reveals obscenity, vindictiveness, cupidity, and other characteristics of the patient' (Ferrero, 1911, p.232). Loos went further, noting that: '[t]hose who are tattooed but are not imprisoned are latent criminals. … If a tattooed person dies at liberty, it is only that he died a few years before he committed a murder' (Loos, 1908, cited in Sullivan, 2009a, p.130). This connection has persisted across time. As late as 1968, *The Journal of Criminal Law, Criminology and Police* published an article alleging that there is 'almost a causal link between tattoos and criminal behaviour' (Post, 1968, p.522).

The concerns of these criminologists are not mere historical idiosyncracies, but are reflective of a wider contemporaneous discursive construction of body modification as a form of socially deviant practice related to 'antisocial behavior' (Putnins, 2002, p.62). Durkin and Houghton's (2000) study of Western Australian children aged six to mid-adolescence found that they held negative perceptions of people with tattoos relative to people without tattoos. This 'deviant' status of body modification is based not just on its supposed links to criminality but also with subcultural affiliation. Homosexual, sadomasochistic and punk subcultures have all historically made wide use of body modifications, marking these body alterations with the social taint of 'disaffection' and 'rebellion' (Pitts, 2003, p.5). This construction is, of course, self-sustaining, as when body modification is discursively presented as a method of distancing oneself from mainstream social values, those wishing to so distance themselves may resort to body modification for that purpose. For example, Modern Primitivism is an American subcultural movement that originated around San Francisco in the 1980s, whose central belief seems to be a rejection of the 'inauthentic' modern Western society in favour of a return to more spiritual, 'authentic' personal space which is to be achieved, at least partly, through body modification (Vale and Juno, 1989).

With the mainstreaming and de-deviantisation of certain forms of tattooing and body piercing since the early 1990s, newer, more 'extreme' body modifications have been required by body modification recipients in order to stand out from the norm (Sanders, 2008). The rise in non-mainstream modifications such as scarification, branding and implantation can be partly explained by this escalation phenomenon. It is important to note that the mainstreaming of tattooing and body piercing is closely associated with a rise in class status of those same practices. Sanders (2008) addresses this issue excellently and at length, documenting the shift in tattoo recipients from predominantly lower-class males to increasingly include middle-class males and females. However, the discursive associations of non-mainstream body modification still reflect a range of socially devalued conceptions: subculture, sexual perversion, criminality, and the lower class. As a result, the body modification industry, unlike the cosmetic surgery industry, is associated with low social status and low social value. Body modifiers, unlike cosmetic surgeons, are not insulated by any recognised qualification, specialised training or dominant social institution from the social taboos that they break by engaging in 'unclean work' (Sanders, 2008, p.92). Body modification's discursive positioning as a socially devalued practice with associations to criminality and deviance inflects its regulation by the criminal law.

Normative and Non-Normative

The current manner in which cosmetic surgery procedures are performed demonstrates a collusive link between cosmetic surgery and the normative discursive structures that frame social life. Contrastingly, body modifications are constructed as oppositional practices that challenge and undermine key conceptions within these discursive structures. Both cosmetic surgery's collusion with the social order and body modification's challenge to it inflect their legal treatment. This section will explore how cosmetic surgery and body modification link to social norms through an exploration of how they negotiate sex/gender.

Before beginning to draw connections between cosmetic surgery, body modification and the wider cultural and discursive terrain, it is important to be mindful of the possible objection that generalised analyses of 'cosmetic surgery' and 'body modification' can omit or obfuscate differences between a whole range of procedures whose individual meanings and political import might vary significantly. Cadwallader (2007, p.382) specifies that whilst 'the variety of cosmetic procedures hang together discursively, each kind of cosmetic surgery functions differently in relation to norms of beauty'. The same point can be made with regard to body modification. While this position seems self-evidently right-minded, it also seems somewhat limited. To play this proposition through to its logical end, should we hold that not only each *kind* of cosmetic surgery but each *individual* cosmetic surgery procedure on each patient functions differently? Should we go so far as to say that even 'no two piercings can be identical'? (Vale and Juno, 1989, p.5). This more individualistic sentiment finds support in Jones' (2008a) analysis of Lolo Ferrari's massively augmented breasts, which she argues, in contrast to feminist writing generally on breast augmentation procedures, subvert rather than support the mainstream aesthetics of the female body. Similarly, Atkinson's (2002) analysis of female tattooing dismisses the simplistic notion that all tattooed women challenge traditional sex/gender stereotypes, arguing that some women, by getting 'feminine' tattoos (those with a certain image, size and placement, such as a small dolphin on the upper back), are actually supporting dominant cultural models of femininity. Whilst there is value in this pluralistic kind of theoretical position and the range of meanings that it can raise against the typically generalising gloss of cosmetic surgery and body modification analyses, it cannot be adopted here for practical reasons. As this book comprises an analytical exploration of the broad positioning of cosmetic surgery and body modification within discourse, it must by necessity deal with abstract generalisations. However, by flagging this issue here I hope to mitigate the erasure of individual meanings that will result from this.

As a general proposition, cosmetic surgeries replicate dominant cultural norms about sex/gender, which, conversely, body modifications challenge and undermine. Clearly, 'women are the primary targets of cosmetic surgery' (Davis, 2002, pp.49–50). Statistically, approximately 91 per cent of all cosmetic surgeries being performed on women (American Society of Plastic Surgeons, 2009), and the vast majority of academic commentary deals almost exclusively with female cosmetic surgery (Fraser, 2003a, p.182).[7] Despite their increasing popularity amongst men, this section will only address how cosmetic surgery negotiates femininity because that is the predominant aspect of the 'gendered context in which cosmetic procedures originated and became popularized' (Braun, 2005, p.420). The overwhelming prevalence of female subjects willing to undergo surgery to alter their bodies speaks to the pervasive cultural norms of beauty that construct the value of the female as a function of her appearance. In an imaginary culture in which the physical appearance of females was not

7 There is evidence that male patients are becoming more common, and some commentators are reorienting their focus to account for this change (Davis, 2002).

emphasised as a factor in their sociocultural value over and above other personal characteristics, this extreme statistical disparity would presumably not exist.

Predictably, cosmetic surgery has proven a fruitful topic for many different kinds of feminist commentators, who have typically argued that not only is cosmetic surgery a method of achieving a culturally appropriate female body but that it also operates 'pedagogically, training women about which aesthetics and attitudes are acceptable and which are not' (Pitts-Taylor, 2009, p.125). The acceptable aesthetic within cosmetic surgery is limited in scope. As a dominant cultural force, the heterosexual male gaze impacts on the types of cosmetic surgery procedures that are carried out. The fact that breast augmentation was the most popular cosmetic surgical procedure carried out in America in 2008 (American Society of Plastic Surgeons, 2009) and the ongoing rise of female genital cosmetic surgery as a cosmetic surgery trend aptly demonstrate the predominant function of cosmetic surgery as a method of producing female bodies that correspond to dominant notions about sexual desirability, as well as reifying this dominant notion itself on the bodies of the patients.

But perhaps the most telling factor that reveals the deep collusion between cosmetic surgery and dominant cultural notions of femininity is not what types of cosmetic surgery procedures are commonly performed, but what possible types of cosmetic surgery procedures are not performed. As Morgan (2002, p.353) insightful reminds us: '[w]hile the technology of cosmetic surgery could clearly be used to create and celebrate idiosyncrasy, eccentricity, and uniqueness, it is obvious that this is not how it is presently being used'. Instead, Morgan (2002, p.364, emphasis in original) imagines a female revolt against dominant beauty norms in the form of:

> [P]ublic participation in Ms. Ugly Canada/America/Universe/Cosmos pageants *and the use of the technology of cosmetic surgery to do so* ... [including b]leaching one's hair white and applying wrinkle-inducing 'wrinkle creams', having one's face and breasts surgically pulled down (rather than lifted), and having wrinkles sewn and carved into one's skin.

By drawing attention to how cosmetic surgery could be used and how it is not being used, in this passage Morgan (2002) deftly highlights the contingent nature of how cosmetic surgery is actually being used. Cosmetic surgery typically operates as a process of 'normalization' and '[m]edical practitioners typically do not perform ... radical cosmetic alterations' that do not accord with cultural ideals of appearance (Karpin, 2008, p.79). There are 'clear limits placed upon what kinds of surgery are available' (Fraser, 2003a, p.71), and these limits work across sex/gender grounds to produce female bodies that correspond to dominant conceptions of appropriately sexed/gendered appearance. Every procedure, then, that (invariably) produces a female body closer to the ideal of 'Ms America' and not 'Ms Ugly America', is a capitulation to the broader discursive framework of sex/gender within which cosmetic surgery is deeply entrenched.

Body modification, on the other hand, is discursively positioned as a culturally oppositional practice that challenges dominant cultural notions such as sex/gender. Body modification is not as explicitly sexed/gendered as cosmetic surgery. Both males and females can and do undergo almost the entire range of body modifications (barring those which rely on sex-specific anatomy, such as clitoral hood and scrotum piercings – though these are discursively and physiologically connected as genital piercings).

Body modifications problematise the dominant cultural conception of heterosexual masculinity and the heterosexual male body as active and impenetrable. If we think about the physical process involved in a body piercing, the male recipient passively awaits the active penetration of his flesh by a body modification artist, who is statistically more likely to also be male, before having first a needle and then jewellery inserted into his body, creating a permanent hole/receptacle. This sexualised description draws on the cultural conception of orifices and cuts in the body as 'erotogenic' zones, which body modification multiplies and extends to the male body (Grosz, 1994, p.139). The male recipient of body modification challenges dominant conceptions about masculinity; he is passive, he is penetrated, and he has erotogenic orifices in his body. Davis (2002) identifies similar anxieties and taboos around dominant cultural norms of masculinity as a factor in the relatively low proportion of male cosmetic surgery patients, but this disproportionality of procedures by sex/gender is abridged within body modification. Makkai and McAllister's (2001) Australian study of tattooing and body piercing found that more men (11.9 per cent) than women (8.5 per cent) had had a tattoo at some point in their lives, and that roughly the same proportion of men (6.5 per cent) and women (7.0 per cent) had had a part of their body other than their ears pierced at some point in their lives. Obviously, with the mainstreaming of some forms of tattooing and piercing, the transgressive nature of these body alterations decreases as the social conception of masculinity stretches to encompass some forms of penetrability. However, undergoing those non-mainstream body modifications involving deeper, or more frequent, penetration and the creation of wider, or more numerous, erotogenic orifices, will remain normative violations.

Female body modifications also challenge dominant cultural conceptions about femininity. Even if we accept Atkinson's (2002) dismissal of some forms of tattooing as collusive with normative conceptions of femininity, and even if we omit any transgressive potential that may be identified in the ubiquitous practice of female ear-piercing, it is self-evident that a heavily tattooed, heavily body-pierced, scarred and/or branded female body runs counter to dominant conceptions about female appearance. This kind of female body is 'profane', as it functions to 'disrupt entrenched cultural images of the beautiful female body' (Atkinson, 2002, p.227). The mere presence of these modifications might transgress female appearance norms, but it is the active decision to choose to become so modified that is most transgressive, as it communicates a conscious decision by the female to distance herself from these norms. Such modifications make 'a bold statement' that 'flies in the face' of 'the "proper" or "normal" construction of the [female] body' (Lentini, 1999, p.34). Similarly to male body modification, the mainstreaming of some body modifications lessens the transgressive potential of the modified female body. However, the more 'extreme' forms of body modification are arguably still sufficient to shift the modified female body out of the normative appearance range.

My decision to explore sex/gender as an example of how cosmetic surgery and body modification negotiate dominant discursive frameworks is based on the existence of extensive feminist engagement with this issue in relation to the cosmetic surgery side of the topic. Arguably, however, the same kinds of conclusions would be reached by using other examples as the analytical foci. Another key discursive framework that I could have chosen to engage with in detail is race. In the same way that sex/gender stereotypes place pressure on women to undergo cosmetic surgeries to bring their bodies into line with cultural standards about appropriate sexed/gendered appearance, so too it has been noted that 'racial stereotypes can coerce a person into seeking cosmetic surgery they would not otherwise feel the need to have' (Bogdanoski, 2009, p.505). Cosmetic surgery typically shifts the patient's body closer towards the dominant cultural ideal of white, Eurocentric appearance (Jones, 2008b, p.33; Kinnun, 2008, p.44), for example through the use of blepharoplasty to increase the visible appearance of 'Asian' eyes or rhinoplasty to reduce the size of 'Jewish' noses (Bogdanoski, 2009, p.505). Body modification typically shifts the recipient's body further away from this ideal, for example the Modern Primitives consciously draw on exoticised body modification practices associated with non-Western, 'traditional' societies that are deviantised as the primitive Other (Fenske, 2007). The collusive links between cosmetic surgery and other discursive frameworks, like sex/gender and race, render every cosmetic surgery procedure an act of 'embodied cultural submission' (Atkinson, 2008, p.78), a form of obeisance to normative ideals. The cosmetic surgery industry is a manufacturer and reifier of normativity that 'tolerates corrections of "unnatural" disorderly bodies, but not challenges to our conception of bodily order' (Weiss and Kukla, 2009, p.128). In contrast, body modifications, particularly non-mainstream modifications, 'are explicitly antisocial'; they are body alterations that mark their recipients 'in accordance with their owners' self-image' (DeMello, 2007, p.xix), or the image of a subculture, rather than in accordance with the normative ideals generated by dominant conceptions of sex/gender and race. Body modification is conceptualised as a conscious rejection of the 'tyranny of habitus formation' and a method of gaining individual 'control over one's body' (Featherstone, 2000, p.3).

Unlike cosmetic surgery's model of cultural submission, body modification is conceptualised as an oppositional practice that challenges and undermines the established norms generated by discursive frameworks (Benson, 2000, p.242). This distinction in cultural status is reflected in the differential regulation of cosmetic surgery and body modification by the criminal law. It should not be forgotten that the legal system, and legal discourse, are not discrete areas disconnected from broader society and the general discursive frameworks that structure social life and dominant cultural conceptions. Feminist legal theorists have long been aware of the deep imbrication of law and the wider cultural landscape, especially with regard to the role normative sex/gender conceptions play in supposedly 'objective' legal reasoning (Edwards, 1981; Eisenstein, 1988; Lacey, 1998). Legal discourse is typically responsive to dominant social norms, such as those around sex/gender, and helps construct and (re)produce them within and through law. Like cosmetic surgery, law colludes with the norms of its sociocultural context. This helps explain the disparate legal treatment of cosmetic surgery and body modification. Cosmetic surgeries are a set of body alterations that construct and replicate cultural norms, they are conceptualised as socially valuable and perform much the same task as the law, and thus they are left free from regulation by the criminal law to churn out conforming docile bodies. Body modifications are a set of body alterations that produce unruly bodies and challenge and undermine cultural norms, they are positioned as a threat to the normative order that law upholds and thus their stricter criminal regulation is necessitated.

The External Discursive Boundaries

The external conceptual boundaries of the categories of 'cosmetic surgery' and 'body modification' are responsive to changes and challenges. These boundaries create divisions between acts that may initially seem to be physically similar but are subsequently rendered discursively dissimilar. Given the disparate cultural and legal statuses of cosmetic surgery and body modification, this external boundary-drawing is self-evidently political. Any body alteration excluded by or included within these discursive categories will correlatively experience social and legal effects. This may entail the social delegitimisation and criminal law regulation of an alteration conceptualised as body modification, or it may entail the social legitimisation and freedom from criminal law regulation of an alteration conceptualised as cosmetic surgery. There is a broad range of body alterations that could be drawn on to problematise the external boundaries of cosmetic surgery and body modification, but this section will focus on three specific areas: the boundary between cosmetic surgery and reconstructive surgery, the boundary between body modification and modifications to the body brought about by things such as diet and exercise, and the boundaries between FGM and both cosmetic surgery and body modification. This section will explore the discursive forces that bind cosmetic surgery and body modification together and maintain the coherency of these classificatory categories, as well as identify the legal implications that arise from challenges to these external boundaries.

Separating Cosmetic Surgery from Reconstructive Surgery

Where does reconstructive surgery end and cosmetic surgery begin? As Naugler (2009, p.226) notes, the difference between these two sets of practices is frequently invoked by '[c]ritical commentators, health care professionals, and everyday folks … [who], when pressed, find the distinction hard to specify'. A central distinguishing factor frequently raised is that cosmetic surgery is about modifying the '*normal* structures of the body' (Cornwall, 2000, p.88, emphasis added), whereas reconstructive surgery modifies the *abnormal* structures of the body, those affected by disease, mutation, or injury. This notion of the '"normal" parameters' (Heyes and Jones, 2009, p.3) of the body is underpinned by the conceptual ideal of a natural, untouched body existing in an unmodified state free from the ravages of physicality. This conception is familiar from previous chapters and functions here like a Platonic form by providing a floating, untouchable bodily signifier as a fixed reference point against which judgements like 'normal' and 'abnormal' can be made. Undercutting any ontological claim about 'normal' and 'abnormal' bodies is the fact that the boundary between reconstructive and cosmetic surgery is 'always being changed' (Gilman, 1999, p, 207). The domain of the 'normal' body has been slowly encroached upon by the pathologising creep of modern medical discourse which is in the 'process of redefining deformity and disfigurement so broadly as to narrow the scope of acceptable variation' (Kennedy, 2012, p.354).

The responsivity of purportedly objective medical diagnoses to the vagaries of cultural taste is evident with regard to cosmetic surgery attitudes towards the breasts. Having small breasts, once in vogue during the 1920s 'flapper' period in the West, has come to be regarded as a medical condition, worthy of not one but multiple pathologising terms: micromastia, breast hypoplasia and hypomastia. Breasts that are too large are now labelled as 'macromastic', and breasts that have 'sagged because of age or breastfeeding' can now be diagnosed as 'suffering from "ptosis"' (Jones, 2008a, p.92). But pathologisation is by no means limited to the breasts. Saggy skin on your upper arms? Excess fat around your waist and abdomen? Excess fat around your outer thigh? You could be diagnosed with, respectively, 'bat wing deformity', 'spare tire deformity' and 'violin deformity' (Haiken, 1997, pp.299–300). Here 'medical terms' are used not only to identify but to pathologise 'particular somatic variation' (Kennedy, 2012, p.354), as healthy parts of the body are constructed as 'grotesque, extraneous and disabling' within discourse around cosmetic surgery (Kennedy, 2009, p.224). Haiken (1997, p.4) warns us that '[a]ging faces, flat breasts, and small penises, which as facts of life were considered undeserving of medical attention, have been progressively redefined as problems worthy of medical concern and more recently as pathologies or deformities requiring medical solutions'. Bodies that have previously been considered as falling within the range of 'normal' bodily contours, shapes and conditions, are continuously being redefined as suffering from medical problems as this range of 'normalcy' narrows.

Correlatively, the purview of what constitutes the 'abnormal' body continues to grow and, as such, the distinction between 'normal' and 'abnormal' that informs the boundaries between cosmetic and reconstructive surgery has become blurred. In practical terms, an economic imperative provides a vested interest to those cosmetic surgeons tasked with maintaining these medical boundaries to feed this expansion of medical symptomatology. Simply put, if a patient's wrinkles or jowls are defined by their cosmetic surgeon as a 'medical condition' and not as a '"natural" characteristi[c] of the aging body' (Balsamo, 1996, p.63), then they will be more inclined to agree to and pay for treatment. The definitional shifting of the medical understanding of the 'normal' body also figures a discursive shift between the categories of reconstructive and cosmetic surgery. The conceptualisation of cosmetic surgery seems to be moving more closely towards reconstructive surgery in terms of rhetoric and cultural positioning, as cosmetic surgery is no longer an extravagance of vanity but rather a form of medical treatment that 'is needed rather than desired' (Haiken, 1997, p.172). Thus, instead of being discursively constructed as a vanity-based enhancement of a 'normal' face, a face-lift has now become a curative treatment for the medical diagnosis that the recipient is suffering from the 'abnormality' of having a 'saggy' face.

As the external boundaries of cosmetic surgery blur into the boundaries of reconstructive surgery, the possible legal ramifications of this discursive shift are probably only minor. Reconstructive surgery holds a lawful position as, like the rest of the medical field, it claims a clear therapeutic effect and provides its patients with clear benefits. Such claims are legally important as they help provide legal defences that absolve surgeons from any criminal liability arising from surgeries they perform. Karpin (2008, p.80) does, however, identify that questions can be raised 'even in the context of so-called abnormal body morphology' as to whether procedures that purport to be reconstructive 'can be classified as treatment, or are also cosmetic'. Nevertheless, it is far more difficult to make a convincing claim for a therapeutic benefit from cosmetic surgery and this has opened up the legal possibility that performing cosmetic surgery is a criminal act, albeit one which is treated practically as being lawful by all social institutions. The shift towards considering cosmetic surgery and reconstructive surgery as more closely connected eases the difficulty in recognising a therapeutic benefit from cosmetic surgery and forecloses this possibility. In this way, cosmetic surgery stands to 'gain legitimacy from a close association with reconstructive plastic surgery' (Kennedy, 2012, p.353). The discursive proximity between the two helps to make cosmetic surgery more clearly identifiable as lawful.

Separating Body Modification from Other Modifications to the Body

From a literal perspective it seems strange that the term 'body modification' does not pertain to the entire range of possible modifications one can make to one's body, such as a haircut, breast augmentation, dieting, exercising, laser eye surgery, and so on. Isn't it the case that these are all body modifications and we are just an entire 'culture of body modificationists'? (Atkinson, 2003, p.3). Maybe. Physical change to the structure and function of our bodies is an integral element of having a body in the first place, regardless of what modificatory regimes one consciously decides to put one's body through. In a sense, every single body is, and will always be, undergoing a process of modification. However, 'body modification' is a discursively constructed category containing particular body altering practices the external boundaries of which are predicated on a common set of meanings and understandings. To try to combine disparate sets of body alterations such as sex reassignment surgery, 'drug abuse, steroid use [and] eating disorders' under the heading of body modification, as Uden (2001, p.5) does, is to fail to grasp the function of discursive frameworks in categorising, separating and assigning different meanings to different alterations.

From the range of all possible modifications to the body, different types of modifications are discursively positioned so as to have different meanings and understandings. This is why body modification studios are understood as different from gyms which, in turn, are understood as different from Jenny Craig or other dieting centres. This is also why texts on 'body modification' typically don't include discussions of anorexia, and texts about bodybuilding typically don't include commentaries about scarification. It is also the reason why different body alterations are subject to different systems of legal regulation. From the milieu of general alterations to the body, discourse forges certain conceptual categories. For example, dieting, anorexia and bulimia are discursively associated in the way they are conceived and written about. Similarly, exercise and bodybuilding are discursively associated through having a similar cultural function and position. This is also how the discursive category of body modification is created; the set of body alterations that constitute 'body modification' are conceptualised as sharing similar meanings, a similar cultural positioning and similar lateral associations with other practices used to alter the body. That is why comments such as Benson's (2000, p.236) that 'it is useful to consider tattooing and piercing in the context of a broader range of practices' such as '[r]unning, working out, dieting and bodybuilding; the astonishing rise of plastic surgery … gender reassignment and third-sexing; anorexia and bulimia' are misleading. Uncritically conflating the highly disparate cultural meanings and positions of different body alterations in order to compare them, simply because they centre on the body, is highly problematic. However, value can be found in reflexively comparing the conceptual category of 'body modification' to other body alterations because it allows the discursive forces that construct and position the divisions between these practices to be drawn out.

This section will identify some of the discursive factors that mark out the external boundaries of body modification, but this is far from a definitive list and it is not necessary for every single factor to always be fulfilled. Firstly, the body alteration must generally cut, pierce, or otherwise transgress the boundary of the skin, and as a result must 'involve pain, bleeding and healing' (Pitts, 2000, p.291). Body modifications literally open up the body, they split the barrier between inside and outside and break social taboos around the spilling of bodily fluids and voluntarily undergoing pain. Secondly, body modifications are a spectacle. They are highly visible procedures that, unlike cosmetic surgery, don't seek to hide the fact that they have been performed. They are spectacular because they have immediate effects, unlike slow processes like exercise or dieting the effects of which only become 'observable over longer periods of time' (Featherstone, 2000, p.1), and are sharply demarcated in terms of how and when they are performed. Thirdly, as discussed above, body modifications are conceptualised as being opposed to dominant cultural norms. Constructed as individualist projects, they are discursively positioned as responding 'to a different set of aesthetic principles' than the norm, and as a form of deliberate distancing from the 'socially determined ideal' of attractiveness (Rosenblatt, 1997, pp.318–319). Fourthly, they are performed by certain people in certain places. This means, generally, the person who performs the modification is a body modification artist or lay person with no special qualification, in a body modification studio or a DIY style-setting. Thus, for example, permanent makeup, as a form of tattooing performed by a beauty therapist in a salon, would not discursively be considered to be a form of body modification as it doesn't take place within a 'body modification' context. Finally, it must not be forgotten that legal discourse is not simply responsive to cultural phenomena but is also constitutive of how they are conceptualised. Thus, the system of criminal and civil legal regulation that governs body modification both informs, and is informed by, the external boundary-drawing around body modification.

Whilst the latter three factors identified above have already been integrated into this chapter's account of the legal treatment of body modification above, it is necessary to further unpack how the first two factors discursively position body modification as a body alteration requiring regulation. The fact that they typically involve breaking the skin is a major factor in law's focus on body modification amidst the plethora of other body alterations, such as dieting and exercise. As discussed in Chapter 2, when considering the criminality of sadomasochistic activities, the law focuses on injury. The act of wounding inherent in body modification and the shedding of blood is a 'peak (visual) experience', an 'extra notch of violence that may seem much more violent than the physical attack' that does not break the skin (Burr and Hearns, 2008, p.10). Bloodshed evokes alarm across 'different cultures … [who] all recognize bleeding as precious fluid leaving the body' (Hewitt, 1997, p.16). Naffine (1997, p.85) summarises the criminal law concept built up to protect this bodily boundary as a form of 'body bag', that is '[p]eople are essentially bounded and separate, they come in closed body bags, and it is vital that one person not interfere with the body bag of another unless there is a positive agreement to make contact. The default position is isolation rather than physical community.' Body modification tears both the body bag and the skin asunder as, even with positive agreement, the wounding inherent in body modification provides a 'universally powerful example of crossing the barrier between the external and internal body' (Hewitt, 1997, p.16). In this way, the transgressive threat of body modification overlaps with the transgressive threat of sadomasochistic injuries. As discussed in Chapter 2, sadomasochism figuratively and literally 'opens' the body up. The threat of sadomasochism and body modification is that they physically connect people constructed legally as discrete entities, blurring the conceptual boundaries between them. The spectacular nature of body modification compounds this transgression, as it not only demonstrates the transgression to the public at large, it draws attention to it and even valorises it. In response to this flagrant disregard for the legal norm of the bounded, discrete body, legal regulation of body modification is necessary to recuperate this transgressive threat.

Separating Cosmetic Surgery and Body Modification from FGM

With the relatively recent criminalisation of FGM in Australia and other Western countries, debate has arisen about the scope of anti-FGM statutory provisions. Some feminist anti-FGM writers have attempted to draw discursive connections between FGM and other body alterations performed on the female genitals, and it has been suggested that some types of cosmetic surgery and body modification may contravene these new laws (see Chapter 3 for the relevant laws on FGM).

Elsewhere, I have addressed the points of similarity and difference that can be drawn between FGM and the practice of cosmetic surgery more generally (Bennett 2012b). Here, however, I want to address the specific issue of the comparison between FGM and female genital cosmetic surgery ('FGCS') in particular. The practice of FGCS in Western countries has been described as 'burgeoning' and includes procedures such as vaginal tightening, vaginal liposuction, vaginal lifts, clitoral unhooding, and labiaplasty (typically the reduction of the labia minora) (Loy, 2000). As a strategic technique, some feminists have likened FGCS to FGM in an attempt to harness anti-FGM sentiment and channel it towards opposing FGCS. For example, Jeffreys (2005b, pp.33–34) argues that FGCS is similar to FGM in the 'degree of mutilation, pain and potential complications'. Essen and Johnsdotter (2004) go further by arguing that laws criminalising FGM should be applied equally to FGCS, effectively criminalising that set of body alterations as well.

These commentators may have a valid legal point. Even the Commonwealth Government has recently recognised that 'female genital cosmetic surgery may involve procedures that are technically very similar to those defined in the legislation' (Attorney-General's Department, 2013, p.9). This is because there are marked physical similarities between FGM and FGCS in that both can involve the cutting and/or removal of part of the female genitalia, or tightening of the vagina (Berer, 2010; Kelly and Foster, 2012; Kennedy, 2009; Veale and Daniels, 2012). Any vaginal tightening procedure would appear to be *prima facie* outlawed in those Australian jurisdictions that prohibit procedures to narrow or close the vaginal opening, just as any clitoral unhooding or labiaplasty procedure would *prima facie* seem to have been criminalised in Australian jurisdictions by the various prohibitions on the excision of any part of female genitals (Mason, 2009a, p.12). Arguably, FGCS may possibly fall under the statutory exception to FGM that exempts surgical operations performed for therapeutic reasons by recognised medical practitioners (Kennedy, 2009), although, as with any cosmetic surgery, it is somewhat difficult to locate therapeutic value in a body alteration that is typically pursued solely for aesthetic or psychological reasons. However, in the same way that both MC and cosmetic surgery may be technically criminal and yet still hold a generally accepted legality, FGCS is treated practically as being lawful within Australia (Kennedy 2009). Kennedy (2009) convincingly argues that the 'inconsistency' between the legal treatment of FGM and FGCS is the result of various discursive processes that align FGCS, and not FGM, with positive notions of psychological benefit, autonomy/agency and identity. As a result, Australian law is left in the same awkward position as the law in the United Kingdom, under which Berer (2010, pp.108–109) concludes that:

> [I]f a woman (probably of African descent) asks a medical practitioner … for her own or her daughter's genitals to be partially or fully excised for traditional or cultural reasons, she will be told it is a criminal offence. Yet if any woman perceives her own genitals to be an abnormal shape or size, even though they are perfectly normal, or wants them to be 'trimmed' or removed for cosmetic

reasons, the surgery is considered legal and brings in a hefty fee, because it is called labia reduction and cosmetic surgery.

Certain types of body modification have also been argued to fall within the ambit of FGM-criminalising legislation (Braun, 2009b). Whilst DeMello (2007, pp.131–132) notes that some Western body modifiers may choose to mimic traditional FGM by having their 'clitorises removed, and sometimes their labia as well', she also points to others who have their clitoral hood removed or who undergo temporary infibulation by sealing their labia with 'glue, piercings, or stitches'. These types of modifications seem clearly criminal under Australian anti-FGM laws on the basis that they excise or infibulate part of the genitalia, regardless of the recipient's consent. However, DeMello (2007) recognises that these types of modification are rare, and the broader argument about the intersection of body modification and FGM typically centres around female genital piercings, and whether or not they can legally be regarded as the 'mutilation' of the female genitalia.

Bibbings (1996), Watkins (1998) and Kelly and Foster (2012) note the technical possibility of FGM charges being brought against those who pierce female genitalia, though Watkins (1998, p, 375) decries this as 'seriously misguided', and constituting 'a serious misconstruction of the intention of the legislation', and Kelly and Foster (2012, p.392) argue that 'there are no medical or ethical objections to [piercing] that are remotely comparable with the objections to FGM or FGCS'. However, John Rau, the then Member for Enfield, when delivering his Second Reading of the *Summary Offences (Tattooing and Piercing) Amendment Bill* on 10 July 2002 before the South Australian House of Assembly, noted that 'in extreme cases the practice of body piercing' should qualify as mutilation under the FGM-criminalising statutes (Hansard, p.688). Statutory interpretation is obviously an important issue here. The coverage of these provisions depends on the application of the *ejusdem generis* rule of statutory interpretation rule (Bibbings and Alldridge, 1993, p.362), which could be used to read down the ordinary meaning of 'mutilation' to simply cover any body alteration 'involving cutting away part of the labia or, narrowing or sealing over part of the vagina' (Greg Parker: Select Committee on the Tattooing and Body Piercing Industries, 2005, Appendix 8). If this was the legal approach, most forms of female genital piercing, such as clitoral hood and labia piercings, would not constitute a statutory offence under anti-FGM laws. However, 'chastity-style' piercings (generally a laddered series of multiple piercings running the length of the labia majora or minora that can be joined together with implements such as rings or padlocks), might be considered mutilation as they are intended to narrow or seal over the vagina.

Legally, then, some forms of cosmetic surgery and body modification may constitute FGM under the anti-FGM statutory provisions. However, linking these body alterations together discursively is problematic as the meanings and cultural positioning of both cosmetic surgery and body modification differ drastically from that of FGM. A number of writers have drawn conceptual connections and disconnections between cosmetic surgery and FGM (Braun, 2009a; Chambers, 2004; Jeffreys, 2005b; Kinnun, 2008; Wilson, 2002), and exploring these in any real depth would probably require a whole article or book on the subject. Briefly, the authoritative Western discursive conceptualisation of cosmetic surgery as a beneficial, non-harmful medical procedure that a woman chooses to undergo is incompatible with the authoritative discursive conceptualisation of FGM as a harmful, painful cultural ritual forced upon unwilling females (Kennedy, 2009). Bridging this conceptual division requires more than merely pointing out the physical '*degrees* of similarity in some procedures', such as the reduction of labial tissue (Braun, 2009a, p.135, emphasis in original). As was demonstrated in Chapter 3's analysis of FGM and MC, physical similarities between body alterations can be overridden by discursive forces that work to conceptualise such alterations as different and even oppositional. Similarly, whilst body modification has predominantly been discursively conceptualised as a deviant, painful and oppositional practice – all characteristics which have also been discursively associated with FGM in the West – it is also strongly associated with other cultural meanings about autonomy, individualism and pleasure. If FGM is seen as a form of cultural submission to non-Western bodily norms of appearance, with those who practice it being depicted as 'lacking agency and autonomy' (Kennedy, 2009, p.211), body modification is constructed as a rejection of normative appearance standards *tout court*, and as an exercise of creative political agency (Lentini, 1999, pp.32–34). Whilst genital piercing may involve pain and physical harm during the procedure, it is also associated with making a statement about one's sexuality and/or enhancing female 'erotic pleasure' (Bibbings and Alldridge, 1993, p.362). In contrast, FGM is typically conceptualised within Western discourse as always harmful to and destructive of female sexuality and female sexual pleasure.

Drawing discursive links between cosmetic surgery or body modification and FGM will prove difficult as their current cultural meanings are almost diametrically opposed. For the criminal regulations prohibiting FGM to be used in the expanded way argued for by some anti-FGM feminist commentators, major conceptual shifts will first be required before cosmetic surgery and body modification can be discursively conceptualised as being similar to FGM.

The Discursive Boundaries Between

Having explored and analysed the internal and external discursive boundaries of both cosmetic surgery and body modification, this chapter now turns towards the discursive boundary that separates these two sets of body alterations from each other. This boundary can be difficult to distinguish as in some places it seems to collapse and join together these two sets of categories, whilst in other places it seems to hold them rigidly apart. In the literature, plastic surgery has been described as a form of 'permanent body modification' (Myers, 1992, p.267), and body modifications have been described as involving the application of 'plastic surgery' (Sanders, 2008, p.179). The social meanings and cultural positioning of both sets of body alteration have been argued to be similar, in that they are 'beauty practices' that typically harm the female body (Jeffreys, 2005b, p.1), and dissimilar, in that cosmetic surgery 'is deemed to enhance or add value to the body whereas body modification procedures are constructed as attempts to devalue the body' (Bogdanoski, 2009, p.508).

The overlap between the types of body alterations that fall within the categories of cosmetic surgery and body modification is significant and has a practical as well as a theoretical element. Whilst the Queensland Health Department (2007, p.2) feels justified in categorically stating that 'tattoos and body piercing … are not commonly regarded as cosmetic surgery', it should be recognised that tattooing 'has been used in the medical field since the early days of plastic surgery' (DeMello, 2007, p.185). Known as 'micropigmentation', it is used by health care practitioners to cover over surgical scars, colour reconstructed areolae, and mask alopecia (De Mello, 2007, pp.185–186). However, Jones (2008b, p.47) rightly recognises that writings on the two sets of body alterations have devolved into separate camps, each with 'their own sets of specialised academics and analysts', such as psychologists and sociologists for body modification, and feminist philosophers and cultural theorists for cosmetic surgery. The only solid conclusion that could possibly arise from this mishmash of contradictory commentary is that cosmetic surgery and body modification are discursively intertwined in some way, and that the boundary between the two body alterations, wherever it lies, is structurally complex.

Throughout this chapter the discursive boundary between cosmetic surgery and body modification has already been addressed in an oblique manner. A number of key points that distinguish the two can be drawn from previous sections, such as that the conceptualisation of 'cosmetic surgery' is confined to practices performed by health care practitioners in a medical setting under the socially legitimising purview of medicine, whereas the conceptualisation of 'body modification' typically covers practices that occur in a non-medical professional or DIY context. Further, cosmetic surgeries are constructed as normalising the body in line with Western dominant cultural norms of sex/gender appearance, whereas body modifications are constructed as distancing their recipients from these norms through an intentionally oppositional bodily aesthetic. Rather than simply repeat these general conclusions from the previous sections, and in order to lend some specificity to the analysis, this section will explore the discursive boundary between cosmetic surgery and body modification by attempting to situate healthy limb amputation within these conceptual categories.

The Problem Case of Healthy Limb Amputation

The term 'healthy limb amputation' refers to the voluntary and non-medically necessary removal of an otherwise healthy limb at the demand of the person to whom the limb is attached. In earlier work I have identified that, at a general level, healthy limb amputation is in a position of 'discursive instability', that is, the meanings and implications of healthy limb amputation are still being negotiated around key sociolegal concepts such as consent, harm and benefit (Bennett, 2011, p.158). Thus, for example, there are a number of unresolved debates around healthy limb amputation, including questions such as: '[i]s the amputation of a healthy body part always harmful and disabling?' and '[s]hould the request to have a healthy limb amputated always be dismissed as symptomatic of a mental disorder, or can it be seen as a meaningful, autonomous claim about a deeply held desire?' (Bennett, 2011, p.158). Despite the efforts of a number of medical, legal and philosophical commentators who have tried to settle its categorisation, healthy limb amputation still occupies an unsettled discursive position today. This section will use the unsettled discursive position of healthy limb amputation to specifically demonstrate how it straddles the conceptual boundary between the categories of cosmetic surgery and body modification, and thus to reveal how and why body alterations are positioned within or outside these categories as well as to highlight the legal consequences that attach to the categorisation process.

What is Healthy Limb Amputation?

Healthy limb amputation received very limited academic attention until widespread news coverage of certain events generated a higher level of general awareness. In 2000, Dr Robert Smith, a Scottish surgeon at the Falkirk and District Royal Infirmary, amputated the legs of two patients at their request. The unusual element of the operations was, as Elliott (2000, p.73) summarises, that '[t]hese patients were not physically sick. Their legs did not need to be amputated for any medical reason. Nor were they incompetent, according to the psychiatrists who examined them. They simply wanted to have their legs cut off.' The surgeries were paid for by the patients, they recovered fully and both later stated that they were happy with the results (Ramsay, 2000). Dr Robert Smith 'received further requests for limb amputation and had six people waiting for surgery' (Elliott, 2009, p.152) when this was effectively foreclosed by the decision of the 'Hospital Board in Falkirk … that no further amputations for

BIID would be carried out … unless the patient lived locally and the procedure was cleared through the local ethical committee' (Smith, 2009, p.155).

The desire to have one's healthy limbs removed seems, from an initial commonsense viewpoint, to be absurd if not obscene. Yet it is a desire that has been identified as being 'on the rise in the West' (Sullivan, 2000, p.325), with a plethora of internet sites devoted to the subject and a growing corpus of academic and medical work putting the procedure under critical scrutiny. The most common desire is 'amputation of one leg above the knee, but some require amputation of an arm or even more than one limb' (Smith, 2009, p.147).

A number of explanatory frameworks have been constructed around healthy limb amputation in an effort to integrate and enmesh this new social phenomenon within medical discourse. The initial explanatory model originates from a 1977 article identifying the desire for healthy limb amputation as being a form of sexual disorder that the article termed 'apotemnophilia', meaning 'amputation love' (Money, et al., 1977). Apotemnophiles were diagnosed as being sexually excited by having a limb amputated – not to be confused with acrotomophiles who are sexually excited by the amputations of others – and their desire to undergo healthy limb amputation was pathologised as a form of aberrant sexuality. Although this explanatory model still holds much weight, it has been recently challenged by the construction of the desire to undergo healthy limb amputation as being the result of BIID (MacKenzie, 2008). Drawing on the discourse surrounding sex reassignment surgery (Lawrence, 2006; this discourse is considered in detail in Chapter 5), this medical category is grounded in the notion that a person who desires to undergo healthy limb amputation was born into the 'wrong' body, that is one with what they perceive is an extraneous limb. Some commentators argue that healthy limb amputation should have its own diagnostic subcategory of Amputee Identity Disorder (AID) (Smith, 2009), whilst other commentators argue that healthy limb amputation is a form of Body Dysmorphia instead (Elliott, 2009). The conflict between these multiple pathologising frameworks exemplifies the discursive instability of healthy limb amputation, as no one explanatory framework has yet succeeded in comprehensively encapsulating the phenomenon of healthy limb amputation.

Cosmetic Surgery or Body Modification?

Given the unstable discursive position of healthy limb amputation, it is possible that it might be ultimately conceptualised as a form of either cosmetic surgery or body modification. Connections between healthy limb amputation and these other body alterations have been drawn by some commentators, but typically not in a detailed manner. For example, Karpin (2008, pp.77–78) notes that '[v]oluntary amputeeism … might arguably fall within the category of radical body modification'. Jeffreys (2005b, p.167) identifies healthy limb amputation as the 'most extreme form of "body modification" presently in vogue, besides amputation of genitals', and the fact that some forms of amputation are practised by people who self-identify as members of the body modification community tends to support this categorisation (Sullivan, 2000, p.326). Alternatively, connections have also been made between healthy limb amputation and cosmetic surgery, with Johnston and Elliott (2002, p.432) pointing out that both types of body alterations are 'invasive, non-therapeutic [and] justified by the patient's own aesthetic preferences'. Kennedy (2012, p.350) identifies further commonalities on the basis that both body alterations are instigated by patients rather than recommended by medical practitioners, 'can only be performed by surgeons', and 'invoke identity construction' as a central concern. However, Kennedy (2012, p.360) also acknowledges a number of differences on the basis that cosmetic surgery is typically conceptualised as a method for 'achieving optimal normalcy of embodiment', whereas healthy limb amputation is conceptualised as leading to 'sub-normal embodiment'. To determine the discursive factors that account for the inclusion or exclusion of a body alteration from the categories of cosmetic surgery and body modification, we can use healthy limb amputation to model the application of the key concepts that underpin these discursive categories. In particular, I want to focus on three factors: therapeutic benefit, the normative implications of these body alterations, and the social status of those who carry them out.

Although it might be questionable whether a therapeutic benefit to a cosmetic surgery patient can be identified at law, the frequently touted potential mental health benefits of cosmetic surgery are a major component of cosmetic surgery discourse. Cosmetic surgery is not seen as therapeutic in a physical, bodily health sense, but rather is conceptualised as a form of 'psychotherapy with a scalpel' (Kennedy, 2009, p.214), in that it can help a patient by relieving issues such as 'psychological stress, low self-esteem, etc' (Skene, 1996, p.277). This conceptualisation is foregrounded in relation to breast augmentation, which Gimlin (2002) identifies as helping females feel more 'womanly' and able to participate in more activities like going to the beach in a bathing suit. In contrast, body modification is typically conceptualised as a form of non-therapeutic mutilation. Rather than providing the recipient with a mental health benefit, body modification is touted as resulting from 'a potential mental health problem' and as a form of 'self-mutilation' (Pitts, 2000, p.293). Physically, body modifications have been argued to 'impair bodily functional ability', as all body modifications 'cause pathological conditions, e.g. destroyed skin tissue' (Schramme, 2008, p.15).

Karpin (2008, p.81) suggests that we 'might consider' the 'amputation of a healthy limb' as 'falling within [the] category of therapeutic modification', but definitively settling this issue is quite difficult. A cursory analysis might suggest that the inevitable harm to the body caused by the amputation of a limb mitigates against the identification of any therapeutic benefit, thus positioning healthy limb amputation discursively closer to body modification. As discussed in Chapter 3, however, MC has long been justified by the purported therapeutic benefits that it provides even though it involves the removal of healthy penile skin. Whilst the amputation of limbs may seem to be simply a process of transforming 'normal, healthy bodies into ones with impairments', those patients who desire such amputation often assert 'that they will not feel physically "whole" until they have had a limb removed' (Elliott, 2009, p.181). Like cosmetic surgery, then, healthy limb amputation can be argued to provide a mental health benefit to the patient that offsets the physical harm caused by the procedure. Indeed, cosmetic surgery itself paved the way for recognising a social benefit from the removal of what is seen as otherwise 'healthy' tissue (Sullivan, 2000, p.326), such as the removal of excess breast tissue in a breast reduction or excess cartilage in a rhinoplasty. This might, however, be too long a bow to draw; if cosmetic surgery is conceptualised as a form of 'psychotherapy with a scalpel' (Kennedy, 2009, p.214), then healthy limb amputation is perhaps more akin to psychotherapy with a hacksaw. It could be argued that whilst the amount of physical harm caused by cosmetic surgery is commensurate to the claimed psychological benefit, the harm caused by amputation of healthy limbs would always outweigh this. Healthy limb amputation seems to straddle the boundary between cosmetic surgery and body modification, as it can be conceptualised as either psychologically beneficial medical treatment or harmful mutilation.

Previous sections have discussed at length how cosmetic surgery is typically conceptualised as shifting bodies towards cultural norms and thus embodies cultural submission, whereas body modification is typically conceptualised as shifting bodies away from cultural norms and is frequently reflexively adopted as an oppositional stance. Locating healthy limb amputation within this duality is difficult because whilst the physical appearance of an amputation recipient may violate cultural norms about the body, those who desire healthy limb amputations do not seem to intentionally want to adopt an oppositional bodily aesthetic. Amputees transgress cultural body norms because they fail to present the 'bounded', untouched body idealised within the West (Naffine, 1997). Instead, their bodies are markedly wounded, open and, to some, 'mutilated'. The dominant ableist rhetoric within Western society devalues wounded bodies: this is what makes 'elective amputees' requests … seem quite so odd' (MacKenzie, 2008, p.405), and it underpins the 'strong reactions of incredulity, disquiet and even disgust' that typically arise when one learns of healthy limb amputation (Elliott, 2009, p.181). Like body modification and unlike cosmetic surgery, healthy limb amputations shift the bodies of the recipients further away from cultural norms.

However, whilst the Modern Primitive or other body modifier may actively engage in body modification because of this transgressive element, using body modification deliberately to place themselves in opposition to the mainstream, those who choose to undergo healthy limb amputation often do so for reasons more akin to recipients of cosmetic surgery. Like the cosmetic surgery patient who gets a facelift because they do not feel old, the elective amputee is constructed as undergoing the procedure in order to have their 'inner self-image matc[h] the outward appearance' (MacKenzie, 2008, p.405). Dr Robert Smith's first patient told the newspapers that 'my left leg was not part of me' (Johnston and Elliott, 2002, p.432), and similarly cosmetic surgery is constructed as being able to 'repair the disjunction that can develop between the internal and the external' (Haiken, 2000, p.88). Rather than being discursively constructed as oppositional, whilst the amputated body itself may transgress cultural appearance norms the motivations of the elective amputee are conceptualised as being similar to that of the culturally collusive cosmetic surgery patient. Again, healthy limb amputation seems to straddle the discursive boundary between cosmetic surgery and body modification.

Healthy limb amputation is already discursively connected to the field of medicine, by virtue of having been recorded in medical writing, carried out in medical practice and linked in the popular consciousness to doctors/hospitals as a result of media reporting on Dr Robert Smith. As such, there is a strong suggestion that healthy limb amputation is discursively located more closely to cosmetic surgery than to body modification. Practically, the skill and equipment required to safely carry out an amputation procedure can typically only be found in a medical setting. Given that these procedures are not medically indicated and are sought on-demand by patients rather than prescribed by doctors as treatments, they seem more similar to cosmetic surgery than any other form of medical procedure. However, given that doctors are currently unwilling (or possibly unable due to codes of medical ethics and/or legal restrictions) to perform elective healthy limb amputations, these procedures are being carried out, like some body modifications, in DIY-style settings by people who are not health care practitioners. Similar to the sadomasochists who performed piercings themselves since the 1970s, some elective amputees attempt their own amputations. Whilst some merely attempt to injure their limb so severely that medical necessity forces medical staff to perform an amputation, others attempt the full amputation procedures, such as the Milwaukee man that Elliott (2000, p.73) mentions who 'severed his arm with a homemade guillotine, and then threatened to sever it again if surgeons reattached it'. The rarity of elective amputations prevents any detailed engagement with the context in which they are usually performed, but we can still note that cultural context is an important factor in distinguishing the boundary between cosmetic surgery and body modification. An elective amputation carried out by a doctor in a hospital, even despite the controversy around Dr Robert Smith, is discursively positioned as a far more legitimate practice than one carried out in a DIY setting. If healthy limb amputations continue to be performed in hospitals and other high-social-status medical contexts they are more likely to be conceptualised as cosmetic surgery. If they continue to be performed outside hospitals and in other lower-social-status contexts they are more likely to be conceptualised as body modification.

My attempt to locate healthy limb amputation within the discursive framework that constitutes the categories of cosmetic surgery or body modification is ultimately fruitless, as it can be seen as neatly straddling the discursive boundary between these two body alterations. Healthy limb amputation might eventually be conceptualised as having a therapeutic effect and thus as being a beneficial cosmetic surgical procedure, or it might be eventually conceptualised as a harmful, oppositional and non-normative form of body modification. What the unsettled discursive position of health limb amputation does make clear, however, are the discursive processes that determine whether a body alteration falls within the conceptual categories of cosmetic surgery or body modification.

The Legal Implications

With the potential remaining for healthy limb amputation to be folded into the conceptual categories of either cosmetic surgery or body modification, it is open to explore how the resolution of this ambiguity would affect the legal status of healthy limb amputation. This reveals the legal stakes that attach to the discursive divisions between the conceptual categories of 'cosmetic surgery' and 'body modification'.

There have been no criminal law cases that address the legality of healthy limb amputation (even Dr Robert Smith was never prosecuted), nor are there any direct statutory sections on point. Indeed, there is 'considerable uncertainty on the amputation of healthy limbs from a legal perspective' (Bryant, 2011, p.287). This, however, has not prevented speculation from a number of commentators on the likely outcome of any potential legal proceedings. I will focus here on two articles in particular that have attempted to trace the legal status of healthy limb amputation.

Firstly, in 'Healthy Limb Amputation: Ethical and Legal Aspects', Josephine Johnston and Carl Elliott (2002, p.432) identify that such a procedure would *prima facie* be considered to be criminal assault. They state that whilst the argument could be made that the law should consider such amputations as similar to 'body piercing, tattoos, sterilisations, abortions and cosmetic surgery' and recognise them as legal on the grounds of autonomy, the legally stronger argument for absolving the criminal liability of the amputator would be that the amputation was 'proper medical treatment' (Johnston and Elliott, 2002, p.432). Drawing on an explanatory model that pathologises the desire for such amputations as a mental disorder, they argue that, like sex reassignment surgery for Gender Identity Disorder ('GID'), the therapeutic benefit of the amputation of otherwise healthy tissue might be locatable in the treatment of a 'psychiatric disorder' (Johnston and Elliott, 2002, p.433). Healthy limb amputations carried out in a medical context for the treatment of a medical issue would be lawful.

Secondly, in 'Body Dysmorphic Disorder, Radical Surgery and the Limits of Consent', Tracey Elliott (2009, p.169) suggests that healthy limb amputation 'surgery may be lawful, provided that certain conditions are met'. She also notes that healthy limb amputations are *prima facie* criminal assaults to which consent is not a defence because they cause wounding or grievous bodily harm. Like Johnston and Elliott (2002) she is troubled by the potential application of the reasonable medical treatment defence where there is a lack of an easily identifiable therapeutic benefit to such operations (Elliott, 2009, p.175). However, she suggests that, as with sex reassignment surgery, treatment of a psychological condition might constitute a benefit at law (Elliott, 2009, p.182). She goes on to consider that cosmetic surgery is frequently undertaken without any therapeutic benefit and is considered lawful, so she argues that healthy limb amputation, when 'conducted by appropriately qualified medical practitioners upon adults who have capacity, and who have consented to the procedure', should similarly be placed outside the purview of the criminal law. Regulation should be left to 'the civil law, and … the medical profession' (Elliott, 2009, p.182).

I have not summarised the legal arguments within these articles on healthy limb amputation in order to comment on their doctrinal correctness. Rather, they have been included because they can be identified as laying the seeds of a possible future trend within legal discourse towards conceptualising healthy limb amputation as cosmetic surgery rather than as body modification. Both articles specifically draw parallels between healthy limb amputation and cosmetic surgery. DIY amputations, or those carried out for aesthetic or sexual reasons, are excluded from consideration, and Johnston and Elliott's (2002) cursory comparison of healthy limb amputation to body modifications such as piercing and tattooing is ultimately abandoned in favour of drawing a comparison to medical procedures like sex reassignment surgery. Furthermore, both articles consider healthy limb amputations as only being lawful when occurring within a similar contextual framework to cosmetic surgery: performed by a health care practitioner, in a medical setting, for the treatment of a medically diagnosed 'condition'. As Kennedy (2012, p.350) notes, it seems as though healthy limb amputation requires 'the imprimatur of the medical profession to be lawful'.

These preliminary legal attempts to discursively position healthy limb amputation draw out the boundaries between cosmetic surgery and body modification. Cosmetic surgery is conceptualised as a lawful, legitimate medical treatment that may provide psychological benefits to the patient, whereas body modification is conceptualised as a criminal, illegitimate body alteration without benefit. All these connotations are at stake, then, in the discursive struggle to locate healthy limb amputation within either of these categories. Whilst this struggle may be no closer to being settled within wider discourse, within legal discourse healthy limb amputation is being drawn towards being conceptualised as cosmetic surgery.

Conclusion

The legal statuses of cosmetic surgery and body modification are inflected by the conceptual categorisations that discursively separate and position these body alterations in particular ways in relation to themselves, other types of body alterations, and each other. Distinguishing these particular body alterations from the almost limitless methods employed by humanity to change the shape and function of their bodies relies upon discourse's capacity to create and maintain distinctions between different kinds of body alterations. These distinctions solidify into conceptual categories, the boundaries of which operate to mobilise the law differentially across the lines that have been drawn. Thus we find that where a body alteration extensively interferes with the body of a patient in extremely invasive and physically harmful ways for no physical benefit, it will be lawful if it is conceptualised as a form of cosmetic surgery but may be criminal if conceptualised as a form of body modification. Three specific conceptual boundaries were considered in this chapter: the internal boundaries within these body alterations, the external boundaries that mark out these body alterations as distinct and the boundary that separates these body alterations from each other.

The internal conceptual boundaries between 'successful' and 'failed' cosmetic surgery and non-mainstream and mainstream body modification reflect this variegated legal response. The creation of unruly bodies that display non-normative appearance is lawful if such bodies are created through cosmetic surgery, but is arguably criminal if they are created through non-mainstream body modification. Accounting for the different ways law is mobilised by discourse here requires consideration of the relative sociocultural positioning of cosmetic surgery as a high status, high social value body alteration that typically colludes with dominant cultural norms surrounding appropriate appearance, whereas body modification is conceived of as a low status, low social value body alteration that functions in oppositional ways to subvert cultural norms.

The external conceptual boundaries that distinguish cosmetic surgery and body modification from other types of body alteration also inflect the ways in which they are dealt with by law. Due to the pathologisation of 'normal' bodies, the growing category of reconstructive surgery now encompasses an increasingly large number of procedures from the category of cosmetic surgery and grants them the protection of its own unassailably lawful status.

Conversely, the criminal regulation of body modification is not extended to other modifications to the body, such as exercise and dieting. Finally, although some cosmetic surgery and body modification alters the female genitalia, strong conceptual boundaries prevent either from being discursively labelled as FGM, which protects them from being criminalised by anti-FGM statutory provisions.

The conceptual boundary that separates cosmetic surgery from body modification carries high discursive and legal stakes. Attempting to fix the discursively unsettled practice of healthy limb amputation into these categories makes these stakes clear. The conceptualisation of a body alteration as cosmetic surgery imports a highly culturally valued medical framework that would legitimate it as lawful, whereas conceptualisation as body modification imports a low cultural value framework of oppositionality and 'perversion' that would delegitimise it as criminal. The problem case of healthy limb amputation also highlights the conceptualisations that are employed to distinguish cosmetic surgery from body modification around issues such as therapeutic benefit, the normative implications of these body alterations, and the social status of those people who perform these body alterations.

Whilst all of our bodies may be in a constant process of change and modification, not all modifications are discursively equal. Cosmetic surgery is constructed as a high-status, socially valued body alteration performed under the venerable auspices of medicine. In contrast, body modification is constructed as a low status, socially oppositional body alteration that is non-medical in character and that demonstrates non-normative individuality or subcultural affiliation. Like the body of the cosmetic surgery patient or the body modifier, the body of the criminal law has been contoured to follow the discursive boundaries within and around these conceptual categories. Thus, cosmetic surgeries are left mostly unregulated by the criminal law, whereas the more 'extreme' forms of non-mainstream body modification attract the regulation of the criminal law. How the boundaries of these categories accommodate challenges, such as the problem case of healthy limb amputation, correlatively structures how the body of the law will sanction such phenomena. It requires strong discursive work not only to construct but also to maintain the categories of cosmetic surgery and body modification, especially in the context of both their increasing popularity and the rapid pace of advances in medical technology and artistic innovation. Given these circumstances, it is only a matter of time until the inevitable next cut is made into the body of the law.

Chapter 5
Sex Surgeries: Defusing Transgression Through Genital Normalisation and Sex Reassignment

The conceptualisation of sex/gender as a binary opposition exerts great influence within both the law and discourse. Male/Female, man/woman, boy/girl: these dyads operate to divide and assign different rights and understandings to what are typically understood as distinctly separate categories and bodies. This conceptualisation is naturalised as simplistic and obvious due to the Western cultural 'truth' that there are 'enormous psychological, biological and social differences between men and women' (Chau and Herring, 2002, p.327). These categories are conceptualised as not only being very different, but also as being 'opposite and incommensurate' (Karkazis, 2008, p.147).

As this fundamental discursive understanding has become 'a fundamental principle of the legal system as well', like Kolbe (2008, p.147) we might expect that this sex/gender division 'would be codified in a prominent place, for example in the constitution'.[1] However, it is conspicuously absent. Marriage, for instance, is currently defined under s5 of the *Marriage Act 1961* (Cth) as 'the union of a man and a woman to the exclusion of all others, voluntarily entered into for life'. The law here identifies two classes of people with separate but corresponding rights: a man, who can legally marry a woman, and a woman, who can legally marry a man. But what we do not have is a clear legal definition of either 'man' or 'woman'. There is a separation of people into different categories, and a differential assignation of rights, but no unambiguous legal criteria set out upon which to effect this separation. Undoubtedly, the parliamentarians responsible for this section were working from their own tacit definitions of 'man' and 'woman', and 'male'/'female' bodies, drawn from thoroughly naturalised sociocultural understandings of sex/gender. Indeed, 'codification in general is only dispensable for circumstances so obvious that no one would call them into question' (Kolbe, 2008, p.147). Thus it could be argued that the

1 Here Kolbe (2008) is discussing German law, but her point is equally applicable to Australian law.

broader discursive division of sex/gender within society becomes embedded in the law and manifests as a legal division. However, what such a view fails to encapsulate is the creative function of the law in the production of sex/gender and the sex/gender division. That is, law does not simply replicate the cultural divide between 'male' and 'female, it also works constitutively by generating appropriately sexed/gendered bodies and actively erasing bodies that transgress this binary.

It is with this understanding in mind that this chapter analyses the legal treatment of people whose sex/gender can be discursively problematic. Specifically, this chapter will deal with the legal and discursive issues that surround intersex and transsexualism. Intersex and transsexual people are seen to challenge normative conceptions about sex/gender because their bodies are identified as having the power to 'raise questions … [about] how people make sense of their bodies … and how we, as … producers of cultural knowledge, make sense of them' (Valentine and Wilchins, 1997, p.219). This chapter deals specifically with the legal status of, and legal discourse around, genital normalisation surgeries performed on intersex people and sex reassignment surgeries performed on transsexual people.

As with Chapter 4, this chapter adopts a broad cultural perspective on legal discourse. This chapter will not engage in a close analysis of specific legal statements in this area, but will rather explore more generally how these body alterations are discursively positioned, utilised and constructed both within law and in relation to other discursive frameworks. Given the subject matter's close connections to conceptions of sex and gender, this broad approach is necessary to engage with these wider issues.

The purpose of this chapter is to chart the discursive forces that have aligned to produce the lawfulness of genital normalisation surgery and sex reassignment surgery and to interrogate the understandings about the body that underpin legal discourse in this area. In order to ground this analysis, the chapter begins by offering definitions of both genital normalisation surgery and sex reassignment surgery, and maps their current legal positions. This chapter then denaturalises the legal status of these body alterations by comparing them to other bodily alterations already discussed in this book. Comparing genital normalisation surgery and sex reassignment surgery to FGM, cosmetic surgery and healthy limb amputation prompts reflexivity about why law treats alterations to 'healthy' bodily tissue carried out under the auspices of sex surgery differently from similar body alterations carried out in the course of these other practices. To address this issue, this chapter then works through three of the dominant discursive conceptualisations that construct and position sex surgeries as lawful: medicine, sex/gender and notions of 'truth'. It argues that legal discourse legitimises particular models of intersex and transsexualism that accord with normative understandings about the body in order to limit the transgressive potentials of intersex and transsexual embodiment. The lawfulness of these surgeries relies upon law's capacity to put such surgeries to work upholding normative aspects of the broader discursive frameworks within which they are imbricated.

Before this analysis can begin it is necessary to clarify some of the language that will be used in this chapter. Within discourse around these areas, the terms 'sex' and 'gender' sometimes tend to be deployed in ways that construct them as having separate and distinct meanings. Thus, for example, the Australian Human Rights Commission (2009a, p.7) identifies that sex is something that is 'biologically determined' and refers to factors such as 'physical attributes, chromosomes, genitals, gonads, hormones and "brain-sex"', whereas gender is something that a person expresses and is 'socially constructed' on the basis of 'how a person looks, dresses or acts'. However, this usage is not consistent and sometimes these terms are instead used interchangeably within statute and case law. Furthermore, academic work has revealed that the uncritical deployment of these categories as separate and distinct is problematic for a number of reasons. Drawing on Judith Butler's work around sex and gender (as mentioned in Chapter 1), it has been argued that not only gender but 'sex itself (the interpretation of bodies) is a social construction' (Cowan, 2005, p.71). This is because biological structures can never be free from enculturated conceptions about them that construct 'gendered' differences, and, correlatively, gender must also be 'sexed' in order to provide points of comparison and differentiation to ground these conceptions (de Castro, 1993, p.17). If even purportedly 'objective' scientific views on 'human biology' are themselves the 'product of the cultural climate in which they work' (Rahman and Jackson, 2010, p.120), then any distinction between sex and gender is blurry at best.

Given the difficulties flagged here, I will adopt the very useful approach set out by Cowan (2005, p.72) that uses the phrase 'sex/gender' to reflect the 'interwoven' nature of these categories. Furthermore, like Cowan (2005) I will also employ some alternative terms at different points within my analysis. For the purpose of this chapter I will use the term 'sex' to refer to biological considerations, 'gender' to refer to social and cultural expressions, and 'gender identity' to refer to a person's psychological identification. Given that genital normalisation surgery and sex reassignment surgery are forms of body alteration I will refer to them collectively as 'sex surgeries', and, because the law has historically demonstrated a close focus on a person's biology as the basis for determining their sex/gender (as will be demonstrated below), I will refer to these legal classifications as constituting a person's 'legal sex'.

Sex Surgeries

Genital Normalisation

Genital normalisation surgery is a type of surgery that is performed on intersex people, and an explanation of such surgeries requires engagement with the concept of intersex as well. The term 'intersex' refers to certain variations in (internal and/or external) sex-specific anatomy, caused by one of 'several dozen congenital conditions, including … hypospadias, Turner syndrome, congenital adrenal hyperplasia, androgen insensitivity syndrome, 5 alpha-reductase deficiency, and sex chromosome mosaicism' (Reis, 2009, p.xi). People who are intersex may possess one or more of the following: chromosomes that are not typically male or female (for example an XYY or XXY karyotype), gonads that are not typically male or female or that seem to contradict typical genital morphology (for example streak gonads or undescended testes), or so-called 'ambiguous genitalia' that are not typically male or female (for example a micropenis or an enlarged clitoris). Given the extent of biological variation within the categorisation of intersex, Karkazis (2008, p.9) identifies the term as a 'catchall category' with the 'defining feature … that intersex bodies in some way violate the commonly understood biological differences between males and females'. Essentially, 'intersex' labels those people whose sex cannot be considered to be 'exclusively "male" or "female"' (Australian Human Rights Commission, 2009b, p.2), at least under orthodox medical understandings of those terms.

The birth of an intersex child is not a particularly rare occurrence. Whilst there are 'few reliable estimates of the frequency of intersexuality' (Karkazis, 2008, p.22), Greenberg (2012, p.2, footnote omitted) identifies that:

> Most experts agree that approximately 1–2 percent of people are born with sexual features that vary from the medically defined norm for male and female. Approximately one in fifteen hundred to one in two thousand births involve a child who is born with genitalia so noticeably atypical that a specialist in sex differentiation is consulted and surgical alteration is considered.

It has been noted that being born with some form of intersex condition is probably more common than being born with albinism (Fausto-Sterling, 2000, p.53), cystic fibrosis or haemophilia (Callahan, 2009, p.7), conditions with much wider public recognition. In 2011, hospitals in Victoria reported approximately 40 new cases of intersex infants and were involved in following up and monitoring some 240 further cases (Department of Health, 2013).

Since the mid-twentieth century the term 'intersex' has mostly replaced the historical term 'hermaphrodite' as the definitive name for this catchall category

(Spurgas, 2009, p.97), hermaphrodite being jettisoned at least partly because of its negative associations with being a 'freak' and a 'mistake of nature' (Reis, 2009, p.154). In turn, the new term 'disorders of sex development' (hereafter 'DSD') was coined at the 2005 Chicago Consensus Conference, convened by the Lawson Wilkins Pediatric Endocrine Society and the European Society for Paediatric Endocrinology. Citing the argument that terms like intersex and hermaphroditism were potentially pejorative and confusing, the new term DSD was proposed to cover all atypical development of chromosomal, gonadal or anatomical sex (Hughes, 2006, p.148). Whilst the term DSD has been adopted by some activists as a 'move toward productive engagement with medical practitioners' (Grabham, 2012, p.3), I have chosen to retain the use of the word intersex in this book. The act of '[l]abeling something a "disorder" places it firmly in the medical world' (Davidian, 2011, p.3), and thus to utilise the terminology of DSD would be to collude with the discursive conceptualisation of intersex as a medical event potentially requiring the attendance and expertise of health care practitioners to administer treatment for a 'disorder' (Reis, 2009, pp.157–158). Such a medicalised construction would positively inflect any analysis of the validity of genital normalisation surgeries, an issue already flagged as being considered critically in this chapter, and would be further undesirable because it would alienate the subjective experiences of intersex people by dismissing their bodies as 'disordered' and in need of treatment (Greenberg, 2012, pp.92–93). Using DSD in this chapter would therefore be inappropriate. The term intersex has also been criticised as being highly politicised and linked to conceptions of a third gender and queer sexuality (Reis, 2009, p.159). However, because of the historical and cultural cachet intersex has developed in the past few decades, and because of its use as a term of identity amongst some intersex people themselves, its adoption here is less problematic. Indeed, despite the recent efforts of medical discourse to supplant the term intersex with DSD, Holmes (2009, p.7) rightly identifies that the term intersex retains its 'historical, social and political import … as a tool for interrogating heteronormative and bionormative presuppositions about proper embodiment'. As such, intersex will be used as the terminology in this chapter.

Intersex is not a recent phenomenon, but surgical treatment of it is. 'Hermaphrodites' featured in the writings of Plato and early biblical scholars, as well as being subject to extensive regulations in Jewish books of law such as the Talmud and the Tosefta (Fausto-Sterling, 1993, p.23). However, whilst surgical intervention on the genitalia of intersex people has occurred since as early as 1833 in the United States of America (Reis, 2009, pp.45–46), such surgical treatment remained rare until the mid-twentieth century (Spurgas, 2009, p.98). In the 1950s, the medical model that dominated modern intersex treatment was developed at Johns Hopkins University under the auspices of psychologist John Money. The 'optimum gender of rearing' model advocated quick assignation of a newborn intersex infant to either male or female and normalisation surgery on their ambiguous genitalia within the first two years of life in order to render their genitalia more clearly male or female, on the basis of the belief that this will assist them in the later development of a clear male/female gender identity and sexual orientation (Dreger, 2006, p.74). Though some intersex conditions go unnoticed and untreated until adolescence, the majority of genital normalisation surgeries occur on infants. Whilst some forms of intersex genital surgery are performed for the health and safety of the infant, such as those born with cloacal exstrophy, this chapter is only concerned with those surgeries whose function is purely '*aesthetic*' (Kessler, 1990a, p.34, emphasis in original).[2] Such genital normalisation surgery can include clitoridectomy or clitoroplasty for those whose clitorises are deemed 'too large', vaginoplasty for those with an absent or 'too short' vagina, various masculinising procedures, the fusing of labia to give them the appearance of a scrotum, and the splitting of the scrotum to give the appearance of labia (Callahan, 2009, pp.120–125). In these cases, the otherwise 'healthy' genital tissue of infants is cut, amputated or rearranged by doctors because its size and/or shape violate normative standards of genital appearance.

To distinguish between medically necessary surgery on intersex infants and that which has no physically therapeutic effect, this chapter will refer to the latter as 'genital normalisation' surgery. Whilst I resist the connotations of this phrasing that intersex genitals are not 'normal', and indeed that there is such a thing as a 'normal' set of genitals, this phrasing has been adopted to refer to the purposive intent that animates the performance of these surgeries and to their discursive effect. Whilst not all intersex people undergo genital surgery or undergo it in infancy (some intersex conditions only manifest later in life), it has been estimated that somewhere between 1.62 per cent and one and two in 1,000 infants are candidates for such surgery (Beh and Diamond, 2005a, p.11). Typically, an infant who is subject to surgical genital normalisation will undergo multiple operations, usually spaced out over a period of time (Ehrenreich and Barr, 2005, p.105).

The dominance of the Johns Hopkins-developed medical model persisted until, under heavy criticism from intersex activists and advocates (Greenberg, 2012), a new protocol was proposed with the formulation of the Consensus Statement on the Management of Intersex Disorders at the 2005 Chicago Conference. The new protocol in this Consensus Statement emphasises that medical personnel consider both the cosmetic outcome of such surgeries as

2 It should, however, be recognised that the boundary between aesthetic surgeries and 'medically necessary' surgeries here is blurry (just as it is in the case of cosmetic and reconstructive surgery, as discussed in Chapter 4), and has been used strategically by both supporters and opponents of genital normalisation surgery (Spurgas, 2009, p.112).

well as the functional outcome for future sexual sensation, and encourages the adoption of a non-surgical approach for minor cases of virilisation and the delay of some types of surgery until adolescence (Hughes, 2006, pp.152–153). However, it is important to note that even under this protocol, early genital normalising surgery is preserved as a medical option. Because it remains a medical option, and '[b]ecause the surgical approach has served as the dominant approach to intersex births for many decades, it is unlikely that this new treatment protocol will result in an end to genital-normalizing surgeries' (Uslan, 2010, p.305). Indeed, there are reports that such surgeries are continuing (Dreger and Feder, 2010). Because this protocol is not mandatory or enforced, it may even be the case that '[m]ost physicians … have not modified their practices to incorporate the recommendations' (Greenberg, 2012, p.83).

Genital normalisation surgeries take place in Australia. Melbourne's Royal Children's Hospital, which is 'recognised for their expertise in the management of DSD' (Warne and Hewitt, 2009, p.612), has long been 'an advocate of early genital surgery for infants with ambiguous genitalia who are to be female. Surgery at the age of 4 to 6 weeks is advised' (Warne and Bhatia, 2006, p.200). Even though it has been years since the release of the Consensus Statement on the Management of Intersex Disorders, 'no institution has yet to fully implement the new standard of care' (Accord Alliance, 2010). The Victorian Department of Health's (2013) recently released *Decision-Making Principles for the Care of Infants, Children and Adolescents with Intersex Conditions* recommends against defaulting to early surgeries and counsels restraint in their use, but also ultimately preserves them as a medical option. The continued practice of these surgeries has proven to be a contentious issue, attracting the attention of a number of government bodies, such as the Australian Human Rights Commission (2009b) and the Tasmanian Commissioner for Children (Mason, 2009b), as well as the media (Russell, 2010).

Sex Reassignment

A transsexual person is someone who has a firmly held and persistent identification of themselves as belonging to a gender which is different from that of their born sex (Dunderdale, 1992, p.23). This identification may be coupled with a desire to live as a person of the gender with which they identify and 'to be fully accepted as such by society' (Finlay and Walters, 1988, p.21). Transsexual people may dress and act in ways culturally associated with their gender identification for periods of time, and may seek various medical and/or surgical procedures to bring their bodies more closely into line with enculturated understandings about sex-appropriate appearance. I will refer to these surgeries collectively as 'sex reassignment' surgery. The process of shifting from openly identifying and acting socially as a member of their born biological sex to a member of their gender identity is typically described as 'transitioning'. During and after transitioning, many transsexual people will identify as simply being 'male' or 'female' in line with their gender identity. However, some transsexual people will identify themselves in ways that convey 'the sense of some element of transition' (Couch, et al., 2007, p.21), such as by describing themselves as a 'trans man' (if they were born biologically female), a 'trans woman' (if they were born biologically male) or a similar term. Under orthodox medical discourse, 'the distress that may accompany the incongruence between one's experienced or expressed gender and one's assigned gender' can be diagnosable as Gender Dysphoria (American Psychiatric Association, 2013, p.451).

Before setting out what sex reassignment surgeries entail, there are some terminological issues that need to be addressed. Whilst this chapter describes this phenomenon with the word 'transsexual' because of its ubiquitous use in medical, legal and popular discourse, there are a number of drawbacks to this term. As Lewins (1995, p.66) notes, some transsexual people find this term inappropriate because they identify themselves simply as male/female (in accordance with their gender identity) and disavow any other categorisation. Another possible motivation for rejecting this term is 'transsexualism's' etymology as a sexological and medical term, generated by doctors with no personal affiliation to transsexualism in an attempt to label and pathologise a particular population (Meyerowitz, 1998, p.160). Valentine's (2007, p.25) response to this was to drop one of the 's' letters from transsexual, thus spelling it 'transexual', in order to 'resist the pathologizing implications of the medicalized two "s" "transsexual"'. Whilst the full word 'transsexual' is retained here, it is not used uncritically. By drawing attention to these issues here, I seek to defuse some of the problems inherent in this term.

A distinction also needs to be drawn between the words 'transsexual' and 'transgender'. Whilst a transsexual person would usually be identified as being transgender, the reverse is not necessarily true. Transgender is an 'umbrella' term developed in the early 1990s that has since become quite popular in queer activism and academic work (Sharpe, 2002b, p.2). It is used to refer to 'a wide variety of bodily effects that disrupt or denaturalize heteronormatively constructed linkages between an individual's anatomy at birth, a nonconsensually assigned gender category, psychological identifications with sexed body images, and/or gender subject positions, and the performance of specifically gendered social, sexual, or kinship functions' (Stryker, 1998, p.149). In addition to transsexualism, other identity categories that the label 'transgender' covers include *inter alia* transvestites, cross-dressers, drag kings/queens, genderqueers and butch lesbians (Valentine, 2007, p.33). The terms, then, are not technically interchangeable, but are sometimes used interchangeably in media reporting and legal discourse.

Furthermore, whilst the surgeries undertaken by some transsexual people in order to align their sex with their gender identity have been termed 'sex reassignment surgeries' or 'sex change surgeries', there has also been a recent push to relabel them as 'sex affirmation surgeries' (Australian Human Rights Commission, 2009a). This new terminology is premised on the notion that transsexual people have always 'really been' the sex/gender indicated by their gender identity and that such surgeries do not 'change' but instead affirm the real sex/gender that has been obscured by their bodies. The strategic value of this new terminology is clear: it constructs the post-operative transsexual body as the 'natural', 'true' body of the transsexual person. This is a discursive position that, if accepted, would allow stronger claims to be made for legal rights and recognition for transsexual people, and enable them to have broader and easier access to medical technologies. This chapter retains the usage of 'sex reassignment surgeries', however, because this terminology is reflective of how these body alterations function, and have functioned, discursively and legally; such surgeries are understood by both medicine and the law to alter the sex of the individual undergoing them.

Surgical attempts to alter the sex of human patients have been documented as occurring as early as 1902 (Meyerowitz, 1998, p.161). However, modern medical and surgical treatments of transsexualism only really began to gain traction from the mid-twentieth century onwards (Bullough, 2007, p.4; Ekins, 2006, p.48; Hausman, 1995, pp.2–3), and it was not until the 1970s that both the classification of GID and the utilisation of sex reassignment surgery as the 'orthodox method of "treatment"' arose (Hines, 2007, p.12). The current protocols developed by World Professional Association for Transgender Health (2011, p.54) set out sex reassignment surgery as being 'often the last … step in the treatment process' that typically requires the transsexual patient to have first undergone counselling, taken doses of hormones, and gained real-life experience living openly for extended periods of time in accordance with their gender identity. Whilst not all transsexual people will choose to undergo surgery, many surgical options are available. A transsexual person who was born biologically male but who identifies as being female may undergo any number of the following:

- removal of the testes (orchiectomy);
- removal of the penis (penectomy);
- creation of a vagina (vaginoplasty);
- creation of a clitoris (clitoroplasty);
- creation of labia (labioplasty);
- breast implantation (mammoplasty);
- reduction of the Adam's apple (thyroid chrondoplasty); and/or,
- facial feminisation surgery (Reed, 2009, p.20).

A transsexual person who was born biologically female but who identifies as being male may undergo any number of the following:

- removal of both breasts (bilateral mastectomy);
- removal of the uterus (hysterectomy);
- removal of the vagina (vaginectomy);
- removal of the ovaries and Fallopian tubes (salpingo-oophorectomy);
- creation of a penis (metoidioplasty or phalloplasty);
- rerouting of the urethral exit (urethroplasty);
- creation of a scrotum (scrotoplasty); and/or,
- testicular implantation (Reed, 2009, p.20).

In addition to the medical risks involved in undergoing such procedures, they are also very expensive. For example, the Melbourne Gender Center, whilst recognising that costs vary between doctors and between countries, estimates that a transsexual person can expect to pay approximately $2,100 to $7,500 for bilateral mastectomies, $10,500 to $18,000 for a hysterectomy, $8,000 to $15,000 for a metoidioplasty, and $15,000 to $150,000 for a phalloplasty (The Gender Center Inc, 2008b, p.25).

In Australia, various sex reassignment surgeries have been performed since the mid-1950s, though more recently such procedures have been concentrated solely in Sydney and Melbourne (Wilson, 2002, p.428). Not all procedures are locally available. Dr Trudy Kennedy, the director of the Gender Dysphoria Clinic in Victoria has recently stated that phalloplasties are not performed in Australia 'because of the high risks and lack of success of the surgery' (*The State of Western Australia v AH* (2010) 41 WAR 431, p.465 per Buss JA). The prevalence of sex reassignment surgeries is difficult to determine for a number of reasons: not all people who experience incongruency between their sex and their gender identity seek medical treatment, not all people who seek medical treatment for this decide to transition, and not all people who decide to transition undergo sex reassignment surgery. Furthermore, data about the transsexual population in Australia is sparse. An early estimate by Finlay (1988, p.28) suggested that there were 400 male and 150 female transsexual people (where sex is described on the basis of born biology) over 15 years of age in Australia, with 25 new cases per year. More recent estimates given by Gina Mather, then president of the Australian Transgender Support Association, are much higher, suggesting that there are between 48,000 and 50,000 transsexual people in Australia and that about 80 patients undergo sex reassignment surgery every year (Hogan, 2003). Estimates from the United Kingdom suggest that 20 out of every 100,000 people are diagnosed with Gender Dysphoria and note that the prevalence of this diagnosis appears to be increasing over time (Reed, 2009, p.4).

The Legal Status of Sex Surgeries

The Legal Status of Genital Normalisation

Greenberg (2012, p.29) notes that '[t]hus far, no country or state has enacted controlling legislation' to govern intersex surgery or hormonal treatment, and Australia is no exception. No specific statutes define the legal status of genital normalisation surgery, and only a handful of cases discuss the legal issues pertinent to intersex people. The most prominent of these cases focus upon civil law issues, such as the legal sex identification of intersex individuals in *W v W (Nullity: Gender)* [2001] Fam 111 and *In the Marriage of C and D (falsely called C)* (1979) 28 ALR 524, but the legality of intersex surgeries has had some consideration in cases such as *In Re A* (1993) 16 Fam LR 715. Because these surgeries require physical intervention on the body of the patient, they will *prima facie* constitute assault. Given the level of harm inflicted by all types of genital normalisation surgery, possible charges of bodily harm, wounding or grievous bodily harm are theoretically available. However, criminal charges have not been brought because these surgeries are carried out by health care practitioners in a medical context and are almost invariably consented to by the parents of the intersex infant. These are all factors which may possibly exclude any criminal liability for the procedure. Clearly, very similar legal issues to those raised in the case of MC are relevant here, and I import the general legal framework raised in Chapter 3 concerning the defences of medical treatment and parental consent.

As with MC, the issue of whether the medical treatment defence is applicable turns on whether genital normalisation surgery can be said to be for the benefit of the infant. Physically, merely having ambiguous genitalia poses 'no immediate threat to life or limb of a child' (Gurney, 2007, p.653). Some types of surgical interventions may be for the medical benefit of some intersex infants, such as in *Re Sean and Another* [2010] FamCA 948, and this can include the removal of undescended testes which may be at a higher risk for developing cancer or the rerouting of the urethral opening to try to minimise recurrent urinary tract infections. However, '[i]n the vast majority of cases [intersex] conditions pose no physical threat' (Ehrenreich and Barr, 2005, p.75). For example, the reduction of a clitoris that is deemed 'too large' can have no possible physical benefit to the infant. Instead, the only possible benefit could be social and cultural. This is neatly encapsulated in the arguments that 'normal'-looking genitalia will reduce 'the risk that the infant will be rejected by parents, discriminated against or ostracised by peers and broader society', and allow the infant to internalise a greater 'acceptance of the sex and gender assigned at birth' (Australian Human Rights Commission, 2009b, p.8). It has been contended that such surgeries 'protect against potential psychosocial stress associated with 'looking different' and being known by others to look different' (Department of Health, 2013). However, such surgeries can also leave 'insensitive, painful, disfiguring or unwieldy scar tissue', make the infant prone to 'lifelong problems with urinary tract infections' (Dreger, 1998, pp.193–194), and potentially harm their orgasmic capability later in life (Karkazis, 2008, p.4). Further, arguments about future social or cultural problems and the reduction of stress have been dismissed as not providing 'a satisfactory rationale for surgical intervention' (Department of Health, 2013, p.22). It remains somewhat doubtful, then, whether such surgeries can be said to be for the benefit of the intersex infant, and the applicability of the medical treatment defence can be questioned.

It is also questionable whether legally valid consent can be given to genital normalisation surgery by the parents of an intersex child. Where the person undergoing the surgery is of the age of majority, or is a legally competent minor, they have the capacity to give legally valid consent. But consideration of the validity of parental consent is necessary because genital normalisation surgery is typically performed on infants or young adolescents who are legally incapable of giving valid consent to such procedures themselves. It seems that some judges may even be reluctant to find adolescent children to be legally competent in intersex cases. For example, in *In Re A* (1993) 16 Fam LR 715 (p.719), whilst Mushin J found that A, a fourteen and a half year old, understood both 'the problem' of their intersex condition and the surgical procedure, and 'expressed a desire' that it take place, he was still not satisfied that A had 'sufficient capacity and maturity to fully appreciate all aspects of the matter and to be able to assess objectively the various options available'.

Whether or not parents are capable of giving legally valid consent for their intersex child to undergo genital normalisation surgery with purely aesthetic results is a difficult question, and it has not been definitively answered at law. Speculation on the possible legal position requires close consideration of the application of *Marion's Case* (1992). Where a non-therapeutic surgical procedure is invasive, irreversible and major, and where there is a significant risk of making the wrong decision about the best interests of the child and the consequences of such a wrong decision are particularly grave, *Marion's Case* (1992) stands as authority that court authorisation is required before it can be lawfully carried out. As discussed above, it is very difficult to locate any therapeutic benefit for this type of surgery. Genital normalisation surgeries are inherently invasive because they involve cutting into the flesh of the patient, aspects of some procedures such as amputation of part of the clitoris or clitoral shaft are clearly irreversible, and they can be considered major because they surgically manipulate a physically sensitive and culturally meaningful area of the body. Furthermore, commentary on genital normalisation surgeries has catalogued the strong sense of 'violation that many' (though not all) 'intersex individuals feel as a result of their surgeries', surgeries that some have argued cause 'physical and psychological harms' whilst lacking 'justification' (Ehrenreich and Barr, 2005, p.132). This kind of reasoning leads to the conclusion that 'it is not clear that parents can consent to surgery' (Lareau, 2003, p.40), and to 'surmise that court authorisation should be sought before non-therapeutic surgery is performed on an infant who is intersex' (Australian Human Rights Commission, 2009b, p.5). Arguably, where these surgeries take place without court authorisation, an indefensible criminal offence may be committed.

Where genital normalisation surgery involves gonadectomy it will also typically render the intersex infant infertile. Because such procedures amount to sterilisation without consent they fall squarely under the prohibitions in *Marion's Case* (1992) as well as additional statutory overview. For example, in NSW it is a criminal offence punishable by seven years imprisonment to sterilise a child unless one abides by the strict legislative guidelines set out in the *Children and Young Persons (Care and Protection) Act 1998* (NSW) s175. Accordingly, if gonadectomy is to form part of a planned genital normalisation procedure then prior court approval must be sought. Recent cases have reiterated this point, with both *Re Lesley (Special Medical Procedure)* [2008] FamCA 1226 and *Re Sally (Special Medical Procedure)* [2010] FAMCA 237 involving parents seeking court authorisation for the orchiectomy of undescended testes in their intersex children who had been assigned, and raised, as female. In *Re Sally (Special Medical Procedure)* [2010] FAMCA 237, Murphy J's orders went further and also included authorisation for additional 'cosmetic treatment' for Sally as part of the overall treatment plan, but it was not decided whether the parents would be required to seek court authorisation for such aesthetic procedures if they were not also seeking authorisation for a sterilisation procedure.

Regardless of the possible technical questions that can be raised about whom, exactly, is capable of consenting to different types of genital normalisation surgeries, these surgeries themselves have a settled legality in Australia. They have been performed for decades, they continue to be performed, and where the procedures involve sterilisation of the intersex child the parents and doctors merely have to seek court authorisation for the procedure (authorisation which the courts seem willing to grant). Despite arguments that these surgical procedures possibly violate international human rights instruments, such as those contained in the *International Covenant on Civil and Political Rights*, the *Convention on the Rights of the Child* and the *Yogyakarta Principles* (Greenberg, 2006), and despite possible arguments that such surgeries performed on patients legally identifiable as female contravene FGM-criminalising provisions (Mason, 2009b, p.12), genital normalisation surgeries are not legally treated as being criminal.

The Legal Status of Sex Reassignment

Legal intersections with transsexualism have undergone pronounced changes in the previous two decades. Since the advent of sex reassignment surgeries, the dominant issue in what Sharpe (2002b) has called 'transgender jurisprudence' has been whether or not it is possible for transsexual people to change their legal sex from a designation that reflects their born biology to one that reflects their gender identity. This issue has been considered with regard to the validity of marriages (*Corbett v Corbett* [1971] P. 83; *Bellinger v Bellinger* [2003] UKHL 21), the distribution of social security benefits (*Scafe v Secretary, Department of Families, Housing, Community Services & Indigenous Affairs* (2008) 100 ALD 131; *Secretary, Department of Social Security v SRA* (1993) 43 FCR 299), and the commission of sex-specific criminal offences (*R v Cogley* [1989] VR 799; *R v Harris and McGuiness* (1988) 17 NSWLR 158; *R v Tan* [1983] QB 1053).

Australian law has moved through several phases of legal tests and legal thought around this issue (Grenfell and Hewitt, 2012; Sharpe, 2002b), including the passage of a swathe of legislation in the 1990s and 2000s that set up administrative pathways for the legal recognition of sex changes.[3] It is now settled that transsexual people can change their legal sex, though there remains contention about what exact preconditions the law should require before recognising this change. In addition, transgender jurisprudence has broadened in scope to encompass new issues such as various human rights claims (Alston, 1999; O'Flaherty and Fisher, 2008), anti-discrimination protection (Gurney and Mills, 2007; Herbert, 2009; Sharpe, 1999b), and a focus on the issues facing transsexual minors (Carrol, 2008–2009; Holman and Golber, 2007; Kennedy, 2008; Parlet and Weston-Scheuber, 2004). It is not within the scope of this book to consider these civil law issues directly, though they will be touched on at several points throughout this chapter. Instead, this chapter will focus on an old and almost forgotten legal issue within transgender jurisprudence: the position of sex reassignment surgery under criminal law. It is important to flag at the outset that my intention in raising and considering this dormant issue is not to suggest that such surgeries are criminal or should be criminalised. Instead, my intention is to highlight and unpack the discursive linkages that underpin the settled lawfulness of these surgeries.

---

3 See, for example, the *Births, Deaths and Marriages Registration Act 1997* (ACT) s24(1)(c), *Births, Deaths and Marriages Registration Act 2005* (NT) s28B(1)(b), *Births, Deaths and Marriages Registration Act 2003* (Qld) ss22–23, *Sexual Reassignment Act 1988* (SA), *Births, Deaths and Marriages Registration Act 1999* (Tas) s28A(1)(b), *Births, Deaths and Marriages Registration Act 1996* (Vic) s30A(1)(c), *Births, Deaths and Marriages Registration Act 1995* (NSW) s32B(1)(b) and the *Gender Reassignment Act 2000* (WA).

Early American legal commentary on transsexualism raised the possible criminality of sex reassignment surgeries by noting that they could arguably constitute the offence of mayhem. This historical offence derived from ancient English statute law that was originally intended to keep citizens 'from dismembering themselves or others so that they would be unable to fight in the service of the Crown', and it prohibited the disfigurement or mutilation of another person regardless of their consent (Smith, 1971, pp.988–989). Whilst no such charges were ever brought in the United States of America on the basis of sex reassignment surgery, the threat of possible prosecution may have prevented some of these surgeries from being performed during the mid-twentieth century (Holloway, 1974). Under modern Australian law, whilst the offence of mayhem may not be relevant anymore, more can be said about the legality of such surgeries. Like any interference with the body, sex reassignment surgery will *prima facie* constitute assault (although factual consent will be given by the recipient) and, given that many sex reassignment surgeries typically involve amputation of certain body parts, the level of harm will be sufficient to ground charges of at least bodily harm and wounding and more likely grievous bodily harm. As with genital normalisation surgeries, the medical treatment and consent defences may apply and need to be considered here.

Sex reassignment surgeries are performed almost exclusively on adult transsexual people. Whilst a number of recent Australian cases have held that court authorisation is required for minors to undergo medical treatment related to their transsexualism, the medical plans considered typically consisted of hormone doses and other non-surgical treatments to prevent the onset of puberty (*Re Alex: Hormonal Treatment for Gender Identity Dysphoria* (2004) 180 FLR 89; *Re Bernadette (Special Medical Procedure)* (2010) 244 FLR 242; *Re Brodie (Special Medical Procedures)* [2008] FamCA 334). Because transsexual surgical patients are typically adults, they are deemed to be legally capable of giving consent to a sex reassignment procedure and this consent could shield their surgeons from criminal liability. However, there are two potential problems with this account.

Firstly, the quality of the consent given by some adult transsexual people to surgery could be legally questioned given that the distress they suffer from as a result of their sex/gender incongruence may be sufficient to diagnose them with Gender Dysphoria. The legal issues here are similar to those discussed in Chapter 4 in relation to the quality of consent given to cosmetic surgery or healthy limb amputation by a person diagnosed with Body Dysmorphia. Not all mental health diagnoses automatically negate all forms of legal consent to surgery, however, and the appropriateness of both medicalising and pathologising transsexualism in this way is a strongly contested issue.

Secondly, sex reassignment surgery functions in a very different way than most other surgeries. The bodily structures amputated or rearranged are not subject to any disease, deformity or disability, and are otherwise 'healthy'.

Chapter 4 also identified a number of legal issues in relation to the lack of physical benefit for cosmetic surgery which are pertinent here too. In relation to the medical treatment defence, sex reassignment surgery clearly cannot be said to be for the patient's physical benefit, as amputating or rearranging body parts that are free from functional disorders can only put a patient's physical health and such functionality at risk. Indeed, these surgeries carry marked physical disbenefits. In addition to the typical medical dangers associated with anaesthesia, complications of sex reassignment treatments can include *inter alia* 'breast cancer in hormonally-treated males; the need for surgical reduction of bloated limbs resulting from hormones; repeated construction of vaginal openings; infections of the urinary system and rectum; haemorrhaging; loss of skin grafts' (Billings and Urban, 1995, p.108). The benefit to the patient cannot be located physically, then, but must be psychological, cultural or social in nature. Medical treatment of transsexualism generally, including surgery, is argued to be beneficial to a transsexual person's 'psychological well-being and identity' (Parlett and Weston-Scheuber, 2004, p.396) by mitigating the distress that many experience. Tobin (2006–2007, p.399) notes that '[f]or many trans people, [sex reassignment surgery] is essential to achieving peace of mind and a successful life in their authentic gender; the alternative is constant anxiety, social maladjustment, depression, and the danger of suicide'. Furthermore, given that sex reassignment surgery is generally accepted as appropriate treatment for Gender Dysphoria, in cases where there is diagnosis of a 'psychological disorder' this may offer a strong argument for a clear therapeutic benefit (Karpin, 2008, p.81) that may render such surgeries lawful under the medical treatment defence. Indeed, a similar kind of argument has been made in relation to certain forms of hormonal medical treatment for transsexual minors, which in the recent decision of *Re Jamie* (2013) 50 Fam LR 369 were held to be 'therapeutic' for the purposes of the application of the test in *Marion's Case* (1992).

Like genital normalisation surgeries, however, any technical legal questions that could be raised about such surgeries are rendered moot by their generally accepted lawfulness. Sex reassignment surgeries have been performed for decades within Australia and continue to be performed today. The fact that there is voluminous legal consideration of issues tangential to the carrying out of these body alterations – such as what effect they have on the legal sex of an individual – demonstrates the strength of the tacit assumption of their lawfulness. Indeed, sex reassignment procedures have been recognised, and thus implicitly legitimated, in other areas of the criminal law. For example, sex reassignment procedures are specifically written in as exceptions to the FGM-criminalising provisions in all jurisdictions (see Chapter 3), and in South Australia hospitals and health care practitioners must be approved before they can lawfully perform sex reassignment procedures (*Sexual Reassignment Act 1988* (SA), s6).

Denaturalising the Lawfulness of Sex Surgeries

Chapters 2, 3 and 4 all considered at least one form of body alteration that contravened the criminal law. The material in this chapter differs in that the bodily alterations that constitute the entire subject matter of the analysis are lawful. This difference should not appreciably change the analysis in this chapter as the contention in this book is that lawfulness and criminality are both produced as an effect of the discursive conditions, and thus they should be able to be unpacked and scrutinised in very similar ways. However, this difference does make the discursively constructed nature of the legal status of sex surgeries more opaque.

If the criminality of an act is conflated with notions of social illegitimacy, then criminal offences are foregrounded as material for analysis because they are seen as instances of rupture. Conversely, lawful acts are backgrounded because they blend into the normative social continuum and thus it is more difficult to conceive of the lawfulness of acts as being produced by discourse because their legal status is naturalised. For example, whilst it seems obvious that we can discuss the discursive positioning that renders killing someone else criminal, it seems highly counter-intuitive to talk about the discursive positioning that renders not killing another person lawful. Previous chapters bypassed the naturalising effect of lawfulness by using comparators to draw attention to the discursively constructed nature of lawfulness. Thus Chapter 2 contrasted the various discursive conceptualisations of sadomasochism generated by authoritative legal discourse to those generated by other competing discourses, Chapter 3 played off discourse around the lawfulness of MC against that around the criminality of FGM, and Chapter 4 did the same with regards to cosmetic surgery and non-mainstream body modification. Comparing the different ways of discursively conceptualising bodily alterations within these chapters helps to denaturalise their legal status by making it clear that their lawfulness or criminality is contingent upon the legal authorisation of certain meanings about them from a range of conflicting meanings. However, genital normalisation surgeries and sex reassignment surgeries are both lawful and the contention in this chapter is that they operate in very similar ways. Whilst obvious differences do exist between the two in practical, medical and legal terms, they have a similar function and effect within legal discourse (as I will demonstrate in detail below).

Because of their lawfulness and the similarities between them they cannot function as effective comparators for each other. As such, further work needs to be done in this chapter to denaturalise the lawfulness of sex surgeries. In order to do this, this section compares sex surgeries to other bodily alterations considered in previous chapters, specifically FGM, cosmetic surgery and healthy limb amputation, in order to demonstrate the range of meanings that could attach to sex surgeries and that law could alternatively embed. It is not the intention of this section to argue that sex surgeries should be criminalised due to any similarity to other already criminal body alterations. Rather, the aim of this section is simply to draw possible points of discursive connection and disconnection between a variety of body alterations in order to encourage reflexivity about the accepted lawfulness of sex surgeries. Doing this allows the analysis of the underlying discursive forces that produce the lawfulness of sex surgeries to proceed.

Connections Between Genital Normalisation and FGM?

As discussed in Chapter 3, there are many different forms of FGM and Australian anti-FGM statutory provisions have been widely drawn so as to prohibit the excision or mutilation of any part of the female genitalia. Genital normalisation surgery and FGM could be argued to be *prima facie* similar. Both involve the cutting and amputation of parts of (typically) an infant's genitalia in order to draw their body closer to cultural norms regarding the appropriate forms of physical genital embodiment (Greenberg, 2012, pp.98–99). Both body alterations aim to ensure the recipient has 'culturally acceptable genitals' (Kolbe, 2008, p.161) and are performed on otherwise healthy bodily tissue, whilst neither provides any form of medical therapeutic benefit. Full or partial clitoridectomies performed on intersex children by Western surgeons to 'normalise' virilised genitalia may even be physically identical to unlawful Type I FGM procedures.

The parallels between these two sets of body alterations have long been noted. In 1996, when the American Congress was considering a federal bill that would criminalise FGM, intersex advocate groups lobbied unsuccessfully for it to also criminalise genital normalisation surgeries (Karkazis, 2008, p.255). Since then, numerous writers have commented on the issue in terms of identifying that Western countries 'protest the practices of genital mutilation in other cultures, but tolerate them at home' (Fausto-Sterling, 2000, p.79, footnote omitted). In an argument remarkably similar to those launched by anti-MC activists, Chase (1998, p.204) notes that Western commentators are quick to point to FGM as a harmful cultural practice whilst neglecting to recognise the enculturated nature of physically harmful genital normalisation surgeries on intersex people. Indeed, such surgeries rely on particular culturally located understandings about the size and function of certain bodily parts that draws on conceptions of sexed difference. Genital normalisation surgeries also cause harms to intersex infants that have been likened to those claimed to be caused by FGM, leaving children 'physically and psychologically scarred' (Green, 2005, p.168). However, '[d]espite the similarities between the surgeries, their harmful physical and psychological effects, and the patriarchal heterosexist norms that support both practices, anti-FGC feminists have excluded intersex concerns from their agenda' (Greenberg, 2012, p.99).

If genital normalisation surgeries were to be discursively conceptualised as a type of cultural harm, they would easily fulfil the requirements for the commission of an offence under Australian FGM-criminalising statutes (Mason, 2009a, p.12). Davidian (2011, pp.12–13) argues that the crucial dissimilarity between genital normalisation surgery and FGM is the legitimisation of such surgeries by a 'sociomedical discourse' that positions them as 'standard medical practice'. The medicalisation of such surgeries is a discursive issue that will be addressed in detail below, suffice it to say here that the sheer physical similarity between lawful genital normalisation surgeries and certain kinds of criminal FGM destabilises the uncritical acceptance of their lawfulness.

Connections Between Sex Surgeries, Cosmetic Surgery and Healthy Limb Amputation?

Comparisons between cosmetic surgery and sex surgeries are frequently drawn in the literature. Both genital normalisation surgeries (Fausto-Sterling, 2000; Holmes, 2002; Kessler, 1990a; Roen, 2008) and sex reassignment surgeries (Hausman, 1995; Nataf, 2006, pp.55–56) have been described as, or conceptually linked to, cosmetic surgery. Indeed, in an information kit prepared for transsexual people undergoing genital-based sex reassignment surgery the Gender Centre (2008, p.6, emphasis in original) notes that the 'appearance of your result is obviously an important part of any *cosmetic procedure*'. Drawing points of similarity between sex surgeries and cosmetic surgery seems to support the discursive positioning of sex surgeries as also being a lawful form of body alteration. However, two key factors problematise this comparison.

Firstly, genital normalisation surgeries are performed almost exclusively on infants. Whilst some cosmetic surgeries are performed on minors, even these are typically performed on adolescents rather than on infants. Indeed, recent legal concern with the growing numbers of such procedures on minors has led to restrictions such as those imposed by the *Health Legislation (Restriction on Use of Cosmetic Surgery for Children and Another Measure) Amendment Act 2008* (Qld). If one condones genital normalisation surgery on an intersex infant's ambiguous genitalia as a form of 'cosmetic surgery', then does this also commit one to condoning cosmetic surgery on a non-intersex infant who has sexually unambiguous but 'ugly' genitalia? If the former surgery is acceptable but the latter surgery is not, then there must be some important distinguishing factor that renders cosmetic surgery and genital normalisation surgery separate and distinct. If these two sets of body alterations are not equivalent in this way, then the lawfulness of genital normalisation surgery cannot be justified on the basis of its similarity to cosmetic surgery.

Secondly, whilst some sex reassignment surgeries are physically identical to some cosmetic surgeries, such as mammoplasty, others seem radically different in scope. Penectomy and orchiectomy, for example, have been identified as seeming to be more akin to healthy limb amputation than cosmetic surgery because they are procedures that amputate 'healthy' parts of the body (Bergelson, 2006–2007, pp.182–183). Lawrence (2006) argues that the desire for sex reassignment surgery and the desire for the removal of a healthy limb are similar, whilst Elliott (2009) and MacKenzie (2008) both consider that healthy limb amputation could be motivated by BIID, a disorder which shares both a similar name and conceptual framework with GID (the historical disorder used to diagnose transsexual people until it was replaced by Gender Dysphoria in 2013). The similarities between some transsexual people and those who desire healthy limb amputation go further than the common goal of having parts of the body removed. '[P]ersonal accounts of both transsexualism and self-demand amputation' share the common 'image of the self trapped in a body that is alien and alienating' (Sullivan, 2008, p.106). For these reasons, it has been argued that sex reassignment surgeries 'are perhaps the closest parallel to voluntary limb amputation because they similarly involve major surgery to the body which is not physically indicated, but which is carried out to satisfy the patient's internal perception of how their body should look', though there is discursive contestation about whether notions of disability and mental health operate in similar or different ways around these body alterations (Bogdanoski, 2009, p.513).

Unlike cosmetic surgery and sex reassignment surgery, healthy limb amputation (as discussed in Chapter 4) has an unsettled status at law and may be criminal. If some forms of sex reassignment surgery are conceptually akin to healthy limb amputation at some level, more work is thus needed to unpack how the two are distinguishable from each other. In order to do this, it is necessary to move beyond a purely physical account of these body alterations, and look instead to the discursive frameworks that work to render such surgeries lawful.

The Discursive Construction of the Lawfulness of Sex Surgeries

By gesturing towards these points of connection and disconnection between sex surgeries and other body alterations, I hope to have demonstrated that the lawfulness of these surgeries results from actualising one contingent possible construction of what they can mean from a pool of possibilities, and to have prompted reflexivity about the accepted lawfulness of sex surgeries. What becomes important, then, are the discursive forces that have aligned to construct and maintain the current lawfulness of sex surgeries, and that have produced their lawfulness as an effect of this discursive framework. Three main discursive linkages inform the lawfulness of sex surgeries: conceptions of health and medicine, conceptions of sex/gender, and conceptions of 'truth'.

Conceptions of Health and Medicine

Intersex and transsexualism are thoroughly enmeshed within medical discourse. Legal discourse colludes in this medicalisation as the legal authorisation of the medical model of treatment for these 'disorders' strongly embeds and naturalises surgical intervention and medicalised understandings about harm and the body within the discursive framework.

Sex surgeries as medical treatment

The lawfulness of sex surgeries is contingent upon the conceptualisation of both intersex and transsexualism within a medical paradigm, wherein the mere existence of intersex and transsexual people is a medical event requiring diagnosis, oversight and treatment. Intersex has not always been regarded this way. Fausto-Sterling (2000, p.40, footnote omitted) reminds us that it was only with the dawn of the twentieth century, and the growth of medical knowledge and surgical technique, that 'physicians were recognized as the chief regulators of sexual intermediacy'. Previously, it had not been seen as 'imperative to catch mixed-sex people at birth and convert them, by any means necessary, to either male or female' (Fausto-Sterling, 2000, p.40). More recently, however, the birth of a child with ambiguous genitalia has typically been 'labelled a medical and social emergency' regardless of whether the intersex condition poses any risk to the infant's health (Karkazis, 2008, p.7). When such conditions are diagnosed, the infant is subjected to tests and treatments administered by endocrinologists, urologists, gynaecologists, psychologists, and surgeons, trapping them in a 'web of relationships that have the potential literally to result in physical incisions, the removal of tissue, and the administration of hormones' (Grabham, 2007, p.39). The mere presence of non-normatively shaped or proportioned genitalia mobilises extensive amounts of medical time and resources, concerned with producing a 'healthy' infant from a 'sick' body that is in need of treatment. This medical fixation on intersex bodies creates the disability it purports to be curing; by disseminating knowledge about the deviance of these bodies and by performing tests and treatments on them, health care practitioners 'convey the message that those born with intersex conditions are abnormal, pathological, and needing correction' (Ehrenreich and Barr, 2005, p.120).

The pathologisation of intersex mirrors the creep of the boundaries of medical treatment to cover previously unremarkable bodily variations (as discussed in Chapter 4 regarding cosmetic surgeries), with bodies being surgically altered not to alleviate physical pain or restore functionality but simply so that they more closely conform to normative ideals. The condition intersex infants are constructed as suffering from is not disabling in the sense that it presents them with 'functional limitations', but rather simply the 'problem' is that their 'corporeal configurations … violate cultural standards' (Karkazis, 2008, p.10). Thus you find arguments justifying genital normalisation surgery on intersex infants on the basis that when these infants are older they may become subject to 'social ridicule, gender-identification and psychological issues, locker-room banter, social discrimination, and moral judgments' (Aliabadi, 2005, p.458), because their bodies differ from normative understandings about embodiment. It is an interesting thought-experiment to consider whether medical treatments should be offered for other bodily variations that may produce similarly negative social outcomes later in life, such as skin-whitening treatments for dark-skinned infants in white-dominated Western countries with racist cultural histories (Kessler, 1998, p.35), or limb-shortening surgeries for infants predicted to grow to be exceedingly tall. Whilst these children have so far eluded what Karkazis (2008, p.8) identifies as an 'increasing tendency to turn social issues into biomedical problems that can be solved by clinical intervention', intersex infants have not.

Transsexual bodies are also thoroughly enmeshed within medicine and medical discourse. This is partly the result of the practical reality that 'many transgender people remain dependent upon physicians and/or surgeons to the extent that they desire sex reassignment surgery, other surgical procedures, and/or regulated hormone treatments' (Sharpe, 2002b, p.8). However, transsexualism as a discursive construct is also constituted through modern medical understandings and methods of medical and surgical treatment. Indeed, Hausman (1995, p.110) locates the demand for sex reassignment surgery as an essential part of transsexualism, identifying that it is the 'mechanism through which transsexuals come to identify themselves under the sign of transsexualism and construct themselves as its subject'. Transsexual people are not just 'dependent on medical caretakers throughout their lives for hormones and surgical repairs to the surgery that is offered as a panacea for their suffering' (MacKenzie, 1994, p.20), the hormones and surgical treatments help constitute the 'disorder' from which they are alleged to be 'suffering'. That the discursive model of transsexualism is at least partly produced through a medicalised system, rather than simply turning upon personal identity claims or subjective lived experience, is most obvious when one is aware that '[g]ender identity clinics administer a battery of tests to candidates for sexual reassignment' and that '[i]t is possible to "fail" these tests for transsexualism, as well as to "pass" them' (Garber, 1992, p.106). If one 'passes' these tests, the scope of medical testing and treatment is extensive and far-reaching. For example, the World Professional Association for Transgender Health (2011, p.106) sets out treatment prerequisites for genital surgery that include the requirement that a candidate complete '12 continuous months of living in a gender role that is congruent with their gender identity'. Thus, even the social, non-physical transitioning of a transsexual person becomes medicalised: it is located within medical discourse as part of a treatment plan and as a treatment prerequisite that unlocks further medical options.

The medicalisation of intersex and transsexual bodies can be understood as strategically defusing the social anxiety created by their sex/gender ambiguities. The ambiguous sex of intersex bodies threatens culturally valued understandings about the separate and opposed nature of 'male' and 'female', and genital normalisation surgeries defuse this transgressive potential by intervening quickly and definitively to surgically transform them into docile 'male' or 'female' bodies. The construction of intersex within medicolegal discourse presents intersex bodies as aberrant and diseased, necessitating this kind of surgical intervention as a form of rehabilitation.

Like intersex bodies, transsexual bodies create social anxiety that medical discourse functions to defuse. The normative understanding that if a person has male genitals then that person will also have a masculine gender identity, and *vice versa*, is contested by transsexualism; transsexual people undermine the cultural 'truth' that gender identity is always congruent with sex. However, medical discourse and its preferred treatment model of hormones, real-life experience and sex reassignment surgery, works to bring the transsexual person back into such normative congruence. Indeed, 'the congruence of physiology and behaviour is … the goal' of sex reassignment surgery (Hausman, 1995, p.132). In this way, transsexualism is put to use within medicolegal discourse as a conservative category that preserves the idea that 'certain gender behaviours are allowed on the basis of whether you inhabit a male or female body, determined by genital anatomy' (MacKenzie, 1994, p.62). MacKenzie (1994, pp.61–62) identifies the 'agenda' behind sex reassignment as being the maintenance of the normative ideal that 'masculine-acting people belong in male bodies and feminine-acting people belong in female bodies'. The medically and surgically fashioned body of the transsexual person thus functions as a 'permanent "spectacle" of truth' (de Castro, 1993, p.58), the 'truth' not only of the transsexual person's sex/gender identity but also the 'truth' of sex-specific bodily structures corresponding in normative ways with gender identity and gendered social behaviours. Medical discourse, then, constructs transsexualism on normative grounds and strategically deploys medical treatments to shut down the transgressive potential of incongruency.

Law's collusion with medical discourse thus functions to manage and contain the sex of potentially 'unruly' or transgressive bodies to ensure that their sex/gender remains 'docile'. In doing so, the patterned medicolegal construction of the specific discursive categories of intersex and transsexualism slots into a broader process of the (re)production of sex more generally. By explicitly determining what is problematic, 'sick' and in need of 'treatment', medicolegal discourse implicitly constructs a model of what is unproblematic, 'healthy' and 'normal'. Law and medicine not only discursively produce the conceptual categories 'intersex' and 'transsexualism' through this process, they also simultaneously (re)produce the conceptual categories of 'male' and 'female'. In this way, the lawfulness of sex surgeries reflects Foucault's recognition that discourse functions creatively, revealing that sex/gender is 'a product of power relations' rather than something that is 'natural' (Cowan, 2005, p.71).

The internalisation of medical discourse

The internalisation of medical discourse into the law in this area is evident in the multiple ways legal discourse privileges medical evidence and utilises medical terminology. Medical evidence is treated as being of primary importance when considering the legal issues surrounding intersex and transsexualism. Harrison-Smith (2007, p.217) identifies that cases involving transsexual issues are characterised by 'the dependence of the judiciary on medical evidence', and the same is true of cases involving intersex issues. Thus, in *Re Bernadette (Special Medical Procedure)* (2010) 244 FLR 242, Collier J found it necessary to consider affidavit material on medical matters from three doctors and four medical professors when determining whether or not Bernadette should begin early-stage medical treatment for transsexualism during her adolescence. This has long been the case with the legal treatment of sex reassignment surgeries, with Ormrod J in *Corbett v Corbett* [1971] P. 83 hearing evidence from four medical professors and two doctors, as well as drawing on his own medical qualifications, as a basis for deciding the legal sex of April Ashley (whose sex at birth was male but whose gender identity was female and who had undergone a number of medical treatments). The use of the medical paradigm as providing the key evidentiary basis for determining legal issues around sex surgeries sets up health care practitioners as having definitive expertise in these issues. Despite the wide-ranging social and political questions about sex, gender and gender identity that intersex and transsexualism raise, sex surgeries become an issue almost purely of medical concern, and medical matters are given primary importance when considering these surgeries.

Legal discourse's adoption of medical terms also supports the pathologisation of intersex and transsexual people. The adoption of 'medical jargon' within legal discourse 'reflects the widespread acceptance of [the] medical paradigm' (Preves, 2002, p.532). For example, in *Re Sally (Special Medical Procedure)* [2010] FAMCA 237 (p.4, emphasis added) Murphy J describes Sally's intersex status in medical terms by noting that what Sally '*suffers* [from] is 5-alpha-reductase deficiency'. Sally is not described as being intersex, in fact the word 'intersex' is not used within the judgment,[4] nor is she described as being locatable in a more central area on the biological continuum between male and female. Rather, she is constructed as a suffering, medically-disordered female child. The underlying message within Murphy J's description of Sally as appearing 'to be a happy and healthy baby girl' at the time of her birth (*Re Sally (Special Medical Procedure)* [2010] FAMCA 237 (p.1) is the implication that the later revelation of Sally's intersex status necessarily makes her both unhappy and unhealthy. In a similar way, Carter J dramatically places a quote from one of the medical professors consulted in *Re Brodie (Special Medical Procedures)* [2008] FamCA 334 in the second last paragraph of her judgment, just before the ultimate decision. When asked what becomes of transsexual minors who do not seek medical assistance, the anonymous 'Professor W' responds: 'They just suffer out there, I think' (*Re Brodie (Special Medical Procedures)* [2008] FamCA 334, p.29).

Legal discourse presents the lawfulness of sex surgeries as simply the natural result of the medical treatment model for intersex and transsexualism. The administration of medication to pre-adolescent minors to block puberty, the administration of hormones that alter biological structures, psychological counselling and surgery are all legally accepted as unremarkable aspects of medical treatment for either intersex or transsexualism, and may indeed even be 'necessary' due to the suffering that intersex and transsexualism are constructed as always causing. Furthermore, this centrality of medical and surgical treatment correlatively constructs the post-treatment intersex or transsexual body as now being 'healthy' and 'fixed'. In this way, the 'successfully integrated' post-sex reassignment surgery transsexual person becomes the 'apex of cross-gender transition' (Halberstam, 1998, p.290). The law has drawn on this pre- and post-operative distinction in a number of ways in its conceptualisation of transsexualism (Sharpe, 2002b), and this distinction figures prominently in law's requirement of medical or surgical intervention as a key prerequisite to 'changing' legal sex. Thus it is a requirement that a transsexual person must have undergone sex reassignment surgery in order to be able to apply to change the sex displayed on their birth certificate in the Northern Territory (*Births, Deaths and Marriages Registration Act 2005* (NT)), Queensland (*Births, Deaths and Marriages Registration Act 2003* (Qld)), Tasmania (*Births, Deaths and Marriages Registration Act 1999* (Tas)) Victoria (*Births, Deaths and Marriages Registration Act 1996* (Vic)), and New South Wales (*Births, Deaths and Marriages Registration Act 1995* (NSW)). In the ACT, this requirement was altered in 2014 to providing medical evidence of 'appropriate clinical treatment' (*Births, Deaths and Marriages Registration Act 1997*

4 The word 'intersex' does not occur in *Re Sally (Special Medical Procedure)* [2010] FAMCA 237, *Re Lesley (Special Medical Procedure)* [2008] FamCA 1226 or *In Re A* (1993) 16 Fam LR 715, although the word 'intersexual' is used once. Tellingly, the judges used medical terms relating to specific names of disorders and biological structures.

(ACT)). In South Australia and Western Australia, surgery is a sufficient but not necessary legal prerequisite as non-surgical medical procedures can also meet the statutory requirements. For example, in Western Australia the requirement is that such applicants undergo a 'reassignment procedure', which is defined as being a 'medical or surgical procedure (or a combination of such procedures) to alter the genitals and other gender characteristics of a person, identified by a birth certificate as male or female, so that the person will be identified as a person of the opposite sex' (*Gender Reassignment Act 2000* (WA), s3). This section was interpreted by the High Court in *AB v Western Australia; AH v Western Australia* (2011) 244 CLR 390 (p.405) to mean that the applicant must undergo sufficient medical or surgical procedures so that their 'appearance' (along with their 'behaviour in the conduct of their life') would 'be accepted by other members of society as conforming to the gender to which the person seeks reassignment'. Even though surgery is not legally required in Western Australia there is clearly still a strong prerequisite for some kind of medicalised body alteration.

These legal body alteration requirements may be problematic for some transsexual people. It should be noted that sex reassignment surgeries can and do have great psychological benefits for many transsexual people who undergo them. The *Tranznation* report, prepared by the Australian Research Centre *in Sex, Health & Society*, found that people who had undergone such surgeries 'often described a deep sense of satisfaction, feelings of relief and completeness with having a body that they have felt to be right for them' (Couch, et al., 2007, p.48). However, the indexation of legal sex recognition to medical and/or surgical prerequisites places pressure on transsexual people to alter their bodies in ways that not all will want or be able to do. As Tobin (2006–2007, p.434) recognises, '[l]arge numbers of trans people live without such surgery due to medical conditions, financial constraints, fear of complications, religious beliefs, or simply by personal choice'.

The discursive coupling of medical and legal discourse around intersex and transsexual bodies also produces the current legal status of sex surgeries as a particularly authoritative and powerful effect. Sharpe (2002b, pp.8–9) recognises that the 'special power enjoyed by law, an effect of the institutional, political and moral authority it commands', is 'bolstered' by this coupling, 'strengthening … the "truth" claims thereby generated'. So what are the truth claims about bodies that are generated by this 'interwoven governance mechanism of [the] legal and medical realms'? (Spade, 2003, p.18). In many ways, the law merely reinforces the medical model's recuperation of the transgressive potential of both intersex and transsexualism through the lawfulness of sex surgeries. Legalising genital normalisation surgeries is tantamount to refusing to admit that the binary opposition of male/female is culturally constructed and non-reflective of even the biological reality of the sex of many individuals. Such surgeries also constitute the 'literal reinscription of sex on to "unruly" bodies' (Hird, 2000, p.349). At one level, the discursively constructed 'need' for such surgeries explains away those bodies that display incongruity between their gender-specific identity/behaviour and their biological structures as being disordered or sick. At another level, such surgeries also literally erase those incongruent bodies by generating such congruence.

Sharpe (2002b, p.37) has argued persuasively that within the broader transgender jurisprudence 'legal concerns cannot be reduced to those of medicine' and that 'law draws heavily, though selectively, on medical knowledge in support of its, often conflicting, propositions' about transsexualism and transsexual people. However, whilst the relationship between law and medicine may be more nuanced around related issues such as legal sex identification and anti-discrimination frameworks, the legal status of sex surgeries as lawful body alterations is the result of a discursive framework in which legal discourse is closely collusively intertwined with medical discursive understandings of intersex and transsexualism. Law and legal discourse may only partially defer to medical experts and medical science 'for the categorization of men and women' (Mayeda, 2009, p.196) at a theoretical level, but it seems to fully defer to their authority to physically (re)inscribe sex at a physical level. The pathologisation of intersex and transsexualism constructs sex surgeries within legal discourse as beneficial treatments that cure sickness and promote wellbeing, rather than as surgical interventions into otherwise 'healthy' flesh without any physical benefit. In return the medical discursive model offers legal discourse a conveniently preset methodology of surgical erasure that defuses the social anxieties caused by intersex and transsexual bodies. Law's 'co-operation' with medical discourse here helps to 'extend its sovereignty' over sex/gender and reflects a 'mode of disciplinary regulation' (Smart, 1989, pp.16–17). By co-opting the medical mechanisms of strict oversight and invasive testing and treatment, the law enhances its power over intersex and transsexual bodies by rendering them both more visible and vulnerable. As in legal discourse around FGM (as discussed in Chapter 3), what is lost in law's close complicity with medical language and conceptualisation is any recognition of the social and political aspects of such body alterations. The role of intersex as a 'sociopolitical phenomenon' (Wilson, 2012) is discursively erased when it is conceived of as a medical disability, as are the identity politics and subjective experience of transsexualism when it is reduced to being a psychological disorder or a physical condition that is 'treated'.

Through sex reassignment surgery transsexual people 'are, literally, "made to fit" within existing sex and gender structures' and this ensures that they are 'no longer a threat to the heteronormative order' (Cowan, 2005, p.72). Genital normalisation surgeries have the same effect with regards to intersex people. This process of erasure folds the transgressive potential of 'unruly' intersex and transsexual bodies back into normative understandings about appropriately-sexed embodiment by working to make them into 'docile' bodies.

Conceptions of Sex/Gender

Legal discourse's treatment of sex surgeries is underpinned by conceptions of sex and gender that simultaneously uphold both a normative set of ideas about the content of these categories and also their configuration as separate and distinct. This section will address three key issues that constitute part of legal discourse around sex surgeries and that relate to sex/gender: the legal requirements to change sex identification, how the law reads ambiguous bodies, and heterosexualism.

The requirements to change legal sex

This chapter has already discussed the legal requirements for a transsexual person to change the legal sex that is registered on their birth certificate, such requirements being phrased to focus predominantly on the transsexual person's biology and whether they have undergone sex reassignment surgery. However, before sex reassignment surgery can be performed, a transsexual person is typically required by health care practitioners to have undergone extensive real-life experience acting in the social role of their psychological sex (World Professional Association for Transgender Health, 2011, p.108). Similarly, some of the birth certificate-altering statutes also include social transitioning requirements, for example the *Gender Reassignment Act 2000* (WA) s15(1)(b)(ii) requires an applicant for a certificate to satisfy the Gender Reassignment Board that they have 'adopted the lifestyle ... of a person of the gender to which the person has been reassigned'. The medicolegal requirements to change sex, then, can be both biological and social.

These social requirements were explicitly considered at length in the celebrated case of *Attorney-General (Commonwealth) v Kevin* (2003) 172 FLR 300 (hereafter '*Attorney-General v Kevin* (2003)'). This case marked the first time a marriage in Australia between a transsexual person and a person of the same born biological sex had been held to be valid. Statutory regimes for changing the legal sex recorded on birth certificates may have overtaken these case law developments, but this is unclear. Indeed, it might not be the case that having your sex changed on your birth certificate definitively changes your sex in all legal circumstances: these legal tests may operate as parallel streams of law that do not intersect. The law has historically been careful to compartmentalise its consideration of legal sex change into different circumstances. For example, in *Corbett v Corbett* [1971] P. 83 (p.106) Ormrod J took pains to note that he was only determining 'what is meant by the word "woman" in the context of a marriage', and that he was 'not concerned to determine the "legal sex" of the respondent at large'. It may be the case that the 'determination of sex for marriage purposes may involve a different set of considerations than for other purposes' (Sharpe, 2002b, p.91). Indeed, the requirements to change the sex noted on a birth certificate are very different from the requirements to change the sex noted on an Australian passport. In the case of a passport, all that needs to be provided is a letter from a medical practitioner – registered with the Medical Board of Australia – noting that the person 'has had, or is receiving, appropriate clinical treatment for gender transition' (Australian Passport Office, 2011). As a result, although it is unclear how much legal value *Attorney-General v Kevin* (2003) holds as a case precedent, it still provides analytic value as an integral part of legal discourse on transsexualism.

The presiding appeal judges in *Attorney-General v Kevin* (2003) extensively quoted from Chisholm J's decision in the same matter in the lower court case of *Re Kevin: Validity of Marriage of Transsexual* (2001) 165 FLR 404 and ultimately approved it. In his decision, Chisholm J focused a lot of attention on the stereotypically masculine aspects of Kevin's social transitioning to live as a man, including his personal life (wife and children), his sartorial choices (shirts and pants), his leisure time (playing sport) and his skills (landscaping and construction) (*Re Kevin: Validity of Marriage of Transsexual* (2001) 165 FLR 404, pp.414–417). Chisholm J used this evidence about Kevin to satisfy himself that Kevin not only had a sufficiently 'masculine' biology but also, importantly, that he had a sufficiently 'masculine' lifestyle: a factor that demonstrated that when people interact with Kevin they 'see him and think of him as a man, doing what men do' (*Re Kevin: Validity of Marriage of Transsexual* (2001) 165 FLR 404, p.417).

I have argued elsewhere that the legal focus on these kinds of social factors is potentially problematic for transsexual people, as it may construct an additional set of social requirements that slot in beside the extant biological requirements and that these social requirements could possibly operate restrictively by trading on stereotypical and outdated notions of 'male'/'female' lives and lifestyles (Bennett, 2013). Here, however, I want to draw attention to a different point. Underlying the existence of any legal attention to social factors is a concern with the visibility of a transsexual person's sex/gender. Whilst sex reassignment surgeries may alter the structure of a person's physical genitalia, this may not be readily apparent to other members of society. Legal consideration of social factors, such as a person's life and lifestyle, supplements this possible deficiency by being directed towards what has been termed 'cultural genitals', that is the genitals that person is assumed to have in wider society because of one's appearance and behaviour (Morland, 2001, p.529). Socially visible gendered expressions work together with sex surgeries to erase the trangressiveness of transsexualism by constructing a visible congruency between physical and cultural genitalia. As such, the legal requirements for gender display can be identified as a necessary part of legal discourse's collusion with broader discursive frameworks around sex and gender. By colluding with the medical model of transsexual 'treatment' that includes a social transitioning process, and by adopting legal tests that look towards gender-appropriate social display, the law ensures that both the biological and the cultural genitals of transsexual people display their sex/gender unambiguously to society. As Sharpe (2002b, p.84) notes, 'there is no suggestion of gender floating free from sex in legal discourse … gender remains very much tied to the notion of sex'. The requirement to display unambiguous 'cultural genitals' is part of this broader process of tethering gender to sex.

Legal discourse sets up a transsexual ideal where the legally valued transsexual subject is one who enacts the sex/gender they are trying to transition into both physically, by undergoing medical and surgical treatment, and socially, by presenting themselves in accordance with, and enacting, normative gender roles. To be legally recognised as having transitioned, a transsexual person must demonstrate that both their sex (understood as their body) and their gender (understood as their social behaviour, identification and recognition) correspond with the legal status they seek. The lawfulness of sex reassignment surgery can be attributed to the way such surgeries function normatively; they uphold Western culture's deep commitment to the male/female binary (Fausto-Sterling, 1993, p.20), and uphold both the sex/gender division and the stereotypical conceptions of masculinity/femininity that surround it.

Legal interpretation of ambiguous bodies

If legal discourse is underpinned by normative conceptions about bodies that require congruence between a person's sex and gender, then how does law deal with people whose bodies fail to unequivocally display sex in the first place? The biological categories of male and female can be understood as mere descriptors pertaining to the most statistically likely patterns of genital and anatomical development. Normative male and female bodies stand as poles 'on the extreme ends of a biological continuum' in between which 'there are many other bodies … that evidently mix together anatomical components conventionally attributed to both males and females' (Fausto-Sterling, 2000, p.31). In contrast, the law typically upholds the stand-point that all individuals, regardless of anatomy, are either male or female. For example, birth certificates in Australia must identify the person in question as either male or female, except 'in rare circumstances such as in the case of stillborn children or premature births where sex could not be determined' and then an identification of 'indeterminate' is allowed (Australian Human Rights Commission, 2009a, p.15) – though in the past year this position has shifted in both NSW and the ACT (as discussed below). This strict legal categorisation of male and female is generally accepted as '[m]ost of us are used to the idea of two sexes, and most of us are used to being only one' (Dreger, 1998, p.6). Intersex and transsexual people subvert this classificatory system as they present legal discourse with bodies that are incommensurable with normative understandings of sexed embodiment and thus deny the biological basis on which sex categorisations are made. However, the law operates as a blunt instrument in this area by forcing intersex and transsexual bodies into these strict categorisations regardless of the problems inherent in doing so.

As Chisholm J notes in *Re Kevin: Validity of Marriage of Transsexual* (2001) 165 FLR 404 (p.473), the law's task is to 'assign individuals to one category or the other, including individuals whose characteristics are not uniformly those of one or other sex'. The case of *The State of Western Australia v AH* (2010) 41 WAR 431, and its appeal decision in *AB v Western Australia; AH v Western Australia* (2011) 244 CLR 390, demonstrate this point. The underlying facts related to two transsexual applicants who sought to have their female birth certificates changed to legally identify them as male because they both self-identified as male, acted socially as males, had had their breasts amputated, and had undergone hormone therapy for years that had deepened their voices, caused male-pattern hair growth, stimulated clitoral growth and increased muscle tone. However, they both retained intact internal reproductive organs, such as their uterus and ovaries, and, it was accepted, could possibly become pregnant and bear children in the (very) unlikely event that they ceased their hormone treatment. The lack of usefulness of such strict demarcations between male and female is highlighted in these cases because the subjects being legally considered defy the discursive frameworks within which they are located. In normative terms, their bodies are not unequivocally male or female. Despite being faced with individuals whose bodies defy these normative understandings, the law necessitates forceful and definitive assignations to the narrow male/female categories regardless. Given the ambiguity of their biology, it is not surprising that different conclusions can be reached as to their legal sex: the Western Australian Supreme Court denied their applications, effectively declaring that they remained legally 'female', whilst the High Court allowed their applications, effectively declaring that they were legally 'male'.

The absurdities that law's reliance on clear-cut binary sex identities can produce are also evident in *W v W (Nullity: Gender)* [2001] Fam 111. This case dealt with the validity of a marriage between a biological male and a person whose birth certificate recorded her as male but who self-identified and lived as a female and who, it was argued, was born intersex. When deciding issues about her history and the medical evidence, Charles J made the following findings in *W v W (Nullity: Gender)* [2001] Fam 111 (p.121):

> (3) The respondent's external genital appearance was ambiguous.
> (4) The respondent has never had a normal penis and without surgery could never have had sexual intercourse using the flap of skin. But if a choice had to

> be made her external genitalia would be categorised as a mini penis rather than an enlarged clitoris ...
> (6) On a purely external genital test the respondent was not, and was not close to being, a normal man or a normal woman. However if a choice had to be made based purely on the respondent's internal and external genitalia the respondent would be on the male side of the line and thus male ...
> (10) Without surgery the respondent would never have been capable of having sexual intercourse as a man or a woman.

These tortured conclusions – that her genitalia can be 'ambiguous', 'not normal', non-functional in a normative sense and yet still be definitively classified as being a 'male' 'mini penis' – result from the law's fixation on the reductive male/female binary. Her genitals are clearly not 'normal', yet they are classified within the normative categories; labelled definitively as male, her genitals are discursively normalised by the law despite the physical ambiguity that Charles J makes so clear.

This passage from *W v W (Nullity: Gender)* [2001] Fam 111 also lays bare two important aspects of legal discourse that inform the legality of sex surgeries. Firstly, the deployment of concepts such as male and female within legal discourse is informed by particular dominant cultural understandings about sexed embodiment. Providing an implicit comparator to all intersex or transsexual bodies, is a conceptualisation of 'normal' male and female sexed bodies. The 'normal' male body envisaged by judges and legislators probably has a penis of a certain minimum size, a scrotum, testicles, certain body hair patterning, whereas the 'normal' female body probably has a vagina, a clitoris of a certain maximum size, labia, a uterus, breasts and ovaries. In this way, 'what are considered intersex genitals depends', at least partly, 'on local standards for penises and clitorises' (Davidian, 2011, p.3). Secondly, even when a body fails to live up to the 'normal' standards for sexed embodiment, the law will still assign them to one category or another. If one has internalised biological understandings such as that '[m]en have penises, women do not', then a person with a 'large clitoris, one that visibly resembles a penis, upsets this primary understanding of sexual differences' (Karkazis, 2008, p.147). The law responds by reconstructing ambiguously sexed bodies as definitively sexed; intersex and transsexual bodies that defy normative classificatory requirements are positioned within the categories they defy. Thus, '[t]he law only recognizes male and female, and coercively assigns intersexuals as male or as female' (Kolbe, 2008, p.147), and so too the law utilises this 'dichotomous framework of sex and gender' to 'make sense of the non-sense' of transsexualism (Cowan, 2005, p.72).

Whilst legal discourse has sliced through the Gordian knot of determining the sex of ambiguous bodies by definitively allocating all bodies to one of two sexes, the cut is not very clean. As Cowan (2005, p.92) identifies: '[t]he perception is still that really there are only two sexes and two genders, even if we are never absolutely clear as to how that distinction is to be made'. The cases discussed above demonstrate this lack of clarity and the reductive nature of the application of the male/female binary within law. Yet this binary is required by the ambiguities and transgressive potentials generated by intersex and transsexual bodies. The certain, definitive legal pronouncements of sex that ignore nuance and erase non-normativity defuse the transgressive potential of intersex and transsexual people by foreclosing the possibility that their 'ambiguity *is* their sex difference' (Morland 2005, p.528, emphasis in original). Sex surgeries are legalised and legitimated by law because they work, like law, to resolve ambiguous bodies into (closer) congruence with normative ideas about 'male' or 'female' bodies.

Heterosexualism

The final sex/gender issue to be considered here is the heterosexualism of legal discourse around intersex and transsexual people. The rationale for considering this here comes from the way in which dominant cultural discourse constructs sexuality as a function of a person's sex/gender. Under a heteronormative conception of sexuality, androphilia is a characteristic that is imputed to and expected from those with a female sex/gender, and gynephilia is similarly linked to those with a male sex/gender. The 'spectre of homosexuality' (Fausto-Sterling, 2000, p.71; Sharpe 2000; 2002b) is raised by those intersex and transsexual people who are difficult to categorise as male or female. After all '[i]f you don't know who is a male and who a female, how will you know whether what you've got is a case of heterosexuality or homosexuality?' (Dreger, 1998, p.9). Legally, this heterosexualism plays out in a variety of ways. The very method of sorting and assigning all individuals into strict legal categories of male and female, regardless of anatomical variation, can be regarded as a method of 'keeping people straight' (Dreger, 1998, p.8). Demarcating male from female in a clear, bright-line manner makes homosexual behaviour highly visible and thus more open to sanction and regulation. Furthermore, by requiring medical oversight and constructing onerous legal tests to establish successful transitions between the categories of male and female, the law protects 'straight' citizens from the threat of covert homosexuality that may arise from hidden or unrecognised cross-gender displays. But the most blatant result of legal discourse's privileging of heterosexuality comes to the fore regarding the intersection of intersex and transsexualism with the legal institution of marriage.

One of the driving forces behind the legal production and reification of binary models of sex/gender is the 'perceived need … to prevent the inadvertent sanctioning of same-sex marriages' (Greenberg 2012, p.54), and it is in the area of marriage that the 'homophobia of law' within 'transgender jurisprudence is rendered most transparent' (Sharpe, 2002b, p.118). As mentioned in the introduction to this chapter, marriage is legally defined as 'the union of a man and a woman to the exclusion of all others, voluntarily entered into for life' (*Marriage Act 1961* (Cth), s5). A lot of ink has been spilled defending the heterosexual male/female binary of the marriage institution from the 'homosexual' aspects that have been identified as existing within the relationships between intersex and transsexual people and their partners (*Bellinger v Bellinger* [2003] UKHL 21; *In the Marriage of C and D (falsely called C)* (1979) 28 ALR 524; *Secretary, Department of Social Security v SRA (1993)* 43 FCR 299; *W v W (Nullity: Gender)* [2001] Fam 111). Much has been made of a passage within the oft-critiqued *Corbett v Corbett* [1971] P. 83 (p.108) in which Ormrod J, when discussing the surgical creation of April Ashley's vagina and whether it could be used to satisfy the then legal test for the consummation of marriage, noted that '[w]hen such a cavity has been constructed in a male, the difference between sexual intercourse using it and anal or intra-crural intercourse is, in my judgment, to be measured in centimetres'. The kind of attitude evident in this judgment is still reflective of the tenor of the law today (Harrison-Smith, 2007). Heterosexism is evident within the sweeping Australian legal reforms of the early 2000s that enabled people to alter the sex registered on their birth certificate (Sharpe 2002b). For example, in Western Australia it is a requirement that an applicant who wishes to have their birth certificate changed must not be married (*Gender Reassignment Act 2000*, s15(3)). The only possible purpose of this requirement is to prevent the heterosexual marriage of two people of 'opposite' legal sexes from continuing through the transition process of one of those persons and becoming a homosexual marriage of two people of the 'same' legal sex. This forces the transitioning partner to make the difficult choice between their marriage and the legal recognition of their gender identity (Sharpe, 2001b). Sharpe (2001b, p.7) has strongly argued that this requirement is the result of the perceived 'threat and [the] fear of homosexuality', and the pointed nature of this requirement makes this position seem inarguably correct. The law here produces appropriately heterosexual bodies by forcing transsexual people to relinquish 'homosexuality' in order to achieve legal benefits and rights.

The heterosexism of legal discourse around intersex and transsexual persons feeds back into the discursive positioning of sex surgeries as lawful body alterations. This is partly the result of law's discursive collusion with medical discourse, which also utilises these surgeries in heterosexist ways. Heterosexism in the medical treatment of intersex has long been flagged by commentators, who note that the medical model of success for genital normalisation surgery has traditionally been the ability to engineer 'female parts [that] fit with male parts' (Karkazis, 2008, p.142), and *vice versa*. Genital normalisation surgeries aim to unambiguously construct their subjects as either male or female, dismissing the 'fears of a connection between intersex and homosexuality' (Mason, 2009a, p.4), and rendering the physical capacities of their subjects suitable for normative heterosexual intercourse. These capacities typically come at the 'expense of genital sensation', thus an intersex child assigned female may end up with a surgically constructed vagina that is capacious enough to receive a penis during heterosexual intercourse but has little pleasurable feeling (Roen, 2009, p.34). However, the Victorian Department of Health's (2013) recently released *Decision-Making Principles for the Care of Infants, Children and Adolescents with Intersex Conditions* possibly mark the beginnings of a move away from this tradition. These principles acknowledge and address the traditional heterosexism in this area of medicine by explicitly recommending that 'decisions about an infant's future sexual functioning should be informed by principles of sexual diversity, rather than being limited to addressing heterosexual sexual function only' (Victorian Department of Health, 2013, p.19).

The lawfulness of sex reassignment surgeries is also a product of anxiety around the pre-operative transsexual body, because such a body is 'too readily associated with homosexuality and homosexual practice' (Sharpe, 2001b, p.7). This '[a]nxiety' about the transsexual bodies' 'proximity to homosexuality is assuaged by the fact of sex reassignment surgery' (Sharpe, 2002b, p.186), due to the physically and discursively transformative effects of this body alteration. Moulding penises and testicles onto the bodies of those who identify as males, and thus are heteronormatively constructed as inclined to have sex with females, and carving vaginas and breasts onto the bodies of those who identify as females, and thus are heteronormatively constructed as inclined to have sex with males, exorcises the spectre of homosexuality by 'heterosexualising' these bodies with the 'right' equipment (Sharpe 2001b, p.21). The lawfulness of sex surgeries is at least partly a function of the heterosexism of law, as they work to defuse anxiety about homosexuality by producing heterosexually-equipped bodies.

Conceptions of 'Truth'

In Western Australia, the Gender Reassignment Board will only issue a recognition certificate allowing an intersex or transsexual applicant to alter the original record on their birth certificate where the Board is satisfied that the applicant 'believes that his or her *true* gender is the gender to which the person has been reassigned' (*Gender Reassignment Act 2000* (WA), s15(b)(i), emphasis added).[5] This specific provision from this particular jurisdiction neatly encapsulates the more general conceptualisation within legal discourse that intersex and transsexual bodies harbour a 'true' sex/gender that can be brought out by medical treatment. Whilst this notion of authenticity is deployed

5 It should be noted here that this Act uses the term 'gender' to refer to biological features. See, for example, s3 in which 'gender characteristics' is defined to mean the 'physical characteristics by virtue of which a person is identified as male or female'.

strategically to validate sex surgeries as a medical treatment that upholds the male/female binary, it is not typically deployed to validate claims that the law should recognise sex/gender identities that deviate from this normative structure. In this way, the lawfulness of sex surgeries works to only produce normatively sexed/gendered bodies as being 'true'.

Intersex and 'true' sex

With the medicalisation of intersex came a series of medical tests designed to root out an intersex person's 'true' sex, that reality of which was considered to be hidden by the medical disorders from which these 'unfortunates' suffered (Reis, 2009). During the so-called 'Age of Gonads', which held sway during the nineteenth century, an intersex person's 'true' sex was determined and allocated based on what type of gonadal tissue they had, either ovarian, testicular or a combination of both (Dreger, 1998). This gradually gave way to the 'Age of Conversion' wherein medical practitioners sought to physically convert intersex bodies into appropriately sexed bodies in order to authoritatively fix their sex/gender (Fausto-Sterling, 2000, p.40). Under the Johns Hopkins 'optimum gender of rearing' model, the 'true' sex of an intersex infant became the sex/gender in which it was most appropriate to rear them, taking into account a variety of factors including their chromosomes, their genital structures, their gonads, and the ease of certain types of genital normalisation surgery. These medical tests and treatments 'hold out the promise of both revealing an answer – the newborn's "true" sex – and providing the solution through medical intervention' (Karkazis, 2008, p. 98).

The internalisation of medical discourse into legal discourse in this area imports this medicalised notion of 'true' sex. Under the law, intersex remains a disordered condition and an intersex person is considered to have a 'deformed' body, a body 'whose "true" sex is obscured' (Bird, 2001, p.21). This is evident in the case of *W v W (Nullity: Gender)* [2001] Fam 111 (discussed above), in which extensive consideration of a subject's genitals, gonads, psychology and social commitments purported to reveal exactly what their sex 'really' was. What is missing in this case is the ability to conceive of bodies outside the narrow confines of the sex/gender binary. The search for a 'true' sex here merely served to replicate normative constructions of sex/gender by disarticulating the possibility of moving outside the frame of the search's reference. As Thomson (2008, p.172) incisively recognises, in this search for a 'true sex' the '"inter" of intersex is erased'. If one is busy seeking to establish whether a particular body is 'really' male or female, what is lost is the very lack of normative maleness and femaleness that initially prompts the search.

The search for 'true' sex in the case of *In the Marriage of C and D (falsely called C)* (1979) 28 ALR 524 went through similar processes and steps to those in *W v W (Nullity: Gender)* [2001] Fam 111, and involved investigation into the history, body and medical treatments of a husband to determine whether they were legally male and thus whether their marriage to a woman was a valid marriage. This search ended, however, with the ultimate conclusion of the court that the husband was 'neither man nor woman but was a combination of both' and could not marry anyone (*In the Marriage of C and D (falsely called C)* (1979) 28 ALR 524, p.42). The important point to note from this judgement is that the husband's intersex status is not acknowledged as their 'true' sex; they are not legally recognised as being 'intersex' or even, to use the language of the time, as being a 'hermaphrodite'. Instead, the husband's sex remains somewhat ambiguous and undefined, and is described only in terms of its problematic relation to the male/female binary. The husband is simultaneously described as being outside this binary ('neither man nor woman') but also inside this binary ('a combination of both'), and these conceptual difficulties result from the fact that the binary remains the central reference point for legal sex. If the search for the 'true' sex of an intersex person cannot locate such a binary sex, the response of the law in this case was not to recognise that the person has a 'true' non-binary sex but rather to conclude they have no 'true' binary sex at all.

In contrast to this legal position, a number of intersex people claim what Kessler (1990a, p.84) calls an 'intersexual identity', by identifying neither as fully male nor as fully female and by recognising the non-normative aspects of their bodies and the uneasy fit caused by forcing them into either sex/gender category. Obviously not all intersex people will identify this way, many may simply identify as being male or female and desire easy categorisation as such, but my contention here is that the law forecloses any identification outside the male/female binary as even a possibility. This foreclosure proceeds at a basic level through illegibility, a discursive tactic that makes claims to an 'intersex' identity unintelligible. The internalisation of medical discourse into legal discourse in this area erases intersex by constructing intersex people as 'simply men and women who happen to have congenital birth conditions; they are not intersex individuals or intersexuals' (Spurgas, 2009, p.104). Law collaborates with the 'medical insistence/assurance that the intersexed child does have one true sex, and is not *actually* intersexed at all' (Holmes, 2009, p.7, emphasis in original). For example, the restrictive circumstances in which a person can have a sex identity other than male or female marked on their birth certificate have already been discussed, wherein intersex has been literally written out of reality in the vast majority of Australian jurisdictions. The result is that, as Kolbe (2009, p.147, footnote omitted) notes, under 'prevailing legal discourses, intersexuals do not exist'. The legal status of genital normalisation surgery supplements this legal discursive erasure of intersex, as the surgical 'normalisation' of genital ambiguity erases the defining characteristic of intersex bodies.

There have been increasing calls since the 1990s from intersex activists who 'claim that they would have been more truly themselves if they had been left "in between"' (Stark, 2006, p.271), but this has had little to no effect on legal erasure of intersex as a valid sex-identity category. A person's 'true' sex has typically been legally conceptualised as only being a binary 'male' or 'female' sex.

Transsexualism and 'true' sex

An explanatory model used by some commentators and transsexual people to conceptualise transsexualism is the notion that a transsexual person was born into the 'wrong body' (Sullivan, 2008). That is, the sex displayed by the transsexual person's born biology does not reflect their 'true' sex/gender experienced as their gender identity. These subjective claims generated by transsexual people about the 'truth' of their own sex/gender are replaced within legal discourse by legal investigation and analysis into their lives and bodies that purports to generate sufficient information for definitive pronouncements of legal sex to be made.

The legal focus on a transsexual person's 'true' sex/gender began with the purely biological model propounded by Ormrod J in *Corbett v Corbett* [1971] P. 83, a model where a person's legal sex was definitively determined by the gonadal, chromosomal and genital makeup they were born with. Ormrod J held that any alteration to these biological features later in life, such as through sex reassignment surgery, 'cannot affect [one's] true sex' as it is static and temporally fixed at birth (*Corbett v Corbett* [1971] P. 83, p.104). Ormrod J's concept of 'true sex' came under criticism by Chisholm J in *Re Kevin: Validity of Marriage of Transsexual* (2001) 165 FLR 404 (p.420) on the basis that it involved rhetorical 'sleight of hand', because 'true sex' was used to refer solely to biological issues without any argument as to why social and psychological issues were omitted. Chisholm J purports to reject this line of thinking, stating that transsexualism:

> [P]resents a question to the individual, and to various social systems, as well as to the law, namely how that person's identity should be defined and managed … [T]he task of the law is not to search for some mysterious entity, the person's 'true sex', but to give an answer to a practical human problem … to determine the sex in which it is best for the individual to live. (*Re Kevin: Validity of Marriage of Transsexual* (2001) 165 FLR 404, p.425)

Surely, however, Chisholm J engages in his own rhetorical sleight of hand here. It matters not whether the legal test for a person's sex draws on biological criteria or considerations as to the 'best' sex for an individual to live in: the result is the same. The broader test that Chisholm J adopts that looks towards biological, psychological and social factors to determine a person's legal sex still sets up a series of legal requirements that some people will overcome and others will fail. In both *Corbett v Corbett* [1971] P. 83 and *Re Kevin: Validity of Marriage of Transsexual* (2001) 165 FLR 404, the law functions as a gatekeeper to rights and privileges that issues definitive pronouncements about a person's legal sex identity. Although the goalposts have shifted, the law is still the arbiter of a person's sex for legal purposes and this was only ever the practical effect of Ormrod J's judgment in the first place. If a person's subjective claim to be male, female or something else is denied by the law, surely this constitutes a pronouncement that they are not 'really' the sex that they have claimed? At the very least, a person's legal sex has the practical effect of a 'truth' within the boundaries of the law. Even if Chisholm J's claim that law has abandoned the search for a person's 'true sex' is taken at face value, it applies only to the common law. As was flagged at the beginning of this section, various pieces of statute law that deal with the implications of sex reassignment surgery on legal identification explicitly retain concepts of 'true' sex/gender, such as the *Gender Reassignment Act 2000* (WA) s15(b)(i) and the *Sexual Reassignment Act 1988* (SA) s8(b)(i).

Within legal discourse, the possibilities of a transsexual person's 'true' sex are limited. As with the legal search for the 'true' sex of intersex people, the search for the 'true' sex of transsexual people uncritically reproduces a frame of reference that reduces the possibilities of sexed embodiment to the male/female binary. Lost in the shuffle of determining and weighing what details and aspects of transsexual lives and bodies should be taken into account when deciding legal sex is the problematic underlying assumption that all bodies have a 'true' sex and that this 'true' sex is always either male or female. In this way, the system of regulation around the legal sex of transsexual people fails to 'acknowledge that there is a spectrum of possibilities of sex/gender' and is instead restrictively structured around a binary model of male/female (Cowan, 2005, p.72).

The motivating force behind the operation of legal discourse in positioning the legal status of sex reassignment surgeries as lawful is revealed by comparing transsexualism to transgender. Transgender, as a category originating in the early 1990s, marks a shift away 'from the identity of transsexualism, which had existed as the dominant Western identity category for transgender individuals' (Hines, 2007, pp.3–4). If transsexualism can be characterised as identifying with and shifting towards one definitive sex/gender categorisation from the other, transgender should be understood more broadly as a category wherein people 'consciously explore the possibilities of creating embodied practices that subvert dominant codes of gender categorisation and sexual classification' (Hines, 2007, p.4). Kessler and McKenna (2000) note that transgender people typically 'place themselves outside the conventional female/male dichotomy'. For example, transactivist Leslie Feinberg (1998, p.1), who identifies as neither male nor female, notes that: 'I'm not at odds with the fact that I was born female-bodied. Nor do I identify as an intermediate sex. I simply do not fit the prevalent Western concepts of what a woman or a man "should" look like.'

Transgender identities deliberately undermine the legal discursive conception that all bodies have a 'true' sex/gender and the assumption that this is always male or female. Some transgender individuals identify as having no sex/gender whilst others identify as shifting between multiple sex/gender categories. Like intersex identities, the law not only fails to recognise but actively erases transgender identities by removing the capacity for articulation within law. The predominant position under Australian law has been that a person cannot be recognised as having no legal sex, or a legal sex other than male or female (though some recent changes on this front will be discussed below). The lawfulness of sex reassignment surgeries operates here to bolster this legal position: by authorising and authenticating transsexualism as a particular model of transgenderism, it works to deauthorise and disauthenticate other models of transgenderism. The legal discursive construction of transsexualism that recognises subjects as only being authentically male or female is superimposed on top of transgender claims as the only legally valid way to articulate a non-normative gender identity. In these ways, the subversive potential of transgenderism and alternative transsexual identities is channelled into the normative ends to which the law puts sex reassignment surgery to work.

Alternative identities?

Here I want to briefly problematise the traditional legal conceptualisation of the male/female binary as the only possible format for the expression of 'true' sex/gender. This will be accomplished by considering the sex/gender possibilities raised by intersex and transgender subjects that legal discourse has historically marginalised and by gesturing towards some recent developments in Australian law that possibly indicate the beginning of a broader legal recognition of non-binary sex/gender identities.

Greenberg (1999, p.277) points out that 'early English law recognized three classifications of human', citing a declaration from Lord Coke that there exists males, females and 'hermaphrodites'. Accounting for exactly why the binary categorisation of male/female hardened into dominant cultural and legal dogma during modern times is perhaps best left to a more history-focused analysis, but commentators on the topics of intersex and transgender have identified the acceptance of non-normative male and female sex/gender identities in other cultures. Kessler and McKenna (1985, pp.36–37) point to the Potok people, whose lack of confusion about the sex/gender status of intersex children 'suggests the possibility of a third gender category' and reflects the culturally constructed nature of the anxiety caused by the birth of such children in Western society. Callahan (2009) identifies the Indian *hijras* and North American *berdache* as examples of potentially third gender social classifications, or at least well-recognised and well-accepted cross-gender classifications, whilst Shapiro (1991) details similar behaviour in the *xanith* of Oman. Nataf (1996, p.13) summarises the reasonable conclusion that can be drawn from this material: '[o]utside the West, an intermediate gender status or third gender category with a special social function exists in many cultures in a variety of forms'.

Two recent surveys demonstrate that a number of Australian trans people also claim sex/gender identities that are neither male nor female. The Australian Research Centre in Sex, Health & Society's *Tranznation* report received a 'wide variety of responses' to a survey question asking for the trans respondent's 'preferred words for gender identity' (Couch, et al., 2007, p.20) Whilst many respondents identified as simply 'male' or 'female', the report also found that it was 'common for transgender people to resist attempts to classify their lived experience through the use of simple categories' and that many respondents claimed non-binary identities or used more than a single term or word to describe their gender identity (Couch, et al., 2007, p.21). Self-reported gender identities included 'transman, transsexed FTM', 'Transgender', 'genderqueer transboi', 'Bi gendered', 'agendered' and 'androgynous' (Couch, et al., 2007, p.21). The 2011 *Gender Diversity in the ACT* report, prepared by *A Gender Agenda*, found that only 'a small number' of the trans respondents to their survey 'self-identified solely as either male or female', and that 'the vast majority … felt that an integral part of their gender identity included a "trans" notion of having "crossed over" or existing "in between" or "outside" the binary notion of either male or female' (David, et al., 2011, p.1). Self-reported gender identities in this survey included 'trans', 'transgender', 'transsexual', 'genderqueer', 'gender neutral', 'indeterminate' and 'inbetween' (David, et al., 2011, pp.5–6).

Yet whilst some people within Australia may self-identify with such intermediate or third gender categories, these identities run counter to dominant cultural notions of binary sex and are delegitimised by the law. Like de Casto (1993, p.56) argues with regard to sex science, legal discourse is 'confronted with invisible or "immaterial" identities waiting to be materialized', but the claims of these intersex and transgender subjects are incommensurable with the authoritative strands of legal discourse. People's subjective understandings of their own identities as being no sex/gender, a third sex/gender, or an intermediate sex/gender, are devalued within legal discourse and have not typically been reflected in the black-letter of the law. Rather than see intersex or transsexual people as 'occupying various points along a sex continuum, our society chooses to see them as having abnormalities that require repair' (Davidian, 2011, p.12). The internalisation of medical discourse into law 'erases alternative identities from legal discourse' (Harrison-Smith, 2007, p.212), as sex surgeries work to literally erase unruly bodies and discursively erase their identity claims in order to uphold the normative male/female binary conception. In this way, the law 'shuts its eyes to the lived experience of many people' because it fails to 'admit the possibility that gender can be lived and expressed in many forms that go beyond the male/female dichotomy' (Mayeda, 2009, p.195). In doing so it perpetuates its privileging of sex surgeries which result in 'painful corporeal experiences and social unease for some, if not many, surgical patients' (Grabham, 2012, pp.21–22), but which also bring transgressive bodies back within normative understandings of sexed embodiment.

Whilst this restrictive binary conceptualisation of sex/gender has historically been strongly embedded in many areas of Australian law, there has been some change on this front in recent years. From 2011, Australians can now have their sex recorded as 'X' on their passport if they can produce a letter from a registered medical practitioner certifying that they are 'intersex and do not identify with the sex assigned to them at birth' (Australian Passport Office, 2011). In 2013, the Commonwealth Parliament amended the *Sex Discrimination Act 1984* (Cth) to prohibit discrimination on the basis of 'intersex status' by passing the *Sex Discrimination Amendment (Sexual Orientation, Gender Identity and Intersex Status) Act 2013* (Cth). In 2014, the High Court held in *NSW Registrar of Births, Deaths and Marriages v Norrie* (2014) 306 ALR 585 that the NSW Registrar of Births, Deaths and Marriages was not restricted to recording only a binary 'male' or 'female' sex on a birth certificate but was also statutorily empowered to record a person's sex as 'non specific'. So too in 2014 the ACT announced amendments to their binary system of recording sex on birth certificates to add an additional third recordable category of 'Unspecified/indeterminate/intersex'.

I have argued elsewhere that these 'recent developments … are beginning to create space for sex identities beyond the male/female binary' in Australian law and policy, and have evaluated the different pathways that could be taken in further, future reform (Bennett, 2014). However, whilst these developments do seem to depart from the traditional binary model of legal sex, it is important to remember that this is neither yet a clean nor a complete break. These developments have proceeded so far in a piecemeal manner: they are spread unevenly across different jurisdictions and different areas of law, and the legal commitment to the male/female binary remains undisturbed in significant areas of law. The continued binary structuration of 'a man and a woman' within marriage law, for example, neither accommodates nor even recognises the existence of non-binary sex/gender identities.

Despite the limited legal scope of these developments so far, they still carry discursive significance. These developments denaturalise binary sex identification within law and legal thinking, and undermine the established role of the male/female binary in legal discourse. They provide evidence of an 'increasing understanding … in the law and in other professional disciplines, that sexual identity is not dependent solely upon physical characteristics and is not necessarily unambiguous' (*Norrie v NSW Registrar of Births, Deaths and Marriages* [2013] NSWCA 145, p.37), and, as such, form the vanguard of a counter-discourse that is pushing for the legal recognition of the broader range of embodied experiences of sex/gender.

Conclusion

Genital normalisation surgery and sex reassignment surgery are both lawful under Australian criminal law, and their legal status is the result of a particular pattern of discursive positioning. Their lawfulness relies upon the discursive construction of sex surgeries as manifestly different in character from other body alterations to which points of possible connection can be drawn, such as FGM and healthy limb amputation. Whilst not wishing to advocate against the lawfulness of such surgeries, the sheer existence of these connections functions to denaturalise and prompt reflexivity about the lawfulness of sex surgeries. The discursive positioning that underlies the lawfulness of these sex surgeries should be recognised as the effect of the deployment of particular conceptualisations of medicine, sex/gender and 'truth'.

Authoritative legal discourse around sex surgeries internalises aspects of medical discourse and dominant cultural notions of appropriate sexed/gendered embodiment, and produces models of intersex and transsexualism that work to replicate normative notions about bodies and the binary nature of sex/gender. Both intersex and transsexualism are conceptualised as medicalised conditions, 'sufferers' of which must undergo 'treatment' in order to return their 'disordered' bodies into acceptable normative states wherein they display the 'appropriate' biology, social functioning and heterosexuality in accordance with the sex/gender to which they have been legally assigned. Through the tests, requirements and considerations set out in various cases and statutes, the law 'firmly … anchors the transsexual person within the realm of medical expertise' (Cowan, 2009, p.248), as it also does with the intersex person. This medicalised model of sex surgeries functions to position such surgeries as lawful; if 'fixing' someone's physical sex is conceived of as no different than setting a broken arm or supplying antibiotics to cure an infection, then it is rendered legally unproblematic. What is elided in this discursive account are the profound social and political questions raised by the performance of sex surgeries – how they can function and what they can mean – as well as the extensive, invasive and potentially harmful nature of the surgeries themselves, especially given that they frequently operate as a legal prerequisite for access to recognition and/or benefits.

Bound up with the lawfulness of sex surgeries is the inherently political function involved in legitimising particular ways of experiencing and expressing both sex/gender and sexed/gendered difference. Ambiguously sexed/gendered bodies, the homosexual desires of the differently sexed/gendered and subjective claims about personal experiences or feelings of sex/gender that contest normative conceptualisations about these topics, are all devalued within legal discourse and erased from the law. The 'medico-legal model of sex/gender … produces certain kinds of transsexual citizens' (Cowan, 2009, p.251), and certain kinds of intersex citizens. The law here 'regulates identities by "producing" a medicalised heterosexual transsexuality' (Harrison-Smith, 2007, p.222) as well as a similarly medicalised heterosexual model of intersex. The restrictive nature of these 'medico-legal conditions' through which they are conceptualised and understood, means that 'transgender people have been granted a limited presence within law' (Sharpe, 2002b, p.4). This 'limited presence' is one in which the transgressive potential of intersex and transsexual embodiment has been defused. In this way, the lawfulness of sex surgeries is strategically utilised to sanction the unruly bodies of intersex and transsexual people, and produce docile bodies that display normative sex/gender.

The ingrained discursive notion that a person has a 'true' sex/gender that can be masked by a medical 'illness' or a biological 'mistake' is reductively reflected in the legal categorisation of all individuals as either male or female. The possibility of third-sex or no-sex identity claims has been backgrounded by a legal regime that has permitted the transference of bodies across the male/female binary, and only then in very limited circumstances, but has not historically permitted challenges to the categories themselves. However, there are recent indications that parts of the law are beginning to recognise that the sex/gender of some individuals falls outside this binary, and legal discourse may be opening up space for a range of possibilities around sexed/gendered difference that have traditionally been erased by law's close reliance on sex surgeries.

Conclusion

This book has analysed a number of case studies of different body alterations, with the purpose of revealing and demonstrating how discursive conditions produce the legality of those alterations. Like a camera lens shifting its focus from the foreground to the background whilst keeping the same shot in frame, as the analysis conducted here progressed across the course of the case studies it moved from emphasising a closer analysis of discourse through language use to emphasising a broader critical discursive analysis of sociocultural forces and positioning. Each chapter speaks individually for its own content, and the conclusions that mark the end of each chapter summarise the findings that are pertinent to the particular case studies considered therein. As such, I do not see value in simply recounting and summarising this material here: this would necessitate steering a perilous path between turgid retelling and reductive summation. In addition, because of the theoretical basis of this book in postmodernism I am wary of attempting to construct a holistic explanatory framework that purports to entirely capture and relate all the different findings from all the different case studies. This runs the risk of introducing into this book the kind of theoretical inconsistency and modernist slippage that plagued Hyde's (1997) 'body fantasia' ideal in *Bodies of Law* (see Chapter 1).

Given the postmodern focus on subjectivity and pluralism adopted in this book, the most appropriate way to draw together the case studies in this Conclusion is to instead recognise and gesture towards the common issues and concerns raised throughout the analysis, identify some promising pathways for future work and address the possibilities for utilising this kind of analysis to reshape legal discourse around body alteration. This provides a way to link together the various chapters without invoking a monolithic explanatory framework that flattens out the differences between the case studies and without undermining the theoretical understandings that informed the analysis.

Common Issues

Three specific issues were consistently raised throughout the case studies: the shortcomings in the legal coverage of body alterations, the collusive interconnections between legal discourse and medical discourse, and the devaluation of alternative accounts of body alterations by authoritative strands of legal discourse. These common issues will be addressed here with reference to the key concepts identified in Chapter 1.

Un(der)worked Legal Coverage

Whilst the analysis in this book has endeavoured to chart the legal status of the body alterations chosen for consideration, it has become clear as the chapters have progressed that this is a problematic process. Unlike the legal coverage of tort law or contract law, or even of other criminal law areas such as those relating to drugs or burglary, the legal coverage of this area is scant, manifestly unclear and confusing. This analysis has raised critical questions about the generally assumed lawfulness of body alterations such as MC, cosmetic surgery, mainstream body modifications and genital normalisation surgery, but these questions remain unanswered and unanswerable due to the dearth of statute and case law on point. Similarly, whilst it is clear that some sadomasochistic activities and some forms of non-mainstream body modification are criminal, it is not clear exactly where the criminal law cuts and divides lawfulness from criminality. Furthermore, despite specifically enacted legislation even the legal scope of FGM provisions are unclear. Is female genital piercing criminalised by FGM-criminalising statute sections? Is female genital cosmetic surgery? This book can only offer speculation.

Compounding this theoretical confusion about the legal status of these body alterations is the practical reality of their everyday performance. Despite the potential technical criminality of some of these body alterations, most of them are not typically actively policed or prosecuted. For example, despite the criminalisation of inflicting sadomasochistic injuries, sadomasochistic subcultural clubs and commercial stores supplying sadomasochistic equipment operate in capital cities across Australia with impunity. So too non-mainstream body modifications, MC and cosmetic surgery are all left largely untouched by police and prosecutors despite their questionable lawfulness. Law in action here is markedly different from law in theory. This disjunction could be leveraged for analytical gain; commentary in this area could benefit greatly from future work that seeks both to explain why bodily alterations are so legally un(der)worked, and to unpack the discursive forces and social realities that cause legal practice and theory to diverge in this area.

Whilst the legal coverage around these body alterations may be markedly lacking, legal and non-legal discourse in this area has been extensively built up. Whilst these body alterations may only occasionally attract the attention of the courts, police and legislators, in contrast legal and non-legal commentators alike have extensively discussed most of the body alterations considered in each of these chapters. Despite the lack of practical legal material such as statutes and case law, it is because the theorising and commentary in these areas is so strong that discourse analysis has a solid basis. Given the gaps in legal coverage, discourse analysis could become quite useful. In areas where the exact legal status of a body alteration is unclear or confusing, there may be some predictive value in the analysis of trends and currents within legal discourse around these body alterations. As flagged in Chapter 1, discourses are conflicted and are subject to internal tensions by differing accounts. Once-strong trends within legal discourse may be displaced by new trends, and these discursive changes could preface or prompt changes to the black-letter of the law. Throughout the analysis a number of counter-discursive currents have been identified that push back against the authoritative legal discursive position. For example, there is a counter-discourse advocating for the legalisation of sadomasochistic activities that cause only moderate injury on the basis of liberal ideals of autonomy, there is a counter-discourse calling for the criminalisation of MC because of the physical harm it can cause, and there is also a growing counter-discourse pushing for the legal recognition of sex/gender identities outside the male/female binary. If these counter-discourses continue to gain traction and manifest support they could very well provide the conceptual impetus for future changes to the black-letter of the law.

The lack of comprehensive legal coverage in these areas complements the predictive value of discourse analysis. Whilst a lack of legal coverage may render definitive statements about the legal position of these body alterations difficult it also correlatively makes changing their current legal position quite an easy process, because the law is not wholly weighed down by precedent or restrained by specific statutory provisions. Apart from FGM, which is criminalised by explicit statutory provisions, the legal position of the body alterations both in common law and Code law jurisdictions could be clarified, shifted or even radically altered by new case law. All it would take is a test case.

Collusion with Medical Discourse

Whilst this book's analysis has highlighted the close ties between legal discourse and other dominant discursive frameworks, such as those around sex/gender, across the course of the various case studies it has become apparent that medical discourse is particularly deeply imbricated with legal discourse around body alterations. Medical terminology and conceptualisations dominate legal discourse around genital normalisation surgery, sex reassignment surgery, cosmetic surgery and MC, whilst medical-based arguments and descriptions (especially around the concepts of 'harm' and 'injury') are key parts of legal discourse around sadomasochism, FGM, MC, and body modification. Smart (1989, p.19) has suggested that law and medicine might have different relationships in respect to different issues, and that whilst they may form a 'coalition' in some areas they may be in 'conflict' in others. For this reason, she warns against 'easily read[ing] off from an individual case the nature of the law/medicine debate' and notes that 'we cannot assume a pattern or clear signposts which will point us to an inevitable feature' (Smart, 1989, p.19). Charting all the discursive interlinkages between medical discourse and legal discourse would require a separate book unto itself, especially because it would necessitate lengthy discussion of the various civil law fields around medicine and the emergence of new biotechnologies. However, the sustained analysis in this book of the specific issue of body alteration has demonstrated a clear and consistent pattern in relation to the operation of medicine and criminal law. I will offer some brief commentary here that goes partway towards explaining and critiquing the close relationship between these discursive frameworks in this area.

Medicine and the law are culturally positioned in remarkably similar ways. As flagged in Chapter 1, law is a core disciplinary institution within society. So too is medicine. They are both dominant, high-status social institutions that function to rehabilitate non-normativity; medicine primarily rehabilitates non-normative physicality by manipulating flesh whilst law primarily rehabilitates non-normative behaviour by manipulating minds. The regulation of body alteration simultaneously polices both flesh and minds because non-normative body alterations are read as a form of physical resistance that inscribes and reifies mental non-normativity. As such, the disciplinary power of law and medicine intersects around body alterations because they are both working towards the same ends. Both law and medicine are structured around producing normative docile bodies and erasing and recuperating non-normative unruly bodies. If the discursive complicity between law and medicine around body alteration can be explained as an effect of their broader, disciplinary function, it follows then that they should respond in similar ways to body alterations. The analysis in this book has shown that they do. Medical discourse constructs certain kinds of bodies as 'anomalous' and as 'needing correction, modification or prohibition', and law colludes in this construction by legalising those 'procedures which serv[e] to settle' the 'disrupted or abnormal boundaries' (Fox and Murphy, 2013, p.255). That is, law and medicine legitimise normative body alterations and delegitimise non-normative body alterations, and through this process of differential legitimisation also (re)produce wider conceptions of normative embodiment. The discursive frameworks surrounding the body alterations considered in this book display marked convergence between the orthodox medical positions and the authoritative legal positions. For example, legal discourse internalises the medical position on genital normalisation surgeries, foregrounding medical issues such as 'disorder' and 'treatment' and backgrounding other issues such as the social significance of sex/gender.

Health care practitioners are trained and acknowledged experts in the 'normal' physiological processes and functioning of bodies, as well as in how to restore and maintain this 'normal' state. But the scope of medical discourse moves beyond the physiological functioning of the body and constructs discursive conceptions about embodiment that inflect the desirability and legitimacy of body alterations in the context of the social functioning of the body. The collusion between legal and medical discourses around body alterations is symptomatic of an inherent slippage between these two types of functioning; medicolegal truth claims (re)produce 'normalcy' and 'health' as normativising ideals. This point is clearly demonstrated by the broadening scope of medicalisation, which has been shown to pathologise both benign bodily variations (under the aegis of cosmetic surgery and genital normalisation surgery) and departures from normative standards of embodiment and embodied identity (such as transsexualism). The analysis in the case studies showed how the expansion of the scope of medicine has proceeded not only without legal sanction but with legal legitimisation, and it also revealed how certain understandings about the body that are (re)produced within medicine are also taken up by law.

This synthesised product of these medical and legal systems of truth-production is powerful, as whatever discursive construction of a particular body alteration they jointly construct has the benefit of a patterned, socially-valued, multi-institutional backing. Thus it would be a difficult feat to undermine or replace the discursive conceptualisations that they authorise. My method of approaching this imposing medico-legal discursive edifice has been to analyse it piece by piece, in order to reveal how it has been put together and how it continues to hold together. This analysis has revealed something fundamentally problematic about the ways in which medical testing and evidence are integrated into general legal reasoning and decision-making around body alteration. Where medical discourse interweaves itself into legal discourse the analysis in this book has shown that it has profoundly reductive effects. Instead of slotting into place besides other considerations within legal arguments about whether a body alteration should be criminal or lawful, medical considerations tend to be conceptualised as being capable of wholly deciding the issue. This totalising effect is perhaps most clear in Chapter 3, where the medical side-effects/benefits arguments about FGM and MC were shown to marginalise and exclude cultural considerations from legal discourse. However, a similar process can also be identified as occurring in the discursive frameworks around all the other alterations, such as in Chapter 5 where medical evidence and testing provided major justifications for the lawfulness of genital normalisation surgery and sex reassignment surgery. In specific relation to body alterations, this book has confirmed the general contention that the '[l]aw has been too ready to defer to scientific and medical expertise', which has meant that law is also correlatively 'opting out of addressing fundamental ethical questions' about such alterations (Sclater, 2002, p.6). In particular, law's deferral to medicine to define 'the scope of medical practice itself, at least in respect to identifying whether particular surgical procedures are therapeutic', has meant that 'prior questions about the legitimacy of an established area of surgery, such as cosmetic surgery, are never raised' (Kennedy, 2012, p.350). By revealing and analysing the lack of critical distance between medicine and the law this book has attempted to pose some of these typically unarticulated questions.

Whilst law may 'not always simply co-opt' or 'rely' on medical science in every area (Sclater, 2002, p.6), this book has established that these dynamics strongly characterise legal discourse around body alterations. However, despite the strongly influential effect of medicine in this area, my contention is that medical factors do not exhaust the list of relevant considerations that should be raised within legal discourse and considered in legal decision-making. The law should look beyond medicine to take other valuable sources of information and understandings about the body into account. Thus, the analysis in this book has highlighted alternative accounts and counter-discourses that the law could and should take into account when negotiating the legality of body alterations. The subjective, embodied experiences of sadomasochists, body modifiers, men who have undergone MC, women who have undergone FGM, intersex people and transsexual people, should all be considered alongside the understandings generated by medical discourse. Whilst I have not offered a thorough methodology for implementing this concept, I have sought to at least challenge authoritative legal conceptualisations of body alteration by presenting some of these accounts as alternative sources of meaning.

Marginalisation of Alternative Accounts

An essential part of being able to open up the law to a wider variety of understandings about bodies and body alterations is the capacity to recognise which meanings are discursively dominant and which are marginalised. If charting the current legal status of the chosen body alterations provided the bulk of the legal content in this book, then unpacking and accounting for the frameworks of meaning surrounding these alterations provided much of the discursive analysis. Chapters 2 and 3 explored how authoritative legal discursive conceptualisations of sadomasochism, FGM and MC marginalise alternative accounts of these body alterations, even those accounts generated by people who are personally involved in or undergo such alterations themselves. Thus authoritative legal discourse devalues subjective claims about the consensuality of sadomasochism, the possible desirability of some forms of FGM and the potential harmfulness of MC. Similarly, Chapters 4 and 5 explored how the various ways cosmetic surgery, body modification, genital normalisation surgery and sex reassignment surgery were discursively positioned in relation to normative conceptualisations of sex/gender and appearance, foreclosed possibilities for not only envisaging but literally creating new types of bodies and understandings about bodies. Authoritative legal discourse renders unintelligible counter-discursive claims as to the possibility of third-sex/gender or no-sex/gender bodies, the monstrosity of inappropriately cosmetic surgery-altered bodies, the aesthetics of non-mainstream body modified bodies and the desirability of the amputation of a healthy limb.

By no means are these alternative, excluded discursive accounts always inarticulable within legal discourse. Whilst some counter-discourses are 'silenced', others are allowed to speak but are transformed within dominant legal discourse either 'into something that law can digest and process' (Smart, 1989, p.11), or that law can simply ignore. Many counter-discourses are clearly articulable because they can be found in secondary legal material and thus they do make up part of legal discourse. However, they should still be understood as marginalised, despite this capacity for articulation, for two reasons. Firstly, they form a devalued, counter-discursive element of the broader legal discursive framework. Typically, they are framed in oppositional terms as 'calls for change' or alterations to current legal thinking and current law, and they lack the influence and power of authoritative legal discursive accounts of these body alterations. Secondly, and more importantly, whilst such claims may take up some legal discursive space they have no black-letter legal effect. The end-point of marginalisation within legal discourse is erasure from the black-letter of the law. The claim that a masochist consented to their injuries may be rearticulated and supported as an important source of meaning by secondary legal material, but the claim itself has no legal bearing on the sadist's court-room treatment by the operation of a legal regime that denies the legal relevancy of factual consent to sadomasochistic activities. Similarly, an intersex person's subjective identification of not belonging to either the 'male' or 'female' sex/gender categories may be championed by legal commentators in articles and books, but the practical reality remains that such a claim is meaningless in a registry office governed by a birth certificate system that only legally recognises identification within the male/female sex/gender binary. Such claims, then, may not necessarily be silenced, but despite being articulable within legal discourse they remain unintelligible before the operation of the law. These alternative accounts about bodies and body alterations are left in a state of rhetorical impotence. The conflict within legal discourse between authoritative discourse and oppositional counter-discourses is adjudged by integration into the legal system, and the legal system has failed to recognise these alternative accounts.

However, the analysis in this book has been committed to reorienting the discursive framing that excludes these alternative accounts about body alterations from the law, because there is value to be found in the subjective accounts offered by those who alter their body in these ways. Karpin and Mykitiuk (2011, p.116) argue that law's 'repertoire of responses' to 'the multiplicity, indeterminacy, and the contingency of the material self … should move beyond regularization, normalization, and stabilization'. So too, legal discourse around body alteration should be more accommodating to the possibilities of embodied difference and less focused on the erasure of alterity and the rehabilitation of transgression. Postmodernism's valuation of subjectivity and mistrust of claims to objective truth can be productively complemented by pluralistic calls for the law to draw on as wide a range of information as possible to more holistically engage with what it regulates. Whilst it is outside the scope of this book to offer specific models for legal reform, the analysis conducted herein carves out further discursive space for these accounts by highlighting how they are marginalised within legal discourse and erased from the law, and by giving them an additional forum from which to speak. If 'any attempt to produce legislation regarding the body is necessarily limited and constrained by what can, as well as by what cannot, be expressed in legal contexts and by what can and cannot be said about the body' (Roberts, 2011, p.349), then it is my hope that this book helps broaden the scope of what can be articulated about the body in a legal context.

The Way Forward

Diverse and highly complex interactions take place at the critical juncture between bodies, discourse and law. Law and the body 'depend on each other' and the relationship between them should be understood as being 'mutually constitutive' (Sclater, 2002, p.1), because whilst law 'shapes the body' it is also the case that a 'diverse range of discourses create the body of and in law' (Karpin and Mykitiuk, 2011, p.129). This book's analysis of the ways in which discourse inflects and impacts on the criminal law's regulation of body alterations reveals the range of ways in which concepts as varied and broad as sex/gender, sexuality, medicine, culture, harm and aesthetics work to create this body of law and are created through the work of this body of law. The legal status of the body alterations engaged with in these case studies should be understood as both the product and (partial) producer of the discursive fields, processes and concepts that circulate within this area. The law here is made up of cases and statutes that are in turn constituted by and through various rhetorical techniques, linguistic devices, cultural understandings, underlying assumptions and collusions with other discursive frameworks. The '[l]aw's truths about the body are multiple and shifting and depend as much upon cultural lore as they do upon the due process of law' (Sclater, 2002, p.8), and underlying this flux is a constant interplay within and between discursive frameworks of meaning that generate and authorise some 'truths' and that silence and/or delegitimise other 'truths'. These discursive forces animate legal discourse and guide the hand of the criminal law, directing it where to cut and divide lawfulness from criminality and social legitimacy from illegitimacy.

Authoritative legal discourse around body alterations not only shapes and controls the law, it shapes and controls the physical reality of our bodies by determining the somatic types that can lawfully be embodied and those that cannot. Whilst 'bodies come in many shapes and sizes' and '[e]very *body* is different' – and this is true of both the material body and of discursive constructions of the body – this diversity is neither socially nor legally accepted, leading to 'the marginalisation of non-conformist, alternate forms of embodiment' (Bogdanoski, 2009, pp.523–524, emphasis in original). The aetiological goal underpinning legal regulation and disciplinary power in this process is the (re)production of normalised docile bodies. The law 'polices and regulates the social and political inscription of the body' and in doing so subjects the 'subversive threat of non-normative body practices' to disciplinary power (Kennedy, 2012, pp.361–362). Unruly non-normative bodies – such as those that display sadomasochistic injuries, female genitalia that have undergone FGM, non-mainstream body modifications or non-binary sex/gender – are marginalised by legal discourse and typically regulated by the criminal law, and are thus erased. By contrast, docile normative bodies – such as those that display male genitalia that have undergone MC, appropriate cosmetic surgical alterations or binary-conforming sex/gender – are legitimised within legal discourse and left unregulated by the criminal law, and are thus (re)produced. By differentially legalising and criminalising body alterations, law and discourse work together to generate and authorise a particular conceptual framework and somatic reality that is more likely to reflect a narrow model of normativity. Thus whilst it may be the case that within the relationship between law and the body generally, 'there is no one body of law, but a multiplicity of contingent and provisional bodies … and laws' (Sclater, 2002, p.1), this book has demonstrated that around body alterations at least there is a distinct narrowing of bodies and a narrowing of laws.

But all is not bleak for those with an oppositional bent, and those with a postmodern affinity for encouraging and supporting a pluralistic range of difference (including somatic difference). There is opportunity for change. For whilst the discursive frameworks surrounding bodies and the criminal law may structure the sociolegal reality of the ways in which we literally shape ourselves through body alterations, it is important to remember that we have the capacity to shape these frameworks too. By revealing how these discursive frameworks are constructed and how they function, and by denaturalising and challenging the results that they generate, this book opens up the possibility to envisage these frameworks embodying different constructions, different functions and different results. By highlighting 'the gaps, inconsistencies and contradictions produced by legal reasoning that seeks to contain unruly bodies', like Sharpe

(2002b, p.196) the book hopes to open up 'opportunities for resisting and rearticulating legal understandings of their bodies and practices'. The kind of 'embodied approach to law' adopted in this book 'allows for a much more careful construction of "strategic" incursions into legal discourse which will not simply be moments of critique and defence, but represent a better understanding of both what is possible now and what potentials might be in play' (Bottomley, 2002, p.146). The specific potentials that this book have been most concerned with are those around creating more discursive room for marginalised counter-discourses to be articulated and heard within legal discourse, and thereby recuperating alternative accounts about bodies and body alteration from their erasure in the black-letter of the law. When the processes of marginalisation within discourse are revealed and made clear, '[o]pportunities present themselves … to attack the visible flaws in the naturalising logic of legal discourse, and they must be tackled using strategies which, at the very least, allow room for other "voices" in the discussion' (Harrison-Smith, 2007, p.239).

As the criminal law cuts and divides the legality and legitimacy of the cuts and divides that we make in our bodies, these incisions take place in the context of a broad discursive framework that has a deep and rich conceptual underpinning. But the sheer wide-ranging variety of conceptual sources that constitute general discourse is not reflected in the narrow range of normative bodily understandings that legal discourse privileges and is not incorporated into the narrow range of normative body types that the law ultimately authorises. Bodies that fall outside this narrow range face delegitimisation, and the body alterations that produce them face criminal regulation. The analysis in this book has demonstrated that the relationship between cuts and criminality is one that is strongly mediated by the complex processes at work within legal discourse. These discursive processes produce the lawfulness and criminality of body alterations because the various ways in which a body alteration is conceptualised (and not conceptualised) within legal discourse fundamentally inflects how it is treated by the criminal law. Given their key importance in determining the legal status of body alterations, these discursive processes lie at the heart of this body of law.

Bibliography

Case Law

AB v Western Australia; AH v Western Australia (2011) 244 CLR 390
Attorney-General (Commonwealth) v Kevin (2003) 172 FLR 300
Attorney-General's Reference (No 6 of 1980) [1981] 1 QB 715
Bellinger v Bellinger [2003] UKHL 21
Commonwealth v Appleby 380 Mass. 296 (1980)
Corbett v Corbett [1971] P. 83
Davis v Chief of Army (2011) 205 A Crim R 521
DPP v Smith [1961] AC 290
Dunning v Scheibner (Unreported, NSW/SC, No 13776 of 1988, 15 February 1994)
Gillick v West Norfolk and Wisbech AHA [1986] AC 112
In Re A (1993) 16 Fam LR 715
In the Marriage of C and D (falsely called C) (1979) 28 ALR 524
Leitner v State 631 So.2d 273 (Ala.Cr.App. 1993)
Lergesner v Carroll [1991] 1 Qd R 206
Mosley v News Group Newspapers Limited [2008] EWHC 1777 (QB)
Neal v R (2011) 32 VR 454
Norrie v Registrar of Births, Deaths and Marriages [2011] NSWADT 102
Norrie v Registrar of Births, Deaths and Marriages [2011] NSWADTAP 53
Norrie v NSW Registrar of Births, Deaths and Marriages [2013] NSWCA 145
NSW Registrar of Births, Deaths and Marriages v Norrie (2014) 306 ALR 585
People v Samuels 250 Cal.App.2d 501 (1967)
Police (NT) v Segeyara [2008] NTMC 19
R *v Adesanya* (Unreported, UK Central Criminal Court, King-Hamilton J, 16 July 1974)
R *v Barker* [2010] 1 NZLR 235
R *v Brown* [1994] 1 AC 212
R *v Cogley* [1989] VR 799
R *v Devine* (1982) 8 A Crim R 45
R *v Dica* [2004] EWCA Crim 1103
R *v Donovan* [1934] 2 KB 498
R *v Emmett* [1999] EWCA Crim 1710
R *v Hancock* 2000 CarswellBC 2703
R *v Harris and McGuinness* (1988) 17 NSWLR 158

R v Holmes (1993) 2 Tas R 232
R v JA 2011 SC 28
R v Jobidon [1991] 2 SCR 714
R v Keeble [2001] EWCA Crim 1764
R v Lee [2006] 3 NZLR 42
R v McIntosh [1999] VSC 358
R v Minor (1992) 2 NTLR 183
R v Morris (Clarence Barrington) [1998] Cr App 386
R v Oversby (Unreported, UK Central Criminal Court, Rant J, December 1990)
R v Raabe [1985] 1 Qd R 115
R v Robinson (2001), 53 O.R. (3d) 448 (Ont. C.A.)
R v Stein (2007) 18 VR 376
R v Tan [1983] QB 1053
R v W 2006 BCPC 300
R v Wilson [1997] QB 47
Re Alex: Hormonal Treatment for Gender Identity Dysphoria (2004) 180 FLR 89
Re Bernadette (Special Medical Procedure) (2010) 244 FLR 242
Re Brodie (Special Medical Procedures) [2008] FamCA 334
Re Jamie (2013) 50 Fam LR 369
Re Jane (1988) 85 ALR 409
Re Kevin: Validity of Marriage of Transsexual (2001) 165 FLR 404
Re Lesley (Special Medical Procedure) [2008] FamCA 1226
Re Sally (Special Medical Procedure) [2010] FamCA 237
Re Sean and Another [2010] FamCA 948
Scafe v Secretary, Department of Families, Housing, Community Services & Indigenous Affairs (2008) 100 ALD 131
Scatchard v The Queen (1987) 27 A Crim R 136
Schloss v Maguire (1897) 8 QLJ 21
Secretary, Department of Health and Community Services v JWB and SMB (Marion's Case) (1992) 175 CLR 218
Secretary, Department of Social Security v SRA (1993) 43 FCR 299
The State of Western Australia v AH (2010) 41 WAR 431
Vallance v R (1961) 108 CLR 56
W v W (Nullity: Gender) [2001] Fam 111

Statute Law

Births, Deaths and Marriages Registration Act 1995 (NSW)
Births, Deaths and Marriages Registration Act 1996 (Vic)
Births, Deaths and Marriages Registration Act 1997 (ACT)
Births, Deaths and Marriages Registration Act 1999 (Tas)

Births, Deaths and Marriages Registration Act 2003 (Qld)
Births, Deaths and Marriages Registration Act 2005 (NT)
Children and Community Services Act 2004 (WA)
Children and Young People Act 2008 (ACT)
Children and Young Persons (Care and Protection) Act 1998 (NSW)
Children and Young Persons (Care and Protection) Amendment (Body Piercing and Tattooing) Act 2008 (NSW)
Crimes Act 1900 (ACT)
Crimes Act 1900 (NSW)
Crimes Act 1958 (Vic)
Crimes Act 1961 (NZ)
Crimes Amendment (Female Genital Mutilation) Act 2014 (NSW)
Criminal Code 2002 (ACT)
Criminal Code Act (NT)
Criminal Code Act 1899 (Qld)
Criminal Code Act 1924 (Tas)
Criminal Code Act Compilation Act 1913 (WA)
Criminal Law Consolidation Act 1935 (SA)
Female Genital Mutilation Act 2003 (UK)
Gender Reassignment Act 2000 (WA)
Health Act 1911 (WA)
Health Legislation (Restriction on Use of Cosmetic Surgery for Children and Another Measure) Amendment Act 2008 (Qld)
Health (Skin Penetration Procedure) Regulations 1998 (WA)
Marriage Act 1961 (Cth)
Police Offences Act 1935 (Tas)
Prohibition of Female Circumcision Act 1985 (UK)
Public Health Act 2005 (Qld)
Sex Discrimination Act 1984 (Cth)
Sex Discrimination Amendment (Sexual Orientation, Gender Identity and Intersex Status) Act 2013 (Cth)
Sexual Reassignment Act 1988 (SA)
Summary Offences Act 1953 (SA)
Summary Offences Act 1966 (Vic)
Summary Offences Act 2005 (Qld)

Other Sources

Abu-Sahlieh, S.A., 1994–1995. Islamic Law and the Issue of Male and Female Circumcision. *Third World Legal Studies*, 13, pp.73–101.

Abu-Sahlieh, S.A. 1999. Muslims' Genitalia in the Hands of the Clergy: Religious Arguments about Male and Female Circumcision. In: G. Denniston, F. Hodges and M. Milos, eds, 1999. *Male and Female Circumcision: Medical, Legal, and Ethical Considerations in Pediatric Practice.* New York: Kluwer Academic. pp.131–172.

Accord Alliance, 2010. *Our Mission.* [online] Available at: <http://www.accordalliance.org/about-accord-alliance/our-mission/> [Accessed 11 March 2014].

Ahmadu, F., 2007. "Ain't I a Woman Too?": Challenging Myths of Sexual Dysfunction in Circumcised Women'. In: Y. Hernlund and B. Shell-Duncan, eds, 2007. *Transcultural Bodies: Female Genital Cutting in Global Context.* New Brunswick, New Jersey and London: Rutgers University Press. pp.278–310.

Aizura, A., 2006. Of Borders and Homes: The Imaginary Community of (Trans)Sexual Citizenship. *Inter-Asia Cultural Studies*, 7(2), pp.289–309.

Aliabadi, S., 2005. You Make Me Feel Like a Natural Woman: Allowing Parents to Consent to Early Gender Assignment Surgeries for their Intersexed Infants. *William and Mary Journal of Women and the Law*, 11, pp.427–459.

Allen, H., 1987 *Justice Unbalanced: Gender, Psychiatry and Judicial Decisions.* Philadelphia: Open University Press.

Allen, M., 1994. Consent and Assault. *Journal of Criminal Law*, 58(2), pp.183–200.

Allison, R., 2010. Aligning Bodies with Minds: The Case for Medical and Surgical Treatment of Gender Dysphoria. *Journal of Gay and Lesbian Mental Health*, 14(2), pp.139–144.

Alston, A., 1999. Transgender Rights as Legal Rights. *Canterbury Law Review*, 7, pp.329–342.

American Academy of Pediatrics, 2010a. Ritual Cutting of Female Minors. *Pediatrics*, 125, pp.1088–1093.

American Academy of Pediatrics, 2010b. Ritual Cutting of Female Minors. *Pediatrics*, 126, p.191.

American Psychiatric Association, 2013. *Diagnostic and Statistical Manual of Mental Disorders.* 5th ed. American Psychiatric Publishing.

American Society of Plastic Surgeons, 2009. *2008 Statistics.* [online] Available at: <http://www.plasticsurgery.org/news/plastic-surgery-statistics/2008-plastic-surgery-statistics.html> [Accessed 11 March 2014].

Anon., 1968. Assault and Battery. Consent. Consent of Masochist to Beating by Sadist Is No Defense to Prosecution for Aggravated Assault. *People v. Samuels*, 58 Cal. Rptr. 439 (Ct. App., 1st Dist. 1967). *Harvard Law Review*, 81(6), pp.1339–1342.

Anon., 2005. Editorial: Consensual Harm. *Criminal Law Journal*, 29(4), pp.197–200.

Armstrong, M., 2005. Tattooing, Body Piercing and Permanent Cosmetics: A Historical and Current View of State Regulations, with Continuing Concerns. *Journal of Environmental Health*, 67(8), pp.38–43.

Asefa, S., 1998. Female Genital Mutilation: Violence in the Name of Tradition, Religion, and Social Imperative. In: R.E. Dobash and R. Dobash, eds, 1998. *Rethinking Violence Against Women.* London and New Delhi: Sage Publications. pp.92–106.

Athanassoulis, N., 2002. The Role of Consent in Sado-Masochistic Practices. *Res Publica*, 8, pp.141–155.

Atkinson, M., 2002. Pretty in Ink: Conformity, Resistance, and Negotiation in Women's Tattooing. *Sex Roles*, 47(5/6), pp.219–235.

Atkinson, M., 2003. *Tattooed: The Sociogenesis of a Body Art.* Toronto: University of Toronto Press.

Atkinson, M., 2008. Exploring Male Femininity in the 'Crisis': Men and Cosmetic Surgery. *Body and Society*, 14(1), pp.67–87.

Atoki, M., 1995. Should Female Circumcision Continue to be Banned? *Feminist Legal Studies*, 3(2), pp.223–235.

Attias, B., 1995. *'Police Free Gay Slaves': Some Juridico-Legal Consequences of the Discursive Distinctions Between the Sexualities.* [online] California State University. Available at: <http://www.csun.edu/~hfspc002/PoliceFreeGay Slaves.html> [Accessed 11 March 2014].

Attorney-General's Department, 2013. *Review of Australia's Female Genital Mutilation Legal Framework: Final Report.* [online] Australian Government. Available at: <http://www.ag.gov.au/Publications/Pages/ReviewofAustralia sFemaleGenitalMutilationlegalframework-FinalReportPublicationandforms. aspx> [Accessed 11 March 2014].

Australian Associated Press, 2008. NSW: Extreme body art to be banned on under 18s. *AAP General News Wire*, May 15.

Australian Bureau of Statistics, 2012. *Reflecting a Nation: Stories from the 2011 Census.* [online] Available at: <http://www.abs.gov.au/ausstats/abs@.nsf/ Lookup/2071.0main+features902012-2013> [Accessed 11 March 2014].

Australian Federation of AIDS Organisations, 2009. *Male Circumcision and HIV.* [online] Available at: <http://www.afao.org.au/__data/assets/pdf_ file/0018/4527/BP09_Circumcision.pdf> [Accessed 11 March 2014].

Australian Human Rights Commission, 2009a. *Sex Files: The Legal Recognition of Sex in Documents and Government Records.* [online] Available at: <http:// www.humanrights.gov.au/genderdiversity/sex_files2009.html> [Accessed 11 March 2014].

Australian Human Rights Commission, 2009b. *Surgery on Intersex Infants and Human Rights.* [online] Available at: <http://www.humanrights.gov.au/gen derdiversity/surgery_intersex_infants2009.html> [Accessed 11 March 2014].

Australian Passport Office, 2011. *Sex and Gender Diverse Passport Applicants: Revised Policy.* [online] Australian Government Department of Foreign Affairs and Trade. Available at: <https://www.passports.gov.au/Web/Sex GenderApplicants.aspx> [Accessed 11 March 2014].

Baer, Z., 1997. Circumcision: Are Baby Boys Entitled to the Same Protection as Baby Girls Regarding Genital Mutilation? In: G. Denniston and M. Milos, 1997, eds, *Sexual Mutilations: A Human Tragedy*. New York and London: Plenum Press. pp.197–204.

Baker, D., 2008. Rethinking Consensual Harm-Doing. *University of Western Sydney Law Review*, 12, pp.21–38.

Baker, D., 2012. *Textbook of Criminal Law*. 3rd ed. London: Sweet & Maxwell.

Baldwin, G., 2003. *Ties That Bind*. 2nd ed. Los Angeles: Daedalus Publishing Company.

Balsamo, A., 1996. *Technologies of the Gendered Body: Reading Cyborg Women*. Durham and London: Duke University Press.

Bamforth, N., 1994. Sado-Masochism and Consent. *Criminal Law Review*, September, pp.661–665.

Barker-Benfield, B., 1975. Sexual Surgery in Late-Nineteenth-Century America. *International Journal of Health Services*, 5(2), pp.279–288.

Barker, M., Gupta, C. and Iantaffi, A., 2007. The Power of Play: The Potentials and Pitfalls in Healing Narratives of BDSM. In: D. Langdridge and M. Barker, 2007. *Safe, Sane and Consensual: Contemporary Perspectives on Sadomasochism*. New York: Palgrave Macmillan. pp.197–216.

Bashir, L., 1995–1996. Female Genital Mutilation in the United States: An Examination of Criminal and Asylum Law. *Journal of Gender and The Law*, 4, pp.415–454.

Bates, F., 2001. Males, Medical Mutilation and the Law: Some Recent Developments. *Journal of Law and Medicine*, 9(1), pp.68–75.

Baudrillard, J., 1988a. Consumer Society. In: M. Poster, trans, 1988. *Jean Baudrillard: Selected Writings*. Stanford: Stanford University Press. pp.29–56.

Baudrillard, J., 1988b. Fatal Strategies. In: M. Poster, trans, 1988. *Jean Baudrillard: Selected Writings*. Stanford: Stanford University Press. pp.185-206.

Baudrillard, J., 1988c. Simulcra and Simulations. In: M. Poster, trans, 1988. *Jean Baudrillard: Selected Writings*. Stanford: Stanford University Press. pp.166–184.

Baudrillard, J., 1988d. The System of Objects. In: M. Poster, trans, 1988. *Jean Baudrillard: Selected Writings*. Stanford: Stanford University Press. pp.10–28.

Baumeister, R., 1988. Masochism as Escape from Self. *The Journal of Sex Research*, 25(1), pp.28–59.

Bean, J., 2004. The Spiritual Dimensions of Bondage. In: M. Thompson, eds, 2004. *Leatherfolk: Radical Sex, People, Politics and Practices*. Los Angeles: Daedalus Publishing Company. pp.257–266.

Beckmann, A., 2001. Deconstructing Myths: The Social Construction of 'Sadomasochism' versus 'Subjugated Knowledges' of Practitioners of Consensual 'SM'. *Journal of Criminal Justice and Popular Culture*, 8(2), pp.66–95.

Beckmann, A., 2009. *The Social Construction of Sexuality and Perversion: Deconstructing Sadomasochism*. Palgrave MacMillan.

Beh, H. and Diamond, M., 2000. An Emerging Ethical and Medical Dilemma: Should Physicians Perform Sex Assignment Surgery on Infants with Ambiguous Genitalia? *Michigan Journal of Gender & Law*, 7(1), pp.1–63.

Beh, H. and Diamond, M., 2005a. David Reimer's Legacy: Limiting Parental Discretion. *Cardozo Journal of Gender & Law*, 12, pp.5–30.

Beh, H. and Diamond, M., 2005b. Ethical Concerns Related to Treating Gender Nonconformity in Childhood and Adolescence: Lessons from the Family Court of Australia. *Health Matrix*, 12(2), pp.239–283.

Beh, H. and Diamond, M., 2006. The Right to be Wrong: Sex and Gender Decisions. In: S. Sytsma, ed., 2006. *Ethics and Intersex*. The Netherlands: Springer. pp.103–113.

Ben-Asher, N., 2006. The Necessity of Sex Change: A Struggle for Intersex and Transsex Liberties. *Harvard Journal of Law & Gender*, 29(1), pp.51–98.

Benjamin, J., 1990. *The Bonds of Love: Psychoanalysis, Feminism and the Problem of Domination*. London: Virago.

Bennett, T., 2011. It's But a Flesh Wound: Criminal Law and the Conceptualisation of Healthy Limb Amputation. *Alternative Law Journal*, 36(3), pp.158–162.

Bennett, T., 2012a. A Polyvocal (Re)Modelling of the Jurisprudence of Sadomasochism. *UWA Law Review*, 36(1), pp.199–221.

Bennett, T., 2012b. 'Beauty' and the 'Beast': Analogising Between Cosmetic Surgery and Female Genital Mutilation. *Flinders Law Journal*, 14(1), pp.49–68.

Bennett, T., 2013. Transsexualism and the Consideration of Social Factors in Sex Identification Law. *Adelaide Law Review*, 34(2), pp.379–402.

Bennett, T., 2014. No Man's Land: Non-Binary Sex Identification in Australian Law and Policy. *UNSW Law Review*, 37(3), pp.847–873.

Benson, S., 2000. Inscriptions of the Self: Reflections on Tattooing and Piercing in Contemporary Euro-America. In: J. Caplan, ed., 2000. *Written on the Body: The Tattoo in European and American History*. New Jersey: Princeton University Press. pp.234–254.

Berer, M., 2010. Labia Reduction for Non-Therapeutic Reasons vs Female Genital Mutilation: Contradictions in Law and Practice in Britain. *Reproductive Health Matters*, 18(35), pp.106–110.

Berg, R. and Denison, E., 2012. 'Does Female Genital Mutilation/Cutting (FGM/C) Affect Women's Sexual Functioning? *Sexuality Research and Social Policy*, 9, pp.41–56.

Bergelson, V., 2006–2007. The Right to be Hurt: Testing the Boundaries of Consent. *George Washington Law Review*, 75, pp.165–236.

Beveridge, F. and Mullally, S., 1995. International Human Rights and Body Politics. In: J. Bridgeman and S. Millns, eds, 1995. *Law and Body Politics: Regulating the Female Body*. Aldershot: Dartmouth Publishing. pp.240–272.

Bibbings, L. and Alldridge, P., 1993. Sexual Expression, Body Alteration, and the Defence of Consent. *Journal of Law and Society*, 20(3), pp.356–370.

Bibbings, L., 1996. Touch: Socio-Cultural Attitudes and Legal Responses to Body Alteration. In: L. Bentley and L. Flynn, eds, 1996. *Law and the Senses: Sensational Jurisprudence*. London and Chicago: Pluto Press. pp.176–195.

Billings, D. and Urban, T., 1995. The Socio-Medical Construction of Transsexualism: An Interpretation and Critique. In: R. Ekins and D. King, eds, 1995. *Blending Genders: Social Aspects of Cross-Dressing and Sex Changing*. London: Routledge. pp.99–117.

Bird, J., 2001. When Sex Means 'Condition' or 'Impairment': Evaluating the Human Rights of Transgender and Intersex Peoples. *Southern Cross University Law Review*, 5, pp.1–26.

Bird, J., 2005. Outside the Law: Intersex, Medicine and the Discourse of Rights. *Cardozo Journal of Law & Gender*, 12, pp.65–80.

Bix, B., 1993. Assault, Sado-Masochism and Consent. *Law Quarterly Review*, 109, pp.540–544.

Bix, B., 1997. Consent, Sado-masochism and the English Common Law. *Quinnipiac Law Review*, 17, pp.157–175.

Blizzard, K., 2005–2006. A Parent's Predicament: Theories of Relief for Deportable Parents of Children who Face Female Genital Mutilation. *Cornell Law Review*, 91, pp.899–926.

Blum, V., 2003. *Flesh Wounds: The Culture of Cosmetic Surgery*. Berkeley and Los Angeles: University of California Press.

Boddy, J., 1998. Violence Embodied?: Circumcision, Gender Politics, and Cultural Aesthetics. In: R.E. Dobash and R. Dobash, eds, 1998. *Rethinking Violence Against Women*. London and New Delhi: Sage Publications. pp.77–110.

Boddy, J., 2007. Gender Crusades: The Female Circumcision Controversy in Cultural Perspective. In: Y. Hernlund and B. Shell-Duncan, eds, 2007. *Transcultural Bodies: Female Genital Cutting in Global Context*. New Brunswick, New Jersey and London: Rutgers University Press. pp.46–66.

Bogdanoski, T., 2009. Every *Body* is Different: Regulating the Use (and Non-Use) of Cosmetic Surgery, Body Modification and Reproductive Genetic Testing. *Griffith Law Review*, 18(2), pp.503–528.

Bordo, S., 1993. *Unbearable Weight: Feminism, Western Culture and the Body*. Berkeley and Los Angeles: University of California Press.

Bottomley, A., 2002. The Many Appearances of the Body in Feminist Scholarship. In: A. Bainham, S. Sclater and M. Richards, eds, 2002. *Body Lore and Laws*. Oxford: Hart Publishing. pp.127–148.

Bourke, E., 2010. Female Circumcision Happening in Australia. *ABC News*, [online] 6 February. Available at: <http://www.abc.net.au/news/2010-02-06/female-circumcision-happening-in-australia/2594496?section=justin> [Accessed 11 March 2014].

Bowra, C., 1994. The Debate on Clitoridectomy: 'Act of Love' or Act of Oppression? *Australian Year Book of International Law*, 15, pp.183–202.

Boyle, E.H. and Corl, A.C., 2010. Law and Culture in a Global Context: Interventions to Eradicate Female Genital Cutting. *Annual Review of Law and Social Science*, 6, pp.195–215.

Boyle, G., Svoboda, S., Price, C. and Turner, J., 2000. Circumcision of Healthy Boys: Criminal Assault?' *Journal of Law and Medicine*, 7(3), pp.301–310.

Bradwell, J., 1996. Consent to Assault and the Dangers to Women. *New Law Journal*, 146, pp.1682–1683.

Braidotti, R., 2011. *Nomadic Subjects: Embodiment and Sexual Difference in Contemporary Feminist Theory*. 2nd ed. New York: Columbia University Press.

Braun, V., 2005. In Search of (Better) Sexual Pleasure: Female Genital 'Cosmetic' Surgery'. *Sexualities*, 8(4), pp.407–424.

Braun, V., 2009a. Selling the 'Perfect' Vulva. In: C. Heyes and M. Jones, eds, 2009. *Cosmetic Surgery: A Feminist Primer*. Burlington: Ashgate Publishing. pp.133–149.

Braun, V., 2009b. The Women are Doing it for Themselves. *Australian Feminist Studies*, 24(60), pp.233–249.

Bridge, C., 2002. Religion, Culture and the Body of the Child. In: A. Bainham, S. Sclater and M. Richards, eds, 2002. *Body Lore and Laws*. Oxford: Hart Publishing. pp.265–287.

Bridgeman, J., 1995. They Gag Women, Don't They? In: J. Bridgeman and S. Millns, eds, 1995. *Law and Body Politics: Regulating the Female Body*. Aldershot: Dartmouth Publishing. pp.22–52.

Bridgeman, J. and Millns, S., 1995. Introduction. In: J. Bridgeman and S. Millns, eds, 1995. *Law and Body Politics: Regulating the Female Body*. Aldershot: Dartmouth Publishing. pp.xix–xxiv.

Bridy, A., 2004. Confounding Extremities: Surgery at the Medico-ethical Limits of Self-Modification. *Journal of Law, Medicine & Ethics*, 32, pp.148–158.

Brigman, W., 1984–1985. Circumcision as Child Abuse: The Legal and Constitutional Issues. *Journal of Family Law*, 23(3), pp.337–357.

Bronitt, S., 1995. The Right to Sexual Privacy, Sado-masochism and the Human Rights (Sexual Conduct) Act 1994 (Cth). *Australian Journal of Human Rights*, 2(1), pp.59–73.

Bronitt, S. and McSherry, B., 2005. *Principles of Criminal Law*. 2nd ed. Pyrmont NSW: Thomson Lawbook.

Broom, D., 2001. Public Health, Private Body. *Australian and New Zealand Journal of Public Health*, 25(1), pp.5–8.

Buhagiar, L., 1997. Criminalising Female Genital Mutilation in Canada: The Excision of Multiculturalism? *Current Issues in Criminal Justice*, 9, pp.184–186.

Buhrich, N., 1983. The Association of Erotic Piercing with Homosexuality, Sadomasochism, Bondage, Fetishism and Tattoos. *Archives of Sexual Behavior*, 12(2), pp.167–171.

Bullough, V., 2007. Legitimizing Transsexualism. *International Journal of Transgenderism*, 10(1), pp.3–13.

Butler, J., 1990. *Gender Trouble*. New York: Routledge.
Butler, J., 1993. *Bodies that Matter: On the Discursive Limits of Sex*. New York: Routledge.
Cadwallader, J., 2007. Suffering Difference: Normalisation and Power. *Social Semiotics*, 17(3), pp.375–393.
Califia, P., 1987. A Personal View of the History of the Lesbian S/M Community and Movement in San Francisco. In: SAMOIS, eds, 1987. *Coming To Power: Writings and Graphics on Lesbian S/M*. 3rd ed. Boston: Alyson Publications. pp.245–283.
Callahan, G., 2009. *Between XX and XY: Intersexuality and the Myth of Two Sexes*. Chicago: Chicago Review Press.
Campbell, F., 2001. Inciting Legal Fictions: Disability's Date with Ontology and the Ableist Body of the Law. *Griffith Law Review*, 10(1), pp.42–62.
Caplan, J. ed., 2000. *Written on the Body: The Tattoo in European and American History*. New Jersey: Princeton University Press.
Chambers, C., 2004. Are Breast Implants Better than Female Genital Mutilation? Autonomy, Gender Equality, and Nussbaum's Political Liberalism. *Critical Review of International Social and Political Philosophy*, 7(3), pp.1–33.
Chan, P.C.W., 2006. Sado-Masochism and the Rule of Law: Brown Re–Examined. *International Journal of Punishment and Sentencing*, 1(4), pp.195–220.
Chancer, L. 1992. *Sadomasochism in Everyday Life: The Dynamics of Power and Powerlessness*. New Jersey: Rutgers University Press.
Chancer, L., 2000. From Pornography to Sadomasochism: Reconciling Feminist Differences. *Annals of the American Academy of Political and Social Science*, 571, pp.77–88.
Chandra-Shekeran, S., 1997. Theorising the Limits of the Sadomasochistic Homosexual Identity. *Melbourne University Law Review*, 21, pp.584–600.
Chase, C., 1998. Hermaphrodites with Attitude: Mapping the Emergence of Intersex Political Activism. *GLQ*, 4(2), pp.189–211.
Chau, P.L. and Herring, J., 2002. Defining, Assigning and Designing Sex. *International Journal of Law, Policy and the Family*, 16(3), pp.327–367.
Cheah, P., Fraser, D. and Grbich, J., 1996. Introduction: The Body of the Law. In: P. Cheah, D. Fraser and J. Grbich, eds, 1996. *Thinking Through the Body of the Law*. NSW: Allen and Unwin. pp.xi–xix.
Cheah, P. and Grosz, E., 1996. The Body of the Law: Notes Towards a Theory of Corporeal Justice. In: P. Cheah, D. Fraser and J. Grbich, eds, 1996. *Thinking Through the Body of the Law*. NSW: Allen and Unwin. pp.3–25.
Chessler, A., 1997. Justifying the Unjustifiable: Rite v. Wrong. *Buffalo Law Review*, 45, pp.555–613.
Cockburn, T., 2008. Legislation Under the Knife. *Lawyers Weekly*, 1(August Issue), p.14.

Cockburn, T. and Madden, B., 2009. Legislative Intervention in Queensland to Restrict Access to Solariums and Cosmetic Procedures by Children and Young Persons. *Journal of Law and Medicine*, 16(4), pp.653–665.

Coello, I., 1999. Female Genital Mutilation: Marked by Tradition. *Cardozo Journal of International & Comparative Law*, 7, pp.213–226.

Cole, A. and Haebich, A., 2007. Corporeal Colonialism and Corporal Punishment: A Cross-cultural Perspective on Body Modification. *Social Semiotics*, 17(3), pp.293–311.

Collier, R., 2002. Male Bodies, Family Practices. In: A. Bainham, S. Sclater and M. Richards, eds, 2002. *Body Lore and Laws*. Oxford: Hart Publishing. pp.149–169.

Commonwealth of Australia, 2013. *Australian Government Guidelines on the Recognition of Sex and Gender*. [online] Available at: <http://www.ag.gov.au/Publications/Documents/AustralianGovernmentGuidelinesontheRecognitionofSexandGender/AustralianGovernmentGuidelinesontheRecognitionofSexandGender.PDF> [Accessed 11 March 2014].

Conaghan, J., 2013. Feminism, Law and Materialism: Reclaiming the 'Tainted' Realm. In: M. Davies and V. Munro, eds, 2013. *The Ashgate Research Companion to Feminist Legal Theory*. Surrey, UK: Ashgate. pp.31–50.

Cooper, D., Wodak, A. and Morris, B., 2010. Editorial: The Case for Boosting Infant Male Circumcision in the Face of Rising Heterosexual Transmission of HIV. *Medical Journal of Australia*, 193(6), pp.318–319.

Cornwall, A., 2000. Facing Up To It: A Review of the NSW Cosmetic Surgery Inquiry. *Australian Health Law Bulletin*, 8(7), pp.87–96.

Cosmetic Surgery Inquiry Committee, 1999. *The Cosmetic Surgery Report: Report to the NSW Minister for Health*. Health Care Complaints Commission.

Couch, M., Pitts, M., Mulcare, H., Croy, S., Mitchell, A. and Sunil, P., 2007. *Tranznation: A Report on the Health and Wellbeing of Transgendered People in Australia and New Zealand*. Australian Research Centre in Sex, Health & Society.

Cowan, S., 2005. Gender is No Substitute for Sex: A Comparative Human Rights Analysis of the Legal Regulation of Sexual Identity. *Feminist Legal Studies*, 13, pp.67–96.

Cowan, S., 2009. Looking Back (To)Wards the Body: Medicalization and the GRA. *Social & Legal Studies*, 18(2), pp.247–252.

Cowan, S., 2011. Criminalizing SM: Disavowing the Erotic, Instantiating Violence. In: R. Duff, L. Farmer, S.E. Marshall, M. Renzo and V. Tadros, eds, 2011. *The Structures of the Criminal Law*. Oxford: Oxford University Press. pp.59–84.

Creighton, S. and Liao, L., 2004. Changing Attitudes to Sex Assignment in Intersex. *British Journal of Urology International*, 93, pp.659–664.

Crockett, G., 1998. The Convict Tattoo. *Social Alternatives*, 17(4), pp.14–17.

Dalton, D., 2006. Surveying Deviance, Figuring Disgust: Locating the Homocriminal Body in Time and Space. *Social and Legal Studies*, 15(2), pp.277–299.

Dalton, D., 2007. Male Circumcision – See the Harm to Get a Balanced Picture. *Journal of Men's Health and Gender*, 4(3), pp.312–317.

Darby, R., 2001. 'A Source of Serious Mischief': The Demonization of the Foreskin and the Rise of Preventive Circumcision in Australia. In: G. Denniston, F. Hodges and M. Milos, eds, 2001. *Understanding Circumcision: A Multi-Disciplinary Approach to a Multi-Dimensional Problem*. New York: Kluwer Academic. pp.153–198.

Darby, R. and Svoboda, J., 2007. A Rose by Any Other Name?: Rethinking the Similarities and Differences Between Male and Female Genital Cutting. *Medical Anthropology Quarterly*, 21(3), pp.301–323.

David, F., Hyndal, L., Hyndal, P., Ion, J. and Yates, J., 2011. *Gender Diversity in the ACT: A Survey of Trans Experiences*. A Gender Agenda.

Davidian, A., 2011. Beyond the Locker Room: Changing Narratives on Early Surgery for Intersex Children. *Wisconsis Journal of Law, Gender & Society*, 26, pp.1–22.

Davies, J., Knight, E., Savage, A., Brown, J. and Malone, P.S., 2010. Evaluation of Terminology Used to Describe Disorders of Sex Development. *Journal of Pediatric Urology*, 7(4), pp.412–415.

Davis, K., 1995. *Reshaping the Female Body: The Dilemma of Cosmetic Surgery*. New York and London: Routledge.

Davis, K., 2002. 'A Dubious Equality': Men, Women and Cosmetic Surgery. *Body & Society*, 8, pp.49–65.

Davis, K., 2009. Revisiting Feminist Debates on Cosmetic Surgery: Some Reflections on Suffering, Agency, and Embodied Difference. In: C. Heyes and M. Jones, eds, 2009. *Cosmetic Surgery: A Feminist Primer*. Burlington: Ashgate Publishing. pp.35–48.

Dawkins, K., 1997. Consent, Tattoos and Taboos. *The New Zealand Law Journal*, May Issue, pp.154–157.

de Castro, O., 1993. *Made to Order: Sex/Gender in a Transsexual Perspective*. The Hague: Het Spinhuis.

DeGagne, J., 1998. Tattoos and Body Piercing: Can Regulations Prevent Health Risks? *McGeorge Law Review*, 29, pp.695–703.

DeMello, M., 2000. *Bodies of Inscription: A Cultural History of the Modern Tattoo Community*. Durham and London: Duke University Press.

DeMello, M., 2007. *Encyclopedia of Body Adornment*. Westport: Greenwood Publishing Group.

Denniston, G., 1999. Tyranny of the Victims: An Analysis of Circumcision Advocacy. In: G. Denniston, F. Hodges and M. Milos, eds, 1999. *Male and*

Female Circumcision: Medical, Legal, and Ethical Considerations in Pediatric Practice. New York: Kluwer Academic. pp.221–240.

Department of Health, 2006. *Cosmetic Surgery: Information for Patients.* United Kingdom Government, [online] Available at: <http://webarchive.nationalarchives.gov.uk/20130107105354/http://www.dh.gov.uk/prod_consum_dh/groups/dh_digitalassets/@dh/@en/documents/digitalasset/dh_4138410.pdf> [Accessed 11 March 2014].

Derrida, J., 1992. Force of Law: The 'Mystical Foundation of Authority'. In: D. Cornell, M. Rosenfeld and D. Carlson, eds, 1992. *Deconstruction and the Possibility of Justice.* New York: Routledge. pp.3–67.

Devereux, J.A. 1987. Consent as a Defence to Assaults Occasioning Bodily Harm: The Queensland Dilemma. *University of Queensland Law Journal,* 14(2), pp.151–159.

Devereux, J. and Blake, M., 2013. *Kenny Criminal Law in Queensland and Western Australia.* NSW, LexisNexis Butterworths.

Diamond, M. and Sigmundson, H. 1997. Sex Reassignment at Birth: Long-Term Review and Clinical Implications. *Archives of Pediatric and Adolescent Medicine,* 151(3), pp.298–304.

Diprose, R., 2005. Community of Bodies: From Modification to Violence. *Continuum: Journal of Media & Cultural Studies,* 19(3), pp.381–392.

Dixon, K., 1996. The Criminalisation of a Cruel Tradition: An Analysis of the *Crimes (Female Genital Mutilations) Act* (New South Wales), 1995. *Australian Feminist Studies,* 11(24), pp.277–293.

Dobber, M., 1995. Hegemon: Tracing Power Through Bodies of Law. *Law/Text/Culture,* 2, pp.61–99.

Donnelly, D. and Fraser, J., 1998. Gender Differences in Sado-Masochistic Arousal Among College Students. *Sex Roles,* 29(5/6), pp.391–407.

Dopico, M., 2007. Infibulation and the Orgasm Puzzle: Sexual Experiences of Infibulated Eritrean Women in Rural Eritrea and Melbourne, Australia. In: Y. Hernlund and B. Shell-Duncan, eds, 2007. *Transcultural Bodies: Female Genital Cutting in Global Context.* New Brunswick, New Jersey and London: Rutgers University Press. pp.224–247.

Douzinas, C., Warrington, R. and McVeigh, S., eds, 1991. *Postmodern Jurisprudence: The Law of Text in the Texts of Law.* London and New York: Routledge.

Downing, L., 2007. Beyond Safety: Erotic Asphyxiation and the Limits of SM Discourse. In: D. Langdridge and M. Barker, eds, 2007. *Safe, Sane and Consensual: Contemporary Perspectives on Sadomasochism.* New York: Palgrave MacMillan. pp.119–132.

Dreger, A., 1998. *Hermaphrodites and the Medical Invention of Sex.* Cambridge and London: Harvard University Press.

Dreger, A., 2006. Intersex and Human Rights: The Long View. In: S. Sytsma, ed., 2006. *Ethics and Intersex.* The Netherlands: Springer. pp.73–86.

Dreger, A. and Feder, E. 2010. *Bad Vibrations*. The Hastings Center Bioethics Forum, [online] Available at: <http://www.thehastingscenter.org/Bioethicsforum/Post.aspx?id=4730> [Accessed 11 March 2014].

Dritsas, L., 2001. Below the Belt: Doctors, Debate, and the Ongoing American Discussion of Routine Neonatal Male Circumcision. *Bulletin of Science, Technology & Society*, 21, pp.297–311.

Driver, B., 2007. Why Trans is Not Intersex and Vice-Versa, With Remarks on the San Francisco Human Rights Report on the Medical Normalization of Intersex People. In: P. Currah, G. Guevara and R. Juang, eds, 2007. *Transgender Justice: Selected Proceedings of the Transgender Politics, Social Change and Justice Conference*. New York: The Center for Lesbian and Gay Studies, pp.48–49.

Duncan, S., 1995. Law's Sexual Discipline: Visibility, Violence and Consent. *Journal of Law and Society*, 22(3), pp.326–352.

Dunderdale, I., 1992. The Human Rights of Transexuals. *Alternative Law Journal*, 17, pp.23–26.

Dunsmuir, W. and Gordon, E., 1999. The History of Circumcision. *British Journal of Urology International*, 83(1), pp.1–12.

Durkin, K. and Houghton, S., 2000. Children's and Adolescent's Stereotypes of Tattooed People as Delinquents. *Legal and Criminal Psychology*, 5, pp.153–164.

Eckert, L., 2009. 'Diagnosticism': Three Cases of Medical Anthropological Research into Intersexuality. In: M. Holmes, ed., 2009. *Critical Intersex*. Farnham and Burlington: Ashgate. pp.41–71.

Edge, P., 2000. Male Circumcision after the *Human Rights Act* 1998. *Journal of Civil Liberties*, 5, pp.320–337.

Edwards, S., 1981. *Female Sexuality and the Law*. Oxford: Martin Robertson.

Edwards, S., 1993. No Defence for a Sado-Masochistic Libido. *New Law Journal*, 143(6592), pp.406–410.

Edwards, S., 2007. Female Genital Mutilation – Violence Against Girls and Women as a Particular Social Group. *Denning Law Journal*, 19, pp.271–278.

Egan, K., 2007. Morality-Based Legislation is Alive and Well: Why the Law Permits Consent to Body Modification but not Sadomasochistic Sex. *Albany Law Review*, 70, pp.1615–1642.

Ehrenreich, N. and Barr, M., 2005. Intersex Surgery, Female Genital Cutting, and the Selective Condemnation of 'Cultural Practices'. *Harvard Civil Rights-Civil Liberties Law Review*, 40, pp.71–140.

Eisenstein, Z., 1988. *The Female Body and The Law*. Berkeley and Los Angeles: University of California Press.

Ekins, R., 2006. *The Transgender Phenomenon*. London: Sage Publications.

Elliott, C., 2000. A New Way to be Mad. *The Atlantic Monthly*, December Issue, pp.72–84.

Elliott, T., 2009. Body Dysmorphic Disorder, Radical Surgery and the Limits of Consent. *Medical Law Review*, 17, pp.149–182.

Ernulf, K. and Innala, S., 1995. Sexual Bondage: A Review and Unobtrusive Investigation. *Archives of Sexual Behavior*, 24(6), pp.631–654.

Essen, B. and Johnsdotter, S., 2004. Female Genital Mutilation in the West: Traditional Circumcision versus Genital Cosmetic Surgery. *Acta Obstetrica et Gynecologica Scandinavica*, 83, pp.611–613.

Everaerd, W., 1983. A Case of Apotemnophilia: A Handicap as Sexual Preference. *American Journal of Psychotherapy*, 37(2), pp.285–293.

Falk, P., 1995. Written in the Flesh. *Body & Society*, 1, pp.95–105.

Family Law Council, 1994. *Female Genital Mutilation: A Report to the Attorney-General.*

Fausto-Sterling, A., 1993. The Five Sexes: Why Male and Female Are Not Enough. *Sciences*, 30(2), pp.20–25.

Fausto-Sterling, A., 2000. *Sexing the Body: Gender Politics and the Construction of Sexuality.* New York: Basic Books.

Featherstone, M., 2000. Body Modification: An Introduction. In: M. Featherstone, ed., 2000. *Body Modification.* London: Sage Publications. pp.1–13.

Feinberg, L., 1992. *Transgender Liberation: A Movement Whose Time Has Come.* New York: World View Forum.

Feinberg, L., 1998. *TransLiberation: Beyond Pink or Blue.* Boston: Beacon Press.

Feldblum, C., 2006. The Right to Define One's Own Concept of Existence: What *Lawrence* Can Mean for Intersex and Transgender People. *The Georgetown Journal of Gender and the Law*, 7, pp.115–139.

Fenske, M., 2007. *Tattoos in American Visual Culture.* New York: Palgrave MacMillan.

Ferrero, G.L., 1911. *Criminal Man, According to the Classification of Cesare Lombroso.* New York: G. P. Putnam's Sons.

Finlay, H., 1998. *Expert Report 4: Transsexualism in a Modern State Options for Reform.* Victorian Attorney-General's Law Reform Advisory Council.

Finlay, H. and Walters, W., 1988. *Sex Change: Medical and Legal Aspects of Sex Reassignment.* Victoria: H.A. Finlay.

Fisher, J., 2002. Tattooing the Body, Marking Culture. *Body & Society*, 8(4), pp.91–107.

Fletcher, R., Foxie, M. and McCandless, J., 2008. Legal Embodiment: Analysing the Body of Healthcare Law. *Medical Law Review*, 16, pp.321–345.

Fogg, K., 2005. Cosmetic Questions. *Australian Doctor*, July Issue, pp.19–20.

Ford, K.K., 2001. 'First, Do No Harm' – The Fiction of Legal Parental Consent to Genital-Normalizing Surgery on Intersexed Infants. *Yale Law & Policy Review*, 19, pp.469–488.

Foucault, M., 1964. *Madness and Civilization.* Translated by R. Howard, 2001. London and New York: Routledge.

Foucault, M., 1972. *The Archaeology of Knowledge.* Translated by A. Sheridan. London: Routledge.

Foucault, M., 1976. *The History of Sexuality: Volume 1.* Translated by R. Hurley, 2008. Camberwell: Penguin Books (Australia).
Foucault, M., 1977. *Discipline and Punish: The Birth of the Prison.* Translated by A. Sheridan. New York: Pantheon Books.
Foucault, M., 1988a. On Power (interview). In: L. Kritzman, ed., 1988. *Politics, Philosophy, Culture: Interviews and Other Writings 1977–1984.* New York and London: Routledge. pp.96–109.
Foucault, M., 1988b. Power and Sex (interview). In: L. Kritzman, ed., 1988. *Politics, Philosophy, Culture: Interviews and Other Writings 1977–1984.* New York and London: Routledge. pp.110–124.
Foucault, M., 1988c. Sexual Choice, Sexual Act: Foucault and Homosexuality (interview). In: L. Kritzman, ed., 1988. *Politics, Philosophy, Culture: Interviews and Other Writings 1977–1984.* New York and London: Routledge. pp.286–303.
Foucault, M., 2003. *'Society Must be Defended': Lectures at the College de France, 1975–1976.* Translated by D. Macey. New York: Picador.
Fox, M. and Murphy, T., 2013. The Body, Bodies, Embodiment: Feminist Legal Engagement with Health. In: M. Davies and V. Munro, eds, 2013. *The Ashgate Research Companion to Feminist Legal Theory.* Surrey, UK: Ashgate. pp.249–265.
Fox, M. and Thomson, M., 2005a. Cutting It: Surgical Interventions and the Sexing of Children. *Cardozo Journal of Law & Gender*, 12, pp.81–97.
Fox, M. and Thomson, M., 2005b. Short Changed? The Law and Ethics of Male Circumcision'. *The International Journal of Children's Rights*, 3, pp.161–181.
Fox, M. and Thomson, M., 2008. Older Minors and Circumcision: Questioning the Limits of Religious Actions. *Medical Law International*, 9(4), pp.283–311.
Fox, M. and Thomson, M. 2009. Foreskin is a Feminist Issue. *Australian Feminist Studies*, 24(60), pp.195–210.
Fox, M. and Thomson, M. 2012. The New Politics of Male Circumcision: HIV/AIDS, Health Law and Social Justice. *Legal Studies*, 32(2), pp.255–281.
Frank, A., 2004. Emily's Scars: Surgical Shapings, Technoluxe and Bioethics. *Hastings Center Report*, 34(2), pp.18–29.
Fraser, D., 1994. Heart of Darkness: The Criminalisation of Female Genital Mutilation. *Current Issues in Criminal Justice*, 6(1), pp.148–151.
Fraser, D., 1995. Father Knows Best: Transgressive Sexualities (?) and the Rule of Law. *Current Issues in Criminal Justice*, 7(1), pp.82–87.
Fraser, S., 2003a. *Cosmetic Surgery, Gender and Culture.* New York: Palgrave Macmillan.
Fraser, S., 2003b. The Agent Within: Agency Repertoires in Medical Discourse on Cosmetic Surgery. *Australian Feminist Studies*, 18(4), pp.27–44.
Freckelton, I., 1994. Masochism, Self-mutilation and the Limits of Consent. *Journal of Law and Medicine*, 2, pp.48–76.
Freckelton, I., 2000. Cosmetic Surgery and Law Reform. *Journal of Law and Medicine*, 7(3), pp.233–238.

Freckelton, I., 2001. Cosmetic Surgery: Challenging the Limits of Medical Negligence Law. *Journal of Law and Medicine*, 8, pp.353–357.

Freeman, M., 1999. A Child's Right to Circumcision. *British Journal of Urology International*, 83(1), pp.74–78.

Funder, A., 1993. *De Minimis Non Curat Lex*: The Clitoris, Culture and the Law. *Transnational Law & Contemporary Problems*, 3, pp.417–467.

Gagne, P. and McGaughey, D., 2002. Designing Women: Cultural Hegemony and the Exercise of Power Among Women who have Undergone Elective Mammoplasty. *Gender and Society*, 16(6), pp.814–838.

Garber, M., 1992. *Vested Interests: Cross-Dressing and Cultural Anxiety*. London: Penguin Group.

Gearhart, S., 1995. Foucault's Response to Freud: Sado-masochism and the Aestheticization of Power. *Style*, 29(3), pp.389–403.

Gebhard, P., 1976. Fetishism and Sadomasochism. In: M. Weinberg, ed., 1976. *Sex Research: Studies from the Kinsey Institute*. New York and London: Oxford University Press. pp.156–166.

George, M.A. 2006. The Modern Mulatto: A Comparative Analysis of the Social and Legal Positions of Mulattoes in the Antebellum South and the Intersex in Contemporary America. *Columbia Journal of Law and Gender*, 15(3), pp.665–709.

Gibbons, J., ed., 1994. *Language and the Law*. London: Longman Group.

Gibson, M., 2006. Bodies Without Histories: Cosmetic Surgery and the Undoing of Time. *Australian Feminist Studies*, 21(49), pp.51–63.

Gilbert, H., 2007. Time to Reconsider the Lawfulness of Ritual Male Circumcision. *European Human Rights Law Review*, 3, pp.279–294.

Giles, M., 1994. *R v Brown*: Consensual Harm and the Public Interest. *Modern Law Review*, 57, pp.101–111.

Gillia, B., 1997. Female Genital Mutilation: A Form of Persecution. *New Mexico Law Review*, 27, pp.579–614.

Gilman, S., 1999. *Making the Body Beautiful: A Cultural History of Aesthetic Surgery*. Princeton: Princeton University Press.

Gimlin, D., 2002. *Body Work: Beauty and Self-Image in American Culture*. Berkeley and Los Angeles: University of California Press.

Glass, J., 1999. Religious Circumcision: A Jewish View. *British Journal of Urology International*, 83(1), pp.17–21.

Glazer, R., 1993. Women's Body Image and the Law. *Duke Law Journal*, 43(1), pp.113–147.

Goldman, R., 1997. *Circumcision: The Hidden Trauma*. Boston: Vanguard Publications.

Goldman, R., 1999. The Psychological Impact of Circumcision. *British Journal of Urology International*, 83(1), pp.93–102.

Grabham, E., 2007. Citizen Bodies, Intersex Citizenship. *Sexualities*, 10(1), pp.29–48.

Grabham, E., 2012. Bodily Integrity and the Surgical Management of Intersex. *Body & Society*, 18(2), pp.1–26.

Grbich, J., 1991. The Body in Legal Theory. In: M. Fineman and N. Thomadsen, eds, 1991. *At the Boundaries of Law: Feminism and Legal Theory*. New York and London: Routledge. pp.61–76.

Green, F., 2005. From Clitoridectomies to 'Designer Vaginas': The Medical Construction of Heteronormative Female Bodies and Sexuality Through Female Genital Cutting. *Sexualities, Evolution and Gender*, 7(2), pp.153–187.

Green, K. and Lim, H., 1998. What is this Thing About Female Circumcision? Legal Education and Human Rights. *Social & Legal Studies*, 7, pp.365–387.

Green, R., 2001. (Serious) Sadomasochism: A Protected Right of Privacy? *Archives of Sexual Behavior*, 30(5), pp.543–550.

Greenberg, J., 1999. Defining Male and Female: Intersexuality and the Collision Between Law and Biology. *Arizona Law Review*, 14, pp.265–328.

Greenberg, J., 2006. International Legal Developments Protecting the Autonomy Rights of Sexual Minorities. In: S. Sytsma, ed., 2006. *Ethics and Intersex*. The Netherlands: Springer. pp.87–101.

Greenberg, J., 2012. *Intersexuality and the Law: Why Sex Matters*. New York and London: New York University Press.

Grenfell, L. and Hewitt, A., 2012. Gender Regulation: Restrictive, Facilitative or Transformative? *Sydney Law Review*, 34(4), pp.761–783.

Griffiths, R., 1999. Current Practices in Foreskin Restoration: The State of Affairs in the United States, and Results of a Survey of Restoring Men. In: G. Denniston, F. Hodges and M. Milos, eds, 1999. *Male and Female Circumcision: Medical, Legal, and Ethical Considerations in Pediatric Practice*. New York: Kluwer Academic. pp.295–302.

Grosz, E., 1994. *Volatile Bodies: Towards a Corporeal Feminism*. NSW: Allen & Unwin.

Grosz, E., 1995. *Space, Time and Perversion: The Politics of Bodies*. New York and London: Routledge.

Gruenbaum, E., 2001. *The Female Circumcision Controversy: An Anthropological Perspective*. Philadelphia: University of Pennsylvania Press.

Gulerce, A., 2007. Agendas for Multicultural Discourse Research. In Shi-xu, ed., 2007. *Discourse as Cultural Struggle*. Hong Kong: Hong Kong University Press. pp.29–45.

Gunning, I., 1991–1992. Arrogant Perception, World Travelling and Multicultural Feminism: The Case of Female Genital Surgeries. *Columbia Human Rights Law Review*, 23, pp.189–248.

Gunning, I., 1994–1995. Female Genital Surgeries and Multicultural Feminism: The Ties that Bind; the Differences that Distance. *Third World Legal Studies*, 13, pp.17–47.

Gurney, K. and Mills, E., 2007. VCAT, *Hanover* and the Transgender Conundrum. *Alternative Law Journal*, 32(4), pp.203–207.

Gurney, K., 2007. Sex and the Surgeon's Knife: The Family Court's Dilemma… Informed Consent and the Specter of Iatrogenic Harm to Children with Intersex Characteristics. *American Journal of Law and Medicine*, 33(4), pp.625–661.

Gustafson, M., 2000. The Tattoo in the Later Roman Empire and Beyond. In: J. Caplan, ed., 2000. *Written on the Body: The Tattoo in European and American History*. New Jersey: Princeton University Press. pp.17–31.

Gutman, J., 1997. *R v Wilson*. *Journal of Law and Medicine*, 4(3), pp.226–228.

Haberfeld, L., 1997a. Responding to Male Circumcision: Medical or Ritual? *Journal of Law and Medicine*, 4(4), pp.379–385.

Haberfeld, L., 1997b. The Law and Male Circumcision in Australia: Medical, Legal and Cultural Issues. *Monash University Law Review*, 23(1), pp.92–122.

Haiken, E., 1997. *Venus Envy: A History of Cosmetic Surgery*. Baltimore: The Johns Hopkins University Press.

Haiken, E., 2000. The Making of the Modern Face: Cosmetic Surgery. *Social Research*, 67(1), pp.81–97.

Halberstam, J., 1998. Transgender Butch: Butch/FTM Border Wars and the Masculine Continuum. *GLQ*, 4(2), pp.287–310.

Hanley, M., ed., 1995. *Essential Papers on Masochism*. New York and London: New York University Press.

Hanna, C., 2001. Sex is Not a Sport: Consent and Violence in Criminal Law. *Boston College Law Review*, 42, pp.239–290.

Harrison-Smith, L., 2007. Changing Sex on the Birth Register – Leave Room for 'I'!: Regulation and Repression of Transsexual Identities in Theory and Law. *Flinders Journal of Law Reform*, 10, pp.211–239.

Hart, L., 1998. *Between The Body and The Flesh*. New York: Columbia University Press.

Hebert, L., 2009. Transforming Transsexual and Transgender Rights. *William and Mary Journal of Women and the Law*, 15, pp.535–590.

Hermer, L., 2002. Paradigms Revised: Intersex Children, Bioethics & the Law. *Annals of Health Law*, 11, pp.195–236.

Hermer, L., 2007. A Moratorium on Intersex Surgeries?: Law, Science, Identity, and Bioethics at the Crossroads. *Cardozo Journal of Gender & Law*, 13, pp.255–272.

Herring, J., 2012. *Criminal Law: Text, Cases and Materials*. 5th ed. Oxford: Oxford University Press.

Hester, J., 2006. Intersex and the Rhetorics of Healing. In: S. Sytsma, ed., 2006. *Ethics and Intersex*. The Netherlands: Springer. pp.47–71.

Hewitt, K., 1997. *Mutilating the Body: Identity in Blood and Ink*. Ohio: Bowling Green State University Popular Press.

Heyes, C., 2007a. Normalisation and the Psychic Life of Cosmetic Surgery. *Australian Feminist Studies*, 22(52), pp.55–71.

Heyes, C., 2007b. *Self-Transformations: Foucault, Ethics, and Normalized Bodies*. New York: Oxford University Press.

Heyes, C., 2009. Diagnosing Culture: Body Dysmorphic Disorder and Cosmetic Surgery. *Body & Society*, 15(4), pp.73–93.

Heyes, C. and Jones, M., 2009. Cosmetic Surgery in the Age of Gender. In: C. Heyes and M. Jones, eds, 2009. *Cosmetic Surgery: A Feminist Primer*. Burlington: Ashgate Publishing. pp.1–17.

Hicks, E., 1993. *Infibulation: Female Mutilation in Islamic Northeastern Africa*. New Brunswick and London: Transaction Publishers.

Hines, S., 2007. *Transforming Gender: Transgender Practices of Identity, Intimacy and Care*. Bristol: The Policy Press.

Hird, M., 2000. Gender's Nature: Intersexuality, Transsexualism and the 'Sex'/'Gender' Binary. *Feminist Theory*, 1(3), pp.347–364.

Hodges, F., 1997. A Short History of the Institutionalization of Involuntary Sexual Mutilation in the United States. In: G. Denniston and M. Milos, eds, 1997. *Sexual Mutilations: A Human Tragedy*. New York and London: Plenum Press. pp.17–40.

Hodgkinson, D., 1999. Cosmetic Surgery Litigation. In: *Plastic, Reconstructive & Cosmetic Surgery Negligence: 1999 Seminar Papers*. Sydney: LAAMS Publications. Paper 1.

Hogan, C., 2003. Trapped in a Sexual Battleground. *The Age*, [online] 31 August. Available at: <http://www.theage.com.au/articles/2003/08/30/1062194758846.html> [Accessed 11 March 2014].

Holloway, J., 1974. Transsexuals: Legal Considerations. *Archives of Sexual Behavior*, 3(1), pp.33–50.

Holman, C. and Goldberg, J., 2007. Ethical, Legal and Psychosocial Issues in Care of Transgender Adolescents. *International Journal of Transgenderism*, 9(3), pp.95–110.

Holmes, M., 2002. Rethinking the Meaning and Management of Intersexuality. *Sexualities*, 5(2), pp.159–180.

Holmes, M., 2005. Distracted Attentions: Intersexuality and Human Rights Protection. *Cardozo Journal of Law & Gender*, 12, pp.127–133.

Holmes, M., 2009. Introduction: Straddling Past, Present and Future. In: M. Holmes, ed., 2009. *Critical Intersex*. Farnham and Burlington: Ashgate. pp.1–12.

Hooley, J., 2006. Normalising Transgender and Policing Transgression: Anti-Discrimination Law Reform Ten Years On. *The Australian Feminist Law Journal*, 25, pp.79–98.

Hoople, T., 1996. Conflicting Visions: SM, Feminism, and the Law. A Problem of Representation. *Canadian Journal of Law & Society*, Spring Issue, pp.177–220.

Hopkins, P., 1994. Rethinking Sadomasochism: Feminism, Interpretation, and Simulation. *Hypatia*, 9(1), pp.116–141.

Horowitz, C. and Jackson, J.C., 1997. Female 'Circumcision': African Women Confront American Medicine. *Journal of General Internal Medicine*, 12(3), pp.491–499.

Hosken, F., 1993. *The Hosken Report: Genital and Sexual Mutilation of Females*. 4th ed. Lexington: Women's International Network News.

Houlihan, A., 2011. When 'No' Means 'Yes' and 'Yes' Means Harm: HIV Risk, Consent and Sadomasochism Case Law. *Law & Sexuality: A Review of Lesbian, Gay, Bisexual and Transgender Legal Issues*, 20, pp.31–59.

Howe, E., 2006. Advances in Treating (or not Treating) Intersexed Persons. In: S. Sytsma, ed., 2006. *Ethics and Intersex*. The Netherlands: Springer. pp.115–137.

Hughes, B., 2002. Female Genital Mutilation: The Complementary Roles of Education and Legislation in Combating the Practice in Australia. *Journal of Law and Medicine*, 3, pp.202–210.

Hughes, I., 2002. Intersex. *British Journal of Urology International*, 90, pp.769–776.

Hughes, I., Houk, C., Ahmed, S.F. and Lee, P.A. 2006. Consensus Statement on Management of Intersex Disorders. *Journal of Pediatric Urology*, 2, pp.148–162.

Hughes, K., 1995–1996. The Criminalization of Female Genital Mutilation in the United States. *Journal of Law & Policy*, 4, pp.321–370.

Humphreys, S., 1985. Law as Discourse. In: S. Humphreys, ed., 1985. *The Discourse of Law*. London: Harwood Academic Publishers. pp.241–264.

Hyde, A., 1997. *Bodies of Law*. Princeton: Princeton University Press.

Ierodiaconou, M.J., 1995–1996. 'Listen to Us!' Female Genital Mutilation, Feminism and the Law in Australia. *Melbourne University Law Review*, 20, pp.562–587.

Irvine, J., 1995. Regulated Passions: The Invention of Inhibited Sexual Desire and Sexual Addiction. In: J. Urla and J. Terry, eds, 1995. *Deviant Bodies*. Bloomington and Indianapolis: Indiana University Press. pp.314–337.

Jeffreys, S., 1993–1994. Consent and the Politics of Sexuality. *Current Issues in Criminal Justice*, 5(2), pp.173–183.

Jeffreys, S., 1996. Heterosexuality and the Desire for Gender. In: D. Richardson, ed., 1996. *Theorising Heterosexuality*. Buckingham and Philadelphia: Open University Press. pp.75–90.

Jeffreys, S., 2000. 'Body Art' and Social Status: Cutting, Tattooing and Piercing from a Feminist Perspective. *Feminism & Psychology*, 10, pp.409–429.

Jeffreys, S., 2005a. Cosmetic Surgery: Beauty and Misogyny. *Arena*, 78, August/September Issue, pp.46–49.

Jeffreys, S., 2005b. *Beauty and Misogyny: Harmful Cultural Practices in the West*. London and New York: Routledge.

Jeffreys, S., 2008. Body Modification as Self-Mutilation by Proxy. In: V. Burr and J. Hearns, eds, 2008. *Sex, Violence and the Body: The Erotics of Wounding.* New York: Palgrave MacMillan. pp.15–33.

Jenkins, R., 2007. To Cut or Not to Cut. *Australian Doctor*, July Issue, pp.21–23.

Johnsdotter, S., 2007. Persistence of Tradition or Reassessment of Cultural Practices in Exile?: Discourses on Female Circumcision Among and About Swedish Somalis. In: Y. Hernlund and B. Shell-Duncan, eds, 2007. *Transcultural Bodies: Female Genital Cutting in Global Context.* New Brunswick, New Jersey and London: Rutgers University Press. pp.107–134.

Johnston, J. and Elliott, C., 2002. Healthy Limb Amputation: Ethical and Legal Aspects. *Clinical Medicine*, 2(5), pp.431–435.

Jones, M., 2004. Mutton Cut Up as Lamb: Mothers, Daughters and Cosmetic Surgery. *Continuum*, 18(4), pp.525–539.

Jones, M., 2008a. Makeover Culture's Dark Side: Breasts, Death and Lolo Ferrari. *Body & Society*, 14(1), pp.89–104.

Jones, M., 2008b. *Skintight: An Anatomy of Cosmetic Surgery.* Oxford and New York: Berg.

Karkazis, K., 2008. *Fixing Sex: Intersex, Medical Authority, and Lived Experience.* Durham and London: Duke University Press.

Karpin, I., 2008. Constructing the Body Inside and Out: Genetic and Somatic Modification. In: Bennett, B., Carney, T. and Karpin, I. (eds) 2008. *Brave New World of Health* (Sydney: The Federation Press). pp.73–92.

Karpin, I. and Mykitiuk, R., 2011. Feminist Legal Theory as Embodied Justice. In: Fineman, M. (ed) 2011. *Transcending the Boundaries of Law: Generations of Feminism and Legal Theory* (Abingdon, Oxon: Routledge). pp.115–130.

Kell, D., 1993. Bodily Harm in the Court of Appeal. *Law Quarterly Review*, 109, pp.199–202.

Kelman, M., 1981. Interpretive Construction in the Substantive Criminal Law *Stanford Law Review*, 33, pp.591–673.

Kennedy, A., 2008. Because We Say So: The Unfortunate Denial of Rights to Transgender Minors Regarding Transition. *Hasting Women's Law Journal*, 19(2), pp.281–301.

Kennedy, A., 2009. Mutilation and Beautification: Legal Responses to Genital Surgeries. *Australian Feminist Studies*, 24(60), pp.211–231.

Kennedy, A., 2012. Regulating Bodily Integrity: Cosmetic Surgery and Voluntary Limb Amputation. *Journal of Law and Medicine*, 20(2), pp.350–362.

Kennedy, R., 1996. The Dangerous Individual and the Social Body. In: P. Cheah, D. Fraser and J. Grbich, eds, 1996. *Thinking Through the Body of the Law.* NSW: Allen & Unwin. pp.187–206.

Kessler, S., 1990a. *Lessons from the Intersexed.* New Brunswick, New Jersey and London: Rutgers University Press.

Kessler, S., 1990b. The Medical Construction of Gender: Case Management of Intersexed Infants. *Signs*, 16(1), pp.3–26.

Kessler, S. and McKenna, W., 1985. *Gender: An Ethnomethodological Approach*. Chicago and London: University of Chicago Press.

Kessler, S. and McKenna, W., 2000. Who put the 'Trans' in Transgender? Gender Theory and Everyday Life. *International Journal of Transgenderism*, 4(3).

Khalafzai, R., 2008a. Female Genital Mutilation. *Chisholm Health Ethics Bulletin*, 14(1), pp.1–4.

Khalafzai, R., 2008b. Male Circumcision – Facts and Fiction. *Chisholm Health Ethics Bulletin*, 13(4), pp.6–9.

Khan, U., 2009. A Woman's Right to be Spanked: Testing the Limits of Tolerance of SM in the Socio-Legal Imaginary. *Law & Sexuality: Rev. Lesbian, Gay, Bisexual & Transgender Legal Issues*, 18, pp.79–119.

Khan, U., 2014. *Vicarious Kinks: S/M in the Socio-Legal Imaginary*. Toronto: University of Toronto Press.

Kim, D.S. and Pang, M.G., 2006. The Effect of Male Circumcision on Sexuality. *British Journal of Urology International*, 99, pp.619–622.

Kingdom, E. 1995. Body Politics and Rights. In: J. Bridgeman and S. Millns, eds, 1995. *Law and Body Politics: Regulating the Female Body*. Aldershot: Dartmouth Publishing. pp.1–21.

Kinnunen, T. 2008. Breast Augmentation Surgery: Carving the Flesh as Female. In: V. Burr and J. Hearns, eds, 2008. *Sex, Violence and the Body: The Erotics of Wounding*. New York: Palgrave MacMillan. pp.34–52.

Klesse, C. 2000. 'Modern Primitivism': Non-Mainstream Body Modification and Racialized Representation. In: M. Featherstone, ed., 2000. *Body Modification*. London: Sage Publications. pp.15–38.

Knouse, J., 2005. Intersexuality and the Social Construction of Anatomical Sex. *Cardozo Journal of Law & Gender*, 12, pp.135–154.

Kolbe, A., 2009. Intersex, a Blank Space in German Law? In: M. Holmes, ed., 2009. *Critical Intersex*. Farnham and Burlington: Ashgate. pp.147–170.

Koso-Thomas, O., 1987. *The Circumcision of Women: A Strategy for Eradication*. London: Zed Books.

Krafft-Ebing, R., 1885. *Psychopathia Sexualis*. 12th ed. Translated by F. Skaf, 1998. New York: Arcade Publishing.

Lacey, N., 1997. On The Subject of 'Sexing' The Subject … . In: N. Naffine and R. Owens, eds, 1997. *Sexing the Subject of Law*. Sydney: LBC Information Services. pp.65–76.

Lacey, N., 1998, *Unspeakable Subjects: Feminist Essays in Legal and Social History*. Oxford: Hart Publishing.

Lacey, N., Wells, C. and Meure, D., 1990. *Reconstructing Criminal Law: Critical Perspectives on Crime and the Criminal Process*. London: Weidenfeld and Nicolson.

Lane, S. and Rubinstein, R., 1996. Judging the Other: Responding to Traditional Female Genital Surgeries. *Hastings Center Report*, May–June Issue, pp.31–40.

Lane, S. and Rubinstein, R., 1997. Circumcision Revisited. *Hastings Center Report*, March–April Issue, pp.4–5.

Langdridge, D., 2006. Voices from the Margins: Sadomasochism and Sexual Citizenship. *Citizenship Studies*, 10(4), pp.373–389.

Langdridge, D., 2007. Speaking the Unspeakable: SM and the Eroticisation of Pain. In: D. Langdridge and M. Barker, eds, 2007. *Safe, Sane and Consensual: Contemporary Perspectives on Sadomasochism*. New York: Palgrave MacMillan. pp.85–97.

Langman, L., 2008. Punk, Porn and Resistance: Carnivalization and The Body in Popular Culture. *Current Sociology*, 56(4), pp.657–677.

Lareau, A., 2003. Who Decides? Genital Normalizing Surgery on Intersexed Infants. *The Georgetown Law Journal*, 19, pp.129–151.

Latham, M., 2008. The Shape of Things to Come: Feminism, Regulation and Cosmetic Surgery. *Medical Law Review*, 16, pp.437–457.

Law Commission, 1994. *Criminal Law: Consent and Offences Against the Person*. Consultation Paper No. 134, United Kingdom.

Law Commission, 1995. *Criminal Law: Consent in the Criminal Law*. Consultation Paper No. 139, United Kingdom.

Law Reform Commission of New South Wales, 2004. *Issue Paper 24: Minors' Consent to Medical Treatment*. [online] Available at: <http://www.lawreform.lawlink.nsw.gov.au/lrc/lrc_publications/lrc_otherpublications/LRC_ips.html> [Accessed 11 March 2014].

Lawrence, A., 2006. Clinical and Theoretical Parallels Between Desire for Limb Amputation and Gender Identity Disorder. *Archives of Sexual Behavior*, 35(3), pp.263–278.

Leigh, L.H., 1976. Sado-Masochism, Consent, and the Reform of the Criminal Law. *The Modern Law Review*, 39(2), pp.130–146.

Lentini, P., 1999. The Cultural Politics of Tattooing. *Arena*, 13, pp.31–50.

Lewins, F., 1995. *Transsexualism in Society: A Sociology of Male-to-Female Transsexuals*. Melbourne: MacMillan Education Australia.

Lightfoot-Klein, H., 1989. *Prisoners of Ritual: An Odyssey into Female Genital Circumcision in Africa*. New York and London: Harrington Park Press.

Lightfoot-Klein, H., 1997. Similarities in Attitudes and Misconceptions About Male and Female Sexual Mutilations. In: G. Denniston and M. Milos, eds, 1997. *Sexual Mutilations: A Human Tragedy*. New York and London: Plenum Press. pp.131–135.

Lindemann, D., 2012. *Dominatrix: Gender, Eroticism, and Control in the Dungeon*. Chicago and London: University of Chicago Press.

Linden, R.R., Pagano, D.R., Russell, D.E.H. and Star, S.L., eds, 1982. *Against Sadomasochism: A Radical Feminist Analysis*. California: Frog in the Well.

Llewellyn, D., 1999. Some Thoughts on Legal Remedies. In: G. Denniston, F. Hodges and M. Milos, eds, 1999. *Male and Female Circumcision: Medical, Legal, and Ethical Considerations in Pediatric Practice.* New York: Kluwer Academic. pp.471–483.

Lloyd, E., 2005a. From the Hospital to the Courtroom: A Statutory Proposal for Recognizing and Protecting the Legal Rights of Intersex Children. *Cardozo Journal of Law & Gender*, 12, pp.155–195.

Lloyd, E., 2005b. Intersex Education, Advocacy & The Law: The Struggle for Recognition and Protection. *Cardozo Women's Law Journal*, 11, pp.283–301.

Lloyd, M., 2004. Life in the Slow Lane: Rethinking Spectacular Body Modification. *Continuum: Journal of Media & Cultural Studies*, 18(4), pp.555–564.

Loy, J., 2000. A Look at Labiaplasty. *AlterNet*, [online] 28 May. Available at: <http://www.alternet.org/story/9217/pushing_the_perfect_pussy/> [Accessed 11 March 2014].

Lyotard, J.F. 1984. *The Postmodern Condition: A Report on Knowledge.* Translated by G. Bennington and B. Massumi. Manchester: Manchester University Press.

McBride, J., 2000. To Make Martyrs of Their Children: 'Female Genital Mutilation', Religious Legitimation, and the Constitution. In: K. Sands, ed., 2000. *God Forbid: Religion and Sex in American Public Life.* New York: Oxford University Press. pp.219–244.

McClintock, A., 1993. Maid to Order: Commercial Fetishism and Gender Power. *Social Text*, 37, pp.87–116.

McDonald, E., 2004. Circumcision and the Criminal Law: The Challenge for a Multicultural State. *New Zealand Universities Law Review*, 21, pp.233–267.

Macdonell, D., 1986. *Theories of Discourse: An Introduction.* Oxford: Basil Blackwell.

McHugh, P., 2004. Surgical Sex. *First Things*, 147, pp.34–38.

Mackay, R., 1983. Is Female Circumcision Unlawful? *Criminal Law Review*, pp.717–722.

MacKendrick, K., 1999. *Counterpleasures.* New York: State University of New York Press.

MacKenzie, G., 1994. *Transgender Nation.* Ohio: Bowling Green State University Popular Press.

MacKenzie, R., 2008. Somatechnics of Medico-Legal Taxonomies: Elective Amputation and Transableism. *Medical Law Review*, 16, pp.390–412.

McSherry, B., 2007. Cosmetic Surgery in Australia: A Risky Business? *Journal of Law and Medicine*, 15(1), pp.14–18.

Mains, G., 2002. *Urban Aboriginals: A Celebration of Leathersexuality.* 3rd ed. Los Angeles: Daedalus Publishing Company.

Makkai, T. and McAllister, I. 2001. Prevalence of Tattooing and Piercing in the Australian Community. *Communicable Diseases Intelligence*, 25, pp.67–72.

Maley, Y., 1994. The Language of the Law. In: J. Gibbons, eds, 1994. *Language and the Law.* London: Longman Group. pp.11–50.

Mantese, T., Pfeiffer, C. and McClinton, J. 2006. Cosmetic Surgery and Informed Consent. *Michigan Bar Journal*, January Issue, pp.26–29.

Markwick, P., 2002. Harming Consent. *Res Publica*, 8, pp.157–162.

Mascia-Lees, F. and Sharpe, P., 1992. The Marked and the Un(re)Marked: Tattoo and Gender in Theory and Narrative. In: F. Mascia-Lees and P. Sharpe, eds, 1992. *Tattoo, Torture, Mutilation, and Adornment: The Denaturalization of the Body in Culture and Text*. New York: State University of New York Press. pp.145–169.

Mason, C., 2001. Exorcising Excision: Medico-Legal Issues Arising From Male and Female Genital Surgery in Australia. *Journal of Law and Medicine*, 9, pp.58–67.

Mason, P., 2009a. 'Pink or Blue?' – A Rights-Based Framework for Medical Intervention with Intersex Infants. In: World Congress on Family Law and Children's Rights, *5th World Congress*, Nova Scotia, Canada, 23–25 August 2009.

Mason, P., 2009b. *Non-Therapeutic Male Circumcision: Issues Paper No 14 June 2009*. Submission to the Tasmania Law Reform Commission, 28 September.

Mayeda, G., 2009. Who Do You Think You Are? When Should the Law Let You Be Who You Want to Be? In: L. Shrage, ed., 2009. *You've Changed: Sex Reassignment and Personal Identity*. Oxford: Oxford University Press. pp.194–216.

Mendelsohn, N., 2004. At the Crossroads: The Case For and Against a Cultural Defence to Female Genital Mutilation. *Rutgers Law Review*, 56(4), pp.1011–1038.

Mertz, E., 1994. Legal Language: Pragmatics, Poetics, and Social Power. *Annual Review of Anthropology*, 23, pp.435–455.

Meyerowitz, J., 1998. Sex Change and the Popular Press; Historical Notes on Transsexuality in the United States, 1930–1955. *GLQ*, 4(2), pp.159–187.

Miller, G., 2002. Circumcision: Cultural-Legal Analysis. *Virginia Journal of Social Policy & the Law*, 9(3), pp.497–585.

Mills, S., 1997. *Discourse*. London: Routledge.

Minter, S. and Keisling, M., 2010. The Role of Medical and Psychological Discourse in Legal and Policy Advocacy for Transgender Persons in the United States. *Journal of Gay and Lesbian Mental Health*, 14(2), pp.145–154.

Money, J., Jobaris, R. and Furth, G., 1977. Apotemnophilia: Two Cases of Self-Demand Amputation as Paraphilia. *The Journal of Sex Research*, 13(2), pp.115–125.

Monro, S., 2005. Beyond Male and Female: Poststructuralism and the Spectrum of Gender. *International Journal of Transgenderism*, 8(1), pp.3–22.

Moran, L. 1995. Violence and the Law: The Case of Sado-Masochism. *Social & Legal Studies*, 4, pp.225–251.

More, S., 1998. The Pregnant Man – An Oxymoron? *Journal of Gender Studies*, 7(3), pp.319–328.

Morgan, K., 2002. Women and the Knife: Cosmetic Surgery and the Colonization of Women's Bodies. In: S. Sherwin and B. Parish, eds, 2002. *Women, Medicine, Ethics and the Law*. Burlington: Ashgate Publishing Company. pp.343–372.

Morgan, M., 1997. Female Genital Mutilation: An Issue on the Doorstep of the American Medical Community. *The Journal of Legal Medicine*, 18(1), pp.93–115.

Morland, I., 2001. Is Intersexuality Real? *Textual Practice*, 15(3), pp.527–547.

Morland, I., 2005. The Injustice of Intersex: Feminist Science Studies and the Writing of a Wrong. In: M. Anderson, ed., 2005. *Toward a Critique of Guilt: Perspectives from Law and the Humanities*. Oxford: JAI Ltd. pp.53–76.

Morland, I., 2009. What can Queer Theory do for Intersex? *GLQ: A Journal of Lesbian and Gay Studies*, 15(2), pp.285–312.

Morris, B., Bailis, S., Castellsague, X., Wiswell, T. and Halperin, D., 2006. RACP's Policy Statement on Infant Circumcision is Ill-Conceived. *Australian and New Zealand Journal of Public Health*, 30(1), pp.16–22.

Morrison, W., 1997. *Jurisprudence: From the Greeks to Post-Modernism*. London: Cavendish Publishing Limited.

Moser, C. and Levitt, E., 1995. An Exploratory-Descriptive Study of a Sadomasochistically Oriented Sample. In: T. Weinberg, ed., 1995. *S&M: Studies in Dominance & Submission*. New York: Prometheus Books. pp.93–112.

Mountbatten, J., 1994. Transsexuals and Social Security Law: the Return of Gonad the Barbarian. *Australian Journal of Family Law*, 8(2), pp.166–177.

Mountbatten, J., 1996. Priscilla's Revenge: Or the Strange Case of Transsexual Law Reform in Victoria. *Melbourne University Law Review*, 20, pp.871–896.

Muller, V., 1994. 'Trapped in the Body': Transsexualism, The Law, Sexual Identity. *The Australian Feminist Law Journal*, 3, pp.103–116.

Murphy, M., 2007. *Philosophy of Law: The Fundamentals*. Victoria: Blackwell Publishing.

Murphy, P., 1994. Postmodern Perspectives and Justice. In: D. Patterson, ed., 1994. *Postmodernism and Law*. New York: New York University Press. pp.3–18.

Murphy, P., 2011. Flogging Live Complainants and Dead Horses: We May No Longer Need to be in Bondage to *Brown*. *Criminal Law Review*, 10, pp.758–765.

Murphy, P. and Sikora, K., 2010. Push to let Australian Doctors Mutilate the Genitals of Baby Girls. *News.com.au*, [online] 28 May. Available at: <http://www.news.com.au/national/push-to-let-australian-doctors-mutilate-genitals-of-baby-girls/story-e6frfkvr-1225872274181> [Accessed 11 March 2014].

Murray, S., 2007. Corporeal Knowledges and Deviant Bodies: Perceiving the Fat Body. *Social Semiotics*, 17(3), pp.361–373.

Murray, S., 2009. Within or Beyond the Binary/Boundary? *Australian Feminist Studies*, 24(60), pp.265–274.

Myers, J., 1992. Nonmainstream Body Modification: Genital Piercing, Branding, Burning, and Cutting. *Journal of Contemporary Ethnography*, 21(3), pp.267–306.

Naffine, N., 1990, *Law & The Sexes: Explorations in Feminist Jurisprudence*, Allen & Unwin Australia, Sydney.

Naffine, N., 1997. The Body Bag. In: N. Naffine and R. Owens, eds, 1997. *Sexing the Subject of Law*. Sydney: LBC Information Services. pp.79–93.

Naffine, N. and Owens, R., 1997. Sexing Law. In: N. Naffine and R. Owens, eds, 1997. *Sexing the Subject of Law*. Sydney: LBC Information Services. pp.3–21.

Nash, S., 1996. Consent: Public Policy or Legal Moralism? *New Law Journal*, 146, p.382.

Nataf, Z., 1996. *Lesbians Talk Transgender*. London: Scarlet Press.

Naugler, D., 2009. Crossing the Cosmetic/Reconstructive Divide: The Instructive Situation of Breast Reduction Surgery. In: C. Heyes and M. Jones, eds, 2009. *Cosmetic Surgery: A Feminist Primer*. Burlington: Ashgate Publishing. pp.225–237.

Negrin, L., 2002. Cosmetic Surgery and the Eclipse of Identity. *Body & Society*, 8(4), pp.21–42.

Newmahr, S., 2008. Becoming a Sadomasochist: Integrating Self and Other in Ethnographic Analysis. *Journal of Contemporary Ethnography*, 37(5), pp.619–643.

Newmahr, S., 2010. Power Struggles: Pain and Authenticity in SM Play. *Symbolic Interaction*, 33(3), pp.389–411.

Newmahr, S., 2011. *Playing on the Edge: Sadomasochism, Risk, and Intimacy*. Bloomington and Indianapolis: Indiana University Press.

Nnamuchi, O., 2012. 'Circumcision' or 'Mutilation'? Voluntary or Forced Excision? Extricating the Ethical and Legal Issues in Female Genital Ritual. *Journal of Law and Health*, 25, pp.85–121.

Norman, S., 2004. I am the Leathefaerie Shaman. In: M. Thompson, ed., 2004. *Leatherfolk: Radical Sex, People, Politics and Practices*. Los Angeles: Daedalus Publishing Company. pp.276–283.

Nugent, K., 2009. Cosmetic Surgery on Patients with Body Dysmorphic Disorder: Cutting the Tie that Binds. *Developments in Mental Health Law*, 28(2), pp.77–104.

Obiora, L., 1996–1997a. Bridges and Barricades: Rethinking Polemics and Intransigence in the Campaign Against Female Circumcision. *Case Western Reserve Law Review*, 47, pp.275–378.

Obiora, L., 1996–1997b. Feminism, Globalization and Culture: After Beijing. *Indiana Journal of Global Legal Studies*, 4, pp.355–406.

Oboler, R., 2001. Law and Persuasion in the Elimination of Female Genital Mutilation. *Human Organization*, 60(4), pp.311–318.

O'Donovan, K., 1997. With Sense, Consent, or Just a Con?: Legal Subjects in the Discourse of Autonomy. In: N. Naffine and R. Owens, eds, 1997. *Sexing the Subject of Law*. Sydney: LBC Information Services. pp.47–64.

O'Flaherty, M. and Fisher, J., 2008. Sexual Orientation, Gender Identity and International Human Rights Law: Contextualising the Yogyakarta Principles. *Human Rights Law Review*, 8(2), pp.207–248.

O'Hara, K. and O'Hara, J., 1999. The Effect of Male Circumcision on the Sexual Enjoyment of the Female Partner. *British Journal of Urology International*, 83(1), pp.79–84.

O'Regan, R.S., 1990. Surgery and Criminal Responsibility Under the Queensland Criminal Code. *Criminal Law Review*, 14, pp.73–83.

O'Regan, R.S., 1993. Consent to Assaults Under the Queensland Criminal Code. *University of Queensland Law Journal*, 17, pp.287–291.

Organisation Intersex International Australia, 2009. On a Third Sex. [online] Available at: <http://oii.org.au/18064/on-a-third-sex/> [Accessed 11 March 2014].

Ozar, D., 2006. Towards a More Inclusive Conception of Gender-Diversity for Intersex Advocacy and Ethics. In: S. Sytsma, ed., 2006. *Ethics and Intersex*. The Netherlands: Springer. pp.17–45.

Pa, M., 2001. Beyond the Pleasure Principle: The Criminalization of Consensual Sadomasochistic Sex. *Texas Journal of Women & the Law*, 11, pp.51–92.

Paltridge, B., 2006. *Discourse Analysis*. London: Continuum.

Parekh, B., 1996. Minority Practices and Principles of Toleration. *International Migration Review*, 30(1), pp.251–284.

Parlett, K. and Weston-Scheuber, K.M., 2004. Consent to Treatment for Transgender and Intersex Children. *Deakin Law Review*, 9(2), pp.375–397.

Patrick, I., 2001. Responding to Female Genital Mutilation: The Australian Experience in Context. *Australian Journal of Social Issues*, 36(1), pp.15–33.

Patterson, D., ed., 1994. *Postmodernism and Law*. New York: New York University Press.

Peterson, D., 1997. The Tattooed Delinquent or the Delinquent Tattoo? A Response to the Typology of Tattooed 'Youth'. *Youth Studies Australia*, 16(3), pp.46–48.

Pitts, V., 2000. Body Modification, Self-Mutilation and Agency in Media Accounts of a Subculture. In: M. Featherstone, ed., 2000. *Body Modification*. London: Sage Publications. pp.291–303.

Pitts, V., 2003. *In the Flesh: The Cultural Politics of Body Modification*. New York: Palgrave MacMillan.

Pitts-Taylor, V., 2007. *Surgery Junkies: Wellness and Pathology in Cosmetic Culture*. New Brunswick and New Jersey: Rutgers University Press.

Pitts-Taylor, V., 2009. Becoming/Being a Cosmetic Surgery Patient: Semantic Instability and the Intersubjective Self. *Studies in Gender and Sexuality*, 10, pp.119–128.

Plant, B., 2007. Playing Games/Playing Us: Foucault on Sadomasochism. *Philosophy & Social Criticism*, 3(5), pp.531–561.

Polhemus, T., 2004. *Hot Bodies, Cool Styles: New Techniques in Self-Adornment*. London: Thames & Hudson.

Post, R., 1968. The Relationship of Tattoos to Personality Disorders. *The Journal of Criminal Law, Criminology and Police Science*, 59(4), pp.516–524.

Post, R., 1991. Introduction: The Relatively Autonomous Discourse of Law. In: R. Post, ed., 1991. *Law and the Order of Culture*. Berkeley and Los Angeles: University of California Press. pp.vii–xvii.

Poulter, S., 1975. Foreign Customs and the English Criminal Law. *International and Comparative Law Quarterly*, 24, pp.136–140.

Povenmire, R., 1998–1999. Do Parents have the Legal Authority to Consent to the Surgical Amputation of Normal, Healthy Tissue from their Infant Children?: The Practice of Circumcision in the United States. *Journal of Gender, Social Policy & The Law*, 7, pp.87–123.

Preves, S., 2002. Sexing the Intersexed: An Analysis of Sociocultural Responses to Intersexuality. *Signs*, 27, pp.523–556.

Price, C., 1996. *Male Circumcision: A Legal Affront*. Brief submitted to the Law Commission of England and Wales, [online] Available at: <http://www.cirp.org/library/legal/price-uklc/> [Accessed 11 March 2014].

Price, C., 1999. Male Non-Therapeutic Circumcision: The Legal and Ethical Issues. In: G. Denniston, F. Hodges and M. Milos, eds, 1999. *Male and Female Circumcision: Medical, Legal, and Ethical Considerations in Pediatric Practice*. New York: Kluwer Academic. pp.425–454.

Putnins, A., 2002. Young Offenders, Tattoos and Recidivism. *Psychiatry, Psychology and the Law*, 9(1), pp.62–68.

Queensland Health Department, 2007. *Have Your Say: Children and Young People Using Cosmetic Surgery and Solariums in Queensland*. Discussion paper.

Queensland Law Reform Commission, 1993. *Circumcision of Male Infants: Miscellaneous Paper No 6*.

Queensland Law Reform Commission, 1994. *Report No 47: Female Genital Mutilation*.

Race, K., 1997. The Beast with Two Backs: Bodies/Selves/Integrity. *The Australian Feminist Law Journal*, 9, pp.24–44.

Rahman, M. and Jackson, S., 2010. *Gender and Sexuality: Sociological Perspectives*. Cambridge: Polity Press.

Ramsay, S., 2000. Controversy Over UK Surgeon who Amputated Healthy Limbs. *The Lancet*, 355, p.476.

Ranson, D., 1996. Female Genital Mutilation. *Journal of Law and Medicine*, 3(3), pp.229–230.

Ras-Work, B., 1997. Female Genital Mutilation. In: G. Denniston and M. Milos, eds, 1997. *Sexual Mutilations: A Human Tragedy*. New York: Plenum Press. pp.137–152.

Raymond, J., 1979. *The Transsexual Empire*. London: The Women's Press.

Raymond, J., 1995. The Politics of Transgenderism. In: R. Ekins and D. King, eds, 1995. *Blending Genders: Social Aspects of Cross-Dressing and Sex Changing.* London: Routledge. pp.215–223.

Reed, B., Rhodes, S., Schofield, P. and Wylie, K., 2009. *Gender Variance in the UK: Prevalence, Incidence, Growth and Geographic Distribution.* Gender Identity Research and Education Society.

Rees, M., 1995. Becoming a Man: The Personal Account of a Female-to-Male Transsexual. In: R. Ekins and D. King, eds, 1995. *Blending Genders: Social Aspects of Cross-Dressing and Sex Changing.* London: Routledge. pp.27–38.

Reis, E., 2009. *Bodies in Doubt: An American History of Intersex.* Baltimore: The Johns Hopkins University Press.

Reischer, E. and Koo, K., 2004. The Body Beautiful: Symbolism and Agency in the Social World. *Annual Review of Sociology*, 33, pp.297–317.

Reti, I., ed., 1993. *Unleashing Feminism: Critiquing Lesbian Sadomasochism in the Gay Nineties.* California: HerBooks.

Richards, D., 1996. Male Circumcision: Medical or Ritual? *Journal of Law and Medicine*, 3(4), pp.371–376.

Richters, J., 2006a. Circumcision and the Socially Imagined Sexual Body. *Health Sociology Review*, 15(3), pp.248–257.

Richters, J., 2006b. Critical Commentary on RACP Policy Statement on Infant Male Circumcision: A Response. *Australian and New Zealand Journal of Public Health*, 30(1), pp.22–24.

Richters, J., Smith, A.M.A., de Visser, R.O., Grulich, A.E. and Rissel, C.E., 2006. Circumcision in Australia: Prevalence and Effects on Sexual Health. *International Journal of STD and AIDS*, 17(8), pp.547–554.

Richters, J., de Visser, R.O., Rissell, C.E., Grulich, A.E. and Smith, A.M.A., 2008. Demographic and Psychosocial Features of Participants in Bondage and Discipline, 'Sadomasochism' or Dominance and Submission (BDSM): Data From a National Survey. *Journal of Sexual Medicine*, 5(7), pp.1660–1668.

Riddell, C., 1995. Divided Sisterhood: A Critical Review of Janice Raymond's *The Transsexual Empire.* In: R. Ekins and D. King, eds, 1995. *Blending Genders: Social Aspects of Cross-Dressing and Sex Changing.* London: Routledge. pp.171–189.

Ridinger, R., 2006. Negotiating Limits: The Legal Status of SM in the United States. In: P. Kleinplatz and C. Moser, eds, 2006. *Sadomasochism: Powerful Pleasures.* New York: Harrington Park Press. pp.189–216.

Rizvi, S., Naqvi, S., Hussain, M. and Hasan, A.S., 1999. Religious Circumcision: A Muslim View. *British Journal of Urology International*, 83(1), pp.13–16.

Roberts, J., 2011. 'Circumcision: Everyone's Talking About It': Legislation, Social Pressure and the Body. *Journal of Gender Studies*, 20(4), pp.347–358.

Roen, K., 2002. 'Either/Or' and 'Both/Neither': Discursive Tensions in Transgender Politics. *Signs*, 27(2), pp.501–522.

Roen, K., 2008. But We Have to *Do Something*: Surgical 'Correction' of Atypical Genitalia. *Body & Society*, 14(1), pp.47–66.

Roen, K., 2009. Clinical Intervention and Embodied Subjectivity: Atypically Sexed Children and their Parents. In: M. Holmes, ed., 2009. *Critical Intersex*. Farnham and Burlington: Ashgate. pp.15–40.

Rogers, J., 2007. Managing Cultural Diversity in Australia: Legislating Female Circumcision, Legislating Communities. In: Y. Hernlund and B. Shell-Duncan, eds, 2007. *Transcultural Bodies: Female Genital Cutting in Global Context*. New Brunswick, New Jersey and London: Rutgers University Press. pp.135–156.

Rogers, J., 2009. A Child is Being Mutilated: Fantasies of Female Genital Mutilation Law. *Australian Feminist Studies*, 24(60), pp.181–194.

Rogers, J., 2013. *Law's Cut on the Body of Human Rights: Female Circumcision, Torture and Sacred Flesh*. Abingdon, Oxon: Routledge.

Rosario, V., 2008. The History of Aphallia and the Intersexual Challenge to Sex/Gender. In: G. Haggerty and M. McGarry, eds, 2008. *A Companion to Lesbian, Gay, Bisexual, Transgender and Queer Studies*. Wiley-Blackwell. pp.262–281.

Rosenberg, J., 2009. Female Genital Mutilation Linked to Sexual Dysfunction. *International Perspectives on Sexual and Reproductive Health*, 35(1), p.5.

Rosenblatt, D., 1997. The Antisocial Skin: Structure, Resistance, and 'Modern Primitive' Adornment in the United States. *Cultural Anthropology*, 12(3), pp.287–334.

Rosenfeld, M., 1992. Deconstruction and Legal Interpretation: Conflict, Indeterminacy and the Temptations of the New Legal Formalism. In: D. Cornell, M. Rosenfel and D. Carlson, eds, 1992. *Deconstruction and the Possibility of Justice*. New York and London: Routledge. pp.152–210.

Royal Australian College of Obstetricians and Gynaecologists, 1997. *Female Genital Mutilation: Information for Australian Health Professionals*.

Royal Australian College of Physicians, 2004a. *Circumcision: A Parents' Guide to Routine Circumcision of Male Infants and Boys*.

Royal Australian College of Physicians, 2004b. *Policy Statement on Circumcision*.

Royal Australian College of Physicians, 2006. Royal Australian College of Physicians Paediatric Policy: Routine Circumcision of Male Infants and Boys – Summary Statement. *Australian and New Zealand Journal of Public Health*, 30(1), p.25.

Royal Australian College of Physicians, 2010. *Circumcision of Male Infants*. [online] Available at: <http://www.racp.edu.au/page/paed-policy> [Accessed 11 March 2014].

Rubin, G., 1987. The Leather Menace: Comments on Politics and S/M. In: SAMOIS, eds, 1987. *Coming To Power: Writings and Graphics on Lesbian S/M*. 3rd ed. Boston: Alyson Publications. pp.194–229.

Russel, A., 2010. Intersex. *The Hungry Beast*, ABC Television, 12 March.

Sagarin, B.J., Cutler, B., Cutler, N., Lawler-Sagarin, K.A. and Matuszewich, L., 2009. Hormonal Changes and Couple Bonding in Consensual Sadomasochistic Activity. *Archives of Sexual Behaviour*, 38, pp.186–200.

Sanders, C., 2008. *Customizing the Body: The Art and Culture of Tattooing*. 2nd ed. Philadelphia: Temple University Press.

Sarwer, D. and Crerand, C., 2004. Body Image and Cosmetic Medical Treatments. *Body Image*, 1, pp.99–111.

Saxe, L., 1992. Sadomasochism and Exclusion. *Hypatia*, 7(4), pp.59–72.

Schramme, T., 2008. Should we Prevent Non-Therapeutic Mutilation and Extreme Body Modification? *Bioethics*, 22(1), pp.8–15.

Sclater, S., 2002. Introduction. In: A. Bainham, S. Sclater and M. Richards, eds, 2002. *Body Lore and Laws*. Oxford: Hart Publishing. pp.1–28.

Scollon, R. and Scollon, S., 2003. Discourse and Intercultural Communication. In: D. Schiffrin, T. Deborah and H.E. Hamilton, eds, 2003. *The Handbook of Discourse Analysis*. Blackwell Publishing, [online] Available at: <http://www.blackwellreference.com/subscriber/tocnode?id=g9780631205968_chunk_g978063120596828> [Accessed 12 March 2014].

Scott, K., 2009. Under the Knife: An Analysis of the Medical Council of New Zealand's Statement on Cosmetic Procedures. *Journal of Law and Medicine*, 16(4), pp.625–652.

Seidler, V., 2007. Masculinities, Bodies, and Emotional Life. *Men and Masculinities*, 10(1), pp.9–21.

Select Committee on the Tattooing and Body Piercing Industries, 2005. *Report of the Select Committee on the Tattooing and Body Piercing Industries*. House of Assembly, South Australian Parliament.

Shapiro, J., 1991. Transsexualism: Reflections on the Persistence of Gender and the Mutability of Sex. In: J. Epstein and K. Straub, eds, 1991. *Body Guards: The Cultural Politics of Gender Ambiguity*. New York and London: Routledge. pp.248–279.

Sharpe, A., 1996. Judicial Uses of Transsexuality: A Site for Political Contestation. *Alternative Law Journal*, 21(4), pp.153–155.

Sharpe, A., 1999a. Imagining the Sexual: Transgendered Desire and Law's Limit. *Flinders Journal of Law Reform*, 3, pp.273–282.

Sharpe, A., 1999b. Transgender Performance and the Discriminating Gaze: A Critique of Anti-Discriminatory Regulatory Regimes. *Social & Legal Studies*, 8(1), pp.5–24.

Sharpe, A., 2000. Transgender Jurisprudence and the Spectre of Homosexuality. *The Australian Feminist Law Journal*, 14, pp.23–37.

Sharpe, A., 2001a. From Functionality to Aesthetics: The Architecture of Transgender Jurisprudence. *Murdoch University Electronic Journal of Law*, 8(1).

Sharpe, A., 2001b. In the Shadow of Homosexual Anxiety: Transgender Law Reform in Western Australia. *Gay and Lesbian Law Journal*, 10, pp.1–25.

Sharpe, A., 2002a. Thinking Critically in Moments of Transgender Law Reform: *Re Kevin and Jennifer v Attorney-General for the Commonwealth*. *Griffith Law Review*, 11(2), pp.309–331.
Sharpe, A., 2002b. *Transgender Jurisprudence: Dysphoric Bodies of Law*. London and Sydney: Cavendish Publishing Limited.
Sheldon, S. and Wilkinson, S., 1998. Female Genital Mutilation and Cosmetic Surgery: Regulating Non-Therapeutic Body Modification. *Bioethics*, 12(4), pp.263–285.
Shildrick, M., 1997. *Leaky Bodies and Boundaries: Feminism, Postmodernism and (Bio) Ethics*. London and New York: Routledge.
Shildrick, M., 2000. This Body Which Is Not One: Dealing with Differences. In: M. Featherstone, ed., 2000. *Body Modification*. London: Sage Publications. pp.77–92.
Shuy, R., 2003. Discourse Analysis in the Legal Context. In: D. Schiffrin, T. Deborah and H.E. Hamilton, eds, 2003. *The Handbook of Discourse Analysis*. Blackwell Publishing, [online] Available at: <http://www.blackwellreference.com/subscriber/tocnode?id=g9780631205968_chunk_g978063120596828> [Accessed 12 March 2014].
Silverman, K., 1992. *Male Subjectivity at the Margins*. New York and London: Routledge.
Silverman, E.K., 2004. Anthropology and Circumcision. *Annual Review of Anthropology*, 33, pp.419–445.
Simon, W., 1996. *Postmodern Sexualities*. New York: Routledge.
Skaine, R., 2005. *Female Genital Mutilation: Legal, Cultural and Medical Issues*. London: McFarland & Company.
Skegg, K., Nada-Raja, S., Paul, C. and Skegg, D.C.G., 2007. Body Piercing, Personality and Sexual Behavior. *Archives of Sexual Behavior*, 36, pp.47–54.
Skene, L., 1996. In Their Mind's Eye: A Different Direction for Cosmetic Surgery Consent Cases? *Torts Law Journal*, 4(3), pp.275–285.
Slack, A., 1988. Female Circumcision: A Critical Appraisal. *Human Rights Quarterly*, 10, pp.437–486.
Smart, B., 1990. Modernity, Postmodernity and the Present. In: B. Turner, ed., 1990. *Theories of Modernity and Postmodernity*. London: Sage Publications. pp.14–30.
Smart, C., 1989. *Feminism and the Power of Law*. London and New York: Routledge.
Smart, C., 1992. The Woman of Legal Discourse. *Social and Legal Studies*, 1, pp.29–44.
Smart, C., 1995. *Law, Crime and Sexuality: Essays in Feminism*. London: Sage Publications.
Smith, D., 1971. Transsexualism, Sex Reassignment Surgery, and the Law. *Cornell Law Review*, 56, pp.963–1009.
Smith, J., 1998. Male Circumcision and the Rights of the Child. In: M. Bulterman, A. Hendriks and J. Smith, eds, 1998. *To Baehr in Our Minds: Essays in Human*

Rights from the Heart of the Netherlands. Netherlands Institute of Human Rights. pp.465–498.

Smith, R., 1992. Female Circumcision: Bringing Women's Perspectives into the International Debate. *Southern California Law Review*, 65, pp.2449–2504.

Smith, R.C., 2009. Less is More: Body Integrity Identity Disorder. In: S. Smith and R. Deazley, eds, 2009. *The Legal, Medical and Cultural Regulation of the Body: Transformation and Transgression*. Ashgate. pp.147–157.

Solomon, D., 2007–2008. Informed Consent for Routine Infant Circumcision: A Proposal. *New York Law School Law Review*, 52, pp.215–245.

Somers, C., 2010. Sexing the Difference in Gender and the Anomalies of Interpretation. *Organisation Intersex International Australia*, [online] Available at: <http://oii.org.au/18131/opinion–sexing–difference–gender/> [Accessed 12 March 2014].

Somerville, M., 1980–1981. Medical Interventions and the Criminal Law: Lawful or Excusable Wounding? *McGill Law Journal*, 26, pp.82–96.

Somerville, M., 1999. Respect in the Context of Infant Male Circumcision: Can Ethics and Law Provide Insights? In: G. Denniston, F. Hodges and M. Milos, eds, 1999. *Male and Female Circumcision: Medical, Legal, and Ethical Considerations in Pediatric Practice*. New York: Kluwer Academic. pp.413–424.

Sorrells, M., 1999. The History of Circumcision in the United States: A Physician's Perspective. In: G. Denniston, F. Hodges and M. Milos, eds, 1999. *Male and Female Circumcision: Medical, Legal, and Ethical Considerations in Pediatric Practice*. New York: Kluwer Academic. pp.331–338.

Spade, D., 2003. Resisting Medicine, Re/Modelling Gender. *Berkeley Women's Law Journal*, 18, pp.15–37.

Spade, D., 2007. Documenting Change: Strategies for De-Medicalizing Trans Identity. In: P. Currah, G. Guevara and R. Juang, eds, 2007. *Transgender Justice: Selected Proceedings of the Transgender Politics, Social Change and Justice Conference*. New York: The Center for Lesbian and Gay Studies. pp.17–19.

Spade, D., 2008. Methodologies of Trans Resistance. In: G. Haggery and M. McGarry, eds, 2008. *A Companion to Lesbian, Gay, Bisexual, Transgender and Queer Studies*. Wiley-Blackwell. pp.237–261.

Spurgas, A., 2009. (Un)Queering Identity: The Biosocial Production of Intersex/DSD. In: M. Holmes, ed., 2009. *Critical Intersex*. Farnham and Burlington: Ashgate. pp.97–122.

Stark, H., 2006. Authenticity and Intersexuality. In: S. Sytsma, ed., 2006. *Ethics and Intersex*. The Netherlands: Springer. pp.271–291.

Stear, N.H., 2009. Sadomasochism as *Make-Believe*. *Hypatia*, 24(2), pp.21–38.

Steele, V., 1996. *Fetish: Fashion, Sex & Power*. Oxford: Oxford University Press.

Stewart, S., 1998. *Sublime Surrender: Male Masochism at the Fin-de-Siecle*. Ithaca and London: Cornell University Press.

Stone, S., 1991. The *Empire* Strikes Back: A Posttranssexual Manifesto. In: J. Epstein and K. Straub, eds, 1991. *BodyGuards: The Cultural Politics of Gender Ambiguity*. New York and London: Routledge. pp.280–304.

Strauss, D., 1989. Modern Primitives. In: V. Vale and A. Juno, eds, 1989. *Modern Primitives*. San Francisco: RE/Search. pp.157–158.

Streets, S., 1993. S&M in the House of Lords – The Criminalisation of Sexual Deviation. *Alternative Law Journal*, 18(5), pp.233–236.

Strengo, C., 2009. Body Modification and the Enlightenment Project of Struggling Against Death. *Studies in Gender and Sexuality*, 10, pp.166–171.

Stryker, S., 1998. The Transgender Issue: An Introduction. *GLQ*, 4(2), pp.145–158.

Stychin, C., 1995. *Law's Desire: Sexuality and the Limits of Justice*. London and New York: Routledge.

Suchet, M., 2009. The 21st Century Body: Introduction. *Studies in Gender and Sexuality*, 10, pp.113–118.

Sullivan, G., 2009. Liberalism and Constraining Choice: The Cases of Death and Serious Bodily Harm. In: S. Smith and R. Deazley, eds, 2009. *The Legal, Medical and Cultural Regulation of the Body: Transformation and Transgression*. Ashgate. pp.205–233.

Sullivan, N., 2001. *Tattooed Bodies: Subjectivity, Textuality, Ethics, and Pleasure*. Westport and London: Praeger.

Sullivan, N., 2005. Integrity, Mayhem, and the Question of Self-demand Amputation. *Continuum*, 19(3), pp.325–333.

Sullivan, N., 2007. 'The Price to Pay for our Common Good': Genital Modification and the Somatechnologies of Cultural (In)Difference. *Social Semiotics*, 17(3), pp.395–409.

Sullivan, N., 2008. The Role of Medicine in the (Trans)Formation of 'Wrong' Bodies. *Body & Society*, 14(1), pp.105–116.

Sullivan, N., 2009a. The Somatechnics of Bodily Inscription: Tattooing. *Studies in Gender and Sexuality*, 10(3), pp.129–141.

Sullivan, N., 2009b. Transsomatechnics and the Matter of 'Genital Modifications'. *Australian Feminist Studies*, 24(60), pp.275–286.

Sussman, E., 1998. Contending with Culture: An Analysis of the Female Genital Mutilation Act of 1996. *Cornell International Law Journal*, 31, pp.193–250.

Svoboda, J., 1997. Routine Infant Male Circumcision: Examining the Human Rights and Constitutional Issues. In: G. Denniston and M. Milos, eds, 1997. *Sexual Mutilations: A Human Tragedy*. New York and London: Plenum Press. pp.205–216.

Svoboda, J., 1999. Attaining International Acknowledgment of Male Genital Mutilation as a Human Rights Violation. In: G. Denniston, F. Hodges and M. Milos, eds, 1999. *Male and Female Circumcision: Medical, Legal, and Ethical Considerations in Pediatric Practice*. New York: Kluwer Academic. pp.455–469.

Svoboda, J., 2001. The Limits of the Law: Comparative Analysis of Legal and Extralegal Methods to Control Child Body Mutilation Practices. In: G. Denniston, F. Hodges and M. Milos, eds, 2001. *Understanding Circumcision: A Multi-Disciplinary Approach to a Multi-Dimensional Problem.* New York: Kluwer Academic. pp.297–366.

Svoboda, J., Van Howe, R. and Dwyer, J., 2001. Informed Consent for Neonatal Circumcision: An Ethical and Legal Conundrum. *Journal of Contemporary Health Law and Policy*, 17, pp.61–133.

Sweetman, P., 2000. Anchoring the (Postmodern) Self? Body Modification, Fashion and Identity. In: M. Featherstone, ed., 2000. *Body Modification.* London: Sage Publications. pp.51–76.

Swensen, G., 1995. Female Genital Mutilation and Human Rights. *Australian Social Work*, 48(2), pp.27–33.

Syrota, G., 1996. Consensual Fist Fights and Other Brawls: Are They a Crime? *UWA Law Review*, 26, pp.169–189.

Sytsma, S., 2006. Introduction. In: S. Sytsma, ed., 2006. *Ethics and Intersex.* The Netherlands: Springer. pp.xvii–xxv.

Tasmania Law Reform Institute, 2009. *Non-Therapeutic Male Circumcision.* Issue Paper No. 14.

Tasmania Law Reform Institute, 2012. *Non-Therapeutic Male Circumcision.* Final Report No. 17.

Tatnell, P., 2010. Circumcising Young Girls is Child Abuse: Goward. *The Sydney Morning Herald*, [online] 28 May, Available at: <http://www.smh.com.au/lifestyle/diet-and-fitness/circumcising-young-girls-is-child-abuse-goward-20100528-wjhc.html> [Accessed 12 February 2014].

Taylor, G., 1997. The Discursive Construction and Regulation of Dissident Sexualities: The Case of SM. In: J. Ussher, ed., 1997. *Body Talk: The Material and Discursive Regulation of Sexuality, Madness, and Reproduction.* London and New York: Routledge. pp.106–130.

Taylor, G. and Ussher, J., 2001. Making Sense of S&M: A Discourse Analytic Account. *Sexualities*, 4(3), pp.293–314.

The Gender Center Inc, 2008a. *M.T.F. Surgery Information Kit.* [online] Available at: <http://www.gendercentre.org.au/resources/kits-fact-sheets-old.htm> [Accessed 12 March 2014].

The Gender Center Inc, 2008b. *Professionals Information Kit.* [online] Available at: <http://www.gendercentre.org.au/resources/kits-fact-sheets-old.htm> [Accessed 12 March 2014].

The Public Policy Advisory Group on Female Genital Surgeries in Africa, 2012. Seven Things to Know About Female Genital Surgeries in Africa. *Hastings Center Report*, 6, pp.19–27.

The World Professional Association for Transgender Health, 2011. *Standards of Care for the Health of Transsexual, Transgender, and Gender Nonconforming People.* 7th ed.

Thomson, M., 2008. *Endowed: Regulating the Male Sexed Body*. Routledge: Taylor and Francis.

Thomson, M., 2011. A Tale of Two Bodies: The Male Body and Feminist Legal Theory. In: Fineman, M (ed) 2011. *Transcending the Boundaries of Law: Generations of Feminism and Legal Theory* (Abingdon, Oxon: Routledge). pp.143–155.

Tiefer, L., 2008. Female Genital Cosmetic Surgery: Freakish or Inevitable? Analysis from Medical Marketing, Bioethics and Feminist Theory. *Feminism & Psychology*, 18, pp.466–479.

Times, 1974. Discharge for Mother in Tribal Cuts Case. *The Times*, 17 July, p.4.

Times, 1974. Mother 'Cut Boys' Faces in Tribal Ritual'. *The Times*, 16 July, p.3.

Tobin, H., 2006–2007. Against the Surgical Requirement for Change of Legal Sex. *Case Western Reserve Journal of International Law*, 38(2), pp.393–435.

Tomlins, C., 2007. How Autonomous is Law? *Annual Review of Law and Social Science*, 3, pp.45–68.

Toubia, N., 1993. *Female Genital Mutilation: A Call for Global Action*. Women Ink.

Toubia, N., 1999. Evolutionary Cultural Ethics and the Circumcision of Children. In: G. Denniston, F. Hodges and M. Milos, eds, 1999. *Male and Female Circumcision: Medical, Legal, and Ethical Considerations in Pediatric Practice.* New York: Kluwer Academic. pp.1–8.

Tractenberg, M., 1999. Psychoanalysis of Circumcision. In: G. Denniston, F. Hodges and M. Milos, eds, 1999. *Male and Female Circumcision: Medical, Legal, and Ethical Considerations in Pediatric Practice.* New York: Kluwer Academic. pp.209–214.

Trueblood, L., 1999–2000. Female Genital Mutilation: A Discussion of International Human Rights Instruments, Cultural Sovereignty and Dominance Theory. *Denver Journal of International Law & Policy*, 28, pp.437–467.

Turner, B., 1984. *The Body and Society: Explorations in Social Theory.* Oxford: Basil Blackwell.

Turner, B., 1990. Periodization and Politics in the Postmodern. In: B. Turner, ed., 1990. *Theories of Modernity and Postmodernity.* London: Sage Publications. pp.1–13.

Turner, B., 2000. The Possibility of Primitiveness: Towards a Sociology of Body Marks in Cool Societies. In: M. Featherstone, ed., 2000. *Body Modification.* London: Sage Publications. pp.39–50.

Turner, S., 1999. Intersex Identities: Locating New Intersections of Sex and Gender. *Gender and Society*, 13(4), pp.457–479.

Uden, J., 2001. *The Right to Freedom of Physical Expression and Body Modification: A Human Rights Perspective.* Masters. Victoria University of Wellington.

United Nations Children's Fund, 2013. *Female Genital Mutilation/Cutting: A Statistical Overview and Exploration of the Dynamics of Change.* [online] Available at: <http://www.unicef.org/media/files/FGCM_Lo_res.pdf> [Accessed 12 March 2014].

United Nations General Assembly, 2012. *Intensifying Global Efforts for the Elimination of Female Genital Mutilations.* GA Res 67/146, UN GAOR, 67th sess, Agenda Item 28, UN Doc A/RES/67/146 (20 December).

Urla, J. and Swedlund, A., 1995. The Anthropometry of Barbie: Unsettling Ideals of the Feminine Body in Popular Culture. In: J. Urla and J. Terry, eds, 1995. *Deviant Bodies.* Bloomington and Indianapolis: Indiana University Press. pp.277–313.

Urla, J. and Terry, J., 1995. Introduction: Mapping Embodied Deviance. In: J. Urla and J. Terry, eds, 1995. *Deviant Bodies.* Bloomington and Indianapolis: Indiana University Press. pp.1–18.

Uslan, S., 2010. What Parents Don't Know: Informed Consent, Marriage, and Genital-Normalizing Surgery on Intersex Children. *Indiana Law Journal,* 85, pp.301–323.

Ussher, J., 1997. Introduction. In: J. Ussher, ed., 1997. *Body Talk: The Material and Discursive Regulation of Sexuality, Madness, and Reproduction.* London and New York: Routledge. pp.1–9.

Vale, V. and Juno, A., 1989. *Modern Primitives.* San Francisco: RE/Search.

Valentine, D., 2007. *Imagining Transgender: An Ethnography of a Category.* Durham and London: Duke University Press.

Van Dijk, T., 2003. Critical Discourse Analysis. In: D. Schiffrin, T. Deborah and H.E. Hamilton, eds, 2003. *The Handbook of Discourse Analysis.* Blackwell Publishing, [online] Available at: <http://www.blackwellreference.com/subscriber/uid=38/tocnode?id=g9780631205968_chunk_g978063120596819> [Accessed 12 March 2014].

Van Howe, R., 1999a. Anaesthesia for Circumcision: A Review of the Literature. In: G. Denniston, F. Hodges and M. Milos, eds, 1999. *Male and Female Circumcision: Medical, Legal, and Ethical Considerations in Pediatric Practice.* New York: Kluwer Academic. pp.67–97.

Van Howe, R., 1999b. Neonatal Circumcision and HIV Infection. In: G. Denniston, F. Hodges and M. Milos, eds, 1999. *Male and Female Circumcision: Medical, Legal, and Ethical Considerations in Pediatric Practice.* New York: Kluwer Academic. pp.99–129.

Van Howe, R., Svoboda, J., Dwyer, J.G. and Price, C.P., 1999. Involuntary Circumcision: The Legal Issues. *British Journal of Urology International,* 83(1), pp.63–73.

Van Leeuwen, T., 2007. Legitimation in Discourse and Communication. *Discourse & Communication,* 1, pp.91–112.

Van Leeuwen, T., 2009. Critical Discourse Analysis. In: J. Renkema, ed., 2009, *Discourse, of Course: An Overview of Research in Discourse Studies*. Amsterdam & Philadelphia: John Benjamins Publishing Company. pp.277–292.

Veale, D. and Daniels, J., 2012. Cosmetic Clitoridectomy in a 33-Year-Old Woman. *Archives of Sexual Behavior*, 41, pp.725–730.

Veitch, S., Christodoulidis, E. and Farmer, L., 2007. *Jurisprudence: Themes and Concepts*. London and New York: Routledge Cavendish.

Vesta, D., 2004. Fantasy, Fetish and the Goddess. In: M. Thompson, ed., 2004, *Leatherfolk: Radical Sex, People, Politics and Practices*. Los Angeles: Daedalus Publishing Company. pp.267–275.

Wade, L., 2009. Defining Gendered Oppression in US Newspapers: The Strategic Value of 'Female Genital Mutilation'. *Gender & Society*, 23(3), pp.293–314.

Wadham, J., 1996. Consent to Assault. *New Law Journal*, 146(6772), pp.1812 and 1823.

Waldeck, S., 2003–2004. Using Male Circumcision to Understand Social Norms as Multipliers. *University of Cincinnati Law Review*, 72, pp.455–526.

Wallerstein, E., 1980. *Circumcision: An American Health Fallacy*. New York: Springer Publishing Company.

Warne, G. and Bhatia, V., 2006. Intersex, East and West. In: S. Sytsma, ed., 2006, *Ethics and Intersex*. The Netherlands: Springer. pp.183–205.

Warne, G. and Hewitt, J., 2009. Disorders of Sex Development: Current Understanding and Continuing Controversy. *Medical Journal of Australia*, 190(11), pp.612–613.

Warren, J., 1999. Foreskin Restoration (Circumcision Reversal). In: G. Denniston, F. Hodges and M. Milos, eds, 1999. *Male and Female Circumcision: Medical, Legal, and Ethical Considerations in Pediatric Practice*. New York: Kluwer Academic. pp 303–309.

Watkins, A., 1998. Score and Pierce: Crimes of Fashion? Body Alteration and Consent to Assault. *Victoria University of Wellington Law Review*, 28, pp.371–398.

Weait, M., 1996. Fleshing it Out. In: L. Bentley and L. Flynn, eds, 1996. *Law and the Senses: Sensational Jurisprudence*. London and Chicago: Pluto Press. pp.160–175.

Weait, M., 2007. Sadomasochism and the Law. In: D. Langdridge and M. Barker, eds, 2007. *Safe, Sane and Consensual: Contemporary Perspectives on Sadomasochism*. New York: Palgrave MacMillan. pp.63–82.

Weinberg, T., 1995. *S&M: Studies in Dominance & Submission*. New York: Prometheus Books.

Weiss, D. and Kukla, R., 2009. The 'Natural Look': Extreme Makeovers and the Limits of Self-Fashioning. In: C. Heyes and M. Jones, eds, 2009. *Cosmetic Surgery: A Feminist Primer*. Burlington: Ashgate Publishing. pp.117–132.

Weiss, M., 2006. Mainstreaming Kink: The Politics of BDSM Representation in US Popular Media. In: P. Kleinplatz and C. Moser, eds, 2006. *Sadomasochism: Powerful Pleasures*. New York: Harrington Park Press. pp.103–132.

Weiss, M., 2008. Gay Shame and BDSM Pride: Neoliberalism, Privacy and Sexual Politics. *Radical History Review*, 100, pp.87–101.

Wellerstein, J., 1999–2000. In the Name of Tradition: Eradicating the Harmful Practice of Female Genital Mutilation. *Loyola of Los Angeles International and Comparative Law Review*, 22, pp.99–141.

White, C., 2006. The Spanner Trials and the Changing Law on Sadomasochism in the UK. In: P. Kleinplatz and C. Moser, eds, 2006. *Sadomasochism: Powerful Pleasures*. New York: Harrington Park Press. pp.167–187.

Whittle, S., 2002. *Respect and Equality: Transsexual and Transgender Rights*. London: Cavendish Publishing Limited.

Wilchins, R., 2004. *Queer Theory, Gender Theory*. Los Angeles Alyson Publications.

Williams, C., 2002. Sexual Harassment and Sadomasochism. *Hypatia*, 17(2), pp.99–117.

Williams, D.J., 2009. Deviant Leisure: Rethinking 'The Good, The Bad, and The Ugly'. *Leisure Sciences*, 31, pp.207–213.

Williams, G., 1962. Consent and Public Policy. *Criminal Law Review*, pp.74–83.

Williams, G., 1997. NOCIRC of Australia. In: G. Denniston and M. Milos, eds, 1997. *Sexual Mutilations: A Human Tragedy*. New York: Plenum Press. pp.189–196.

Wilson, G., 2012. A Conspiracy of Deceit: Alice Dreger, ISNA, the Invention of DSD and Dix Poppas of Cornell who Cuts up Intersex Babies' Clitorises. *OII Intersex Network*, [online] 25 January, Available at: <http://oiiinternational.com/2528/conspiracy-deceit/> [Accessed 12 March 2014].

Wilson, M., 2002. 'I am the Prince of Pain, for I am a Princess in the Brain': Liminal Transgender Identities, Narratives and the Elimination of Ambiguities. *Sexualities*, 5(4), pp.425–448.

Wilson, T., 2002. Pharaonic Circumcision Under Patriarchy and Breast Augmentation Under Phallocentric Capitalism: Similarities and Differences. *Violence Against Women*, 8(4), pp.495–521.

Wise, T. and Kalyanam, R., 2000. Amputee Fetishism and Genital Mutilation: Case Report and Literature Review. *Journal of Sex & Marital Therapy*, 26, pp.339–344.

Wood, A., 2001. A Cultural Rite of Passage or a Form of Torture: Female Genital Mutilation from an International Law Perspective. *Hastings Women's Law Journal*, 12(2), pp.347–386.

World Health Organisation, 1998. *Female Genital Mutilation: An Overview*.

World Health Organisation, 2007. *Male Circumcision: Global Trends and Determinants of Prevalence, Safety and Acceptability*.

World Health Organisation, 2008a. *Eliminating Female Genital Mutilation: An Interagency Statement*.

World Health Organisation, 2008b. *Fact Sheet No 241: Female Genital Mutilation*.

World Health Organisation, 2010. *Regarding the 'Policy Statement – Ritual Genital Cutting of Female Minors' from the American Academy of Pediatrics.* [online] Available at: <www.who.int/reproductivehealth/topics/fgm/fgm_app_statement.pdf> [Accessed 11 March 2014].

Wright, S., 2006. Discrimination of SM-Identified Individuals. In: P. Kleinplatz and C. Moser, eds, 2006. *Sadomasochism: Powerful Pleasures.* New York: Harrington Park Press. pp.217–231.

Wright, S., 2008. *Second National Survey of Violence and Discrimination Against Minorities.* National Coalition for Sexual Freedom, [online] Available at: <https://ncsfreedom.org/images/stories/pdfs/BDSM_Survey/2008_bdsm_survey_analysis_final.pdf> [Accessed 12 March 2014].

Yost, M., 2007. Sexual Fantasies of S/M Practitioners: The Impact of Gender and S/M Role on Fantasy Content. In: D. Langdridge and M. Barker, eds, 2007. *Safe, Sane and Consensual: Contemporary Perspectives on Sadomasochism.* New York: Palgrave MacMillan. pp.135–154.

Young, P.W., 2011. Is There any Law of Consent with Respect to Assault? *Australian Law Journal*, 85, pp.23–36.

Zoske, J., 1998. Male Circumcision: A Gender Perspective. *Journal of Men's Studies*, 6(2), pp.189–208.

Zoske, J., 1999. Celebrating Phallos: Healing Men and Culture. In: G. Denniston, F. Hodges and M. Milos, eds, 1999. *Male and Female Circumcision: Medical, Legal, and Ethical Considerations in Pediatric Practice.* New York: Kluwer Academic. pp.279–284.

Zwang, G., 1997. Functional and Erotic Consequences of Sexual Mutilations. In: G. Denniston and M. Milos, eds, 1997. *Sexual Mutilations: A Human Tragedy.* New York and London: Plenum Press. pp.67–76.

Zwang, G., 1999. Motivations for Modifications of the Human Body. In: G. Denniston, F. Hodges and M. Milos, eds, 1999. *Male and Female Circumcision: Medical, Legal, and Ethical Considerations in Pediatric Practice.* New York: Kluwer Academic. pp.201–208.

Index

For Product Safety Concerns and Information please contact our EU representative GPSR@taylorandfrancis.com Taylor & Francis Verlag GmbH, Kaufingerstraße 24, 80331 München, Germany

Batch number: 10725973

Printed by Printforce, the Netherlands

विठ्ठला!

विजय तेंडुलकर यांची नाटके

नाटक
अशी पाखरे येती
एक हट्टी मुलगी
कमला
कन्यादान
कावळ्यांची शाळा*
कुत्रे
गिधाडे
गृहस्थ*
घरटे अमुचे छान
घाशीराम कोतवाल
चिमणीचं घरं होतं मेणाचं
चिरंजीव सौभाग्यकांक्षिणी
झाला अनंत हनुमंत
त्याची पाचवी***
दंबद्वीपचा मुकाबला
नियतीच्या बैलाला**
पाहिजे जातीचे
फूटपायरीचा सम्राट
बेबी
भल्याकाका
भाऊ मुरारराव
मधल्या भिंती
माणूस नावाचे बेट
मित्राची गोष्ट
मी जिंकलो! मी हरलो!
विठ्ठला
शांतता! कोर्ट चालू आहे
श्रीमंत
सखाराम बाइंडर
सफर**
सरी ग सरी

एकांकिका
समग्र एकांकिका : भाग १
समग्र एकांकिका : भाग २
समग्र एकांकिका : भाग ३

बालवाङ्मय
इथे बाळं मिळतात
चांभारचौकशीचे नाटक
चिमणा बांधतो बंगला
पाटलाच्या पोरीचं लगीन
बाबा हरवले आहेत
बॉबीची गोष्ट
राजाराणीला घाम हवा

अनुवादित
आधे अुरे
(मूळ लेखक : मोहन राकेश)
तुघलक
(मूळ लेखक : गिरीश कार्नाड)
मी कुमार
(मूळ लेखक : मधु राय)
लिंकन यांचे अखेरचे दिवस
(मूळ लेखक : मार्क फॉन डॉरन)
लोभ नसावा ही विनंती
(मूळ लेखक : जॉन पॅट्रिक)
वासनाचक्र
(मूळ लेखक : टेनेसी विल्यम्स)

---

* 'गृहस्थ'चे पुनर्लेखन : 'कावळ्यांची शाळा'
** ध्वनिफितीच्या रूपानेही प्रकाशित
*** मूळ इंग्रजी : His Fifth Woman (अनु. चंद्रशेखर फणसळकर)